The Money Problem

The Money Problem

Rethinking Financial Regulation

MORGAN RICKS

THE UNIVERSITY OF CHICAGO PRESS   CHICAGO AND LONDON

MORGAN RICKS is associate professor at Vanderbilt Law School. Previously, he was a senior policy advisor and financial restructuring expert at the US Treasury Department, a risk-arbitrage trader at Citadel Investment Group, and vice president in the investment banking division of Merrill Lynch & Co.

The University of Chicago Press, Chicago 60637
The University of Chicago Press, Ltd., London
© 2016 by The University of Chicago
All rights reserved. Published 2016.
Printed in the United States of America

25 24 23 22 21 20 19 18 17   3 4 5

ISBN-13: 978-0-226-33032-7 (cloth)
ISBN-13: 978-0-226-33046-4 (e-book)
DOI: 10.7208/chicago/9780226330464.001.0001

Ricks, Morgan, author.
The money problem : rethinking financial regulation / Morgan Ricks.
     pages ; cm
     Includes bibliographical references and index.
     ISBN 978-0-226-33032-7 (cloth : alk. paper)—ISBN 978-0-226-33046-4 (ebook) 1. Money market—United States.   2. Monetary policy—United States. 3. Banks and banking—United States. 4. Informal sector (Economics)—United States. 5. Financial crises—Prevention. I. Title
HG540. R534 2016
332.4'973—dc23
2015017766

⊚ This paper meets the requirements of ANSI/NISO Z39.48-1992 (Permanence of Paper).

TO MOLLY

Contents

Preface

This book found its genesis at the US Treasury Department in the fall of 2009. I had joined Treasury earlier that year as a member of the newly created Crisis Response Team. We were a small group of Wall Street professionals—investment bankers, traders, and buyout specialists—whom Secretary Timothy Geithner had brought on board to help engineer the Obama administration's response to the financial crisis. That fall, with the financial system in fairly stable condition, Geithner asked us to turn our attention from financial rescue to financial reform. The team gathered one afternoon to review some ideas.

We quickly found ourselves converging on a key issue. We called it "shadow banking." That term has come to mean different things to different people. Indeed, it has become so vague as to render it almost meaningless. Sometimes it is used as a synonym for nonbank credit intermediation; other times it is an all-purpose reference to unregulated or lightly regulated parts of the financial system. To us, though, the term meant something very different, and quite specific. When we talked about shadow banking, we were referring to the financial sector's use of vast amounts of *short-term debt* to fund portfolios of financial assets.

The short-term funding markets are enormous, but they are fairly obscure. They exist largely in the background, as part of what might be called the "operating system" of modern finance. These markets have weird names—like repo, Eurodollars, and asset-backed commercial paper—but this confusing terminology belies their simplicity. These markets are not exotic at all. They are as simple as can be: they are just short-term debt. Borrowings in these markets mature very soon, often in a single day. Financial institutions that rely on these markets typically must continuously renew (or "roll over") large quantities of short-term borrowings.

Failing to do so on any given day would result in the immediate default and collapse of the firm.

In 2007 and 2008 the short-term funding markets unraveled in dramatic fashion. The unraveling started in mid-2007 with the failures of a number of big investment conduits that relied heavily on short-term borrowings. The following spring the crisis spread to the giant repo market—a multitrillion-dollar market in which Wall Street firms finance their securities portfolios on a very short-term basis, typically overnight. Bear Stearns, a major investment bank, collapsed that spring when it lost access to overnight repo funding. Finally, with the bankruptcy of Lehman Brothers in the fall of 2008, all the short-term funding markets seized up at once. Many key financial markets stopped functioning. The economy promptly went into free fall. Governments in the United States and abroad launched massive financial rescue operations. With few exceptions, these emergency measures were aimed at stabilizing the short-term funding markets.

To our team at Treasury, the short-term funding markets seemed dysfunctional: they were prone to damaging panics. We were not alone in reaching this conclusion. On the contrary, we had been deeply influenced by others. A few months before our fall meeting, Federal Reserve chairman Ben Bernanke had publicly described the acute phase of the financial crisis as a "classic panic," which he defined as "a generalized run by providers of short-term funding to a set of financial institutions."[1] Several Fed economists had been promoting this thesis for some time. Gary Gorton had done pioneering work in this area as well; his writings on the short-term funding markets were very influential in the financial policy community. Paul Krugman had also been an early and perceptive analyst of this problem. Our views at Treasury had been influenced by all these thinkers.

By no means did we think that shadow banking was the only problem with the financial system. There were other problems too, particularly in the consumer protection area. But our sense was that the fragility of the short-term funding markets was a central problem—perhaps *the* central problem—for financial stability policy. Any serious program for financial reform, we thought, should address this area directly. In fact, we believed that a coherent regulatory approach to shadow banking might go a long way toward addressing other major issues, such as the vexing "too big to fail" problem. But what if anything should be done?

After our team meeting I drew up a memo titled "Liability Reform." The memo proposed a system of explicit federal guarantees for the short-term borrowings of financial firms. In return for this guarantee, financial firms that relied on short-term borrowings would pay periodic fees to the government. (Others later offered broadly similar proposals.)[2] The reasoning behind the proposal was straightforward. During the financial crisis, taxpayers had stood behind the short-term funding markets on a staggering scale, with commitments in the trillions of dollars. If the public was going to stand behind these markets, the memo reasoned, then the public should be compensated for bearing this risk. By the same token, the fees (if properly priced) would end the massive public subsidies that accrue to big financial firms by virtue of the prospect of public support. Furthermore, an explicit guarantee presumably would remove the incentive for short-term creditors to run. In this regard the long-standing US deposit insurance system provided an instructive model. The establishment of federal deposit insurance in 1933 put a stop to the recurring panics that had previously beset the US banking system.

The memo generated a fair amount of discussion within Treasury. To be honest, the memo was not very good. (Geithner called it wacky.) The proposal as conceived was crude and unworkable, and there were serious drawbacks—moral hazard in particular. Over the subsequent months, the financial reform process went in a very different direction. July 2010 saw the enactment of the Dodd-Frank Act, the most far-reaching financial reform bill since the Great Depression. The act was intended to address the root causes of the financial crisis and prevent a recurrence. It was a massive piece of legislation, with over eight hundred pages of dense statutory text. But the new law left the short-term funding markets practically untouched.

I doubted we had succeeded in striking at the root of financial instability, and I believed the failure had been mostly conceptual, not political. When I left Treasury in 2010 to join academia, I sought to improve on my initial analysis of the shadow banking problem. This book is the result. The direction of this project was shaped by a conclusion I reached early on— that shadow banking should be viewed as a problem of monetary system design. (Just what I mean by this will soon become clear.)

My professional background has had a big influence on the way I think about these matters. Before joining Treasury I worked on Wall Street. My career there had three phases. I was first a corporate takeover lawyer, then an investment banker, and finally a risk arbitrage trader at a big hedge fund. I had a particular specialty, which on Wall Street is known as FIG (pronounced like the fruit). FIG stands for Financial Institutions Group, and it refers to teams that specialize in investments in financial firms (as opposed to, say, industrial firms or health care firms). My career has afforded me considerable practical experience in asset pricing, transaction structuring, and the valuation of banking and securities firms. This experience provides a useful vantage point from which to approach the topics addressed in this book.

Recent years have seen no shortage of analyses of the problems with modern finance. I suppose this book represents yet another entry in this already overpopulated genre. I believe it is unique in framing the issue as one of monetary system design. In addition, I hope it will distinguish itself by conceptual clarity, a trait not always in evidence in the recent and ongoing financial reform debates.

Emblematic of the problem has been the recent fashion for analyzing and measuring something called "systemic risk." This nebulous concept has yet to be defined, let alone operationalized, in anything approaching a satisfactory way. In a well-known line from a Molière comedy, a doctor explains that opium puts people to sleep because it contains a "dormitive property." This explanation says nothing at all—that's the joke. It is a kind of tautology: the phenomenon is "explained" in terms of itself. The concept of systemic risk has roughly the same status. If the term were used merely as a catchall for theories about the sources of financial instability, it would be harmless shorthand. But systemic risk has now been "thingified"[3] into something that supposedly can be measured and monitored, and even managed through various regulatory techniques. This reflects, in my view, a lack of discipline and conceptual development in the financial reform process. We have moved forward based on vague ideas about the nature of the underlying problem.

Greater conceptual clarity makes possible, I think, an approach to reform far simpler than the one currently being pursued. Simplicity is of course essential to good design. This is as true in the design of institutions as in the design of anything else. Unfortunately, recent and pending financial reforms have been anything but simple; they are mind-numbingly complex. Some might interpret this technical complexity as a hallmark of sophistication, but I take exactly the opposite view: it is a sure sign of poor design. We should be aiming for something far simpler. Bear in mind that simple does not mean simplistic. Justice Oliver Wendell Holmes once distinguished between the simplicity on *this* side of complexity and the simplicity on the *other* side of complexity.[4] It is the latter kind that he considered worthwhile, and it is not easy to get there. Steve Jobs, one of the greatest product designers in business history, made the same point: that simple is *harder* than complex. "It takes a lot of hard work," Jobs said, "to make something simple, to truly understand the underlying challenges and come up with elegant solutions."[5]

This book offers a blueprint for an updated monetary system—a fairly simple one at that. It is not a vague statement of principles but rather a concrete and realistic institutional design. The design is not radical or exotic; indeed, it is fairly conservative. It is best understood as a modernization of the current monetary architecture. I believe the approach described here would enable us to substantially scale back our existing unwieldy approach to financial stability regulation.

Apart from serving as a possible basis for reform, this blueprint offers another advantage: it helps to illuminate the logic and historical development of existing institutions. The analysis will reveal that, despite its design flaws, the existing US system of money and banking in many ways embodies a coherent economic logic—one that has not previously been clearly articulated. Surprisingly, much of this terrain has never been systematically explored. Many of the components of the analysis already exist in the literature, but in fragmentary form. A central task of the book (and a source of its novelty) will be to assemble these elements into a coherent and integrated whole.

Portions of this book draw on my previous work. Parts of the introduction and chapters 1, 2, 9, and 10 draw on "Regulating Money Creation after the Crisis," *Harvard Business Law Review* 1, no. 1 (2011): 75–143; parts of chapters 4, 6, 7, and 8 draw on "A Regulatory Design for Monetary Stability," *Vanderbilt Law Review* 65, no. 5 (2012): 1289–360; parts of chapter 5 draw on "Money and (Shadow) Banking: A Thought Experiment," *Review of Banking and Financial Law* 31, no. 2 (2012): 731–48; parts of chapter 10 draw on "Reforming the Short-Term Funding Markets," Harvard John M. Olin Discussion Paper 713 (2012); and parts of chapters 1, 9, and 10 draw on "A Simpler Approach to Financial Reform," *Regulation*, Winter 2013–14, 36–41.

I have amassed many intellectual debts in formulating the ideas presented here. Without implicating any of them in my conclusions, I want to thank Margaret Blair, Christine Desan, Gary Gorton, Sam Hanson, Mike Hsu, Howell Jackson, Matt Kabaker, Roy Kreitner, Perry Mehrling, Andrew Metrick, Geoff Miller, Jim Millstein, Nadav Orian Peer, Zoltan Pozsar, Jim Rossi, Nick Rowe, Ian Samuels, David Scharfstein, Ganesh Sitaraman, David Skeel, Jeremy Stein, Adi Sunderam, Randall Thomas,

Yesha Yadav, and participants in workshops and seminars at Vanderbilt Law School, Harvard Law School, NYU Law School, Fordham Law School, University of Colorado Law School, and Duke Law School. Thanks also to Luke Meyers for research assistance.

As this book neared publication, Chris Rhodes, my editor at the University of Chicago Press, passed away. Chris was a superb editor—a wise and honest critic, a patient sounding board, an advocate and cheerleader, a skillful project manager. This book owes much to him.

Introduction

I am tempted to believe that what we call necessary institutions are often no more than institutions to which we have grown accustomed.—Alexis de Tocqueville, 1850[1]

This book is about the structure of monetary institutions. It is also about financial instability. These two topics are closely related; in fact they are inseparable. I argue that our existing monetary framework is outdated and defective—and that revamping it is a prerequisite to financial stability. More than that, such a revamp could pave the way for a dramatic reduction in the scope and complexity of modern financial stability regulation.

In short, financial instability is at bottom a problem of monetary system design. In a sense, this statement reflects the traditional wisdom. During the Great Depression, the academic debates over what had gone wrong centered on the monetary architecture. Reform-minded scholars, including many of the leading economists of the era, sought above all to stabilize the "circulating medium" of bank-issued money. They understood the core problem in distinctly monetary terms.[2]

Today's prevailing viewpoint is quite different. The global financial crisis of 2007 to 2009 has produced a flood of literature on the sources of financial instability. With very few exceptions, though, that literature has neglected the topic of monetary system design. Instead, under today's dominant line of thinking, financial instability is understood to be an inherent feature of capitalist economies. In the words of Hyman Minsky, a pioneer of this point of view, "serious business cycles are due to financial attributes that are essential to capitalism."[3] The financial system, we are told, has a built-in tendency to get badly out of kilter, endangering the broader economy.

In my view the prevailing viewpoint is not a useful way of thinking about financial instability. Just what is wrong with it is not easily stated in a few words. The case against the prevailing view won't reach fruition until part 3 of the book. For now, let's just say that the prevailing view has sent us on a wild goose chase, searching for "systemic risk" and other mythical creatures. I argue instead that the traditional wisdom still applies. When it comes to financial stability policy, our top priority should be to follow through on building a stable and efficient monetary framework. This project is not a new one, of course. Monetary system design is an age-old challenge of government. It is a discrete task of institutional engineering, not an open-ended search for "systemic risk" or anything like that.

This book is by no means the first to address monetary system design. As we'll see later, though, the topic hasn't been thought through as well as one might expect. To be clear, this book isn't about the conduct of monetary policy—a topic that has received vastly more attention over the years. The conduct of monetary policy and the design of monetary institutions are distinct subjects. The latter analytically precedes the former: monetary policy takes place within a given institutional setting.

If my argument is right, then the financial stability reforms of recent years—in the United States and, by extension, abroad—have mostly been on the wrong track. We will look at those reforms in part 3. To the extent that they reflect an underlying theory, it is the prevailing viewpoint just described. Recent reforms have touched virtually every part of the US financial system, but they have left the monetary architecture practically untouched. I fear they could turn out to be both costly and ineffective.

The idea that financial instability is largely a problem of monetary system design is counterintuitive. It doesn't mesh with the usual narratives about the recent financial crisis. Indeed, many readers may be wondering what this proposition even means. So this is where we need to start.

One View of the Challenge

It is useful to begin by discussing a subject that might initially seem unrelated to monetary system design: "shadow banking." This term has taken on a variety of meanings lately, but I will use it in a very precise way. For our purposes, a shadow bank is an entity that uses large quantities of short-term debt to fund a portfolio of financial assets and that is not a chartered deposit bank. The shadow banking system is just the set of entities that meet these two criteria.[4]

The concept of shadow banking, as used here, is more or less interchangeable with the (nondeposit) short-term debt of the financial sector. Practically speaking, they are the same thing. The markets for this short-term debt—often called the short-term funding markets, the wholesale funding markets, or just the funding markets—are described in some detail in chapter 1. These markets are huge, and they were at the center of the recent financial crisis. In 2007 and 2008 the short-term funding markets unraveled in a series of classic panics. From the perspective of finance practitioners and policymakers, these panics were virtually synonymous with the financial crisis. The panics themselves *were* the emergency, and they coincided with the start of a severe economic slump.

This book argues that, when it comes to financial stability policy, panics—widespread redemptions of the financial sector's short-term debt—should be viewed as "the problem" (the main one, anyway). More to the point: *panic-proofing*, as opposed to, say, asset bubble prevention or "systemic risk" mitigation, should be the central objective of financial stability policy—at least insofar as financial stability policy is about preventing macroeconomic disasters. I will have much more to say about this later.

We do of course have a policy response to panics, but it has major problems. The modern answer to panics consists of an implicit commitment of open-ended public support for the financial sector's short-term debt, via the lender of last resort and other facilities. The very prospect of public support introduces potentially severe distortions into the financial system. It encourages the growth of individual financial firms and the financial sector as a whole; it rewards high degrees of leverage and generates an oversupply of credit; and it perversely subsidizes the financial sector through artificially low funding costs. These are not novel claims, but they do suggest that our modern approach to fighting panics might *itself* bear substantial responsibility for many of the apparent pathologies of modern finance.

So what does the financial sector's short-term debt (shadow banking) have to do with the monetary system? Gary Gorton, a leading expert in this area, has said that "the shadow banking system is, in fact, real banking."[5] This is an important insight. Shadow banking clearly bears a close resemblance to ordinary deposit banking. Both shadow banks and deposit banks hold portfolios of financial assets that they fund largely with very short-term IOUs. In deposit banking those IOUs take the form of deposit liabilities. In shadow banking those IOUs consist of the myriad instruments of the short-term funding markets. But the basic structure is the same. Because of this heavy reliance on short-term debt funding, both business models are inherently susceptible to a liquidity crisis or "run" in which short-term claimants simultaneously seek to redeem.

So far so good; this comparison between shadow banking and deposit banking has become fairly standard. But the comparison can be taken one step further. It is a truism of finance that deposit banks are in the *money creation* business. Every student of introductory economics learns how this works. Deposit banks issue special instruments called "deposits" that function as money.[6] This is a legally privileged activity: only chartered deposit banks are authorized to issue these instruments. And they issue them in amounts that far exceed their holdings of government-issued (or "base") money. Deposit banks, then, really do augment the money supply.

Here we come to a threshold conceptual step. It turns out that the shadow banking system creates money too. The short-term IOUs that are issued by shadow banks are widely understood to be close substitutes for deposit instruments. For accounting and other purposes, these short-term debt instruments are called cash equivalents. Corporate treasurers and other businesspeople just call them cash. Economists sometimes refer to them as near money or quasi money. Central bankers include many of these instruments in their broad measures of the money supply. And, not coincidentally, the market for these short-term IOUs is known in the financial world as the *money* market, as distinct from the more familiar *capital* market in which stocks and ordinary bonds are traded.

Now, these cash equivalent instruments might not really seem like "money." In particular, they are not typically used as a means of payment—a textbook attribute of money. In this respect cash equivalents look like ordinary bonds. An important task ahead will be to clarify what it means to say that cash equivalents have monetary attributes, whereas other financial instruments—like longer-term Treasury bonds, or shares in equity mutual funds—do not. The answer is not obvious, and it is not just a matter of asset "liquidity." I will address this central topic in chapter 1.

Shadow banking, then, appears to be a *monetary* phenomenon, not just a financial one. This distinction might seem subtle, but it is conceptually significant. It implies that the shadow banking problem is bound up with the institutional structure of the monetary system. In other words, the question of what to do about shadow banking is inseparable from the question of how our monetary system should be designed. This recognition should not be very controversial; it emerges naturally from the analogy between shadow banking and deposit banking. Interestingly, though, shadow banking is seldom discussed in this way.

What would it mean to take this monetary perspective on shadow banking seriously? Deposit banks have long been viewed as special by virtue of their monetary function. In particular, disruptions in the deposit banking sector can and do inflict severe damage on the broader economy. In a classic analysis, Milton Friedman and Anna Schwartz argued that the Great Depression was largely the product of a monetary contraction caused by waves of banking panics.[7] Those panics, they wrote, "were the mechanism through which a drastic decline was produced in the stock of money." And the economic devastation that followed was "a tragic testimonial to the importance of monetary forces." (Subsequent research on the Depression has stressed the causal role of the international gold standard. Note that these two explanations are complementary[8]—and both implicate the monetary framework.) The impact of Friedman and Schwartz's study was profound. Ben Bernanke has described their achievement as "nothing less than to provide what has become the leading and most persuasive explanation of the worst economic disaster in American history, the onset of the Great Depression."[9] The relevance of the Friedman-Schwartz thesis to shadow banking is not hard to see. If the shadow banking system performs a monetary function similar to that of deposit banking, presumably it also presents similar macroeconomic risks.

This line of reasoning raises fundamental questions of institutional design. For the *legal* distinction between deposit banking and shadow banking is striking. Consider deposit banks first. In recognition of their special role in money creation, deposit banks have long been required to submit to a uniquely extensive regulatory regime. No other industry is subject to remotely comparable constraints and oversight. In the United States, deposit banks face detailed chartering criteria; strict limits on permissible activities and investments; leverage limits (capital requirements); special restrictions on affiliations and affiliate transactions; base money reserve requirements; extensive on-site supervision; a vigorous enforcement regime; special receivership in the event of failure; and so on. Deposit banks are also the beneficiaries of government stabilization facilities—central bank loans and deposit insurance—that are (normally) unavailable to other firms.

By virtue of submitting to this regulatory regime, deposit banks are endowed with an extraordinary legal privilege: they are licensed to issue deposit instruments. This privilege is accompanied by a logical corollary: enterprises *other* than chartered deposit banks are legally *prohibited* from issuing these instruments.[10] This remarkable prohibition might be described, both logically and historically, as the "first law of banking." It is worth dwelling on this point for a moment. In formal terms, a deposit instrument is merely a variety of IOU. The first law of banking thus establishes a sweeping limitation on freedom of contract. Parties not licensed as deposit banks are legally ineligible to be obligors under this particular type of IOU. The authority to issue them is the very legal privilege that a banking charter conveys.[11]

Contrast the shadow banking system. Shadow banking entities have no legal or regulatory status as such. Issuing cash equivalent instruments—the hallmark of shadow banking—requires no license. This activity takes place pursuant to generally applicable background rules of property and contract (maybe with a dash of commercial law and organizational law thrown in). It is not legally confined, nor is it surrounded by the elaborate institutional architecture of the deposit banking system. What justifies this differential legal status? Assume for the moment that the monetary function of deposits is, in one way or another, what justifies the extraordinary regulation of their issuers. If cash equivalents perform a monetary function too, then perhaps the law of banking rests on an arbitrary and formalistic distinction. That is to say, perhaps the starting point for banking law should be not the deposit instrument but rather the broad array of short-term IOUs that serve a monetary function.

This analysis reveals a basic point that has vital implications for monetary system design: *given* the existence of some established medium of exchange, entrepreneurs can set up a distinctive "money creation" business model whose liabilities consist largely of instruments that are redeemable for that existing money on demand or in the very near term. (Why entrepreneurs would want to use such a funding model will be discussed in chapters 2 and 3; the short answer is that it is very profitable.) The portfolios of these enterprises tend to consist mostly of longer-term financial assets like loans and bonds. This is the familiar business model of banking—or shadow banking, as the case may be. Crucially, *in the absence of any special legal impediments*, this business model can arise through the operation of standard rules of property and contract. The law of deposit banking, however, establishes just such a legal impediment. It is the first law of banking: no person or entity may issue redeemable instruments styled as "deposits" unless it has a special charter to do so.

One sometimes hears that banking regulation should be "extended" to the shadow banking system, but this argument misapprehends the basic structure of banking law. To see why, imagine what it would mean to "extend" banking regulation to, say, a big securities dealer that relies heavily on short-term debt funding. I noted above that US deposit banks are strictly limited in their permissible activities and investments. Let's now be a little more specific. In the United States, deposit banks are basically limited to holding diversified portfolios of credit assets—loans and investment-grade bonds. They generally may not buy equity securities or junk bonds, for example.[12] So deposit banks are not allowed to own many of the kinds of assets that securities dealers hold as a part of their core business. More fundamentally, deposit banks are explicitly prohibited by statute from *engaging in securities dealing*, subject to very narrow exceptions.[13] Simply put, if deposit banking regulation were "extended" to a securities dealer, it could no longer be a securities dealer.

One might argue that these activity and portfolio constraints should be relaxed in the case of a securities dealer. But this is a strange argument; those constraints are part of the very core of banking regulation! Remember, banking law starts by *confining* the issuance of deposit instruments to a class of specially chartered entities that must abide by all sorts of requirements, including strict activity and portfolio constraints. If cash equivalents function as deposit substitutes, then the natural question is whether their issuance should *also* be so confined. In other words, the question isn't whether banking regulation should be "extended" to (for example) securities dealers, but rather whether securities dealers should be *prohibited from issuing cash equivalents*, just as they are now prohibited from issuing deposits. We are talking here about updating the first law of banking—the general prohibition that is the starting point for banking law.

Here is another way of thinking about it. Imagine that the statutory definition of "deposit"[14] were amended to encompass all the various types of short-term debt instruments on which the financial sector relies for funding. In that case, only chartered deposit banks would be authorized to issue such instruments. This would mean the end of "shadow" banking; the business of funding portfolios of financial assets with large quantities of short-term debt would be coextensive with the deposit banking system. We would then have a single set of chartered money creation firms, operating under terms and conditions established by the state.

It should now be apparent what it means to say that financial instability is a problem of monetary system design. The short-term IOUs of the financial sector are monetary instruments, and a panic—what Bernanke called a "generalized run by providers of short-term funding to a set of financial institutions"—is a defining feature of financial crises. To quote

University of Chicago economist Douglas Diamond, a leading theorist in this area, "Financial crises are everywhere and always about short-term debt."[15] This is perhaps an exaggeration, but only a slight one.

The Broader Context

This discussion has offered a glimpse of the kinds of questions this book is occupied with. To bring these questions fully into view, it is useful to situate the foregoing discussion within a more general context. Some taxonomy will help. Consider the "cash and equivalents" line on the asset side of the balance sheet of an operating company, say IBM. We tend to think of this as just "cash" or "money"—and that is what IBM's managers surely call it—but of course in reality it consists of specific kinds of instruments. What are they exactly? There are three basic categories. First, there is government-issued physical currency; IBM has only a tiny amount of this. Second, there are (checkable) bank deposit instruments, which the company uses to make virtually all its payments. Third, there are the various instruments of the short-term funding markets: cash equivalents.

Let's look more closely at these three categories. Table 1 summarizes some of their essential legal-institutional attributes (the focus here is on the United States, but other jurisdictions are similar). The first row, physical currency, has been lurking in the background so far; we can now bring it forward. In modern monetary systems, physical currency is "fiat" currency, meaning it lacks intrinsic value and isn't redeemable for anything else.[16] The table indicates that issuing physical currency is legally *privileged*: having issued currency, the state prohibits others from producing identical instruments. This of course is the subject of anticounterfeiting

TABLE 1. **Characteristics of Existing Monetary Instruments**

Monetary Instrument	Privileged Issuance?	Sovereign vs. Private
Physical currency	Yes	Sovereign
Bank deposits	Yes	Sovereign (insured) and
		Private (uninsured)
Cash equivalents	No	Private (mostly)

law.[17] Physical currency is also *sovereign* in status. This just means it represents a "commitment" of the state and not of any private entity.

Next consider bank deposits, which are the predominant medium of exchange in modern economies. We have already seen that their issuance is a privileged activity, inasmuch as it is legally confined to a class of specially chartered entities. In addition, most deposit instruments—those that are federally insured—are sovereign in status, meaning the government commits to honor them. Uninsured deposits, on the other hand, are private obligations and are susceptible to default.

The third category is cash equivalents. As we saw above, their issuance generally is *not* a legal privilege. Most cash equivalent instruments have no legal or regulatory status as such. They are issued (in immense quantities) pursuant to standard rules of property and contract. There are no legal restrictions on issuing cash equivalents, and they reside outside the purview of monetary authorities. In addition, cash equivalents generally are private obligations and are susceptible to default.

These three categories of monetary instruments roughly correspond to conventional measures of the money stock: the "monetary base," "M1," "M2," and "M3." Physical currency belongs to the monetary base, which under current arrangements is issued directly by the central bank. Bank deposits that are payable on demand belong to M1, which consists of types of money commonly used for payment. Some important cash equivalents are included in M2 and M3, which are broader measures of the money stock. The Federal Reserve stopped reporting M3 in 2006, but other central banks, including the European Central Bank, do report M3 measures (see chapter 1).

The taxonomy in table 1 raises some basic questions of institutional design. The most fundamental question is why the government should involve itself in monetary matters to begin with. We can safely stipulate that money serves a vital function in a market economy: it makes exchange much easier. But it doesn't follow that the state needs to have a role here. The state could exit the monetary business altogether—including the issuance of physical currency—leaving it entirely to "the market" to establish a monetary framework.

In the area of money, however, the pure laissez-faire approach has few advocates.[18] Even the most ardent proponents of laissez-faire usually concede that "the market" (as constituted by the legal institutions of property and contract) should not be expected to generate satisfactory monetary arrangements through some kind of spontaneous process. Consider the views of Milton Friedman, a champion of laissez-faire in other areas: "Something like a moderately stable monetary framework seems an essential prerequisite for the effective operation of a private market economy. It is dubious that the market can by itself provide such a framework. Hence, the function of providing one is an essential governmental function on a par with the provision of a stable legal framework."[19] More recently, another Nobel Prize–winning economist with equally impeccable laissez-faire credentials made a similar argument. "The market will not work effectively with monetary anarchy," wrote James M. Buchanan. "Clearly some defined process and institutional structure must be established" over monetary affairs.[20]

If the government is going to establish a monetary framework, it must decide how best to do so. In this regard it faces some fundamental design choices. An initial set of choices is evident in the "privileged issuance" column in table 1. Let's suppose the state has successfully put some amount of fiat paper money into circulation, by whatever means. Assume also that it has established anticounterfeiting laws and is enforcing them adequately. As we have already seen, *given* the existence of this established medium of exchange, entrepreneurs can set up a money creation business (in other words, a bank) using generally available legal technologies. A threshold question for the state is whether to impose any limitations on this private activity.

The notion that the state should leave this activity unhindered—a proposal that sometimes goes by the name free banking—embodies a commitment to freedom of contract in this area. Note, however, that both theory and history suggest this business model is prone to damaging panics. (We will examine this topic in detail in part 1.) Perhaps for this reason, free banking has not been the historical norm. The issuance of deposit instruments and their historical predecessors, bank notes, has almost always been a legal privilege.[21]

Suppose the state were to conclude that free banking is dubious—that legal constraints should be placed on issuing redeemable instruments that function as money. (This is the first law of banking.) The state might then adopt the familiar licensing approach, permitting only selected third parties to issue these instruments under specified terms and conditions. But if the state sees problems with this activity—problems that justify curtailing freedom of contract—why let any third parties do it at all? After all, the state could make itself the *exclusive* issuer of monetary instruments, whether through a state-owned "bank" or through some other institutional arrangement. This would mean prohibiting all third parties from creating money; money creation would be a public monopoly. Lest this idea seem far-fetched, it is worth noting that one version of this proposal, called "100% reserve banking," has a very distinguished intellectual lineage.[22]

Either way—whether the government grants the privilege of issuing monetary instruments to selected third parties or retains it exclusively for itself—the government needs to specify the precise contours of the privilege. A legal privilege logically implies a legal prohibition; parties without the privilege are prohibited from doing *something*.[23] So what, exactly, is the government prohibiting? Is it just the issuance of redeemable instruments styled as "deposits"? Or should the prohibition extend to issuing cash equivalents, defined on some functional basis? This is the question we encountered above in the shadow banking discussion: whether there is a respectable basis for the differential legal status of deposits and cash equivalents. It is clear now that this is just one aspect of a broader design challenge.

Turning to the "sovereign vs. private" column, we encounter another set of design choices. Government-issued fiat money is inherently sovereign in status; dollar bills are not susceptible to default. But if the government chooses to license third parties to issue redeemable monetary instruments, those instruments are another matter. The state has two options here. The first would be to leave such instruments as private (defaultable) contractual obligations. The second would be to accord them sovereign status: think deposit insurance.

This is a much debated topic. Historically, deposit insurance systems seem to have had remarkable benefits in preventing banking panics. At the same time, such systems give rise to well-known incentive problems, encapsulated by the term moral hazard. Whether such incentive problems can be successfully mitigated through various regulatory techniques is an important question. A related question is whether the government should limit the scope of its commitment. Under the current US system, federal deposit insurance is capped at $250,000 per account.[24] This coverage limit reflects a consumer protection philosophy; small retail account holders presumably lack the capacity to monitor bank solvency. But if we view deposit insurance through the lens of panic prevention instead of consumer protection, then the justification for coverage limits becomes far murkier. As we will see in future chapters, sophisticated institutional accounts are far *more* likely than small retail accounts to redeem en masse, precisely *because* they are paying closer attention. If panic prevention is a key goal, then coverage limits may very well undermine it.[25] Finally, the subject of cash equivalents arises here too. If the government sees fit to accord sovereign status to "deposit" instruments, does the same logic apply to cash equivalents?

Still other questions suggest themselves. If the government chooses to license third parties to engage in money creation, under what terms and conditions should they operate? How should we think about the relation between this activity and the direct issuance of base money by an arm of the state, such as a state-owned central bank? And how (if at all) should the government exercise control over the supply of monetary instruments? These questions subsume a variety of others: about the operation of monetary policy; about the administrative independence of the monetary authority from the fiscal authority; about the mechanics of the payment system; and about "seigniorage," or government revenue that arises from money creation.

It should be clear that we are dealing with a multifaceted institutional design challenge. Given the importance of the topic, one could be forgiven for assuming that these issues must already have been fully thought through. Surprisingly, they have not. The basic legal-institutional design considerations that are pertinent to the establishment of a monetary system have never been well articulated. Look, for instance, at the standard textbooks on money and banking, on macroeconomics, and on bank regulation. This is where one might expect to see a systematic treatment of these issues, but it is not to be found.

Looking beyond the textbooks, one finds a handful of book-length treatments of the topic of monetary system design.[26] These include such classic works as Walter Bagehot's astounding *Lombard Street: A Description of the Money Market* (1873) and Milton Friedman's *A Program for Monetary Stability* (1960). Despite their remarkable insights, these and other scholarly efforts in this area have major shortcomings (or so I will argue). And these shortcomings in turn explain the inadequacies of the standard textbooks. The textbooks reflect the state of the theory, but the theory is seriously underdeveloped.

A Design Sketch

The core question this book seeks to answer is deceptively simple: How would we design a fiat monetary system if we were starting from scratch?

In the interest of concreteness, this section lays out a blueprint for a fiat monetary system, which I will call the reformed monetary system or just the reformed system. The analysis of this book will suggest that it is a *good* system: it compares favorably with the realistic alternatives. The blueprint will be fleshed out in chapter 9.

The system described here is not radical. On the contrary, I will show in chapter 9 that it is fairly conservative. It could be implemented through a series of incremental changes to the existing US system of money and banking. For purposes of exposition, it is easier to describe the reformed system from the ground up rather than as an evolutionary transformation of the current US framework. Existing US deposit banks would be grandfathered into the reformed system as "member banks," and their current business models would remain mostly intact.[27]

Medium of Exchange

In the first instance, we will imagine the reformed monetary system to be one without *physical* currency. That is, the medium of exchange does not exist in tangible (bearable) form. By no means is this an essential feature of the reformed system. Physical currency can easily be accommodated, and there may be good reasons to do so in practice. But the system is much easier to describe if we imagine there is no physical currency. And clearly there is no magic to bits of paper.[28]

Also, in describing the reformed system we will not use the term "deposit." That term is questionable on a number of levels. For one thing, it connotes a place of storage, which brings to mind misleading imagery.[29] For another, it is commonly used to refer both to instruments that serve as a medium of exchange (checkable deposits) and to a very different class of instruments that resemble ordinary bonds (time deposits). So we will do without this term.

In the system described here, the medium of exchange exists only in *record* form, not physical form. Because it exists only in record form, we will refer to it as r-currency. R-currency is issued only by member banks of the system, and it is denominated in the standard monetary unit (e.g., dollars in the United States). It functions just like today's demand deposit instruments. Agents in the economy hold r-currency accounts. Each member bank maintains a ledger (presumably an electronic ledger or database) reflecting its customers' accounts. Payments in the economy are made through assignments (transfers) of r-currency. The technology of assignment—whether it is a check, an electronic transfer, a card swipe, or some other mechanism—is not important. This is a minor detail of transaction processing; any or all of those technologies would work.

Why does anyone ascribe value to r-currency? For the same reason that people ascribe value to fiat physical currency today. In the reformed system, the government declares r-currency to be legal tender and, more important, accepts it in payment of taxes. The legal-institutional environment thus ensures that r-currency is valued. That is how fiat money always works, of course.[30] Because it is fiat money, r-currency is not susceptible to default, any more than today's dollar bills can default. There is no "coverage cap" on the sovereign status of r-currency. In this respect r-currency differs from today's federally insured demand deposits, with their cap of $250,000 per account. Thus all r-currency is sovereign, fiat money, and r-currency bears no interest—again, like today's physical currency.

This description raises an important point of contrast. Under today's system of money and banking, there are two common media of exchange: physical currency and demand deposit instruments. They are not of equal status. The latter are redeemable for the former, but not vice versa.[31] This asymmetry is encoded in the basic vocabulary of money and banking. Modern physical currency is a form of "base money," "high-powered money," or "outside money," whereas demand deposits are a form of "bank money" or "inside money." In the reformed system this two-tiered structure does not exist. There is one homogeneous medium of exchange. Even if physical currency were introduced, it would have precisely the same legal and economic status as r-currency. And even if the state chose to maintain a "central" bank (a topic we will come to shortly), r-currency issued by that entity would be exactly the same as r-currency issued by member banks. The reformed system thus establishes a legally and economically uniform medium of exchange.

If r-currency seems weird or exotic, it shouldn't. At the risk of belaboring the point, it works just like a fully insured checkable deposit. Instead of committing to honor these instruments with some kind of fiat "base" money, the government simply declares these instruments to be fiat money. In economic substance, these two approaches amount to the same thing. So r-currency should seem quite familiar. Readers who find this weird may just be grappling with the weirdness of fiat money itself, rather than with its particular institutional realization in the reformed system.

At any rate, readers who find this weird are the very reason for introducing the r-currency terminology and for omitting physical currency from this discussion. The word deposit and the presence of bits of paper tend to be conceptually distracting—even for many specialists.[32] They encourage us to think of money as something the bank "takes" and then "lends out," instead of as an *instrument* the bank *issues*. The goal here is to declutter the institutional environment; we need to strip away the inessentials in order to clarify the basic mechanics. Once this is accomplished, then introducing physical currency, or reverting to the unfortunate "deposit" terminology, becomes a trivial matter.

Member Banks

Member banks in the reformed system are chartered by the government and owned by private shareholders. They are authorized to issue r-currency in exchange for financial assets, under terms and conditions established by the state. By acquiring financial assets in exchange for newly issued r-currency, member banks augment the money supply and put downward pressure on market interest rates. Conversely, by selling financial assets or allowing them to mature, they shrink the money supply and put upward pressure on market interest rates.

In addition to this issuance function, member banks assist commerce by managing the circulation of r-currency. In particular, they effect transfers of r-currency among account holders through bookkeeping entries, just as deposit banks do today. (Again, the precise payment processing technology is unimportant; the related topic of "clearing and settlement" among member banks will be addressed briefly below.) In effect, member banks are engaged in a joint venture with the state: a public-private partnership for the issuance and circulation of the money supply.

Why involve the private sector in this monetary function? After all, the state could reserve to itself the exclusive privilege of issuing r-currency. We can imagine, for example, a system under which the state would spend r-currency into circulation through its normal fiscal operations, without involving private agents at all. However, for reasons I will discuss later (chapter 5), that approach to distribution would present serious practical problems in terms of both fiscal management and the administration of monetary policy. By comparison, issuing r-currency in exchange for (nonmonetary) financial assets—*lending* the money supply into circulation rather than *spending* it into circulation—turns out to have significant practical advantages. Of course, the state could pursue this lending strategy without involving the private sector; it could undertake these investments on its own. But there are reasons the state might find it advantageous to outsource this function. That is, the state might want to hire investment specialists and provide them with incentive contracts that reward them for investing well. Such an arrangement should be expected to improve asset allocations while also insulating the investment process from political influence. This is the core rationale for the joint venture.

Like any joint venture, this one needs to be structured. Two key terms of the structure are worth highlighting here. First, member banks in the reformed system are required to abide by portfolio constraints, which confine them to diversified portfolios of relatively high-quality credit assets (loans and bonds). So member banks are not permitted to engage directly in commercial activities, and they are disallowed from investing in equity securities, real estate, or commodities. Instead, their portfolios consist almost entirely of *senior* claims on other economic agents.[33] The objective here is to limit portfolio risk. Second, member banks are subject to equity capital requirements. This just means that at least some specified proportion of each member bank's financing structure must consist of a residual (or shareholders' equity) claim. As residual claimants, member bank shareholders benefit from good portfolio performance, but they also absorb "first loss" in the event of portfolio losses. A supervisory regime monitors compliance with these risk constraints. How to optimize the risk constraints is an important topic that will be clarified in subsequent chapters. For now, it's enough to note that the risk constraints need to be permissive enough to accommodate the desired money supply.[34]

As this discussion illustrates, member banks' investment activities are merely incidental to the system's public purpose, which is to issue and circulate money. Member banks in this system should not be viewed as financial "intermediaries." The system's purpose is not to link savers and borrowers but rather to efficiently accomplish the state's monetary objectives. Put differently, r-currency does not represent claims on portfolios of assets. Rather, all r-currency is uniform, sovereign, noninterest-bearing, fiat money—just like today's physical currency. In the reformed system, member banks coexist with many other types of credit investors that *are* financial intermediaries: finance companies, insurance companies, securities firms, hedge funds, pension funds, mutual funds, and so forth. The aggregate size of member banks, and thus their relative share of the total credit market, is entirely a function of monetary policy; more on this below.

Unauthorized Banking

A central objective of the reformed monetary system is to *confine* money creation to the member banking system. This presents a significant challenge. As I noted above, given the existence of some existing medium of exchange (in this case, r-currency), entrepreneurs can establish money creation firms using standard tools of property and contract. The business model is straightforward. It involves issuing and continuously rolling over large quantities of IOUs that are redeemable on demand or in the very near term for the established form of money.

The reformed system includes a prohibition on this fragile funding model: it constitutes unauthorized banking. To see how this legal restriction works, it is useful to introduce a point of terminology. This book uses the functional term *money-claims* to denote short-term debt instruments (excluding trade credit)[35] that are payable in the medium of exchange or its equivalent. The meaning of *short-term* is a central question and will be analyzed in detail in chapter 1; for now, think maturities of less than one year—the traditional dividing line between the money market and the capital market. I will add some further refinements to the money-claim definition in chapter 9. It is enough for now to note that the definition encompasses such instruments as demand deposits and cash equivalents. It covers the money markets but not the capital and derivatives markets.

Under the reformed system, entities other than member banks are prohibited from issuing money-claims, subject to de minimis exceptions. A more precise specification of the prohibition, and relevant antievasion measures, will be discussed in chapter 9. But the general idea should be clear. This prohibition might initially seem radical, but it is just a functional modernization of banking law's current prohibition on issuing deposit instruments without a special charter. In an earlier era, similar prohibitions applied to the issuance of circulating bank notes. As I noted above, these prohibitions are the "first law of banking"—they are the essential starting point for banking law. The reformed system is no exception. I will argue in this book that the prohibition described here would allow for a substantial reduction in the scope and complexity of modern financial stability regulation. By doing this one thing reasonably well, we could stop trying to do a bunch of other things.

Many readers will no doubt object to this prohibition on grounds of feasibility. Chapter 9 will address this objection in some detail. In the meantime I hope readers will give me the benefit of the doubt. I don't think I'm naive about the potential for "regulatory arbitrage"—a fancy term for avoidance. I used to do it for a living. Just to be clear, my claim is not that specifying and enforcing a general prohibition on money-claim issuance would be easy. It would be challenging, of course. But it is worth pointing out that *every* financial regulatory regime—securities laws, investment company laws, insurance laws, capital regulation, derivatives regulation, proprietary trading limits, and so forth—raises difficult anti-avoidance challenges. Such challenges are an inevitable problem of economic regulation; they are not unique to the reformed monetary system. And regulatory effectiveness doesn't require zero arbitrage.

Of course, this kind of prohibition should not be undertaken lightly. A commitment to market allocation of resources leads naturally to a presumption in favor of freedom of contract. Nonetheless, it is only a presumption. The law curtails freedom of contract when contractual enforcement would produce inefficient or otherwise undesirable outcomes. Antitrust law's prohibition of contracts in restraint of trade is only the most obvious example.[36] Another example comes from bankruptcy law, which usurps individual creditor remedies in order to make creditors as a whole better off.[37] The unauthorized banking provision described here is conceptually analogous to these other cornerstones of the legal structure of capitalism.

The unauthorized banking provision has the effect of requiring all entities that are not member banks to finance their operations in the capital markets and not the money markets. As we will see later, this prohibition would have major consequences for the financial system as it exists today. The direct effect on the nonfinancial sector, however, would be very modest. Contrary to what many people think, commercial and industrial firms rely hardly at all on money market funding. They finance themselves overwhelmingly with equity and longer-term debt (see chapter 1).

Hence, in our design member banks are the exclusive issuers of monetary instruments—both r-currency *and* cash equivalents.[38] In addition, all monetary instruments are sovereign in status. This includes cash equivalents; they simply become r-currency at maturity. Because cash equivalents in this system have no default risk, they bear interest at risk-free short-term rates, as determined by market forces.

Affiliations

Member bank charters are granted entity by entity, just like today's deposit bank charters. This means that a member bank charter confers no privileges on the member bank's "affiliates": other entities in its corporate group (parent companies, sister companies, and subsidiaries). Such affiliates, like any other unlicensed entity, are prohibited under the reformed system from issuing money-claims.

We saw above that member banks face strict limitations on their permissible activities and investments. But should member banks be allowed to affiliate with entities whose portfolios or activities would be impermissible for the member bank itself? For example, should a member bank be allowed to be held in the same corporate group with, say, a securities firm? This type of question has long figured prominently in US banking regulation. Under the famous Glass-Steagall regime, a deposit bank could not be held in the same corporate group as a securities firm (also known as an investment bank).[39] This Depression-era prohibition was repealed in 1999.[40] To be clear, the repeal of Glass-Steagall did *not* mean deposit banks *themselves* could engage in investment banking. Even today they remain largely prohibited from doing so. This is a common point of confusion: restrictions on affiliations should not be conflated with the basic activity and portfolio constraints that apply directly to deposit banks.

Arguably, the importance of affiliations has been vastly overemphasized in US banking regulation. Suffice it to say that there are reasonable arguments both for and against letting member banks affiliate with other types of financial enterprises. This issue is not very important in the grand scheme of things. At any rate, if member banks are allowed to affiliate with securities firms and the like, then transactions with affiliates will need to be restricted. Such restrictions are nothing new; they are a core part of modern deposit bank regulation.[41]

It may be useful here to visualize what the reformed system would mean for a giant financial conglomerate like JPMorgan, Bank of America, or Citigroup. (Assume we have decided to allow affiliations between member banks and securities firms.) In basic terms, we can picture the conglomerate as consisting of a holding company with two subsidiaries: a big deposit bank and a big securities firm. In the reformed system, the deposit bank would become a member bank. This would require some changes to its business model, but not major ones. The securities firm, though, would be required to end its reliance on unstable short-term debt funding. Nor would the conglomerate be able to just move its securities business into its member bank; as noted above, member banks are subject to activity and portfolio constraints that would be incompatible with a securities business. And restrictions on affiliate transactions would preclude the conglomerate's member bank from lending to the securities affiliate in meaningful amounts.

Seigniorage

Member banks in the reformed system were described above as joint ventures with the state. But what are the *economic* terms of the joint venture?

This is a key issue and a major point of contrast from today's system of money and banking.

In the reformed system, the returns from each member bank's portfolio are split between the member bank and the state, as follows. Each member bank pays a periodic (say, quarterly) fee to the state based on its quantity of issued and outstanding r-currency and cash equivalents. The member bank's earnings net of the fee flow to shareholders' equity. The fee is risk-based, meaning it is tailored to the individual member bank's risk characteristics—in particular, its asset quality and capital adequacy.[42] Fee obligations are secured by a lien on each member bank's investment portfolio. In effect, the state holds a senior claim on each member bank's assets. The state's fee stream from the member banking system constitutes seigniorage, or government revenue from money creation.

It should be obvious that this seigniorage fee system is essential. Without it, member banks would earn windfall profits. Member banks have the privilege of funding their portfolios by issuing sovereign monetary instruments, consisting of r-currency that bears no interest at all and cash equivalents that bear interest at short-term risk-free rates. In the absence of fees, member bank shareholders would extract enormous rents from the public. And recall the core logic of the reformed system. The state has decided to invest the money supply into circulation. Investing requires expertise, so the state outsources to specialists; it wants to harness private incentives to invest well. The state's goal should be to earn a fair return, not give its returns away.

These seigniorage fees bear a superficial resemblance to today's deposit insurance fees. The latter, however, are not a source of fiscal revenue. Existing US deposit insurance fees are used only to cover deposit insurance payouts; when the deposit insurance system is fully funded, deposit banks are relieved of further contributions.[43] The US government today earns seigniorage only on the *central* bank's assets—assets acquired through issuing base money. In the reformed system, by contrast, there is no base money/bank money distinction. All monetary instruments are sovereign and nondefaultable, and the state receives seigniorage revenues from the entire system of member banks.

This discussion of seigniorage fees illuminates the rationale for the reformed system's risk constraints—the portfolio constraints and capital requirements described above. Think about it this way: if an arm of the state could reliably charge perfect fees, there presumably would be no need for portfolio constraints or capital requirements. A member bank with a very risky portfolio and/or very low capital would simply be charged a very high fee. The state would be indifferent, since it would be fully compensated for bearing the risk.[44] In reality, though, the state should be expected to have imperfect valuation capabilities. And these very deficiencies give member banks an incentive to ramp up portfolio risk in order to extract value from the state. This, of course, is the moral hazard problem. The reformed system's portfolio constraints and capital requirements are designed to counteract these moral hazard incentives. As we will see in part 2, the challenge is to implement risk constraints without impairing member banks' money creation function.

If a member bank incurs portfolio losses that render it unable to honor the state's senior claim, the state suffers a capital loss—a reduction in the present value of its expected seigniorage fee stream. In the event of critical undercapitalization, a member bank enters a special insolvency system under which r-currency and cash equivalents are seamlessly honored while ordinary debt and equity claims on the member bank are subject to impairment or extinguishment.

Administration

How is the aggregate quantity of outstanding monetary instruments determined? The reformed system employs a cap and trade system. Each member bank holds a permit entitling it to issue a certain nominal quantity of "broad" money (r-currency and cash equivalents). The system's aggregate permit capacity constitutes a cap on the quantity of broad money outstanding. Permit capacity is tradable among member banks. Accordingly, those member banks with more attractive credit investment opportunities can acquire capacity from member banks with less attractive investment prospects. For diversification and competition purposes, no member bank is permitted to hold more than some specified percentage of outstanding permit capacity, say 10%.

The system is administered by a monetary authority—an independent federal agency. The monetary authority establishes the cap on the quantity of broad money outstanding. It may adjust this cap in the conduct of monetary policy, pursuant to its legal macroeconomic policy mandate.[45] To generate a monetary expansion, the monetary authority may increase outstanding permit capacity. Member banks may then expand their portfolios by acquiring more credit assets (subject to the applicable portfolio restrictions and capital standards), thereby putting more money into circulation.

A monetary contraction works the other way around, requiring member banks to reduce new originations relative to maturing assets or perhaps even to shed assets in the secondary market. Thus the size of the member banking system is determined by the conduct of monetary policy.[46]

The reformed system would also include certain other administrative functions. There would need to be a rulemaking apparatus, a supervisory function, and a special insolvency regime. These functions might be allocated to the monetary authority, or they might be allocated to one or more other agencies specializing in such matters. These administrative particulars are secondary issues and need not be addressed here.

Conspicuously absent from this design sketch has been the core institution of modern monetary systems: the central bank. This omission is intentional. While the reformed system is certainly *compatible* with a central bank, it arguably could get along fine without one. As we have just seen, it should be possible for the monetary authority to conduct monetary policy through an administrative apparatus without resorting to a state-owned central bank that transacts directly in the market. Member banks transact on the monetary authority's behalf—their raison d'être. In addition, other key functions of modern central banks, including payment system (clearing and settlement—see below) and lender of last resort functions, should also be rendered unnecessary.

On reflection, this should not be surprising. As I noted above, a core characteristic of existing monetary arrangements is that the central bank issues "base," "high-powered," or "outside" money while other banking entities issue redeemable monetary instruments that are of lower monetary status. By eliminating this dichotomy—by making all money equally sovereign—the reformed system calls into question the need for a "central" bank of which the state is the residual claimant. I hasten to emphasize that the reformed system can certainly accommodate a central bank, and there are good practical arguments for keeping one (see chapter 9). The point is that a central bank is not strictly necessary in this system.

Clearing and Settlement

We can conclude this design sketch by addressing a rather technical issue, one that is a common source of confusion. To see the issue, first imagine that the state charters just one member bank, which is the sole issuer of r-currency. In this scenario, all payments in the economy would be effected through bookkeeping entries. Upon instruction from a payer, the member bank would debit the payer's r-currency account and credit the payee's r-currency account by an equivalent amount. The member bank's balance sheet would be unaffected by these two book entries.

Presumably, though, the government wants to charter multiple member banks to achieve diversification and competition. This circumstance makes the payment mechanics more complicated. What happens when the payer and the payee hold accounts with different member banks? Under today's system of money and banking, here is how it usually works. The payer's bank debits the payer's account, and the payee's bank credits the payee's account. In the absence of any other transactions, the payer's bank would see its liabilities reduced, making it better off, and the payee's bank would see its liabilities increased, making it worse off. To offset these effects, the payer's bank delivers an asset to the payee's bank. In most cases this asset is base money (in the form of a central bank reserve balance). This is the process of clearing and settlement in the payment system. It is generally done through electronic systems managed by the Federal Reserve, and it is coupled with a system of intraday credit whereby the Fed advances base money to deposit banks to enable them to settle payments with other deposit banks throughout the day.[47]

The reformed system makes possible a far simpler method of clearing and settlement. Member banks don't need to hold reserves of base money; indeed, there is no such thing as "base" money in the system. When the payer's member bank debits the payer's r-currency account by $X, it does not deliver an $X asset to the payee's member bank. Instead it books a new $X liability, which we can call a "sovereign debit." The functional significance of the sovereign debit is this: in calculating seigniorage fees, sovereign debits are added to the member bank's outstanding r-currency. Accordingly, after the payment is made, nothing of substance has changed at the payer's member bank. Its investment portfolio is unchanged, its capital ratio is unchanged, and its seigniorage fee obligations are unchanged.[48]

What about the payee's member bank? It credits $X to the payee's account, but it does not receive an asset from the payer's member bank. Instead it books a new $X asset, called a "sovereign credit." Its functional significance is this: in calculating seigniorage fees, sovereign credits are netted against the member bank's outstanding r-currency. In addition, sovereign credits are not counted as assets when calculating capital ratios.[49] Accordingly, after the payment is made, nothing of substance has changed at the payee's member bank. Its investment portfolio is unchanged, its capital ratio is unchanged, and its seigniorage fee obligations are unchanged.

These clearing and settlement mechanics are designed to make the system work "as if" there were just a single member bank. The system does not require any complicated, centralized processes to manage interbank asset transfers or provide intraday credit. By eliminating the base money/bank money dichotomy, the reformed system makes it possible to replace this complicated apparatus with a simple and elegant device.

Some Observations

The foregoing broad-brush description leaves a number of questions unanswered. How does the monetary authority go about calibrating the system's portfolio constraints, capital requirements, and risk-based fees? How are the relative outstanding quantities of r-currency and cash equivalents determined? What is to stop the financial industry from just innovating around the system? What are the international ramifications? These questions are very important, but they can be deferred for now. These and related matters are addressed in chapter 9.

In 1960 Milton Friedman observed that "federal deposit insurance has performed a signal service in rendering the banking system panic-proof."[50] The reformed system is designed to do the same, but on a functional basis. The issuance of broad money is confined and administratively capped; the broad money supply becomes fully sovereign and nondefaultable. And here we reach a point that often encounters strong pushback. This book argues that once the monetary-financial system has been made panic-proof, other forms of stability-oriented financial regulation could be dramatically scaled back.

This is another way of saying that, when it comes to financial stability policy, panics are "the problem" (so to speak). Panics represent far and away the biggest threat that the financial system poses to the broader economy. In particular, I will argue that in a panic-proof system we could worry far less about a lot of other things: "excessive debt," "debt-fueled bubbles," "excessive risk taking," "disorderly failures," "too big to fail," "interconnectedness," "systemic risk," and so forth. Simply put, the problem of financial instability and the problem of panics are one and the same, which is to say that financial instability is (mostly) about private money. A major task of part 1 is to make this case.

Of course, even if one accepts that panics are the central problem for

financial stability policy, one might not favor a design like the reformed system sketched above. Other potential policy responses are available. Part 2
reviews the most promising alternatives. In particular, it looks at using regulatory risk constraints and/or a lender of last resort to deal with the panic
problem. I conclude that these approaches have serious drawbacks.

While the reformed system is essentially conservative in its basic design, its practical implications for the existing financial sector would be
profound. To a far greater extent than is commonly understood, our financial sector funds itself with extremely short-term debt. These instruments
are cash equivalents: they are money-claims. And the market for them is
vast, far exceeding the insured deposit market in size. Under the blueprint
sketched above, many financial firms that currently rely heavily on money-
claim funding, such as the major Wall Street securities firms, would be pre-
cluded from doing so. Their current funding models would be incompatible with the reformed system.[51] In practical terms, such firms would be
required to "term out" their funding structures, that is, finance their operations in the longer-term debt and equity capital markets and not the
money markets. This requirement would be costly for these institutions
and could bring significant changes to their business models. But there appears to be little reason to regard Wall Street's current funding model as
sacrosanct—particularly in view of the events of recent years.

That said, nothing in the reformed system should be expected to make
the financial system any less dynamic or innovative. The blueprint above
says nothing about what activities can take place outside the member
banking system. It only says that those activities can't be financed with
run-prone debt. In principle, we could imagine a very wide degree of lati-
tude for nonbank firms, subject of course to appropriate standards of disclosure, antifraud, and consumer and investor protection. So securities
firms and other nonbanks might be given free rein to engage in structured
finance, derivatives, proprietary trading, and so forth. But they would not
be allowed to "fund short."

Before the recent financial crisis, our monetary system was characterized by the absence of legal restrictions on issuing cash equivalents,
coupled with an implicit government commitment to honor these instruments. This dubious structure remains basically unchanged. Rather than
addressing the structural defects in the existing monetary framework, we
have opted for a staggeringly complex and hypertechnical financial regulatory overlay. These reforms' prospects for success are doubtful: I argue
in part 3 that the system that has emerged is unworkable.

It seems we have been making financial stability policy much more complicated than it needs to be. Panics are a centuries-old problem. They are not about cutting-edge developments in contemporary finance. Private money is not complex. On the contrary, these instruments—most of which are zero-coupon IOUs—are *the most primitive* financial instruments in existence. The upshot is that panic-proofing does not entail extending regulatory oversight or control over the outer reaches of modern finance. Nor does it entail taking aim at nebulous targets like "systemic risk" or "excessive risk taking." It is not clear that these are even meaningful concepts, much less that they can provide a sound basis for policy. Before embarking on a vast array of costly and speculative interventions in the financial system, then, we might be well served by trying to get money right. It might then turn out that many of the supposed problems of finance are not as big as we thought.

PART I
Instability

CHAPTER ONE

Taking the Money Market Seriously

Pure money ... is nothing else but the most perfect type of security. Bills of short maturity form the next grade, being not quite perfect money, but still very close substitutes for it.... The rate of interest on these securities is a measure of their imperfection—of their imperfect "moneyness."—John Hicks, 1946[1]

Are the instruments of the money market—the short-term debt instruments we have been calling cash equivalents—really *money*? The question seems to invite a semantic debate. It obviously depends on how one defines "money." Still, semantic debates can sometimes be useful; they can help to sharpen concepts. This is one of those cases.

Start with the textbook definition of money. That definition can be rehearsed by any student of introductory economics. Money is conventionally defined as the set of assets that can be readily used in transactions. In this regard the *medium of exchange* function of money is commonly said to be paramount. But cash equivalent instruments, unlike checkable bank deposits, generally do not function as a medium of exchange. Rather, they must be converted into the medium of exchange—by selling them or waiting for them to mature—before they can be used in transactions. In this respect, cash equivalents resemble other (nonmonetary) financial assets like stocks and longer-term bonds.

So, under the textbook definition, cash equivalents are not money. And some experts—perhaps many—favor sticking to this usage. Consider the following observations from a prominent macroeconomist regarding the Federal Reserve's (now discontinued) M3 monetary aggregate, which consisted of several important classes of cash equivalents: "Economists define 'money' as an asset that is used to pay for transactions. ... I have to confess that in a quarter century of teaching and research, I never had any occasion to make use of M3. It always seemed to me that this unambiguously failed the definition of an asset that is used to pay for transactions. If you're going to include such assets in your concept of 'money,' why stop there?"[2]

Along the same lines, another well-known monetary economist recently had this to say about "money market": "I know that finance people and business people frequently use the words 'money market' to mean the market for short term bonds/loans. But when you are talking about models of monetary exchange, it is a really bad idea to use the words 'money market' in that way. What you really mean is 'bond market.'"[3] This same economist has also said that "money market" is "just a weird slang name for the market in short-term bonds."[4] And two other influential economists recently opined that referring to short-term debt as money is "an abuse of the word 'money.'"[5] To all these experts we are dealing with a binary categorization. An instrument either is used in transactions or is not; it is either money or something else, such as a bond.

Other monetary theorists, however, have defined money rather differently. Milton Friedman and Anna Schwartz devoted part 1 of their 1970 book, *Monetary Statistics of the United States*, to the "Definition of Money."[6] They remark that it is "tempting ... to try to separate 'money' from other assets on the basis of a priori considerations alone." They go on to note that "perhaps the most common" version of the a priori approach "takes as the 'essential' function of money its use as a 'medium of exchange.'" But Friedman and Schwartz decline to tie their definition of money to this function: "We see no compelling reason to regard the literal medium-of-exchange function as the 'essential' function of the items we wish to call 'money.'" They conclude instead that "the definition of money is an issue to be decided, not on grounds of principle as in the a priori approach, but on grounds of usefulness in organizing our knowledge of economic relationships." Friedman and Schwartz see varying degrees of what they call "moneyness" in different assets.

They are not alone. It has long been common, both within economics and in the broader financial and commercial world, to use "money" in reference to assets that are *not* a medium of exchange. Invariably such assets have consisted of various kinds of short-term debt. They are commonly seen as occupying a kind of intermediate status between cash and bonds. Hence economists sometimes call them "near money," a term that is roughly synonymous with cash equivalent or money market. Moreover, as we will see shortly, many nondeposit short-term debt instruments are commonly classified "as if" they were cash (and differently from stocks and longer-term bonds) in a variety of legal, accounting, and financial market contexts.

This broader usage stands in tension with the binary, textbook definition of money we saw above. The textbook definition does not admit of gradations; it does not envisage a spectrum of moneyness. Is this just a matter of loose terminology, or is something more at stake? This chapter suggests that this terminological ambiguity points toward something that is economically significant. For there *is* something special about cash equivalents; they have a property that distinguishes them from longer-term bonds and other financial instruments. This property can be usefully described as moneyness—but the challenge is to specify precisely what this means in functional terms.

So what does it mean to say that cash equivalents are "money," or that they are "moneylike," or that they have "moneyness," even though they are not a medium of exchange? A common answer is that these instruments are very *liquid*: they can be traded quickly and cheaply for the medium of exchange. But this can't be the whole story. All sorts of financial assets apart from cash equivalents are extremely liquid. Ten-year Treasury securities, many large-cap stocks, and interests in equity mutual funds all exhibit high liquidity. They can be exchanged for cash at a moment's notice and at negligible cost. Yet unlike cash equivalents, these other liquid instruments are not classified with cash in any of the myriad contexts alluded to above. So liquidity alone doesn't seem to be the answer.

Another common answer is that cash equivalents are *safe*. Now, this gets us into the right zone—or so this chapter will argue—but it is important to specify just what is meant by safe. This is not entirely obvious. After all, high-quality *long-term* bonds are often said to be "safe" assets, but they are not generally thought to be cash substitutes. At the same time, cash itself isn't necessarily "safe" over any given period; it may fall in value relative to other things.

This chapter offers a specific, functional explanation. It starts with the observation that economic agents generally find it desirable to hold an inventory of liquid assets to facilitate near-term transactions, which we will call a "transaction reserve." (Milton Friedman called it a "temporary abode of purchasing power.")[7] And this chapter argues that, in a monetary economy where prices tend to be "sticky" in the short run, agents will generally want their transaction reserves to have a very stable value *in relation to* cash. Cash equivalents have this special property: unlike, say, longer-term Treasuries, they have practically no nominal price risk. For this reason they make particularly good transaction reserve assets. This leads to a seemingly paradoxical conclusion: the expectation of potential near-term transactions is one source of demand for cash equivalents, even though cash equivalents are not a medium of exchange.

I believe there is novelty in this argument,[8] but the more important contribution of this chapter is something else. I aim to bring together various fragmentary pieces of theory and institutional practice into a coherent and integrated account of the role of short-term debt in the financial system. There is a remarkable lack of any unified treatment of these matters in the existing literature. Consequently, many discussions in this area are characterized by vagueness, inconsistent usage of terminology, and occasional confusion. The topics discussed here are a cornerstone for the rest of the book.

This chapter concludes that cash equivalents serve a function that can usefully be described as monetary: they satisfy an aspect of money demand. When drawing a line between money and bonds, it sometimes makes sense to place cash equivalents on the money side of the line. A corollary is that the moneyness property of short-term debt disappears on default. The latter point is straightforward enough, but this idea plays a crucial role in the next chapter, so it needs to be stated explicitly.

Bear in mind that the proposition that cash equivalents are moneylike has *not* been taken seriously in the actual design of our monetary institutions. We saw this in the introduction. Issuing deposits (the predominant medium of exchange) is a privileged activity. You need a special charter to do it, and chartered entities are surrounded by an elaborate institutional apparatus. Issuing cash equivalents, by contrast, is not a legal privilege but a legal right. Cash equivalents have no legal-institutional status as such; their issuance is a matter of property and contract. A key inquiry for this book's design project is whether there is a respectable policy rationale for the stark institutional dichotomy between deposits and (nondeposit) cash equivalents.[9] This chapter begins the task of calling that dichotomy into question.

The Contemporary Monetary Landscape

We can start by looking at the universe of US dollar–denominated money-claims, a term that was defined in the introduction as, essentially,

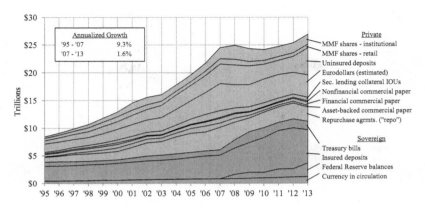

FIGURE I.I. Gross money-claims outstanding
Source: See chapter appendix.

short-term debt instruments apart from trade credit.[10] Figure I.I shows the evolution of this asset class over the past two decades. The top nine series (lighter shading) represent *private* money-claims, in that the issuer (obligor) is a private firm, not a public institution. The bottom four series (darker shading) are *sovereign* money-claims, meaning the federal government is either issuer or guarantor.

Some of these instruments are more familiar than others. Details about them are supplied in the appendix to this chapter, but the details are not important. All these instruments are quite simple. They are dollar-denominated short-term debt. (Whether currency in circulation is properly viewed as a form of "debt" is a subject of debate—a largely metaphysical one at that—but I include it here for completeness.) The maturity cutoff is one year. Note that the figure is underinclusive, inasmuch as several categories of private money-claims are absent because data are not available.[11]

I should emphasize that the figure depicts *gross* quantities: every distinct instrument is counted. That is to say, the figure doesn't "net out" those money-claims that are held by issuers of money-claims. For example, the figure includes money market mutual fund (MMF) shares, even though MMF portfolios consist almost entirely of other types of instruments that appear in the figure. If the figure were presented on a net basis, it would include MMF shares but exclude instruments held by MMFs. Unfortunately, the data required to present each series on a net basis are not available. The figure therefore can't be compared apples to

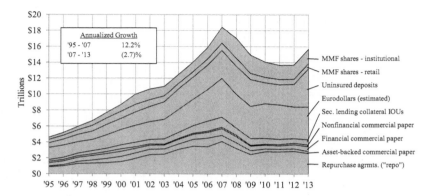

FIGURE I.2. Gross private money-claims outstanding
Source: See chapter appendix.

apples with standard measures of the money stock, which employ netting. While net quantities would be useful for certain purposes, gross quantities are instructive in their own right. The use of gross quantities should not be confused with "double counting." The figure counts each distinct instrument exactly once: this is single counting. The figure might be said to reflect double counting if any of the relevant issuers were mere pass-through entities, but this is not the case. MMFs, for example, issue demandable (zero maturity) claims, whereas the weighted average maturity of their assets may be as high as sixty days. Accordingly, their shares are distinct instruments and belong in a gross aggregate.

Figure I.I gives rise to a few immediate observations. First, the market for US dollar–denominated money-claims is huge, exceeding $25 trillion on a gross basis. (By way of comparison, total outstanding US mortgage debt is about $14 trillion.) Second, this market grew rapidly in the run-up to the financial crisis. The 9.3% annualized growth rate of this market from 1995 to 2007 far exceeded the 5.4% annualized growth rate of nominal GDP over the same period. Third, this is primarily an institutional market, not a retail one. Apart from deposits, MMF shares, and physical currency, very few of these instruments are held directly by individuals.

It is worthwhile to look separately at the private and sovereign components of this asset class. As shown in figures 1.2 and 1.3, from 1995 to 2007 private money-claims grew at an annualized rate of 12.2%, far outstripping the 3.9% growth rate of sovereign money-claims over the same period. This trend reversed itself with the government's intervention during the financial crisis. The private aggregate plunged after 2007, while the sovereign aggregate soared. Interestingly, most of the crisis-related

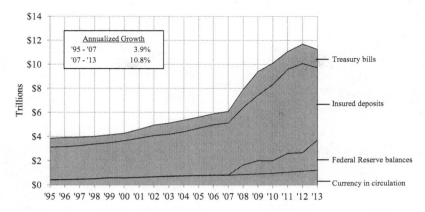

FIGURE I.3. Gross sovereign money-claims outstanding
Source: See chapter appendix.

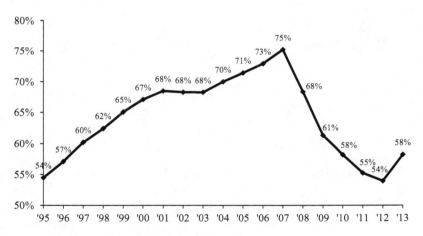

FIGURE I.4. Private money-claims as percentage of total
Source: See chapter appendix.

growth in sovereign money-claims came not from the Federal Reserve's
balance sheet expansion—indeed, the figures reveal the modest size of the
Fed's balance sheet (the bottom two sovereign series) in relation to the
overall market for money-claims—but rather from emergency increases
in deposit insurance coverage.[12] Still, as shown in figure I.I, the postcrisis
growth in sovereign money-claims was insufficient to offset the massive
contraction in private money-claims over the same period.

During the years preceding the crisis, private money-claims came to
represent a steadily increasing share of the total. Figure I.4 illustrates this

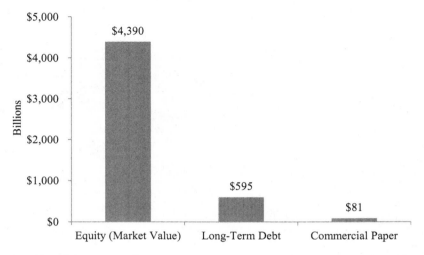

FIGURE 1.5. Selected sources of financing for the twenty-five largest US nonfinancial public companies by equity market capitalization
Source: Company 10-K filings for the 2013 fiscal year.
Note: General Electric is excluded on account of its large financial operations (GE Capital).

trend and its sudden reversal with the onset of the crisis. The increasing private share from 1995 to 2007 can be understood as an increasing privatization of the broad money supply in the precrisis years.

The figures above highlight an additional fact that is crucial from an institutional design perspective: for at least the past two decades, practically all money-claims have been issued by the financial sector and the government. That is to say, nonfinancial (commercial or industrial) issuers have been virtually nonexistent. In particular, only one series in figure 1.1 above—nonfinancial commercial paper—represents issuance by commercial or industrial firms. And that market is trivial—it is by far the smallest series in the figure. This fact comes as a surprise even to many financial specialists. It is commonly supposed that the money market consists largely of commercial paper issued by real-economy firms to finance their working capital. This could hardly be further from the truth.[13]

But isn't commercial paper nonetheless an important source of financing for the nonfinancial sector? The answer is no. Figure 1.5 shows selected sources of financing for the twenty-five largest nonfinancial US public companies. It is apparent that commercial paper is not a significant source of financing for corporate America today.[14] This will be important later in the book, when we discuss the practical implications of imposing legal restrictions on money-claim issuance.

Finally, the figures above raise an important conceptual point. It is typical to think of "money" as a neutral, default-free, uniform asset. But the figures show that the reality is more complicated. A large institution doesn't have the luxury of holding its entire cash balance in the form of insured deposits; the $250,000 cap on deposit insurance coverage makes this impracticable. And a large *uninsured* bank account presents unacceptable credit risk.[15] The "cash and equivalents" line on the balance sheet of any large institution therefore consists of some combination of the instruments shown in figure 1.1. This is the institutional reality of money today.

What's Different about the Money Market?

I noted above that even though cash equivalents do not generally function as a medium of exchange, they are nonetheless classified with cash (and differently from longer-term bonds) in a variety of disparate settings. Before turning to a fuller discussion of why this might be, it is useful to do a quick survey of what those settings are. We will first look at four contexts: accounting, financial markets, law, and monetary aggregates. We will then take a closer look at how this issue is treated within the field of economics, including the curious stance of the standard textbooks.

First there is accounting. "Cash equivalents" is an accounting term of art. The accounting definitions are instructive and worth reproducing substantially in full. Under US generally accepted accounting principles, the definition is as follows:

> Cash equivalents are short-term, highly liquid investments that are both: (a) Readily convertible to known amounts of cash [and] (b) So near their maturity that they present insignificant risk of changes in value because of changes in interest rates. Generally, only investments with original maturities of three months or less qualify under that definition.
>
> Examples of items commonly considered to be cash equivalents are Treasury bills, commercial paper, money market funds, and federal funds sold (for an enterprise with banking operations). Cash purchases and sales of those investments generally are part of the enterprise's cash management activities rather than part of its operating, investing, and financing activities, and details of those transactions need not be reported in a statement of cash flows.[16]

The corresponding definition under international accounting standards is similar:

> Cash equivalents are held for the purpose of meeting short-term cash commitments rather than for investment or other purposes. For an investment to qualify as a cash equivalent it must be readily convertible to a known amount of cash and be subject to an insignificant risk of changes in value. Therefore, an investment normally qualifies as a cash equivalent only when it has a short maturity of, say, three months or less from the date of acquisition. Equity investments are excluded from cash equivalents unless they are, in substance, cash equivalents, for example in the case of preferred shares acquired within a short period of their maturity and with a specified redemption date.[17]

To classify as a cash equivalent under either of these accounting standards, it is not enough that an instrument be liquid; it must also have an insignificant risk of changes in price. This means we are talking about short-term debt, since long-term debt fluctuates in price with changes in market interest rates. The maturity cutoff is three months.[18] An instrument with a longer maturity is not a cash equivalent but an investment security. The financial reporting implications are significant. Unlike investment securities, cash equivalents are classified with checkable deposits and currency on the balance sheet. Furthermore, purchases and sales of cash equivalents (unlike investment securities) need not be reported in the statement of cash flows; they are treated as exchanges of cash for cash. Both of the accounting standards above indicate that cash equivalents are held as part of the cash management function rather than for investment purposes. In fact, corporate treasurers, institutional investors, and other businesspeople typically refer to cash equivalents as just cash.

Second, consider financial markets terminology. "Money market"—which obviously suggests monetary attributes—has long been used in the financial and business world to signify the market for debt instruments that mature in a year or less. The market for longer-term claims, such as stocks and longer-term bonds, is of course called the *capital* market. A similar distinction prevails in the international financial markets. The international market for short-term debt instruments that are issued by financial institutions and denominated in nondomestic currencies is called the "Eurocurrency" market—again suggesting a functional similarity to cash.[19] By contrast, the "Eurobond" market generally consists of longer-term obligations. Thus financial markets terminology distinguishes between short-term and long-term debt. In these cases the customary maturity cutoff is one year.

Third, consider the law. US federal securities and investment company laws accord special status to short-term debt. Debt securities are generally exempt from registration under the Securities Act of 1933 so long as their maturities do not exceed nine months.[20] This exemption aligns the treatment of nondeposit short-term debt with that of bank deposits for securities registration purposes.[21] Obligations that mature in nine months or less are also generally exempt from the Securities Exchange Act of 1934, including its antifraud provisions.[22] Likewise, under the Investment Company Act of 1940, holders of short-term paper (maturity of nine months or less) are not counted in determining whether an issuer qualifies for the private issuer exemption (generally available only to entities with a hundred or fewer securities holders).[23] Moreover, the Securities and Exchange Commission staff has indicated that when interpreting the term "cash items" in the Investment Company Act, the "essential qualities" it looks for are "a high degree of liquidity and relative safety of principal"[24]—a characterization that basically tracks the accounting definition of cash equivalent quoted above. Note that the essential quality of a cash item is *not* that the instrument function as a medium of exchange.

Fourth, consider the treatment of short-term debt in monetary aggregates. Central bankers have long included various types of short-term debt in their broad measures of the money stock. In particular, M3 monetary aggregates consist of some categories of nondeposit cash equivalents, albeit not all of them. The Federal Reserve stopped reporting its M3 aggregate in 2006, but other central banks, including the European Central Bank (ECB), do still report M3 measures. The ECB's M3 aggregate includes debt instruments with maturities of up to two years that are issued by what it calls "monetary financial institutions" (MFIs). The ECB refers to MFIs located in the euro area as the "money-issuing sector." According to the ECB, "Broad money (M3) comprises M2 and marketable instruments issued by the MFI sector. Certain money market instruments, in particular money market fund (MMF) shares/units and repurchase agreements are included in this aggregate. A high degree of liquidity and price certainty make these instruments close substitutes for deposits."[25] Note the reference here to "price certainty" as an essential feature. As with the accounting standards, liquidity is not enough.

Now let's return to economics. This chapter began by noting a definitional tension. Some economists reject using "money" to refer to instruments that do not function as a medium of exchange; they have called it "weird slang," "an abuse of the term," and "unambiguously" wrong. Other economists, though, have taken a different view. We saw that Milton Friedman used a broader conception of money. Notably, so did Henry Simons, another towering figure in University of Chicago economics. "Much is gained by our coming to regard demand deposits as virtual equivalents of cash," Simons wrote in 1934. "But the main point is likely to be lost if we fail to recognize that savings-deposits, treasury certificates [short-term Treasury securities], and even commercial paper are almost as close to demand deposits as are demand deposits to legal-tender currency."[26] Simons opined that "short-term debts ... are ... closely akin to money and demand deposits, since they provide in normal times an attractive and effective substitute medium in which the liquid 'cash' reserves of individuals may be held."[27]

This broader usage is common within economics today. Consider a few examples from prominent thinkers. Robert Lucas and Nancy Stokey observe that certain types of securities are "close to cash" and that the repo market performs for large institutions "the same function that commercial banks perform for smaller depositors."[28] Paul Krugman says that "repo and other kinds of short-maturity obligations are, from an economic point of view, more or less equivalent to deposits."[29] Gary Gorton refers to various types of short-term debt as "forms of money" and "private money."[30] Jeremy Stein says that the financial sector's short-term debt obligations are a form of "private money" and offer "monetary services."[31] Marvin Goodfriend says that short-term debt instruments offer "monetary services."[32] John Cochrane says that "short-term debt *is* money."[33] In short, many leading economists use terms like money and cash in reference to short-term debt instruments that are not a transactions medium.[34] Their usage aligns with the accounting, legal, and financial markets usage I described above.

Given this widespread recognition that nondeposit short-term debt serves a monetary function, one might expect this topic to receive some attention in the leading textbooks on macroeconomics and on money and banking. Interestingly, this is not the case. Consider the leading macro text, Gregory Mankiw's *Macroeconomics*.[35] That text devotes an early chapter to the monetary system, including discussions of money supply measurement, the role of banks in money creation, and central banking operations. The institutional setting is very much front and center here. Yet a reader of Mankiw's textbook never learns of the existence of cash equivalents, by this or any other name ("near money" doesn't appear either). Having defined money as the stock of assets used for transactions, the text informs us that "the quantity of money is the quantity of those assets." While Mankiw's textbook does acknowledge that there can be some ambiguity in determining which assets to include in measures of the money supply, it mentions only two examples of close calls: savings deposits that "are almost as convenient [as demand deposits] for transactions" and MMF accounts that offer check-writing privileges and therefore "can be easily used for transactions." The emphasis here is clearly on the medium of exchange function. After briefly mentioning these borderline cases, the textbook turns to an extended description of the institutional structure of the monetary system—one in which currency and demand deposits are presented as the only components of the money supply. Cash equivalents and their issuers make no appearance.

The leading money and banking text, Frederic Mishkin's *The Economics of Money, Banking, and Financial Markets*,[36] offers a very similar analysis. That text devotes a chapter to the question, "What is money?" It defines money as anything that is generally accepted in payment for goods and services, more or less in line with Mankiw. Promisingly, the chapter notes that "the problem of measuring money has recently become especially crucial because extensive financial innovation has produced new types of assets that might properly belong in a measure of money." Curiously, though, the chapter contains no discussion of cash equivalents or near monies. It merely notes in passing that the Federal Reserve includes in its broadest monetary aggregate certain assets "that have check-writing features" and other assets "that can be turned into cash quickly at very little cost." The latter phrase is suggestive, but it is vague—after all, many *equity* securities can be turned into cash quickly at very little cost—and there is no elaboration. Readers learn nothing here about cash equivalents/near monies. When the Mishkin text turns to an analysis of institutional structure of the monetary system, the money supply again consists exclusively of currency and checkable deposits, and cash equivalents and their issuers are completely absent.

What is particularly interesting about the Mishkin textbook is that it *does* offer a fairly detailed description of the money markets. However, that description appears in a separate chapter that surveys the financial system. It is completely disconnected from the discussions of the attributes of money, the measurement of the money supply, and the institutional structure of the monetary system. Organizationally, the discussion of the money markets is treated as a matter of finance, not money; there is no recognition that the money markets and money might be related in some way. Indeed, Mishkin goes out of his way to emphasize that they are different things. "Note that the term *market for money* refers to the market for the medium of exchange, money," he writes. "This market differs from the *money market* referred to by finance practitioners, which, as discussed in [another chapter], is the financial market in which short-term debt instruments are traded."

It is a commonplace to say that money market instruments have basic properties of money. Yet clearly there is a degree of cognitive dissonance about this proposition—a conceptual tendency to group these instruments with nonmonetary instruments like longer-term bonds rather than with acknowledged forms of money like checkable deposits. This conceptual tension may stem from the lack of a clear articulation of what it means to say that short-term debt instruments have monetary attributes. We turn now to this topic.

The Function of Cash Equivalents

Most economic agents (people, businesses, etc.) hold reserves of assets for near-term transactions, which I referred to above as transaction reserves. Such assets need not be cash itself. As James Tobin noted in a famous 1956 article, "It is not obvious that [transactions] balances must be cash. By cash I mean generally acceptable media of payment, in which receipts are received and payments must be made. Why not hold transactions balances in assets with higher yields than cash, shifting into cash only at the time an outlay must be made?"[37]

While transaction reserves need not be cash, it is equally true that not all financial assets will do. What are the characteristics of good transaction reserve assets? Presumably such assets need to be liquid, or easily traded for cash at negligible cost. But I want to suggest that liquidity alone is not enough; there is another characteristic that is equally if not more important. "Liquidity" and "moneyness" are not synonyms.

The point can be illustrated by considering the typical firm's transaction reserve practices. For any given firm, allocating resources to transaction reserves is costly. These resources are both diverted from the firm's operating activities and withheld from distributions to shareholders. But shortfalls in transaction reserves are expensive too. Such shortages can interfere with production or even lead to default. To determine the optimal size of its transaction reserve, the firm makes its best estimate of future transactional needs and seeks to minimize the sum of its carrying costs and shortage costs.[38]

Why not invest transaction reserves in very liquid equity securities, which have a higher expected return than cash? The problem is that stock prices often fluctuate significantly from day to day. By putting its transaction reserve in, say, Google stock, the firm would run a material risk of experiencing a costly shortfall. Now, the firm could reduce this risk by increasing the size of its transaction reserve—holding *more* Google stock. But this strategy would tie up resources that could be put to better use. Presumably the firm's shareholders are equally well equipped to invest in liquid equities, and they probably do not have uniform preferences in this regard. They would be better off if these assets were returned to them. Accordingly, cash—despite its lower expected return—may dominate Google stock as a transaction reserve asset. And this may be true even if Google stock is perfectly liquid and brokerage costs are zero.

The foregoing analysis has rested on an important assumption: I have tacitly assumed that the value of cash (relative to the firm's inputs) is reasonably stable in the near term. If this were not the case—if the purchasing power of cash relative to the firm's inputs tended to fluctuate wildly over short periods—then a firm that held its transaction reserves in cash would run a high risk of incurring a costly shortfall. It might then do just as well putting its transaction reserves in Google stock. Fortunately, the assumption that the purchasing power of cash tends to be reasonably stable in the near term is empirically sound. This is just another way of saying, as economists do, that "prices are sticky" in the short run.[39]

To be sure, the prices of some kinds of goods do fluctuate from day to day. Many firms rely on marketable commodities for production, and commodity prices can be volatile. But firms typically shield themselves from commodity and other price risks through contractual arrangements. They sign long-term supply contracts with fixed prices, for example, or they lock in their input prices through futures markets. These contractual precautions ensure that, from individual firms' perspectives, key input prices will remain fairly predictable for the near future.

Hence, in a world of sticky prices, agents should be expected to allocate transaction reserves to stable-price assets. This rules out equity securities, no matter how liquid. It also rules out long-term debt securities—no matter how minuscule the credit risk—because long-term debt fluctuates significantly in price owing to changes in market interest rates. By contrast, short-term debt has negligible interest-rate risk. So it should not be surprising that in the real world economic agents typically hold their transaction reserves in cash and cash equivalent instruments. According to the leading treatise in this area, *Stigum's Money Market*, "conservative" holders of cash equivalents "believe that the correct way to manage a portfolio is to reduce their accounting risk to *zero*. In other words, they attempt to run the portfolio in such a way that they will *never* book a loss."[40] Another reference work notes that "economic units . . . supplement [bank transaction account balances] with holdings of money market instruments that can be converted to cash quickly and at a relatively low cost and that have low price risk due to their short maturities."[41]

This analysis implies that there is *instrumental* value in holding cash equivalent instruments, distinct from their intrinsic value as investments. Put differently, cash equivalents satisfy a demand (we might call it money demand) that longer-term bonds, no matter how liquid and high in quality, do not satisfy. This is not just a theoretical conjecture. According to a recent study by three Harvard economists,[42] "a growing body of evidence suggests that safe short-term debt securities provide significant monetary services to investors." This inference is drawn from the fact that "yields on short-term T-bills are often quite low relative to those on longer-term [Treasury] notes and bonds." The authors provide a graph illustrating this, reproduced in figure 1.6.

It is important to interpret this figure correctly. It depicts the extent to which yields on short-term Treasuries *differ* from "what one would expect based on an extrapolation of the rest of the yield curve."[43] It shows that yields on short-term Treasuries are much lower (i.e., prices are higher) than such an extrapolation would predict. "The differences are large," the authors note. "Our preferred interpretation of these [spreads] is that they reflect a money-like premium on short-term T-bills, above and beyond the liquidity and safety premia embedded in longer term Treasury yields." The authors stress that this moneyness is a function of low interest-rate risk. Short-term Treasuries offer "absolute stability of near-term market value," they note, whereas long-term Treasuries are exposed to "interim repricing risk."

The idea that there is a trade-off between holding money and earning investment returns is standard in economics. It traces its lineage back at least to John Maynard Keynes, who *defined* the interest rate as the "re-

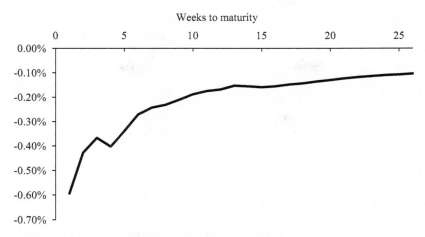

FIGURE I.6. The money premium on short-term Treasury bills
Source: Robin Greenwood, Sam Hanson, and Jeremy Stein, Harvard University.

ward for parting with" money.[44] The important point here is that both logic and empirical evidence suggest that money demand applies not just to currency and checkable deposits but also to high-quality short-term debt instruments that are *not* a medium of exchange. In this light, calling the holders of these instruments "investors" is somewhat misleading. Holders of cash equivalents usually think of these instruments, together with currency and checkable deposits, as precisely the resources they are *not* investing. As *Stigum's Money Market* observes, "The [money market] portfolio manager's job is first to ensure that the funds he invests will be available whenever his firm needs them and only second to maximize the return he earns on these funds."[45] A research report issued by a leading Wall Street firm during the early stages of the recent crisis makes the same point: "Actions that short-term investors view as rational behavior [do] not always align with what other investors might view as rational," because short-term creditors "care mainly about being able to get their money back when they want it." Their actions, the report says, must be "viewed through the lens of different priorities."[46]

It is customary to say that money serves a threefold function: it is a medium of exchange, a unit of account, and a store of value. The third of these functions is sometimes treated as an embarrassment—a characteristic that doesn't distinguish money from other things. Thus Mishkin's textbook says that "money is not unique as a store of value; any asset—

whether money, stocks, bonds, land, houses, art, or jewelry—can be used to store wealth."[47] Mankiw's introductory textbook says that "stocks and bonds, like bank deposits, are a possible store of value."[48] More colorfully, Nick Rowe says "my canoe is a store of value."[49] But maybe it would clarify matters if we said that money is a *reliable* store of *nominal* value. Apart from cash itself (a dollar is always worth a dollar), cash equivalents are unique in possessing this attribute. It is in this sense that cash equivalents are monetary instruments. In a sticky-price world, agents can economize on transaction reserves by holding stable-price assets.

Moneyness and Line Drawing

The reformed monetary system described in the introduction would require drawing a line between cash equivalents and bonds—not merely for analysis but as the basis for an operative legal standard. There is always an element of arbitrariness in drawing a dividing line along a continuum. This is a familiar problem in the design of legal systems: think voting ages and statutes of limitation. It comes down to a practical judgment.

In this regard, look again at figure 1.6. The spread there reflects the moneyness of short-term US Treasuries. The larger the spread—the greater the absolute distance between the curve and the x-axis—the greater the monetary content of the instrument. The figure shows a negative relation between spread and maturity, with much larger spreads at very short maturities. The one-week spread is about sixty-five basis points, whereas the six-month spread is only about ten basis points. We can infer from the figure that the moneyness of Treasuries is likely to be very small at maturities above, say, one year. It is probably fair to assume that this holds true for private debt securities too.

For our purposes, a one-year cutoff is probably in the right zip code. There is no magic to one year, but it does have the advantage of aligning with traditional financial markets terminology; as I noted above, one year is the dividing line between the money market and the capital market. And it is worth pointing out that the Basel Committee on Banking Supervision has embraced the one-year cutoff in its new international liquidity standards, which define financing as "stable" (not runnable) so long as its maturity is one year or more.[50]

This discussion of maturity cutoffs helps clear up one point of potential confusion. In recent years the topic of "safe assets" has become a hot area in the financial stability literature.[51] The term safe assets is basically a synonym for AAA-rated bonds. It refers to debt securities that are perceived to have negligible risk of default. This category includes high-quality sovereign bonds, certain corporate debt securities, and senior tranches of certain loan securitizations and other structured products. Some scholars argue that "excess demand" for safe assets played an important role in the run-up to the recent crisis. In their view, financial and macroeconomic policies should therefore take safe assets into account in one way or another.

The merits of these safe asset theories are debatable, and it remains to be seen how the scholarly debate will play out. Let me just say that safe assets are not what I've been talking about in this chapter. The standard examples of safe assets are *long-term* bonds—they are capital market securities, not money market instruments. It is true that such long-term bonds sometimes serve as collateral for certain kinds of money-claims (such as repo), but this is incidental. After all, many money-claims are uncollateralized. Hence money-claims and safe assets are distinct categories; our focus here is on the former, not the latter.

To John Maynard Keynes, the long-term/short-term distinction was crucial. Indeed, in laying out his famous "liquidity preference" theory of money demand, Keynes devotes most of the discussion to the interest-rate risk of long-term bonds.[52] If bonds were not susceptible to interest-rate risk, he writes, then "it must always be more advantageous" to store wealth in the form of bonds instead of money. (Keynes assumes for this analysis "that the risk of default is the same" as between monetary assets and bonds.) In reality, though, future interest rates are uncertain—which is to say that the price of even a nondefaultable bond may fall after purchase—and "a need for liquid cash may conceivably arise" before the bond matures. Bonds are therefore ill suited to satisfy the precautionary motive for holding money, which Keynes defines as "the desire for security as to *the future cash equivalent* of a certain proportion of total resources" (emphasis added). Keynes's point is that a bond that matures in ten years, even if easily sellable and free from default risk, can't provide any such "security," say, next week. Note that Keynes's analysis has nothing to do with transaction costs or anything like that.

For Keynes, then, the critical distinction was not between the medium of exchange and other assets but rather between short-term and long-term debt. He is explicit on this score. In teeing up the liquidity-preference discussion, he frames the question as one of holding "money *or its equivalent*" (emphasis added) versus other assets. Keynes then gets more specific:

> We can draw the line between "money" and "debts" at whatever point is most convenient for handling a particular problem. For example, we can treat as *money* any command over general purchasing power which the owner has not parted with for a period in excess of three months, and as *debt* what cannot be recovered for a longer period than this. . . . It is often convenient in practice to include in *money* time-deposits with banks and, occasionally, even such instruments as (*e.g.*) treasury bills.

Axel Leijonhufvud wrote in 1968 that "the distinction between 'shorts' and 'longs' to which Keynes attached almost exclusive significance has been largely neglected in the subsequent Keynesian literature."[53] Friedman and Schwartz agreed. "When Keynes distinguished between 'money' and 'bonds' in *The General Theory*," they wrote, "he intended [the] distinction [between short- and long-dated assets] rather than the distinction that has been used by later writers between money, interpreted as noninterest-bearing assets, and all other assets of whatever period."[54]

It is worth pointing out how different Keynes's treatment of money demand is from the standard textbook treatment. The Baumol-Tobin model of money demand—developed independently in the 1950s by William Baumol and James Tobin[55]—is a staple of economics textbooks. In their model an agent decides how to divide its resources between an "investment" (or "bond") and a cash balance. But the "investment" in their model has a special property: it *cannot* fall in price. It is a continuously accreting asset—in effect, an interest-earning savings account. So not only does it bear no default risk, it bears no interest-rate risk either. In this model the only motivation for holding cash balances stems from the assumption that liquidating the "investment" entails transactions costs. By contrast, Keynes was concerned with a much richer setting in which even nondefaultable bonds *do* have price risk, which is to say that future interest rates are uncertain.

It is useful to conclude with an issue that will feature prominently in the next chapter: the consequences of money-claim defaults. Upon an issuer default, the holders of its money-claims may encounter serious practical problems. They may have payments due very soon to suppliers, employees, or lenders, for example. Unless the affected money-claimants can monetize other assets right away, they may have trouble meeting near-term transactional requirements. And a sudden inability to meet transactional needs may lead to *consequential* losses—opportunity costs, operational disruption, reputational damage, or even default.

These difficulties don't ordinarily arise for holders of *capital* market securities, such as long-term bonds. Capital market securities are seldom held as transaction reserves, and their defaults seldom create immediate practical problems for their holders. Money-claims are different in this regard. Money-claims lose their moneyness on default, and moneyness is what they were held for in the first place.[56] When this moneyness abruptly disappears, the consequences can be dire—in much the same way that a firm may incur large consequential losses from an unexpected failure of its power supply or computer systems. The harm to a money-claimant from an issuer default may far exceed the loss sustained on the money-claim itself.

Nor will these consequential losses be retroactively mitigated if the money-claims are ultimately honored in full. Walter Bagehot, writing in 1873, emphasized this very point. "Ultimate payment is not what the creditors of a bank want," he wrote. "They want present, not postponed, payment; they want to be repaid according to agreement; the contract was that they should be paid on demand, and if they are not paid on demand they may be ruined."[57] The moneyness of money-claims and the consequential losses that arise when their issuers default are two sides of the same coin.

*   *   *

Ludwig Wittgenstein famously cautioned against categorizing things in terms of "essential" properties. The essentialist approach, he said, tends to obscure our view of reality, causing us to miss important connections. Better to classify things in terms of "family resemblances" instead. Wittgenstein's antidote to essentialism was "don't think, but look!"[58]

When we look at real-world cash management practices, we see the predominance of cash equivalents (or near monies, or the money market; these are all basically the same thing). This is the institutional reality. Yet the notion that these instruments have monetary attributes has yet to be taken seriously in the actual design of our monetary institutions. Rather, the essentialist approach—under which the medium of exchange function is taken to be money's defining attribute—still has a tenacious hold. As a legal-institutional matter, cash equivalents today have the status of ordinary bonds. Their issuance is a legal right, not a legal privilege. This institutional configuration is not fixed by nature; it is the product of a policy choice. Subsequent chapters aim to show that we have chosen poorly.

Appendix to Chapter 1: Sources for Money-Claim Figures

Sovereign Money-Claims

Currency in circulation. Source: Federal Reserve Economic Database, series
   MBCURRCIR.
Federal Reserve balances. Source: Federal Reserve Economic Database, series
   BOGMBBM.
Insured deposits. The series represents insured deposit obligations of all FDIC-
   insured institutions. The maturity breakdown is not available. The series may
   therefore include some certificates of deposits with maturities longer than one
   year, but it is unlikely that the amounts are large. Sources: *FDIC Quarterly
   Banking Profile*, 4Q'13 (for 2010–13), 4Q'09 (for 2006–9), 4Q'05 (for 1999–
   2005), and 4Q'01 (for 1995–98).
Treasury bills. Source: Economic Report of the President (2014), table B-25.

Private Money-Claims

Repurchase agreements ("repo"). A repo transaction consists of the sale of a security coupled with an agreement to buy the security back at a slightly higher
   price. It is economically equivalent to a secured borrowing. The series represents repo obligations of the primary dealers. The maturity breakdown is not
   available. The series may therefore include some repo instruments with terms
   longer than one year, but it is unlikely that the amounts are significant. Sources:
   Financial Stability Oversight Council, *2014 Annual Report* (for 2011–13) and
   2011 Annual Report (for 1995–2010).
Asset-backed commercial paper. Asset-backed commercial paper consists of short-
   term IOUs issued by special-purpose conduits, including structured investment
   vehicles, that invest in longer-term bonds (typically structured credit). Sources:
   Federal Reserve Economic Database, series ABCOMP (for 2001–13); Federal
   Reserve Data Download Program (for 1995–2000).
Financial commercial paper. The series represents commercial paper issued by
   financial institutions. Sources: Federal Reserve Economic Database, series
   FINCP (for 2001–13); Federal Reserve Data Download Program (for 1995–
   2000).
Nonfinancial commercial paper. The series represents commercial paper issued
   by nonfinancial firms. Sources: Federal Reserve Economic Database, series
   COMPAPER (for 2001–13); Federal Reserve Data Download Program (for
   1995–2000).
Securities lending collateral IOUs. In a typical securities lending transaction, an

asset manager lends a security to a third party, who then sells the security with the expectation of buying it back later at a lower price (shorting) and then returning it to the asset manager. Securities borrowers post cash collateral with securities lenders. Securities lenders usually reinvest the collateral rather than holding it on a custodial basis. They thereby incur what amounts to a demandable debt obligation. Sources: Financial Stability Oversight Council, *2014 Annual Report* (for 2013) and *2013 Annual Report* (for 1995–2012).

Eurodollars. Eurodollars are dollar-denominated short-term IOUs that are issued by financial institutions domiciled outside the United States. Reliable estimates of the size of the Eurodollar market are hard to come by. A recent study reports dollar deposits of banks outside the United States of \$4.1 trillion as of year-end 2008.[59] My Eurodollar estimate is \$4.2 trillion at that date. One textbook estimates a Eurodollar market size of "more than \$5 trillion in the first decade of the 2000s."[60] My series peaked at \$4.9 trillion in 2007. A 1998 study estimated \$1.5 trillion in Eurodollars as of 1996, based on unspecified data from the International Securities Market Association.[61] My estimate for 1996 is likewise \$1.5 trillion. My data series is derived from global bank data compiled by the Bank for International Settlements (BIS). It consists of the product of (1) banks' dollar-denominated cross-border liabilities that are designated as foreign currency liabilities and (2) the ratio of (A) banks' consolidated outstanding international claims up to and including one year for all countries and (B) banks' total consolidated outstanding international claims for all countries. Source: BIS Banking Statistics, tables 5A, 9A(A), and 9A(B).

Uninsured deposits. The series represents the difference between (1) the sum of total checkable deposits (series TCDNS), small time deposits (series STDNS), savings deposits (series SAVINGNS), and large time deposits (series LTDACBM027NBOG), all from Federal Reserve Economic Database, and (2) insured deposits (see above). The maturity breakdown is not available. The series may therefore include some time deposits with maturities longer than one year, but it is unlikely that the amounts are large.

Money market fund shares—retail. Source: Federal Reserve Economic Database, series RMFNS.

Money market fund shares—institutional. Source: Federal Reserve Economic Database, series IMFNS.

CHAPTER TWO

Money Creation and Market Failure

Anytime you ask me about the biggest risk the firm faces, you're always going to hear me give the same answer, which is: liquidity, liquidity, liquidity.—David Viniar, CFO, Goldman Sachs, 2012[1]

The previous chapter centered mostly on the *demand* for money-claims. We now turn to the supply. The goal here is to shed light on a particular business model, which I will call banking. This term is used here in a precise way. It is not a synonym for financial intermediation. Instead, it refers to the business of issuing large quantities of money-claims— short-term debt instruments, excluding trade credit—to fund portfolios of nonmonetary (or at least *less* monetary) financial assets. The issuance of large quantities of money-claims that are continuously rolled over is the defining feature of our concept of banking.[2]

Not everyone uses this definition. To take a typical example, Richard Posner writes, "'banking' has become virtually synonymous with financial intermediation" and "I . . . use the words 'bank' and 'banking' broadly, to encompass all financial intermediaries."[3] His definition has no necessary connection to any particular funding model; it is much broader than mine. Compare Walter Bagehot, who wrote in 1873 that "Messrs. Rothschild are immense capitalists, having, doubtless, much borrowed money in their hands"—but they are *not* engaged in banking, since their money is "borrowed for terms more or less long."[4] My usage resembles Bagehot's.

This definition of banking obviously encompasses deposit banking; deposit instruments are one type of money-claim. But as we have just seen, there are other money-claims—nondeposit cash equivalents—and their issuers too are generally engaged in banking under this definition. These issuers constitute what we have called the shadow banking system. We will look closely at this system in the next chapter.

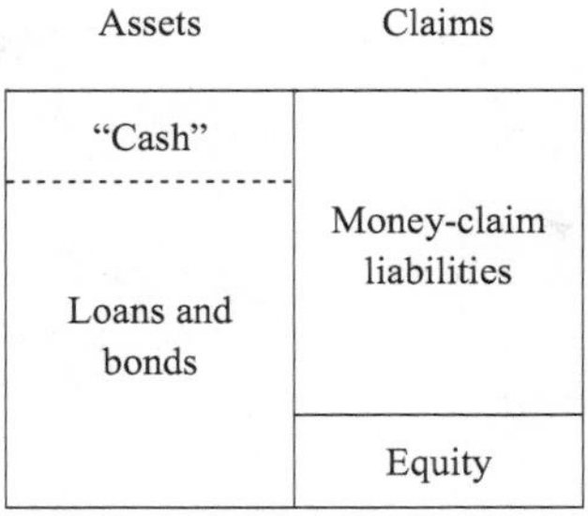

Assets   Claims

FIGURE 2.1. Illustrative bank balance sheet

For now the important point is that the business model of banking is distinctive and identifiable. Figure 2.1 is a typical balance sheet of this kind of firm, familiar to anyone who has studied banking. On the right side we see a large quantity of money-claim liabilities, coupled with a smaller residual claim: shareholders' equity. On the left side is the firm's asset portfolio. It consists mostly of loans and/or bonds. It also includes a small "cash" reserve. Cash is in quotation marks because the precise nature of this reserve depends on what the firm's money-claim liabilities are redeemable for. For deposit banks, cash reserves consist of government-issued base money. For shadow banks, cash reserves consist mostly of account balances with deposit banks.

In looking at this balance sheet, a natural question arises: What do the two sides have to do with each other? Why do they "go" together? We saw in the previous chapter that commercial and industrial firms do very little money-claim issuance. We will want to understand why this is so—why money-claim issuance is so closely associated with financial asset portfolios (*credit* portfolios in particular). And a second, more fundamental question is, Why does this business model exist at all? That is, why would *any* business choose to fund itself with large quantities of money-claims instead of exclusively with longer-term debt and equity? These basic questions turn out to be surprisingly hard to answer. We will address them in chapter 3.

In the meantime we will take it for granted that the banking business model is viable. This chapter argues that this business model presents special problems that can be illustrated with basic game theory. In particular, I argue that banking involves a *coordination game* that is characterized by self-fulfilling bank runs. Those who are familiar with modern banking theory will find this argument familiar. As I show in the next chapter, though, my analysis is fundamentally different from the canonical model of bank runs. Specialists in banking theory should not be deceived by the simplicity of the analysis: this chapter's model of bank runs is novel.

As a prelude to the game theory analysis, we will walk through a stylized story about the emergence of the banking business model. The goal is not to provide an account of the actual historical development of banking but rather to clarify the economic logic of this activity. The story will begin in a standard way, but it will quickly depart from the textbook version. As we are about to see, when it comes to banking the most elementary propositions are disputed to a surprising extent, even among experts. Money and banking debates often boil down to very basic conceptual issues. So it is essential to start from first principles.

The Business Model of Money Creation

For this discussion, we will posit the existence of some amount of fiat money in the form of physical currency. How it got into circulation does not matter for now. Physical currency is the only form of money in this hypothetical economy. Holding physical currency is expensive. It must be kept physically secure; it must be counted manually; its authenticity must be verified to exclude counterfeit bills; it must be physically transported to counterparties to serve as a basis for exchange. Making large payments, particularly across long distances, is risky, time-consuming, and costly.

Given the impediments to trade in this hypothetical world, it would only be natural if a market innovation arose to make trade easier. As a first step, an entrepreneur might set up a specialist firm with expertise in the secure storage and management of physical currency. For a fee, the specialist firm would hold physical currency in trust for its customers in secure vaults. Customers of this firm (and let's assume for now that there is just one such firm) would no longer need to engage in costly storage and transportation of physical currency. These tasks would be outsourced to the specialist.

If large numbers of economic agents began to use the specialist firm, a collateral benefit would arise: payments could be accomplished through bookkeeping entries. To make a payment, a buyer of some good or service would instruct the specialist firm to debit the buyer's account and credit the seller's account. Currency is fungible, so no particular bits of paper need be earmarked for any particular customer. Nothing more than a ledger entry is required. In this way the specialist—a "currency warehouse"[5]—would relieve economic agents of the problems of currency management and delivery, making trade easier. Even after the emergence of this warehousing firm, however, our hypothetical financial system still has no bank-issued money. The specialist firm described here is not a bank as we have defined it; it is only a custodian.

The currency warehouse will do business only if it is profitable. At first it will generate earnings by charging its customers fees. Inevitably, though, the specialist will perceive a second source of potential income. Once it has a large customer base—with no single customer accounting for more than a small fraction of its business—it will find that its aggregate holdings of currency are remarkably stable from day to day. This stability arises from two sources. The first is the "law of large numbers," which says that a very large number of independent events (such as coin tosses) will converge toward an expected outcome (50% heads). The law of large numbers ensures that so long as the firm has many account holders, and so long as those account holders make *independent* deposit and withdrawal decisions, the firm can be very confident that its currency holdings will stay within a specified range for the near future. The second source of stability is actually more fundamental. It stems from the fact that customers seldom see any need to withdraw currency at all. They find it convenient to "use" the currency by assigning their account balances among themselves.

This circumstance presents the currency warehouse with a compelling profit opportunity. It no longer needs to hold currency dollar-for-dollar against its customers' account balances. Instead, it can operate with fractional reserves: it can get away with holding physical currency equal to only a fraction of outstanding account balances. How does this result come about? So far the specialist has created new account balances only upon receiving physical currency from customers. But now the specialist can begin to create account balances in exchange for assets *other than* physical currency—like loan receivables (promissory notes) and bonds. Bear in mind that these newly created account balances are no different from the preexisting ones. They are redeemable on demand for physical currency, and they function as a medium of exchange. Because they can be reliably redeemed on demand, they trade at par with physical currency.

As a result of this business innovation, the firm's outstanding account balances now exceed currency on hand. Even so, for the reasons I noted above, the specialist does not incur a material risk of failing to meet redemption orders. If the specialist's physical currency holdings are quite stable, it can implement this innovation on a large scale. Imagine the ware-

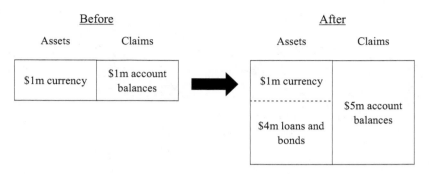

FIGURE 2.2. Warehousing to banking

house starts with $1 million in physical currency and a corresponding $1 million in account balances. It might, for example, acquire $4 million in loans and bonds in exchange for $4 million in newly issued account balances. The balance sheet effect is shown in figure 2.2.

If account holders were willing to accept this new arrangement on the same terms and conditions as under the pure warehousing arrangement—with no modification to the fees they pay to the specialist— then the expected returns from this business innovation should be very substantial for the entrepreneur. But this would be an odd thing for account holders to do. They are assuming risk in this arrangement and will need to be compensated for it. In fact, it is not obvious that this business innovation will be profitable for the entrepreneur. All the returns from investing might be absorbed by account holders. This fundamental issue can be tabled for now; we will return to it in the next chapter.

Let's step back and make sure we understand what has happened here. Readers may have been expecting the warehouse to begin "lending out" a large proportion of the physical currency it holds, with the currency actually leaving its custody. And this is the usual story that is presented in the textbooks and elsewhere. But recall why the currency warehouse came into existence in the first place. Businesses and individuals generally don't want to hold physical currency; they find it inconvenient. They prefer to hold account balances with the specialist and make payments via bookkeeping entries. So when the specialist firm makes a loan, instead of "lending out" physical currency, it simply credits the borrower's account in exchange for a loan receivable. (Presumably the borrower then spends this account balance by assigning it to payees, through the usual bookkeeping procedures.) The result is the same as if the specialist firm "lent out" physical currency to the borrower and the borrower immediately returned it to the specialist in exchange for a credit to the borrower's account balance. Clearly there is no point in introducing this intermediate step. The specialist (which we can now call a bank) just issues the account balance in exchange for the loan receivable. From the borrower's perspective, the account balance *is* the borrowed money. (This portrayal of banking mechanics is sometimes associated with the phrase "loans create deposits."[6] For some historical articulations of this view, see the appendix to this chapter.)

Note that this bank has created money "out of thin air," so to speak. Its account balances function as a medium of exchange, even after they are no longer backed dollar-for-dollar by physical currency. And the firm is now creating these balances at the stroke of a pen (or a computer key) in exchange for valuable assets. To be sure, there are economic constraints on the bank's ability to do this. The bank needs to ensure that it can honor redemptions in the ordinary course. A ratio of five to one ($5 in account balances for every $1 in currency) might be fine; a ratio of fifty to one might not be.

This picture of banking mechanics is rather different from the way banking is usually described—not only in ordinary conversation but also in textbooks and scholarly writings. For instance, banks are commonly said to "take," "accept," "receive," or "hold" deposits. But it may be more accurate, or at least more useful, to say that deposits are *instruments* that the bank *issues*. What a bank "takes" in exchange for issuing a deposit instrument is another matter altogether; it might very well be a loan receivable or a bond. Along the same lines, the phrase "deposits in banks"—which the Federal Reserve uses in its money supply reports—gets the imagery backward. A deposit instrument is not "in" a bank, any more than a bond or equity share is "in" its issuer. Thus "deposit" is often used in a curious dual capacity, to refer both to the monetary instruments a bank issues and to the assets it receives in exchange for those instruments. This ambiguous terminology is a bad idea, and it is a common source of mistakes.

It is worth pointing out that no one would have used this misleading imagery in an earlier era, when banks' liabilities consisted mostly of physical bank notes instead of deposit instruments. From an economic standpoint, bank notes and checkable deposits are basically the same thing. Both are demandable instruments (puttable to the bank at par) that circulate as money. As every commercial lawyer knows, a security can be either "certificated" or "uncertificated" and can be held in either "bearer form" or "registered form."[7] These distinctions do not carry any economic substance; they relate merely to the legal mechanics of determining ownership and effecting transfer. It is useful to think about bank deposit liabilities through this lens. A deposit instrument is just an uncertificated bank note that is held in registered form and that can be denominated in any amount. So deposit instruments and bank notes are substantively identical. Yet the owner of a bank note would never have said it was "in" the bank or that the bank was "holding" it. Nor would anyone have said that such a bank was in the business of "taking" or "receiving" bank notes that are then lent out.[8]

The discussion so far has imagined there is just one bank. Does anything change when more banks are introduced into the picture? Yes and no. Consider a more realistic setting in which there are many banks but most people want to hold an account with just one bank. So if Bank A extends a loan to a customer by crediting the customer's deposit account (in exchange for a loan receivable), and the customer then "pays away" some or all of that deposit balance to an account holder at Bank B in exchange for some good or service, then a set of background mechanics comes into play: Bank A debits the payer's account, Bank B credits the payee's account, and Bank A delivers an asset (typically base money) to Bank B. This is the process of clearing and settlement in the banking system, and it requires Bank A to have enough base money to ensure that, when the time comes, it can settle with counterpart banks. Thus a bank may experience a "clearing drain" when it makes a new loan. This issue didn't arise when there was just one bank.

The standard textbook description of bank money creation brings this clearing drain to the forefront. Take the leading macro textbook.[9] Its description of money creation starts with a currency warehouse with $1,000 in currency and a corresponding $1,000 in customer accounts. The bank then "lends out" $800 in currency. The borrower spends the currency, and the recipient of the currency "deposits the $800 in another bank," which then "loans out" most of it. Thus, we are told, "the process of money creation continues," and "the process goes on and on," such that "with each deposit and subsequent loan, more money is created." In fact, "this process of money creation can continue forever." Notice that deposits *themselves* do not function as a medium of exchange in the textbook story. All exchange is conducted directly with currency.

My claim is not that the textbook story is "wrong." It isn't. My point is that it emphasizes the clearing drain while downplaying the monetary function of deposit instruments themselves. To see why this might matter, let me make a slight adjustment to the textbook story. Instead of starting with one currency warehouse with $1,000 in currency, imagine an economy with ten currency warehouses, each with $100 in currency. Now imagine that, in lockstep, each warehouse makes $400 in loans by crediting customers' accounts in exchange for loan receivables. They have now become banks. Each bank is now vulnerable to a clearing drain as borrowers pay away their new balances. However, because *all* the banks have made loans, each bank should expect to receive clearing inflows that approximate its outflows, per the law of large numbers. The net clearing drain for each bank will therefore be approximately zero. This modified story sounds a lot more like our single-bank hypothetical, with money being created through bookkeeping entries. Note that in our modified story money creation is *instantaneous* with loan formation, whereas in the textbook story money is created through a gradual, ad infinitum process of "lending out" and "depositing in."

Incidentally, we might refer to our modified story as the "Keynes story" because it was (to my knowledge) first articulated by John Maynard Keynes. Keynes offered a careful analysis of these issues near the beginning of his *Treatise on Money*, published in 1930.[10] "A modern bank," Keynes writes, creates deposits "in two ways." First, customers' accounts may be credited in exchange for currency itself. "But there is a second way" that a bank may create a deposit. The bank "may itself purchase assets, *i.e.* add to its investments, and pay for them, in the first instance at least," by crediting a deposit account. "In *both* cases the bank creates the deposit," Keynes observes, "and there is no difference between the two except in the nature of the inducement offered to the bank to create the deposit."

Keynes goes on to analyze the clearing drain issue. The second (or "active") method of deposit creation, he notes, will "diminish the reserves" of the bank as balances are "paid away to the customers of other banks." He continues:

> Practical bankers ... have drawn from this the conclusion that for the banking system as a whole the initiative lies with the depositors, and that the banks can lend no more than their depositors have previously entrusted to them. But economists cannot accept this as being the common-sense which it pretends to be. I will, therefore, endeavor to make obvious a matter which need not, surely, be obscure.

Keynes explains that, while a bank will experience a clearing drain when it creates deposits actively, by the same token the bank "finds itself strengthened whenever the other banks are actively creating deposits"—that is, it will receive clearing inflows. He concludes that banks can safely create deposits on their own initiative *"provided that they move forward in step"*:

> Every movement forward by an individual bank weakens it, but every such movement by one of its neighbor banks strengthens it; so that if all move forward together, no one is weakened on balance. . . . Each Bank Chairman sitting in his parlour may regard himself as the passive instrument of outside forces over which he has no control; yet the "outside forces" may be nothing but himself and his fellow-chairmen, and certainly not his depositors.

Keynes concludes as follows:

> It is certainly not the case that the banks are limited to that kind of deposit, for the creation of which it is necessary that depositors should come on their own initiative bringing cash or cheques. But it is equally clear that the rate at which an individual bank creates deposits on its own initiative is subject to certain rules and limitations;—it must keep step with the other banks and cannot raise its own deposits relatively to the total deposits out of proportion to its quota of the banking business of the country. Finally, the "pace" common to all the [banks] is governed by the aggregate of their reserve-resources.

Keynes's account is quite similar to our modified story above. He is very much aware of clearing drains, but he nonetheless argues that banks can create deposit balances "actively" by making loans or other investments—subject, of course, to economic constraints. "I have endeavoured," he writes, "to say enough to show that the familiar controversy as to how and by whom bank-deposits are 'created' is a somewhat unreal one."

Perhaps surprisingly, the "familiar controversy" has continued, and it shows no sign of abating. In a classic 1963 article, James Tobin criticized as "superficial and irrelevant" the notion that "a bank can make a loan by 'writing up' its deposit liabilities."[11] After all, he writes, the new deposit balance stays with the bank only for "a fleeting moment" because "the borrower pays out the money, and there is of course no guarantee that any of it stays in the lending bank." I believe Keynes had already given a satisfactory answer to this objection, but reasonable people can disagree. More recently, the economics blogosphere has erupted on more than one occasion with heated debates over these basic mechanical issues. Paul Krugman (channeling Tobin) wrote in 2012 that "any individual bank does, in fact, have to lend out the money it receives in deposits. Bank loan officers can't just issue checks out of thin air; like employees of any financial intermediary, they must buy assets with funds they have on hand."[12] It is not clear whether Krugman meant for this statement to be taken at face value; his broader point seems to have been that banks face economic constraints on their ability to create money (which is indisputable). In any case, several other economists responded that banks *do* create money "out of thin air."[13] Two years later, three economists at the Bank of England wrote that it is a "common misconception ... that banks act simply as intermediaries, lending out the deposits that savers place with them."[14] They argued instead that "the act of lending creates deposits— the reverse of the sequence typically described in textbooks," and they challenged "the notion that banks can only lend out pre-existing money." Macroeconomist Stephen Williamson called the article "confused," remarking that the notion that banks simply lend out the deposits savers place with them is "not a misconception, but a very useful way to begin thinking about what a bank does."[15] Keynes was right that these debates have a "somewhat unreal" quality. It is not always clear what the disputants think is at stake.

My point is simply that, as a matter of banking mechanics, it is important to understand *both* the textbook story and the modified (or Keynes) story. These dual views of banking mechanics reflect the dual nature of the medium of exchange in the current monetary framework. Today we have two primary media of exchange, namely government-issued fiat base money and bank-issued checkable deposits. The textbook story puts primary emphasis on base money: base money constitutes the "funds" that go into and out of commercial banks. By contrast, the modified story puts the focus on deposits: deposits *are* the "funds," and they are *issued* by commercial banks; clearing and settlement are pushed into the background. Both perspectives are perfectly valid, and they are not incompatible.

Under a different institutional configuration, however, we might not need two stories—the "familiar controversy" could evaporate. In the reformed monetary system I described in the introduction, there was no base money/bank money distinction. The system envisioned a single, homogeneous medium of exchange. Member banks in the reformed system don't need to "get" r-currency before they "lend it out," any more than the Federal Reserve needs to "get" dollars before buying a bond. There is no such thing as a clearing drain; the system operates as if there were just one bank. So the textbook story no longer fits. It should now be clear why I have stressed the modified view of banking mechanics. It offers a better way of thinking about the institutional direction I think we should be heading toward.

Now that we have developed this perspective on banking mechanics, we are in a position to turn to the core question of this chapter: What exactly is the problem with this activity? Given the existence of an established medium of exchange, the banking business model can be established pursuant to background rules of property and contract. As we are about to see, this business model is associated with a distinctive kind of problem, one that can be illustrated with basic game theory.

Toy Games and the Bank Game

Let's start with a little intellectual history. In 1948 the sociologist Robert K. Merton published "The Self-Fulfilling Prophecy."[16] The essay begins with a parable about a bank. "It is the year 1932," Merton says, and the Last National Bank—a "flourishing institution" with substantial liquid resources—opens to an unusually long line one morning. It turns out that a rumor of insolvency has begun to circulate. "A situation has been defined as real," Merton writes. "The stable financial structure of the bank had depended upon one set of definitions of the situation." But now things had changed. "Once depositors had defined the situation otherwise, once they questioned the possibility of having these promises fulfilled, the consequences of this unreal definition were real enough." Merton's fictional bank meets a sad fate. Redemption orders pour in, and the Last National Bank fails the next day.

Merton uses the bank run parable to introduce a more general point: that there are areas of human activity in which expectations can influence outcomes. Merton coined the term self-fulfilling prophecy for this phenomenon. As he put it:

> The parable tells us that public definitions of a situation (prophecies or predictions) become an integral part of the situation and thus affect subsequent developments. This is peculiar to human affairs. It is not found in the world of

nature. Predictions of the return of Halley's comet do not influence its orbit. But the rumored insolvency of [the] bank did affect the actual outcome. The prophecy of collapse led to its own fulfillment.

Had Merton written not in 1948 but a few years later, he might have connected his insight to a thriving new area of scholarly inquiry. Game theory was still in its early infancy when Merton wrote his essay. (The foundational concept of Nash equilibrium, owing to mathematician John Nash, would not be formulated until 1949.) And game theory takes as its subject precisely the sorts of situations Merton had in mind. The self-fulfilling prophecy would later become an important concept in game theory. In particular, it would figure prominently in the study of *coordination games*—games with two or more Nash equilibria that occur when players choose the same strategy. Merton did not have access to the methods and terminology of game theory, but implicitly and informally he was modeling coordination games. And he referred to the bank run as his "case in point."

It is perhaps surprising, then, that that the formal methods of game theory were not brought to bear on the topic of bank runs until 1983. That year saw the publication of "Bank Runs, Deposit Insurance, and Liquidity," a now classic article by Douglas Diamond and Philip Dybvig.[17] The Diamond-Dybvig article has come to stand for the proposition that bank account holders are involved in a coordination game. Banks in their model exhibit multiple Nash equilibria, one of which is a bank run. This means that banks are potentially unstable under laissez-faire conditions, since rational account holders redeem if they expect others to redeem. "Once they have deposited," say Diamond and Dybvig, "anything that causes them to anticipate a run will lead to a run."

This sounds an awful lot like what Merton was saying in his 1948 essay and what others like Walter Bagehot had said long before that.[18] (Franklin D. Roosevelt's iconic "the only thing we have to fear is fear itself"—uttered in 1933 at the apex of, and in reference to, the worst banking panic in US history—is about as concise a description of self-fulfilling equilibria as one can imagine.) This would seem to suggest that the Diamond-Dybvig model served primarily to formalize a widely held intuition. Yet the stature of the Diamond-Dybvig paper implies that it accomplished something more. Paul Krugman, for instance, has described it as "one of those papers that just opens your mind to a wider reality."[19]

We will take a critical look at the Diamond-Dybvig model in the next chapter, when we discuss modern banking theory. Before we get there, though, it will be useful to build our own game-theoretic model of bank runs. Our model will differ from the Diamond-Dybvig model in two key respects. First, it starts with a completely different theory of banking. As the next chapter will show, the Diamond-Dybvig model has no apparent role for *money*—or if it does, only in a strained sense of what "money" is. By contrast, in our model the monetary function of banks will prove to be central. In this respect the two models are completely different.

Second, unlike the Diamond-Dybvig model—which is expressed in the arcane mathematical language of academic economics—the following analysis uses only the simplest of game-theoretic tools. This is a feature, not a bug. One of the appealing aspects of game theory is that deceptively simple and intuitive games can yield rich insights. As one prominent game theorist, Ken Binmore, has said, "The crucial step in solving a real-life strategic problem nearly always consists of locating a toy game that lies at its heart."[20] This chapter adheres to a toy game approach.

Our goal is to construct a bank game, and we don't have to start from scratch. Game theory gives us a big head start by offering a set of heavily studied games that we can take off the shelf. We will look at two such games, starting with the most famous game of all: the prisoner's dilemma. This will turn out not to be the game we are looking for, but I cover it here for two reasons. The first reason is frankly didactic: some readers may be unfamiliar with game theory, and this game provides a convenient way to briefly introduce some basic concepts. (Readers who already know the basics can skip ahead a few pages to the bank game.) Second, and more important, it is sometimes said that bank runs reflect a prisoner's dilemma scenario.[21] This strikes me as a mistake. For there are no self-fulfilling prophecies in the prisoner's dilemma. If we're going to use basic game theory to shed light on banking, we may as well pick the right toy game.

The Prisoner's Dilemma

The standard story is as follows. Two criminals—call them Alice and Bob—are arrested for a joint crime. The prosecutor puts them in separate rooms and tells each one this: "If one of you confesses and the other does not, the confessor will go free, and the other will get the maximum sentence (ten years). If you both confess, you will both get a reduced sentence (nine years). If neither confesses, you will both be prosecuted on a lesser charge for which conviction is certain (one year)."

	Bob	
	Silent	Confess
Alice Silent	−1, −1	−10, 0
Alice Confess	0, −10	−9, −9

FIGURE 2.3. Prisoner's dilemma

It is assumed that each prisoner cares only about minimizing his or her own time in prison; each is indifferent to the other's fate. Figure 2.3 illustrates this situation in standard matrix form, called "strategic form" in game theory lingo. The numbers within in each quadrant represent the "payoffs" to Alice and Bob, respectively. Because this is a two-person game with two strategies, there are four possible outcomes: both stay silent; both confess; Alice stays silent and Bob confesses; and vice versa.

Obviously, both prisoners would be better off if they both remained silent than if they both confessed. But game theory tells us that if they are rational, both prisoners will confess. How can this be? Consider Alice's inner monologue: "If Bob remains silent, I'm better off confessing and going free. If Bob confesses, I'm better off confessing and avoiding the maximum sentence. I'm better off confessing no matter what!" Bob's inner monologue is exactly the same. For each prisoner, confessing is the *dominant* strategy: it is each player's best strategy no matter what the other player does.

Thus the "solution" of the prisoner's dilemma is the lower right quadrant, where both Alice and Bob confess. This outcome is a *Nash equilibrium*, a profile of strategies in which each player's strategy is his or her best response to the other player's strategy. And it is this game's *only* Nash equilibrium. The outcome in which both Alice and Bob remain silent— clearly better for them both—is not a Nash equilibrium, because each player could have improved his or her position given the other player's strategy. The prisoner's dilemma thus encapsulates situations in which individual rationality and group rationality diverge. It illustrates why two people might not cooperate even if cooperation would make them both better off.

This game has introduced all the game theory concepts we will need, including most importantly the Nash equilibrium. But it doesn't seem to be the toy game we are looking for. If we have a sense that banks are characterized by multiple Nash equilibria—as Diamond and Dybvig argue, and as Merton implied—then we need to look elsewhere.

The Stag Hunt

This takes us to a second toy game, the stag hunt, which traces its lineage to Jean-Jacques Rousseau.[22] The stag hunt bears a superficial resemblance to the prisoner's dilemma, but it presents an entirely different strategic problem. A typical statement of the game goes like this. There are two hunters; let's say Alice and Bob again. They must simultaneously decide whether to hunt stag or rabbit. A rabbit can be caught by one hunter alone, but catching a stag requires two hunters. Each hunter would rather have half a stag than a single rabbit. A hunter is more likely to catch a rabbit if he or she alone is hunting rabbits. Assigning payoffs to each outcome, figure 2.4 illustrates this situation in strategic form.

Does either Alice or Bob have a dominant strategy in this game—a strategy that is the player's best response no matter what the other player does? This time, unlike the prisoner's dilemma, the answer is no. Consider Alice. If Bob hunts stag, she is better off hunting stag (payoff of 10 instead of 5). But if Bob hunts rabbit, she is better off hunting rabbit (payoff of 3 instead of 0). Bob is in the same situation: if Alice hunts stag he is better off hunting stag; if she hunts rabbit he is better off hunting rabbit.

These two outcomes—where Alice and Bob both hunt stag (upper left quadrant) and where they both hunt rabbit (lower right quadrant)—are *both* Nash equilibria, meaning that each player's strategy is his or her best response to the other player's strategy. So what will Alice and Bob decide to do? The game itself can't tell us the answer. We are faced with what is called an "equilibrium selection problem," which is discussed below. For now, the important point about the stag hunt is that each player's decision depends on what he or she expects the other player to do. This game has diverse applications. It has been used to shed light on national security

| | | Bob | |
		Stag	Rabbit
Alice	Stag	10, 10	0, 5
	Rabbit	5, 0	3, 3

FIGURE 2.4. Stag hunt

policy, constitutional theory, and even our moral intuitions.[23] We will see now that it sheds light on banking too.[24]

The Bank Game

The stag hunt above has something of the feel of Merton's self-fulfilling prophecy. It is a situation in which expectations influence outcomes— precisely Merton's point. And for Merton, the most obvious example of this phenomenon was a bank run.

What would a bank game look like? We can start by developing a scenario to set the stage for our game. The previous section gives us the basic setup. Recall that we are imagining an economy with a fiat money system. An entrepreneur establishes a "bank" that issues obligations called money-claims (think of them as checkable deposits). Money-claims are redeemable on demand for currency, and they too function as a medium of exchange. The bank's existence depends on account holders' preference for holding money-claims over physical currency; money-claims are more convenient. The bank holds a fractional reserve of currency against its outstanding money-claims. The rest of its asset portfolio consists of loans and bonds, which are not perfectly liquid.

At any given moment, each money-claimant must decide whether to continue holding his money-claim (that is, whether to "roll over" his money-claim) or redeem it for currency. So long as the bank has enough currency reserves to honor redemptions, all is well. But a big surge in redemptions will exhaust the bank's currency reserves and lead to default. This is a bad outcome for the remaining money-claimants, since their claims no longer function as money. We saw at the end of chapter 1 that money-claimants may experience large *consequential* losses when the issuer defaults. Such consequential losses play a pivotal role in the bank game.

Let's assign some payoffs. (The numbers themselves are arbitrary; what matters is their rank ordering.) It must be the case that economic agents derive some value from holding money-claims in lieu of physical currency. Otherwise the bank would not exist in the first place. So we can assign payoff = 1 to agents who own money-claims issued by a nondefaulting bank. Agents who choose not to own money-claims get payoff = 0. We can imagine that this reduced "payoff" represents the inconvenience of holding physical currency directly or the fee charged by an alternative, 100% reserve bank.

What if the bank defaults on its money-claims? For any money-claimant, the worst-case scenario is that he idly rolls over his money-claim

| | Agent 2 | |
	Roll Over	Redeem
Roll Over	1, 1	−10, 0
Redeem	0, −10	−6, −6

FIGURE 2.5. Bank game

while others redeem. In that case he may experience large consequential losses. Let's assign payoff = −10 to this "sucker" outcome. The final permutation is the one in which the money-claimant redeems when other agents also redeem. We can assign payoff = −6 to this outcome (again the numbers are arbitrary); the difference between −6 and −10 represents the possibility that, by seeking to redeem when others are redeeming, the money-claimant might succeed in exchanging at least a portion of his money-claim for physical currency.

Figure 2.5 depicts the bank game in strategic form. In this matrix we envision that each agent is "playing" against all other agents. So, when examining agent 1's payoffs, imagine that agent 2 represents all other money-claimants, and vice versa. It should be apparent that this game has a lot in common with the stag hunt. Indeed, they are the same game: they share precisely the same strategic form. So any conclusions we can draw about the stag hunt will apply equally to our bank game. Most important, like the stag hunt, the bank game has multiple Nash equilibria, one where everyone rolls over (upper left) and another where everyone redeems (lower right). We can call these the good equilibrium and the run equilibrium, respectively.

In some respects the bank game is a gross oversimplification. First, as I mentioned above, we are depicting a multiplayer game in a two-player matrix. This is a common convention in game theory but one we should remain cognizant of. Second, we have completely abstracted away from the *fundamental* condition of the bank. If the bank has sustained substantial investment losses, then the harm to money-claimants from a bank default would presumably be more severe, since money-claimants' ultimate recoveries would be reduced. Bear in mind, though, that the consequential losses to money-claimants discussed at the end of chapter 1 are entirely distinct from the bank's investment losses. Crucially, such consequential losses can arise even if the bank has positive net worth.

The Equilibrium Selection Problem

The good equilibrium in the bank game is clearly better for the players than the run equilibrium. Doesn't this mean that the rational outcome will always be the good equilibrium? Why would rational money-claimants ever run when it's bad for them in the aggregate? The answer is not so simple. There is no "correct" or "rational" Nash equilibrium. In the stag hunt, Alice and Bob will select their strategies based on what each expects the other to do, and there is no a priori reason to expect them both to hunt stag. A leading game theory textbook elaborates on this point:

> What prediction should one make about the outcome of Rousseau's game? Cooperation—both hunting stag—is an equilibrium, or more precisely a "Nash equilibrium," in that neither player has a unilateral incentive to change his strategy.... However, Rousseau ... also warns us that cooperation is by no means a foregone conclusion. If each player believes the other will hunt hare, each is better off hunting hare himself. Thus, the noncooperative outcome—both hunting hare—is also a Nash equilibrium, and without more information about the context of the game and the hunters' expectations it is difficult to know which outcome to predict.[25]

Binmore makes a similar point. When there are multiple Nash equilibria, he writes,

> one is then faced with the *equilibrium selection problem*, for which no satisfactory solution is yet known. The reason may be that there is something self-defeating in formulating our difficulties in this way. If we knew everything we need to know to solve the equilibrium selection problem, perhaps we wouldn't want equilibria to be our central concept any more. In practice, we solve many coordination games by appealing to focal points that are determined by the context in which the game appears.[26]

Both of these passages highlight the fact that, when multiple equilibria exist, predicting outcomes depends on context.

This way of thinking about equilibrium selection was pioneered by Thomas Schelling in his seminal work *The Strategy of Conflict*.[27] Schelling suggested that a choice among Nash equilibria may be determined by a "clue" or "focal point" that affects how players expect other players to behave. The prominence of any such focal point can't be derived from reason; it "may depend on imagination more than on logic." Accordingly, the outcome of a coordination game "cannot be discovered by reasoning a priori. This corner of game theory is *inherently* dependent on empirical evidence." Because focal points are necessarily contextual and therefore extrinsic to the game, they may have no fundamental significance at all—which is why economists sometimes refer to them by the code word "sunspots." Focal points affect outcomes purely because they are expected to.

The takeaway for our bank game is that the shift from one equilibrium to the other is inherently a psychological matter. We might very well expect this shift to be related to some change in the fundamental condition of the bank—but maybe not. For instance, a commonly observed run at another bank may be a natural focal point. The expectation of a run will start a run, returning us to Merton's concept of the self-fulfilling prophecy. Schelling makes the same point. "What is most directly perceived as inevitable is not the final result but the *expectation* of it, which, in turn, makes the result inevitable," he writes. "Everyone expects everyone else to expect everyone else to expect the result; and everyone is powerless to deny it."[28] Furthermore, focal points may induce nervousness and thereby have a compounding effect, as Schelling illustrates in the context of a "surprise attack" game. "The intuitive idea [is] that initial probabilities of surprise attack become larger—may generate a 'multiplier' effect—as a result of [the] compounding of each person's fear of what the other fears," he writes. "People may vaguely think they perceive that the situation is inherently explosive, and respond by exploding."[29]

Game theory thus confirms Merton's intuition. The shift from good equilibrium to run equilibrium in the bank game depends on expectations—and the game itself doesn't tell us how expectations are formed. It is an empirical matter. Note that none of this has anything to do with irrationality. On the contrary, we have assumed throughout that agents are perfectly rational.

A Market Solution?

The prisoner's dilemma is often analogized to situations of market failure—situations in which the market fails to allocate resources efficiently. A classic example is the "tragedy of the commons," a form of collective action problem. The idea is that if large numbers of people have the right to use some common resource, such as fishing in a lake, then they will overuse and deplete it. A sole owner, by contrast, would maximize the value of the lake by fishing in a measured way, allowing the fish to multiply and replenish their numbers.[30] Hence the rational but uncoordinated actions of individuals lead to an inefficient outcome, just as in the prisoner's dilemma. These are situations in which government intervention may be warranted on efficiency grounds.

It should be clear that the stag hunt represents a possible market failure too. We saw two Nash equilibria in the stag hunt, one of them efficient, the other inefficient. The game itself can't tell us which equilibrium will be realized; we have an equilibrium selection problem. But there is a possibility of a bad equilibrium in this game. So, situations that resemble the stag hunt—such as the bank game—may warrant government intervention too.

If a run is bad for money-claimants, then why doesn't the market offer a solution? We can imagine a hypothetical bargain under which the bad equilibrium would never be realized. Money-claimants could agree in advance never to "run" on an issuing firm, even if they feared that investment losses had wiped out its equity. If honored, this deal would ensure that the law of large numbers would remain operative so that the firm could continue to meet its obligations regardless of any investment losses. The deal would also specify that if at any point there turned out to be insufficient value (as ascertained by an agreed procedure) to make money-claimants whole, they would each take a haircut on their money-claims (perhaps a few pennies on the dollar) to recapitalize the firm. The bargain described here is just a prenegotiated financial restructuring in which money-claimants agree not to exercise their contractual rights to redeem outside the ordinary course. The bargain would of course have no effect on the issuer's investment losses, but it would avoid the *consequential* losses to money-claimants that arise from a sudden loss of money services. Such a bargain might be significantly welfare-enhancing in the aggregate for holders of money-claims.

It is obvious that reaching such a bargain would be impossible in the real world. If money-claimants waited until liquidity strains emerged before starting to negotiate, it would be too late. Bargains take time, and runs are fast. More realistically, the issuing firm itself might require all its money-claimants to agree to the terms of this bargain before becoming account holders. But there is an even more fundamental problem: any effort to monitor and enforce compliance with the terms of this bargain would encounter insuperable practical obstacles. The effectiveness of such an agreement would depend critically on money-claimants' not altering their ordinary redemption patterns, even if the issuing firm incurred substantial investment losses. But each money-claimant would have an incentive to skew toward redemptions. Even a modest skew by a substantial number of money-claimants would deplete the issuer's currency reserves, which are equal to only a small fraction of its outstanding money-claims. And the large number of money-claimants—a necessary precondition to the operation of the law of large numbers that makes the banking business model possible in the first place—presents daunting problems when it comes to enforcing compliance. Proving in court that any given money-claimant submitted more redemption orders than she would have under normal conditions would be very challenging, to say the least. Such lawsuits might need to be pursued against tens of thousands of money-claimants, some with very small balances. Clearly this would not be realistic. Unless the contract could be effectively enforced—through ex ante judicial compulsion or through a meaningful threat of ex post damages—it would not do any good.

The point is that the costs of transacting can stand in the way of bargains, even when a deal would make the prospective bargainers better off. This was a central theme of the famous work of economist Ronald Coase, who wrote that

> in order to carry out a market transaction it is necessary to discover who it is that one wishes to deal with, to inform people that one wishes to deal and on what terms, to conduct negotiations leading up to a bargain, to draw up the contract, to undertake the inspection needed to make sure that the terms of the contract are being observed, and so on. These operations are often extremely costly, sufficiently costly at any rate to prevent many transactions that would be carried out in a world in which the pricing system worked without cost....
>
> ... There is no reason why, on occasion ... governmental administrative regulation should not lead to an improvement in economic efficiency. This would seem particularly likely when ... a large number of people are involved and in which therefore the costs of handling the problem through the market or the firm may be high.[31]

Before considering government intervention in banking, we should ask whether any other *private* solutions to the bank run problem suggest themselves. What about private insurance? Money-claimants know they may experience consequential losses in the unlikely event of an issuer default. Presumably they would be willing to pay something to insure against such losses. This circumstance presents an opportunity for a trade in risk.

For a fee, an insurance firm could agree to promptly deliver to money-claimants, in the event of an issuer default, "good" money-claims in exchange for their now-distressed "bad" ones. Consequential losses would then be avoided.

No such insurance policy is available in the real world. It isn't hard to see why. Imagine the characteristics of this insurance firm. It would need to be prepared to experience sudden demands for large quantities of money-claims from its policyholders. To credibly withstand these demands, the insurance firm would need to hold large quantities of extremely safe money-claims on standby. It would also need to have a very stable funding structure so that its own financing sources could not deplete its assets at an inopportune time, rendering the firm unable to meet its obligations to policyholders. This insurance firm would be the opposite of a bank; it would finance itself in the capital markets and park the proceeds in the low-yielding money markets (or in currency itself). It would essentially undo bank money creation. To make this "negative carry" business model viable, the fees charged to policyholders would need to be substantial. Recall from the start of this chapter that our specialist had to compensate money-claimants in order to transition from currency warehousing to banking. If the bank's customers are willing to pay high fees to make their money-claims perfectly safe again, then presumably they never would have consented to the shift from warehousing to banking in the first place.

*   *   *

This chapter has made a prima facie case that the banking business model is associated with a market failure. This argument will be solidified in chapter 4 (which discusses the consequences of panics) and in part 2 (which turns to institutional design). In the meantime, the next chapter refines this chapter's insights—and offers a critical overview of what modern banking theory has to say about these matters.

Appendix to Chapter 2: Accounts of Bank Money Creation Mechanics, 1790–1930

The present chapter described John Maynard Keynes's account of bank money creation mechanics in his *Treatise on Money*. Keynes was not the first to dwell on these matters. Below I produce some examples that appeared before the publication of Keynes's *Treatise* in 1930. I have made no attempt to be comprehensive; these are just examples I have come across. Two themes stand out. The first is an insistence that banks can create deposits "actively" (to borrow Keynes's term) in the process of acquiring investment assets. The second is the observation that checkable deposits are more or less economically equivalent to bank notes. The thinkers below clearly believed that bank money creation mechanics were a common source of confusion—and that there was something at stake in understanding these mechanics.

Alexander Hamilton (1790)

Alexander Hamilton included a discussion of bank money creation mechanics in his report to Congress recommending the establishment of a national bank:

> Every loan which a bank makes, is, in its first shape, a credit given to the borrower on its books, the amount of which it stands ready to pay, either in its own notes, or in gold or silver, at his option. But, in a great number of cases, no actual payment is made in either. The borrower frequently, by a check or order, transfers his credit to some other person, to whom he has a payment to make; who, in his turn, is as often content with a similar credit, because he is satisfied that he can, whenever he pleases, either convert it into cash, or pass it to some other hand, as an equivalent for it. And in this manner the credit keeps circulating, performing, in every stage, the office of money.[32]

Notice that Hamilton describes banks as issuing account balances (which function as money) directly in exchange for loan receivables, rather than as lending out only what has been entrusted to them.

Albert Gallatin (1831)

Albert Gallatin, the longest-serving treasury secretary in US history, rejected the distinction between bank notes and demand deposits:

> The bank-notes and the deposits rest precisely on the same basis.... We can in no respect whatever perceive the slightest difference between the two; and we cannot, therefore, but consider the aggregate amount of credits payable on demand, standing on the books of the several banks, as being part of the cur-

rency of the United States. This, it appears to us, embraces not only bank-notes, but all demands upon banks payable at sight. . . . If, in comparing the amount of currency in different countries, we have only included specie and actual issues of paper, it was partly in conformity with received usage, and partly from want of information respecting the amount, in other countries, of the bank credits, which may be considered as perfectly similar to our deposits.[33]

Henry Dunning MacLeod (1883)

In the nineteenth century it was common to distinguish between "banks of deposit" and "banks of issue." The latter category referred to banks that issued bank notes. Scottish economist Henry Dunning MacLeod argued that this was a distinction without a difference. "To Issue an instrument is to deliver it to any one so as to give him a Right of action against the deliverer," he wrote. "It in no way increases the banker's liability to write the liability down on paper. Such is only done for the convenience of transferring the Right of action to some one else." MacLeod concluded, "It is, therefore, a fundamental error to divide banks into 'Banks of Deposit' and 'Banks of Issue.' All banks are 'Banks of Issue.'"[34]

Charles Dunbar (1887)

In an article titled "Deposits as Currency," Harvard economist Charles Dunbar pointed to the equivalence of deposits and bank notes: "The ease with which we ignore deposits as a part of the currency seems the more remarkable, when we consider that few men in business fail to recognize the true meaning of this form of bank liability; that it is a circulating medium in as true a sense and in the same sense as the bank-note, and that, like the bank-note, it is created by the bank and for the same purposes." Dunbar acknowledged MacLeod as a precursor. "MacLeod's remark, that 'every bank is a bank of issue,' may seem a hard saying," he wrote. "Still, every man of affairs would be found applying it in practice and recognizing the essential truth contained in it in a tolerably distinct manner."[35]

J. Laurence Laughlin (1903)

J. Laurence Laughlin, a monetary expert at the University of Chicago, wrote that deposits originate in "two ways":

(1) Obviously, deposits originated from carrying money to the bank, the depositor receiving in return a credit exactly corresponding to the money added to the reserves; and this is often thought to be the usual manner in which the deposit item is made up.... (2) On the other hand, it is literally true that in these days most of the enormous deposits of banks in the United States and Great Britain do not result from the actual deposit of money in a bank. By far the largest part of deposits in a commercial bank are the consequences of a discount operation. A loan is inevitably followed by the creation of a deposit account in favor of the borrower; as yet no money is paid out or comes in.[36]

Frank Vanderlip (1908)

Frank Vanderlip, a prominent early twentieth-century banker and a key figure in the debates surrounding the establishment of the Federal Reserve, had this to say about deposit creation:

It is a misconception to suppose that a bank first accumulates deposits and then loans them out to borrowers. The operation is the reverse. The bank first makes a loan to the borrower and in so doing creates a deposit. The borrower exchanges his credit, his evidence of indebtedness, for the bank's credit, a deposit balance....

... That is the true business of a modern bank. It swaps its credit, which has a wide currency, for the credit of its customers, and the bank deposits thus created become the medium of exchange for the greater part of the transactions of commerce....

Obviously erroneous is the conception that so-called deposits represent an actual deposit of money. When the nature of fundamental banking transactions is understood, the error is made plain; but the conception is a persistent one and confuses much discussion of banking questions.[37]

Ludwig von Mises (1912)

Austrian economist Ludwig von Mises wrote that "banknotes, say, and cash deposits differ only in mere externals, important perhaps from the business and legal points of view, but quite insignificant from the point of view of economics."[38]

Irving Fisher (1913)

Irving Fisher wrote that a bank can issue a "right to draw" (a deposit instrument) directly in exchange for "a promissory note" (a loan receivable or a bond). "This operation most frequently puzzles the beginner in the study of banking," he said. But Fisher regarded it as "a needless complication" to say that the bank's currency reserve exits the bank when the loan is made. He went on to note that "a bank depositor ... has not ordinarily 'deposited money.'"[39]

Joseph Schumpeter (1927)

Joseph Schumpeter offered the following description of bank money creation mechanics:

> Even if banks ... only lent out what customers entrusted to them, there would be "manufacture of credit" as far as current accounts are concerned.... There would be ... creation of new purchasing power, even if banks did only lend what they receive.
>
> But this is not the case.... Over and above this supply at their command, banks can and do extend their credits; and that part of the savings entrusted to them, which they can count upon for lending, is not so much the fund they have to lend, but the reserve against the sum they actually lend.

Schumpeter noted that "there are, of course, limits to this creation of additional purchasing power."[40]

CHAPTER THREE

Banking in Theory and Reality

There is no sphere of human thought in which it is easier for a man to show superficial cleverness and the appearance of superior wisdom than in discussing questions of currency and exchange.—Winston Churchill, 1949[1]

The analysis of the previous chapter turns out to hold answers to some pretty big puzzles: whether standard corporate finance principles apply to banks; why money-claim issuance tends to be dominated by entities that hold portfolios of credit assets as opposed to other types of assets; and why this business model—whose principal feature is the large-scale issuance of money-claims—exists in the first place. This chapter takes on these challenging issues. It articulates a money-centric theory of banking and compares it with other leading theories.

As a point of entry, let's return to an issue we tabled in the previous chapter. When the specialist began issuing account balances in exchange for loan receivables or bonds, it exposed existing account holders to a risk they did not previously bear. We noted that account holders should be expected to require compensation for assuming this risk. They paid fees to the specialist when it was just a warehouse. Now that it is engaged in banking, they presumably will require, as a condition of their continued business, that these fees be reduced. In fact the "fee" could go negative: account holders may now require the bank to pay *them* to stick around. How can we be sure this compensation (understood to include fee reductions plus any outright payments) won't cost the specialist more than it expects to earn from its investment portfolio? In other words, why does the banking business model exist in the first place?

To answer these questions, we need to think about how much compensation account holders will require. Recall that account holder claims "mature" continuously and are rolled over each instant they are not re-deemed. The compensation account holders will require to induce them to roll over from any given moment to the next depends largely on their judgments about the likelihood of default the next moment. And these judgments, in turn, depend on the probabilities that each account holder attaches to what *other* account holders will do. This was the key lesson of the bank game, and it means that the probability of default at any given in-stant is not necessarily solely a function of "fundamentals" (the character-istics of the bank's asset portfolio). So long as each account holder thinks it is extremely unlikely that others will redeem en masse, no account holder has reason to redeem.

It should not be surprising that account holders' judgments about whether to redeem should depend on what they expect other account holders to do. After all, fiat money itself has a similar quality. Paper money is "intrinsically" worthless, but people value it at least in part because they expect others to value it. Fiat money, then, is an equilibrium in a coor-dination game.[2] And banking—the business model of money creation—essentially replicates this "outside" money phenomenon at the level of "inside" money. To imagine that this phenomenon is possible only when it comes to physical currency is to fetishize bits of paper.

Hence there is no *necessary* connection between the characteristics of the specialist's asset portfolio and the amount of compensation account holders will require to roll over from any given instant to the next.[3] And this conclusion suggests that, when we talk about the liabilities of banking firms, we are not in a "corporate finance" world. In the study and practice of corporate finance, the value of a firm (and thus the value of the financial claims on the firm) is said to be equal to the present value of the firm's ex-pected future *cash* flows. In corporate finance analysis, cash is blackboxed; its value is taken for granted. What makes banks distinctive, though, is that they are *issuers* of cash (and/or cash equivalents). Banks therefore need to be looked at with a "money view" and not just a "finance view."[4] This chapter will show that applying standard corporate finance principles to banks can lead to big mistakes.

The upshot is that, despite the need to compensate account holders, the banking business model may very well beat the warehouse model. The coordination game is essential here; it is not possible to make sense of money and banking without understanding the power of this concept. Importantly, the logic above sheds light on not just issuers of transaction accounts but also issuers of cash equivalents. Recall from chapter I that

very safe short-term debt offers a nonpecuniary convenience yield; its pecuniary yield is exceptionally low. Accordingly, an issuer of cash equivalents (such as a shadow bank) can capitalize on an extraordinarily cheap
source of funding, so long as its risk of default is perceived to be sufficiently remote. And the risk of default for such an issuer depends on what
money-claimants expect other money-claimants to do. The coordination
game applies here too.

In the real world, of course, money-claimants do care about portfolio
characteristics. They ascribe some positive probability to the bank's default at any given instant, and the bank's portfolio is their collateral in the
event of default. By holding a higher-quality portfolio, the bank increases
each account holder's confidence that other account holders will roll over
and thus reduces each one's required compensation for the bank's shift
away from warehousing. Still, it would be a mistake to conclude that there
is any *mechanical* or deterministic relation between portfolio characteristics and required compensation. Bear in mind that we are not doing corporate finance analysis here. We are talking instead about Schelling focal
points in a coordination game.

This analysis suggests that the specialist might *maximize the value of
the firm* by confining its portfolio to fairly high-quality assets. The coordination game framework doesn't give us an analytic way to determine what
the optimal level of portfolio risk might be. But it should not be surprising
to find that issuers of large quantities of money-claims tend to hold fairly
high-quality portfolios: say, diversified portfolios consisting mostly of senior claims on other economic agents. At some point, dialing up portfolio
risk would reduce the specialist's profits, because the incremental compensation that must be paid to account holders would exceed the expected
incremental portfolio returns. At that point it would no longer pay to increase portfolio risk.

What we have here is a *money-centric* theory of banking—one that
views banks first and foremost as monetary institutions. Modern banking
scholarship, however, tells a different story. Over the past thirty-odd years,
a number of leading banking scholars have offered answers to the questions we are asking here: Why would *any* firm choose to finance itself with
large amounts of short-term debt? And why would the issuers of short-
term debt want to limit themselves, by and large, to portfolios of credit assets? Their answers are very different from the ones offered here.

A Brief Look at Modern Banking Theory

It is worth taking a look at the existing scholarship in this area. This tour will be brief and admittedly selective, but it will touch on what are widely seen as the key theoretical advances.[5] We will look at three major strands in modern banking theory. The first strand sees money-claim funding as a "commitment device" to "discipline" banking firms. The second strand views banking as a response to information asymmetry. The third strand views banks as providers of a kind of consumption insurance. The third strand forms the basis for the famous Diamond-Dybvig model of bank runs mentioned in the previous chapter. Because of the importance of that model in modern banking theory, the third strand will receive in-depth treatment in the next section.

Commitment Device Models

The first major strand of the literature views money-claim funding as a "commitment device" to "discipline" banking firms. The idea is that banking firms rely on fragile funding as a deliberate strategy to constrain their own activities. The pioneering contribution here is a 1991 article by Charles Calomiris and Charles Kahn.[6] In their model the banker has the ability to abscond with the bank's assets. Knowing this, agents are reluctant to hold claims on the bank. Demandable debt makes it difficult for the banker to abscond, which in turn enables the bank to attract funding. So short-term debt funding is a way of solving an agency problem.

While this logic does offer an explanation for why firms might use short-term debt funding, taken alone it doesn't explain why this liability structure should be coupled with any particular *asset* profile. The authors refer to the issuer of demandable debt as a "banker," but this is essentially arbitrary, as the logic of their model doesn't impose limits on the issuer's asset portfolio. Indeed, they say that "claimants to short-term senior debt in modern [nonfinancial] firms may play a similar role to that of the monitoring depositors in our model."[7] Two other experts in this area likewise point out that the Calomiris-Kahn model implies that demandable debt "should be as effective in industrial firms as in banks."[8]

Can commitment device models provide an explanation for the observed *combination* of short-term debt funding and portfolios of credit assets? Some scholars have answered yes. Mark Flannery argues that short-term debt is a particularly effective incentive alignment device for firms whose portfolios consist of "bank-type assets."[9] Bank-type assets in his model are "relatively illiquid" and "nonmarketable" and have "high information costs." Investors in these assets specialize in relationship lending and borrower monitoring, and they earn profits by lending in imperfectly competitive markets. These firms, says Flannery, present serious agency problems for which short-term debt is a particularly good solution. Similarly, Douglas Diamond and Raghuram Rajan develop a commitment device model that associates short-term debt funding with "relationship lenders" that make "loans to difficult, illiquid borrowers."[10] They note that there might appear to be a "fundamental incompatibility" between illiquid loans and short-term debt funding, but they contend that there is a "logic, hitherto unnoticed" to combining these activities. Their model is complicated, but essentially the relationship lender, who has unique "collection skills" with respect to the loans she makes, can commit to use those skills efficiently by employing a fragile funding structure.

Note how different the commitment device story is from the money-centric theory of banking sketched above. The commitment device story has nothing to do with money, at least not in any straightforward way. Banks in these models are not monetary institutions at all—or if they are, it is only incidentally. Indeed, Calomiris and Kahn are explicit that "liquidity demand is absent" in their model and that "there is no demand for transactability." They further observe that "it may be possible to view the liquidity of bank claims as a *by-product* of the solution to the agency problem" (emphasis added).[11] At most, then, liquidity and transactability are emergent properties in these models. By contrast, in our account the monetary function was the starting point—we got to fractional reserve banking by way of currency warehousing. If one is inclined to think that the monetary function of banking is central rather than incidental, then the commitment device theory might seem to have an air of unreality.

The commitment device theory has another problem. We don't really have a theory of banking unless we can explain why short-term debt funding is so closely related to portfolios of credit assets—that is, unless we can explain how the two sides of the banking balance sheet relate to each other. This would seem to be a minimal requirement of any theory of banking. As noted above, attempts to tie the commitment device model to particular asset profiles have emphasized "relationship lenders" with unique "collection skills" or lenders that acquire illiquid financial assets and engage in extensive borrower monitoring.

The problem is that, while in practice short-term debt funding is associated with *credit* portfolios, it clearly is *not* specific to relationship lenders or illiquid loans. For example, consider a prototypical shadow bank: the asset-backed commercial paper (ABCP) conduit. These entities invest in highly rated bonds that trade in the secondary market. They fund these bond portfolios with very short-term debt. This became a massive business in the years preceding the crisis, with over $1 trillion in outstanding short-term paper. It would be odd to think of an ABCP conduit as a "relationship lender" with special "collection skills." They don't make loans to individual borrowers, nor do they have any responsibility for individual borrower monitoring or collection. Commitment device models do not offer much traction in understanding why such an entity would use short-term debt funding. Nor, for that matter, do these models help us understand modern repo-funded securities firms, whose assets consist primarily of marketable securities purchased in the secondary markets.[12] Thus, even setting aside questions of intuitive plausibility, the commitment device model seems to have serious limitations.

The commitment device theory is nonetheless quite influential. In a 2009 speech, Ben Bernanke cited both the Calomiris-Kahn paper and the Diamond-Rajan paper for the proposition that "short-term creditors can help to impose market discipline on financial institutions." He viewed this to be a "good economic reason" for short-term debt funding.[13] A recent report by fifteen illustrious economists also views this theory favorably. "The disciplining effect of short-term debt ... makes management more productive," these economists note. "Capital requirements that lean against short-term debt push banks toward other forms of financing that may allow managers to be more lax."[14] Despite the influence of these models, I question whether they provide a suitable basis for policy analysis in the real world.[15]

Information Asymmetry Models

The second key strand in the literature views banking as a response to information asymmetry. This class of models has much more in common with the money-centric model presented here, but there are important differences. The canonical work here is a 1990 paper by Gary Gorton and George Pennacchi.[16] Their model posits the existence of uninformed "noise" traders who trade with and lose money to informed traders. Recognizing this problem, noise traders prefer securities with low default risk. Such "information insensitive" securities do not afford informed traders the opportunity to take advantage of superior information.[17] Because no one has an information advantage, these securities exhibit superior liquidity in the model. And the natural issuer of these securities is an intermediary that owns a diversified portfolio of credit assets—that is, an entity whose total asset value is not very volatile. So this theory, unlike the commitment device theory, does link the issuance of "liquid" claims to a particular asset profile in a clear and intuitive way.

Note the stark difference between these two theories. The commitment device model envisions that short-term creditors are keeping a watchful eye on the bank, and that those who are paying the most attention are rewarded by getting out first. By contrast, under the information asymmetry model, the whole point of the bank is to produce claims for which producing information is *not* rewarded. Remarkably, then, these two leading theories of banking are polar opposites. "Paradoxically, these two literatures give contradictory and inconsistent accounts of the banks' short-term creditors," write Anat Admati and Martin Hellwig. "The two visions, one of creditors constantly on the watch for problems and the other of creditors trusting that banks are safe, are not compatible with each other."[18] If you buy one of these theories, there is no buying the other.

The information asymmetry theory has at least one major limitation: it has no necessary connection to *short-term* debt. Long-term debt may be information insensitive too, so long as its likelihood of default is perceived to be very remote. Thus the information asymmetry theory can be understood as a general theory of capital structure or "safe assets" (see chapter 1) rather than a theory of banking proper. It applies to any set of cash flows that is tranched into senior and junior components, irrespective of whether the funding comes from short-term IOUs that are continuously rolled over. In this sense, the theory does not seem to get at the distinctive qualities of the banking business model. As we saw in chapter 1, moneyness is unique to short-term claims.

Design Implications

Before turning to the third major theory, it is useful to pause and take stock. The differences among these models have crucial implications for regulatory policy. Consider first the design implications of the commitment device theory. That theory implies that the fragility of banks may be a *good* thing. Stability policies, such as the lender of last resort and deposit insurance, deprive money-claims of their disciplinary power and may lead to less-efficient resource allocations. Thus Diamond and Rajan contend that "financial fragility" may be "a desirable characteristic of banks" and that "stabilization policies . . . may reduce liquidity creation."[19] Flannery's view is similar. "Banking firms' exposure to liquidity risks ('depositor runs') has traditionally been considered a social 'bad,'" he writes. "However, if short-funding bank assets provides important incentive benefits, regulations that limit a bank's ability to employ this funding device may reduce social welfare rather than increase it."[20]

As for the information asymmetry theory, it too suggests a certain way of thinking about bank regulation. Gary Gorton, the leading proponent of the information asymmetry theory of banking, argues that a panic occurs when information insensitive assets become information sensitive. Holders of these assets lack the capacity to evaluate them, since the whole point was to hold assets that don't require such evaluation. When they find themselves needing to do such evaluation, they face a serious problem, and systemwide consequences ensue. In Gorton's model, banking is not characterized by self-fulfilling prophecies; there is no coordination game.[21] Naturally, Gorton's preferred policy solution involves strict regulation of portfolio quality—in effect, a form of narrow banking.[22] When we turn to design alternatives in part 2, we will find big problems with the narrow banking strategy.

The Standard Model of Bank Runs

We now turn to the final theory of banking, which sees banks as providers of a special type of insurance. This theory forms the basis for the Diamond-Dybvig model of bank runs.[23] Because of the stature and continuing influence of this model, it is important to look at it in some detail.

The important features of the Diamond-Dybvig model can be described in a few paragraphs. Their model has three periods ($T = 0, 1$, and 2). There are two types of consumers: those who want to consume only at $T = 1$ (type 1 consumers) and those who want to consume only at $T = 2$ (type 2 consumers). There is "a single homogeneous good" in the model, called the consumption good.[24] Each consumer starts with one unit of the consumption good, and each has an opportunity at $T = 0$ to lend his unit to a third party. All loans are identical. Loans mature at T = 2 and produce positive returns at maturity (payable in the consumption good) with no risk of default. The model thus abstracts away from credit risk, inasmuch as nobody ever loses money on a loan. If a consumer declines to lend his consumption unit, he earns no return. In that case he can store his unit and consume it later. Notice that there is nothing called "money" in this setup.

If consumers knew their types at T = 0, then type 2 consumers obviously would lend their consumption units and type 1 consumers presumably would not. After all, type 1 consumers would not want to have their consumption units tied up in loans at T = 1. But here's the rub: consumers don't discover their types until T = 1. This is a problem, because consumers must decide at T = 0 whether to lend.

Owing to this uncertainty, we might expect that consumers would be hesitant to make loans at all. However, Diamond and Dybvig make one other crucial assumption: all loans can be risklessly *called* at T = 1. If a loan is called, the consumer gets his consumption unit back with no interest but also no penalty. With this call feature, there can never be any downside in lending. If a consumer lends his unit (at T = 0) and later discovers (at T = 1) that he is of type 1, he will just call the loan and consume the unit—putting him in the same position as if he hadn't lent the unit at all. On the other hand, if the consumer discovers that he is of type 2, he won't call the loan at T = 1. Instead, he will allow the loan to mature at T = 2, earning a positive return.

So what role do banks play in this strange economy? For Diamond and Dybvig, the answer is that they offer consumers a form of insurance. Here is how it works. In the scenario described above, any consumer would rather be of type 2 than type 1. This is because type 2 consumers get positive returns from lending, whereas type 1 consumers get no return.[25] Assuming consumers are risk-averse, they can benefit from a bargain at T = 0, before they learn their types. Specifically, consumers can pool their consumption units into a "bank" at T = 0. The bank promptly lends out all the deposited units. It keeps no units in reserve; it has no need for reserves, since all loans can be called with no penalty. When T = 1 rolls around, each consumer discovers his type. Naturally, all type 1 consumers go to the bank to withdraw their consumption units—first come first served—and the bank must call loans to make these payouts. Here is the innovation: the bargain that was struck at T = 0 specifies that consumers who withdraw at T = 1 are entitled to something slightly *more* than one consumption unit. They now get a positive return. So, type 1 consumers who withdraw at T = 1 will clearly be better off than if they had lent their units directly.

What about type 2 consumers? Assuming none of them withdraws at T = 1, they will still receive positive returns at T = 2. However, such returns are necessarily smaller than they would have been had those consumers lent directly—because some of their returns were, in effect, shared with type 1 consumers. Clearly, then, considered from an ex post perspective, type 2 consumers are worse off than they would have been in the absence of the bank. Keep in mind, though, that everyone agreed to this deal back at T = 0, when nobody knew his or her type. Ex ante, behind the T = 0 veil of ignorance, the bargain makes consumers better off in the aggregate. (Insurance is always "expensive" ex post if the risk did not materialize.) Like any insurance contract, this contract is welfare enhancing because consumers are assumed to be risk-averse. As Diamond and Dybvig put it, the point of the bank is to "allow agents to insure against the unlucky outcome of being a type 1 agent."[26]

In a moment we will see why the bank described here might be vulnerable to a bank run, in which both type 1 and type 2 consumers seek to withdraw at T = 1. But it is worth stepping back for a moment and asking a basic question: What does this model of banking have to do with *actual* banking? These banks don't augment the supply of credit; the quantity of loans is exactly the same whether or not the banks exist, because all consumption units are lent in either case. Even more noteworthy are the monetary aspects of the model—or, more accurately, their absence. For there is no money in the model. Banks don't hold fractional reserves in the model; there is nothing called money to be held in reserve. Banks have no use for such reserves anyway, since all loans can be risklessly called. Nor do these banks issue monetary instruments. Consumers in this model are in no need of money, since they inhabit a world with just one homogeneous good. As Gary Gorton and Charles Calomiris have pointed out, "the banks' liabilities do not circulate as a medium of exchange in this model, so there is no sense in which demand deposits function like money. This appears to be a weakness of the model."[27] In a subsequent paper, Gorton and Andrew Winton elaborate on this point: "There is no notion of exchange in the model, no sense in which transactions are taking place where bank 'money' is being used to facilitate the [consumption] smoothing. Instead, agents are essentially isolated from each other; there is no trade with other agents where 'money' buys goods.... Agents trade only with the bank."[28]

Of course, this is only a model, and all models are simplifications of reality; the map is not the territory, as they say. Perhaps the model can help us gain a better understanding of some feature of the world. So let's turn to what the model says about bank runs.

Diamond and Dybvig show how a run can arise at their bank. Suppose some type 2 consumers—in addition to all type 1 consumers—ask for withdrawals at $T = 1$.[29] (We will see in a moment why they might do so.) These withdrawals by type 2 consumers at $T = 1$ create a problem. Withdrawals at $T = 1$ eat into the returns left over for consumers who do not withdraw. Remember, consumers withdrawing at $T = 1$ get *more* than one unit—that was the whole point of the bank—while loans called by the bank at $T = 1$ to meet those withdrawals are called at par. Accordingly, if enough type 2 consumers join type 1 consumers in withdrawing at $T = 1$, the bank's assets will be completely exhausted, leaving the remaining type 2 consumers with nothing. This outcome is clearly bad for consumers in the aggregate, since all loans get called at $T = 1$, leaving no positive returns to be split among consumers.

But why would a type 2 consumer ever withdraw at $T = 1$? The answer is, if he suspects that other type 2 consumers will do so! The type 2 consumer doesn't want to *consume* at $T = 1$, but he can still withdraw his consumption unit at $T = 1$ and store it for consumption at $T = 2$. If he thinks there is a significant chance that he might be left worse off if he doesn't get in line at $T = 1$, then he will get in line for withdrawal.

This run risk raises the question why banks exist in the first place. Here is Diamond and Dybvig's answer—one that echoes several of the themes we discussed in the previous chapter in developing our bank game:

> No one would deposit anticipating a run. However, agents will choose to deposit at least some of their wealth in the bank even if they anticipate a positive probability of a run, provided that the probability is small enough, because the good equilibrium dominates holding assets directly. This could happen if the selection between the bank run equilibrium and the good equilibrium depended on some commonly observed random variable in the economy. This could be a bad earnings report, a commonly observed run at some other bank, a negative government forecast, or even sunspots. It need not be anything fundamental about the bank's condition. The problem is that once they have deposited, anything that causes them to anticipate a run will lead to a run. This implies that banks with pure demand deposit contracts will be very concerned about maintaining confidence because they realize that the good equilibrium is very fragile.[30]

This all seems quite sensible; the "observed variable" that Diamond and Dybvig refer to here is just a Schelling focal point (they use the code word "sunspots" for this). And their conclusion that "anything that causes [agents] to anticipate a run will lead to a run" is, as we have seen, a basic property of coordination games like the stag hunt. They're talking about a self-fulfilling prophecy of the type described by Robert K. Merton.

The obvious question, though, is whether it was necessary to build an elaborate mathematical model in order to get here—whether the Diamond-Dybvig model sheds any more light on the real world than our bank game did. At a certain level of abstraction, the two models get you to the same place; both are characterized by self-fulfilling bank runs. One might therefore be tempted to conclude that they are just two ways of saying the same thing. Nonetheless, I see three reasons to prefer the bank game to the Diamond-Dybvig model of bank runs.

First, the Diamond-Dybvig model is subject to at least one trenchant criticism from which the bank game is exempt. The criticism comes from Gary Gorton. Gorton notes that the coordination game in the Diamond-Dybvig model arises from the fact that the bank's assets constitute a "common pool" backing depositors' claims. But Gorton points out that in the real world we see runs even when there is no common pool of assets; some money-claims (like repo) are *collateralized*. To Gorton, this fact calls into question the real-world relevance of the Diamond-Dybvig model. In a collateralized setting, "the actions of other depositors are irrelevant; beliefs about other agents' beliefs then do not matter."[31] He sees no multiple equilibria, no coordination game. Note however that our bank game isn't susceptible to Gorton's common pool critique. In the bank game it was the fact that money-claims lost their moneyness on default, resulting in consequential losses, that set the stage for the coordination game. This problem doesn't disappear when money-claims are secured by specific collateral. Even if the collateral can be seized immediately on default, the collateral lacks the moneyness property that was the very reason for holding the money-claim in the first place. Accordingly, receiving the collateral is a distinctly unwelcome outcome for money-claimants.[32] The coordination game remains in effect.

A second reason to prefer the bank game to the Diamond-Dybvig model is methodological. The bank game is simple and accessible, whereas the Diamond-Dybvig model is esoteric. There is no doubt that, for many types of economic questions, difficult math is indispensable. I just question whether this is one of those cases. All else equal, a simple and accessible model is better.

The third reason to favor the bank game is the most fundamental. It is that the bank game's underlying (money-centric) theory of banking arguably has a far better claim to reality than does the insurance-type model of Diamond and Dybvig. The Diamond-Dybvig banks just don't *look* like banks as we know them. They don't issue claims that function as money; they don't facilitate payments among agents in the economy; they don't augment the supply of credit; they don't hold fractional reserves. They exist in a moneyless world. To bring this point into sharp relief, consider that, for most of the nineteenth century, US banks' short-term liabilities consisted mostly of circulating bank notes that paid *no* interest to their holders (whether "type 1" or "type 2"). It strains the imagination to try to understand such banks through the Diamond-Dybvig insurance lens. Yet such banks existed and were susceptible to runs.

One might argue that, at a high enough level of abstraction, our money-centric theory of banking can be interpreted through an insurance lens—one could interpret bank accounts as insurance policies. But it isn't clear what one would gain by doing so. For centuries, banks have been understood to be monetary institutions. That is how they are described in every introductory textbook on macroeconomics and on money and banking. (That the field is called "money and banking" is telling in itself.) This alone should make us leery of models, like the Diamond-Dybvig model, in which there is something called banking but nothing called money. The proponents of such nonmonetary theories of banking seem to bear the burden of persuasion here. I am arguing for the traditional wisdom and against the theoretical detours of recent decades.

Does Financing Structure Matter for Banks?

I suggested above that viewing banks through a corporate finance lens can be misleading. Now let's pin this down more precisely. Among the cornerstones of modern finance theory is the famous Modigliani-Miller theorem.[33] The essence of the theorem is that, in the absence of tax and other distortions, the financing structure of a firm does not affect its value. To use the (somewhat simplistic) slogan, "capital structure doesn't matter." Replacing debt with equity, or equity with debt, can't affect the value of a firm or its overall cost of funds. Such adjustments merely redistribute the firm's economic profits among various claimants.

Does the Modigliani-Miller theorem apply to banks? A number of prominent economists have said yes. Indeed, one of the theorem's authors has argued that it applies in principle as much to banks as to any other type of firm. "In a capital market left to its own devices," Merton Miller writes, "it's hard to see anything about demand securities so special as to rule out the application of the M & M Propositions to the banking industry."[34] Gregory Mankiw has suggested much the same, and so has Raghuram Rajan.[35] Along the same lines, in their influential recent book and related writings, Admati and Hellwig argue forcefully that the Modigliani-Miller theory applies to banks.[36] They acknowledge that deposit liabilities are special because they are bundled with payment services, but they insist that the Modigliani-Miller logic applies to banks' other sources of funding, including nondeposit short-term debt funding.[37]

Our money-centric theory of banking suggests a different conclusion. The argument is straightforward. If the Modigliani-Miller theorem holds, then a firm's overall cost of financing must remain constant, regardless of its financing structure (again, in the absence of tax or other distortions). But we saw in chapter 1 that money-claims have instrumental value to their holders that is distinct from their intrinsic value. This conclusion applied not just to checkable deposits but also to nondeposit short-term debt instruments (cash equivalents). Because they satisfy an aspect of money demand, they are characterized by extraordinarily low pecuniary yields. Necessarily, then, replacing money-claims with capital market financing—whether equity or longer-term debt—would *increase* banks' overall financing costs. So the financing structure of a bank does affect its value.[38]

To drive this point home, it may be useful to draw an analogy to an insurance company. The main liability of insurance companies is typically their policy reserves. To suggest that it would not be costly for an insurance company to replace its policy reserves with equity or long-term debt financing—in other words, for the firm to stop writing insurance policies—would be absurd. The same logic applies to banks: the liabilities (cash and cash equivalents) *are* these firms' distinctive product.[39] Standard capital structure principles therefore don't apply.

There is a broader perspective from which to look at this topic. Consider again the shift from currency warehousing to banking that was discussed in chapter 2. In particular, consider how the emergence of banking—the business model of money creation—affects the *financing market*. The financing market is the market in which individuals and businesses issue nonmonetary claims (such as bonds or shares) in exchange for money. (It is sometimes called the "loanable funds" market; think of it as the rental

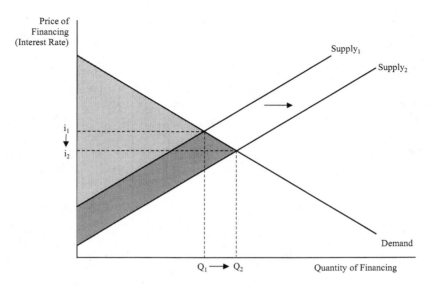

FIGURE 3.1. Financing market

market for purchasing power.) Recall that, when our specialist firm became a bank, it began acquiring loan receivables and/or bonds in exchange
for newly issued account balances. Holding everything else constant, this
business innovation—banking—increases the supply of financing in the
economy. The effect is shown in figure 3.1. The supply curve for financing
shifts rightward (from Supply$_1$ to Supply$_2$). The equilibrium quantity of
financing increases (from Q$_1$ to Q$_2$). Given a downward-sloping demand
curve, the equilibrium price of financing (the interest rate) declines (from
i$_1$ to i$_2$). Economic surplus—the difference between the respective reser-
vation prices of financing recipients and financing providers—increases by
an amount equal to the dark gray area.

Now, this analysis needs to be seriously qualified. When one examines
the effects of a supply curve shift, it is assumed that everything else is
held constant. However, to the extent that the specialist firm increases the
supply of financing, it necessarily also increases the quantity of account
balances outstanding. The money supply, then, is not held constant in the
figure. And this raises a key point about the relation between our hypothetical bank and the state. We posited the existence of some amount of
fiat physical currency at the very beginning of our hypothetical in chapter 2. Presumably the state was pursuing some public objective in deter-

mining both the quantity of physical currency it issued and the method of issuance. But the emergence of the banking business model may have significant ramifications for the state's pursuit of this public objective. In particular, the state may find that, since base money is now being multiplied through the issuance of bank money, the state can get away with issuing a smaller quantity of base money to begin with.

So perhaps the appropriate comparison is between two worlds with equal quantities of money—one without banking (and a correspondingly larger quantity of base money, perhaps held in currency warehouses) and one with banking (and a smaller quantity of base money, supplemented by bank-issued money). But then we can no longer say that the supply of financing is *necessarily* greater in the second world than the first. For now we need to know how the state goes about issuing base money. If the state issues base money in exchange for financial assets (just like the bank), then both the supply of money and the supply of financing are exactly the same in the two worlds.

From this standpoint, the question whether the value of a bank depends on its financing structure—whether the Modigliani-Miller theorem applies to banks—takes on a rather strange light. In the absence of the banking business model, the state would need to issue a correspondingly larger quantity of base money to achieve any given money supply. But this only sidesteps the question whether there might be good reasons to let banks create money instead. This is not a question that can be answered by theories of corporate finance.

Panics, Shadow Banking, and the Crisis of 2007 to 2009

It is widely accepted that the recent crisis involved a *panic* in the *shadow banking system*. As I noted in the introduction, I use "panic" in a very specific sense. To quote Ben Bernanke, it is "a generalized run by providers of short-term funding to a set of financial institutions."[40] The presence of short-term funding is definitional. Firms that finance themselves solely in the capital markets—with equity and long-term debt—are not vulnerable to runs. Such firms can *default* of course, but the concept of a run obviously implies something more than just a default.

Stock market crashes—think October 19, 1987—are sometimes called panics, as in "panic selling." But they do not qualify as panics under the definition used here; they have no necessary connection to short-term debt redemptions. To be sure, widespread redemptions of short-term debt may *cause* massive sales of financial assets (see chapter 4). Still, these phenomena are distinct. The term panic may seem to contain overtones of irrationality; however, as I emphasized in chapter 2, the coordination-game model of bank runs assumes that agents are perfectly rational. Nothing in this book depends on irrationality or "animal spirits."

How does a run at one bank turn into a panic? It will happen if a commonly observed run at one bank serves as a Schelling focal point for money-claimants at other banks. In other words, an observed run at one bank causes money-claimants at other banks to anticipate that their fellow money-claimants may redeem. In these circumstances, one would expect money-claim redemptions to happen in generalized fashion, affecting many issuers at the same time. This perspective gives concrete meaning to the notion of financial "contagion," which often comes up in discussions of financial crises. Contagion is often said to arise from "linkages" or "interconnectedness" among financial institutions.[41] Note that the contagion phenomenon described here does not rely on these things.

Some analysts have disputed the notion that bank runs or panics have a self-fulfilling dimension. They purport to prove their point by showing that, historically, panics have been triggered by fundamental developments—business cycle downturns, portfolio losses, and so forth. For example, Charles Calomiris and Joseph Mason studied the US banking panics of the early 1930s and found that, until the nationwide panic in early 1933 (which occurred near the trough of the Great Depression), bank failures were highly correlated with weak fundamental condition. They conclude on this basis that public liquidity support wouldn't have accomplished much. "It is doubtful whether the Federal Reserve System ... could have done much in the way of traditional microeconomic *liquidity* assistance ... to rescue failing banks during 1930–1932," they write. "Only a combination of expansionary monetary policy and bank bailouts ... could have prevented banks from failing in 1930–1932."[42]

Subsequent research, however, has suggested otherwise. In a 2009 paper, Gary Richardson and William Troost analyze banking distress in Mississippi during the Great Depression. Mississippi was split between two Federal Reserve districts. The state's southern half fell under the Atlanta Fed, which was an aggressive lender of last resort. The northern half fell under the St. Louis Fed, which was noninterventionist. Richardson and Troost find strikingly different outcomes in the two districts during the late 1930 panic. Banks in the (stingy) St. Louis Fed's district failed in much larger numbers; that district also saw much larger contractions in commercial credit and real economic activity. The authors point out that in the (aggressive) Atlanta Fed's district "recovery began earlier and progressed swifter than anywhere else in the United States." The Atlanta Fed's robust support, they write, may help to explain "the South's sudden, singular recovery" from the Depression.[43] The striking success of liquidity support suggests that runs hit banks that were fundamentally solvent: there were "unwarranted" redemptions.

More generally, the "fundamentals" versus "panic" dichotomy needs to be treated with extreme caution. Some have argued that the idea that banking involves a coordination game with self-fulfilling equilibria implies that panics must be *random* events; they have called it the "random withdrawal theory of panics."[44] But nothing in the coordination game model implies that panics must occur "randomly" or that fundamentals are irrelevant. Indeed, Schelling's argument was precisely that equilibrium selection in a coordination game may *not* be random. Money-claimants redeem when they expect others to redeem, and fundamentals may be an important determinant of such expectations. Further, as many others have pointed out (and as we will see in chapter 4), short-term debt redemptions depress asset prices, so runs may be a *source* of "fundamental" insolvency—not just vice versa.

Supporters of laissez-faire often attribute banking instability to unwise laws and government policies. They have a point. There can be little doubt that the excessive fragmentation that characterized the English and US banking systems for much of their histories—a consequence of various laws—made them more fragile. But it does not follow that free banking is wise policy. Free banking proponents usually cite Scotland from 1716 to 1844 and Canada before 1934 as leading examples of free-ish banking systems that performed well. Spared from the artificial fragmentation of their English and US counterparts, those systems were relatively concentrated and fairly stable. The degree to which they approximated free banking is, however, a subject of debate. The Scottish case seems ambiguous;[45] the Canadian case dubious.[46] Both systems appear to have enjoyed a measure of government support, which may very well have enhanced their stability. One should therefore be cautious about interpreting them as vindications of laissez-faire banking.

With this analysis as a backdrop, let's turn now to the shadow banking system. Recall from chapter 2 that this book defines banking as the business model under which portfolios of financial assets (typically credit assets) are funded largely with short-term debt that is rolled over continuously. As used here, "shadow banking" just refers to the existence of this activity—the large-scale issuance of private money-claims—*outside* the licensed deposit banking sector.[47] Note that some analysts use the term shadow banking rather differently. The Financial Stability Board, for example, says that "the 'shadow banking system' can broadly be described as 'credit intermediation involving entities and activities (fully or partially) outside the regular banking system' or non-bank credit intermediation in short."[48] Their concept of shadow banking is far broader—and in my view less useful—than the one we are using here. Theirs has no necessary connection to short-term debt.

It is worth pointing out that the idea of shadow banking (as used here) is not remotely new. The concept was presaged by Walter Bagehot in his 1873 masterpiece *Lombard Street: A Description of the Money Market*.[49] Bagehot observed that the great London banks were accompanied by a parallel set of financial firms, known as "bill brokers," which in some ways resembled modern-day securities firms. The bill brokers financed themselves with borrowings that, Bagehot informs us, were "repayable at demand, or at very short notice." Formally speaking, these firms were not banks—but to Bagehot they might as well be. "The London bill brokers do much the same [as banks]," he says. "Indeed, they are only a special sort of bankers who allow daily interest on deposits, and who for most of their money give security [collateral]. But we have no concern now with these differences of detail." At times Bagehot is careful to note that the short-term obligations of bill brokers were not technically deposits; he observes that the maturing of these liabilities "is not indeed a direct withdrawal of money on deposit" although "its principal effect is identical." Other times, however, Bagehot dispenses even with this distinction: "It was also most natural that the bill-brokers . . . should become, more or less, bankers too, and should receive money on deposit without giving any security for it." Here we have a clear identification of the shadow banking phenomenon—about 140 years ago.

The US shadow banking system has existed outside the explicit banking safety net and, for the most part, with minimal regulatory constraints. Naturally this freedom has been conducive to high returns, but the system has also proved fragile. The crisis that began in 2007 eventually tore through the entire shadow banking sector. ABCP conduits (including structured investment vehicles), repo markets, financial commercial paper markets, Eurodollars, auction-rate securities, prime brokerage free credit balances, securities lending collateral reinvestments, money mar-

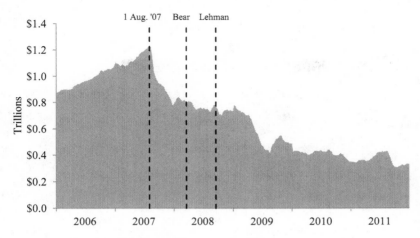

FIGURE 3.2. US asset-backed commercial paper outstanding
Source: Federal Reserve Economic Database, series ABCOMP.

ket mutual funds (MMFs), and uninsured bank deposits all experienced modern-day bank runs.

Let's look at some of the key panic events and the US government's response. Developments in the subprime mortgage markets prompted a marketwide run on ABCP in August 2007. As shown in figure 3.2, during the second half of 2007 the volume of outstanding ABCP plummeted, as many investors declined to roll over their positions.[50] Figure 3.3 shows a similar phenomenon occurring a few months later in a different segment of the money-claim market. The proximate cause of the Bear Stearns failure was a run on the firm's overnight financing through the giant repo market. Despite the Fed-assisted rescue of Bear Stearns in March 2008 and the simultaneous establishment of special lending facilities to support the repo market, the period after Bear's failure saw an abrupt reduction in repo volumes.[51]

Finally, the bankruptcy of Lehman Brothers in September 2008 triggered a broad panic in the market for private money-claims. Among other things, Lehman's default precipitated a run on the MMF sector—one of the core distribution channels for money-claim funding. Practically overnight, institutional investors redeemed nearly half a trillion dollars of claims on prime MMFs, as shown in figure 3.4. Notably, there was no comparable run on *retail* money funds; the panic was overwhelmingly institutional. Figure 3.5 shows that the panic events in 2007 and 2008 coincided with a drastic widening of short-term funding spreads, as cash parkers

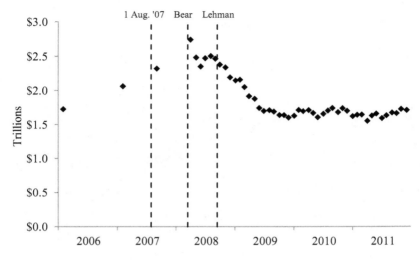

FIGURE 3.3. US triparty repo outstanding
Source: Financial Stability Oversight Council, *2014 Annual Report*.
Note: Data availability is limited before April 2008.

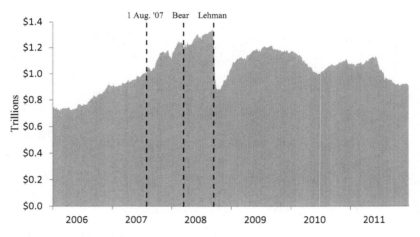

FIGURE 3.4. US prime institutional money market fund shares outstanding
Source: Financial Stability Oversight Council, *2012 Annual Report*.

sought the safe haven of sovereign money-claims in lieu of private money-claims.

If the shadow banking system played a prominent role in the recent crisis, it was also at the center of the government's emergency policy response. At the height of the crisis, the government's paramount objective

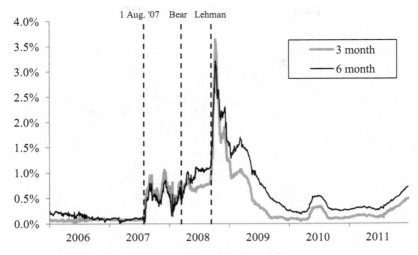

FIGURE 3.5. Short-term funding (LIBOR-OIS) spreads
Source: Bloomberg.

was to halt the spreading panic by holders of money market instruments, the vast majority of which were issued by shadow banking institutions.[52] The scale of these policy measures was staggering. At its peak, the Federal Reserve extended about $1 trillion of liquidity through an arsenal of emergency lending programs (evident in fig. 3.6). The FDIC issued over $1 trillion in guarantees of financial firm liabilities, including nondeposit obligations. The Treasury Department supplied $0.3 trillion in equity capital infusions, which were designed mainly to stabilize diversified financial firms that relied heavily on short-term wholesale funding. Finally, Treasury officials engineered a dramatic $3 trillion guarantee of MMF obligations.

The success of these policy measures in arresting the panic was a remarkable achievement. Over the course of 2009, short-term funding spreads moved back toward precrisis levels. The emergency measures were accompanied by extraordinary monetary policy initiatives by the Fed, which slashed the federal funds rate effectively to zero and conducted additional expansionary monetary policy through "quantitative easing" (evident in the buildup of securities in fig. 3.6). Nonetheless, as we will examine in some detail in the next chapter, these measures were not enough to avert an abrupt and severe macroeconomic contraction.

The US government's crisis response measures were aimed, with few exceptions, at propping up the private money-claim markets. As shown in table 2, *every* major category of private money-claim was specifically tar-

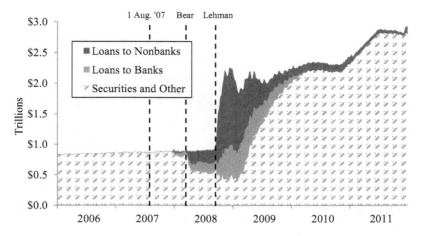

FIGURE 3.6. Federal Reserve assets
Source: Federal Reserve Economic Database.
Note: Loans to nonbanks consists of series WPDF, TERMFAC, WABCMMF, WCPFF, WLIQSWP, WMAIDEN1, WMAIDEN2, WMAIDEN3, WALICO, and WAIG. Loans to banks consists of series WPC, WSC, WSB, and WTERAUC. Securities and other consists of total Federal Reserve assets (series WALCL) less the sum of loans to nonbanks and loans to banks.

TABLE 2. **The US Policy Response**

Private Money Claim Category	Emergency Policy Measures
Money market mutual fund shares	MMF guarantee (Treasury)
	Money market investor funding facility (Fed)
Uninsured deposits	Transaction account guarantee (FDIC)
	Term auction facility (Fed)
	Deposit insurance limit increase (EESA)*
Eurodollars	Central bank liquidity swaps (Fed)
Financial and nonfinancial commercial paper	Temporary liquidity guarantee program (FDIC)
	Commercial paper funding facility (Fed)
Asset-backed commercial paper	ABCP MMF liquidity facility (Fed)
Primary dealer repo	Primary dealer credit facility (Fed)
	Term securities lending facility (Fed)

* Emergency Economic Stabilization Act of 2008, Pub. L. No. 110-343, § 136, 122 Stat. 3765, 3799.

geted with emergency stabilization programs in 2008. Moreover, the key emergency policy measures that are not reflected in this table—equity capital infusions and the FDIC's massive debt guarantee program for longer-term debt—were used primarily to stabilize diversified financial firms that relied heavily on nondeposit short-term debt funding. It is no exaggeration to say that practically the entire emergency policy response to the recent crisis was aimed at stabilizing the short-term funding markets.

I contend that the shadow banking panic just described involved waves of self-fulfilling redemptions. Money-claimants redeemed, at least in part, because they expected other money-claimants to redeem. This does not mean fundamentals were irrelevant. Developments in the real estate and mortgage markets were clearly the spark, but the money-claim markets were the dry tinder that transformed the spark into a raging fire.

*   *   *

As this chapter has shown, modern banking scholarship has gone off in some odd directions. The essence of my argument is actually quite traditional: that banking is first and foremost a monetary activity. This shouldn't be a controversial statement, but we have seen that it is. The next chapter builds on the preceding analysis. It makes the case that, when it comes to financial stability policy, panics should be viewed as "the problem."

Panics and the Macroeconomy

If money isn't loosened up, this sucker could go down.—President George W. Bush, September 25, 2008[1]

A central argument of this book is that, insofar as financial stability policy is about avoiding macroeconomic disasters, it should concern itself mostly with *panic-proofing*. This claim often meets with fierce resistance, generally on two grounds. The first objection is that the problem of financial instability is about much more than panics. (Panics, to repeat, are widespread redemptions of short-term debt, period.) Panic-proofing, it is said, would not necessarily mitigate problems like "asset-price bubbles," "overleverage," "excessive risk taking," "interconnectedness," "disorderly failures," and so on. And these other things are taken to pose a serious danger to the broader economy in themselves, irrespective of any connection to panics.

The second objection complements the first. It holds that, even if panics were indeed "the problem" (so to speak), panic-proofing—suppressing run-prone funding structures in one way or another—would not be desirable. For there would be costs to such an approach, and implementation would be challenging. Besides, the argument goes, there are other ways to deal with panics. For example, we might leave fragile short-term funding untouched while seeking to forestall the types of events that trigger panics (collapsed bubbles and so forth). Or we could just deal with panics as they arise; that's what the lender of last resort is for, after all.

This chapter addresses the first of these objections. (The second objection raises questions of comparative institutional design—the topic of part 2.) The argument of this chapter is not merely that panics harm the broader economy. Most—though, as we will see, not all—experts would agree with that proposition. My claim is quite a bit stronger. I argue that panics constitute far and away the biggest threat the financial system poses to the broader economy, and avoiding them should therefore be the predominant focus of financial stability policy. This is a much more controversial proposition, and it is a crucial threshold issue for policy.

There is a widespread tendency in this area to lump various phenomena into a complex and multifaceted "financial crisis." The financial crisis, taken as a whole, then becomes the unit of analysis and the thing to be prevented. This methodological tendency has huge effects on how policy analysis is done. It inevitably draws attention away from the panic and toward the various "excesses" that preceded it. This chapter insists on disaggregation—on treating the panic itself as a distinct event.[2] The distinction I am drawing here loosely resembles one Anna Schwartz once drew between "real" and "pseudo" financial crises. Schwartz equated "real" financial crises with runs on banks and "a scramble for high-powered money." She classified other phenomena, like stock market crashes and burst bubbles, as merely "pseudo" crises.[3] (I depart from Schwartz inasmuch as her classification scheme would not treat *shadow* bank runs as real crises.)

As a starting point, consider the close association between panics and economic disasters in US history.[4] From 1825 until the Civil War the United States saw four major panics (1833, 1837, 1839, and 1857). They coincided with four of the five biggest output contractions during that time span, including the largest one. Between the Civil War and World War I there were three major panics (1873, 1893, and 1907). They coincided with three of the five largest output contractions during that period, including the two largest. In the interwar years the United States saw one major cluster of panics (1930–33). They coincided with the biggest output contraction in US history, the Great Depression. Finally, since World War II the United States has had one cluster of panics: the shadow banking panics of 2007 and 2008. They coincided with the onset of the Great Recession—by far the worst slump of the postwar period (see fig. 4.1). Correlation does not establish causation, of course. Maybe panics are caused by severe recessions, or maybe panics and severe recessions are jointly caused by something else. But one must at least entertain the hypothesis that panics do massive damage to the real economy. Every major panic in US history has been accompanied by a severe recession, and most of the worst recessions have been accompanied by panics.

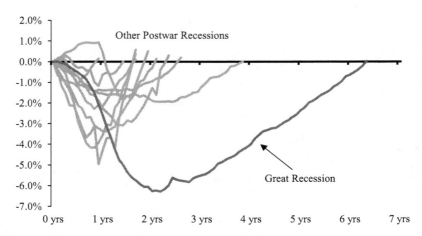

FIGURE 4.1. Change in US employment in post–World War II recessions
Source: Federal Reserve Economic Database, series PAYEMS.
Note: Recession start dates (per NBER): November 1948, July 1953, August 1957, April 1960, December 1969, November 1973, January 1980, July 1981, July 1990, March 2001, and December 2007 (the Great Recession).

A point of clarification: to say that panics are the central problem for financial stability policy is *not* to say that financial institution *failures* are the central problem. These phenomena are logically distinct. In principle it is possible to have widespread short-term debt redemptions without any financial institution failures at all. That is, the whole financial industry might survive a panic. I will argue that such an event might nonetheless be very damaging to the broader economy. Conversely, it is possible to have large numbers of financial institution failures without a panic. For example, the bank and thrift debacle of the 1980s resulted in the failures of over 2,600 US depository institutions holding over $700 billion in combined assets.[5] Thanks to deposit insurance, however, there was no panic. Notably, the ensuing recession was quite mild. I am arguing that panics, not financial institution failures per se, are what we should be most concerned about.

At the risk of belaboring the point, figure 4.2 offers a way to think about what this chapter is getting at. Let's posit that there exists something called a debt-fueled bubble in asset prices. (Substitute some other type of financial "excess" if you want to.) Further posit that the collapse of such a debt-fueled bubble tends to be accompanied by both panics and severe recessions. If there is a causal relation here, how might it work?

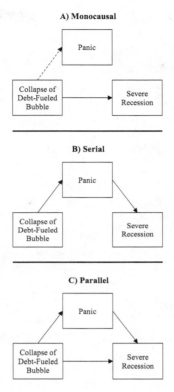

FIGURE 4.2. Alternative causal scenarios

Figure 4.2 shows three alternatives. In panel A the debt-fueled bubble's collapse leads directly to a severe slump, whether or not a panic happens. In this scenario the panic has no independent causative significance in relation to economic performance; it is a mere symptom of the bubble's collapse. Panel B shows the other extreme: a serial link between debt-fueled bubbles, panics, and severe recessions. In this scenario a debt-fueled bubble crashes the economy *only* if its collapse triggers a panic.

Whether panel A or panel B is closer to reality has vital implications for regulatory policy. If panel A is right, then panic-proofing would do nothing to prevent severe recessions, because panics just aren't a source of macroeconomic damage. In that case we would do better to direct our efforts toward fending off debt-fueled bubbles. If panel B is right, then we have an entirely different situation. Panic-proofing would break the causal chain, rendering debt-fueled bubbles far less troubling.

Most experts would probably agree that panel C has a lot to be said for it. It shows a parallel link: the collapsed bubble damages the economy directly, but it may also trigger a panic, which adds to the damage. If panel C is right, then panic-proofing would be only a partial solution. Yet this is not the end of the discussion. For it may still be that one of the channels of harm predominates. That is essentially what this chapter argues: that most of the damage probably comes from the panic. In other words, the serial scenario (panel B) is more nearly accurate than the monocausal scenario (panel A). The upshot is that a successful approach to panic-proofing would allow us to worry far less about debt-fueled bubbles and the like.

These claims are at odds with the prevailing view. As I noted above, most analysts do not decompose the financial crisis into its component parts. Even when they do, they often treat the debt-fueled bubble (or other purported excesses) as the "deeper" or more "fundamental" problem and thus as the primary evil that financial regulation is supposed to address. By contrast, this chapter offers reasons to doubt that debt-fueled bubbles and the like pose a grave threat to the real economy *in the absence of a panic*. This argument is counterintuitive: it implies that the search for "deeper" or more "fundamental" problems may in fact be leading us astray. From a regulatory standpoint it would be hard to overstress the importance of these basic issues.

A common objection to the claim that panics are "the problem" is that panics are brief, whereas the economic slumps that follow financial crises tend to be long-lasting.[6] Why doesn't the economy just bounce right back to full employment once financial markets have returned to normal? Surely something must be "holding the economy back," the argument goes, and surely that something is the "real" problem. A common culprit in this regard is said to be excessive debt loads. This chapter raises questions about this line of reasoning. I argue that it is far from clear that the economy would bounce back much more quickly from severe trauma if only debt loads were lower. Nor does ex post stimulus, whether monetary or fiscal, appear to be a reliable solution. Better, then, to avoid severe trauma in the first place.

The chapter proceeds as follows. We will start by looking at a number of prominent analysts, stretching back to Walter Bagehot, who have stressed the central role of panics in causing economic disasters. That viewpoint certainly isn't unique to this book. I then discuss causal mechanisms. I place special emphasis on one mechanism, which I call the panic-induced financing crunch (or just the "panic crunch"), that appears to have significant explanatory power. The chapter then zeroes in on the recent crisis. We will review evidence that the panics of 2007 and 2008 were a major source of damage to the US economy—despite the government's aggressive emergency measures. This point is surprisingly controversial, so I want to present the evidence in a straightforward way.

After that, we will look at several theories challenging the view that panics play a significant role in major economic contractions. We will take a particularly close look at various "debt cycle" theories, which have been very influential. The chapter will question whether things like "overleverage" or "debt-fueled bubbles" are likely to seriously imperil the broader economy in the absence of a panic. In short, I argue that panel B gets us closer to the truth than panel A. The chapter concludes that there is a strong case for making panic avoidance our top financial stability priority. This argument sets the stage for part 2, which turns to how we might go about that task. The task will turn out to be inextricably bound up with the larger project of monetary system design.

Panics as "the Problem"

A long and venerable literature examines panics and their effects on the broader economy. Panics were a central concern of Walter Bagehot,[7] who observed in 1873 that panics pose a "great danger" to the "industrial system." He went on to note that "the problem of managing a panic must not be thought of as mainly a 'banking' problem. It is primarily a mercantile one." When reading Bagehot one is struck by his distinct lack of interest in the events and circumstances that precipitate panics. "Some writers have endeavoured to classify panics according to the nature of the particular accidents producing them," he writes. "But little, however, is, I believe, to be gained by such classifications. There is little difference in the effect of one accident and another upon our credit system." To be sure, Bagehot does devote a few pages to investment "manias," or bubbles. "At some times there are more savings seeking investment than there are known investments for," he writes. A speculative mania may ensue, and investment losses are sure to follow. Yet Bagehot does not view this process as particularly problematic in itself. Such booms and busts are just "the inevitable vicissitudes" of the market, he says. It is in the event of a panic that "the public may be exposed to disaster."

Milton Friedman and Anna Schwartz sound a similar note in their seminal study of nearly a century of US monetary history.[8] "Banking panics," they conclude, "have occurred only during severe contractions and have greatly intensified such contractions, if indeed they have not been the primary factor converting what would otherwise have been mild contractions into severe ones." Zeroing in on the Great Depression, they stress the causal role of the waves of banking panics that struck the United States from 1930 to 1933. They acknowledge that the downturn began before the panics but contend that without them the Depression would have been far milder. Like Bagehot, Friedman and Schwartz show little interest in the *origins* of the banking panics. They devote only four pages to the topic, and they find others' preoccupation with the banking sector's investment losses to be largely beside the point. "Any runs on banks for whatever reason became to some extent self-justifying, whatever the quality of assets held by banks," they write. "The composition of assets held by banks would hardly have mattered if additional high-powered money had been made available from whatever source to meet the demands of depositors for currency without requiring a multiple contraction of deposits and assets. The trigger would have discharged only a blank cartridge." Friedman and Schwartz point out that many Federal Reserve officials at the time regarded the banking crises "as inevitable reactions to prior speculative excesses, or as a consequence but hardly a cause of the financial and economic collapse in process." The authors reject these views. "Pursuit of the policies outlined ... by Bagehot in 1873," they write, "would have prevented the catastrophe." So too with deposit insurance: "Had federal deposit insurance been in existence in 1930, it would very likely have prevented ... the tragic sequence of events" that followed. As with Bagehot, with Friedman and Schwartz it is the panic itself, as distinct from the various supposed excesses that preceded it, that is the central focus.

More recently, other prominent analysts have stressed the same distinction. Gary Gorton has been particularly influential in interpreting the recent crisis as a banking panic resembling those of the early 1930s and before. Gorton uses "panic" the same way I use it here: a panic is a situation in which "holders of short-term liabilities ... [refuse] to fund 'banks.'"[9] Gorton observes that the United States enjoyed a long panic-free period from the inception of deposit insurance in 1934 until the recent crisis. He refers to this as the "Quiet Period" in US banking, and he points out that this was an unusually stable time for the US economy. Gorton suggests that this is no random coincidence: the absence of panics was a major factor behind the absence of economic disasters. Echoing Bagehot, as well as Friedman and Schwartz, Gorton cautions against lumping panics with other events into a generic conception of financial crisis or "systemic event." Indeed, Gorton *defines* a financial crisis as a panic.[10]

Ben Bernanke expresses a similar point in a slightly different way. In his analysis of the recent crisis, Bernanke distinguishes between what he calls "triggers" and "vulnerabilities."[11] The triggers of the crisis consisted of developments in the US housing and mortgage markets. Bernanke argues that these triggers alone can't explain the magnitude of the accompanying economic downturn. Losses on subprime mortgages just weren't big enough: "It is not especially uncommon for one day's paper losses in global stock markets to exceed the losses on subprime mortgages suffered during the entire crisis, without obvious ill effect on market functioning or on the economy." Even if the focus is broadened to the housing sector as a whole, Bernanke says, we are still left with a puzzle. The losses of US housing wealth—totaling about $7 trillion—do not seem adequate to explain the slump that followed. "Any theory of the crisis that ties its magnitude to the size of the housing bust," he says, "must also explain why the fall of dot-com stock prices just a few years earlier, which destroyed as much or more paper wealth—more than $8 trillion—resulted in a relatively short and mild recession and no major financial instability." In Bernanke's view, the triggering events in the housing and mortgage markets must have "interacted with deeper vulnerabilities in the financial system in ways that the dot-com bust did not." And one of the biggest vulnerabilities, he contends, was the financial sector's heavy reliance on "short-term wholesale funding." In line with Gorton, Bernanke suggests that "the crisis is best understood as a classic financial panic—differing in details but fundamentally similar to the panics described by Bagehot and many others."

Thus a substantial body of expert opinion supports the view that panics can and do inflict severe damage on the real economy. (We will see later that this view is far from universal among economists.) But to build a convincing case, we need to specify a plausible *mechanism* by which panics affect output and employment.

This question of causal mechanisms has engendered some controversy. Friedman and Schwartz posited a monetary mechanism. They argued that banking panics reduce the money supply, which in turn reduces economic activity. "Here was the famous multiple expansion process of the banking system in vicious reverse," they wrote in reference to the Depression-era panics.[12] (One could make a similar argument about the US experience in the Great Recession; as shown in chapter 1, gross aggregates of broad money peaked in 2007 and then abruptly shrank as a result of the shadow banking panics.) But the Friedman-Schwartz monetary explanation is subject to criticism on various grounds. Among other things, the monetary mechanism—which presumably operates at an aggregate level—does not explain *local* output effects arising from local bank runs. Yet there is evidence that such local effects were significant during the early 1930s.[13]

These local effects suggest a possible role for *nonmonetary* effects of banking panics on economic output. Ben Bernanke advanced this thesis in a famous 1983 paper.[14] In Bernanke's stylized description, banks "specialize in making loans to small, idiosyncratic borrowers whose liabilities are too few in number to be publicly traded." The banking system functions to "differentiat[e] between good and bad borrowers," which is costly. According to Bernanke, banking distress in the early 1930s "forced a contraction of the banking system's role in the intermediation of credit." While "some of the slack" was taken up by other credit channels, "the rapid switch away from the banks (given the banks' accumulated expertise, information, and customer relationships) no doubt impaired financial efficiency" and raised the cost of credit intermediation. The result was a reduction in economic output: "An increase in the cost of credit intermediation reduces the total quantity of goods and services currently demanded." Notably, Bernanke was not talking just about bank failures. "The bankers' *fear* of runs" (emphasis added), he wrote, "had important macroeconomic effects."

A more recent literature offers a somewhat different—and, I think, more convincing—way of thinking about how panics might damage the real economy.[15] The story goes like this. Imagine that some kind of shock, perhaps losses on financial assets, triggers a panic. When the panic happens, financial firms that rely on large amounts of short-term debt funding go into survival mode: they must meet redemptions. They begin to sell some of their existing portfolios in the secondary markets. In the economic literature, this is called a fire sale.[16] Because financial assets are dumped on the market all at once during a fire sale, they temporarily trade at artificially depressed prices.

At first blush, fire sales might not seem to present much of a policy problem. True, sellers take losses, but buyers reap a corresponding gain—they get to buy assets on the cheap—so it's just a wealth transfer. But let's think more carefully about the implications. When financial assets are sold in a fire sale, their prices fall; equivalently stated, their yields rise. And here is the crucial point: these elevated yields then serve as the hurdle rate for *new* financing in the primary capital markets. Providers of fi-

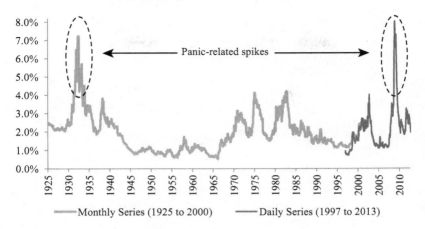

FIGURE 4.3. US "BBB"-rated corporate bond spreads, 1925–2013
Source: Federal Reserve Economic Database.
Note: Monthly series consists of Moody's Seasoned Baa corporate bond yield (series BAA) minus Long-Term US Government Securities (series LTGOVTBD). Daily series is the BofA Merrill Lynch US Corporate BBB Option-Adjusted Spread (series BAMLC0A4CBBB).

nancing will not originate new financing transactions whose risk-adjusted returns are below those available on comparable secondary market assets. So when the fire sale happens, firms and consumers find that financing rates have suddenly skyrocketed. This is the *financing crunch*: for some period, the supply of new financing shrinks dramatically. Because overall economic activity relies heavily on external financing, economic output plummets. Hence the panic is the proximate cause of the severe recession. I refer to this mechanism as the panic-induced financing crunch, or just the panic crunch.

The panic crunch story suggests we should see big spikes on bond spreads in a panic (assuming the financing crunch has little or no effect on risk-free rates). In this regard, look at figure 4.3, which shows US corporate bond spreads since 1925. There are huge—and strikingly similar— spikes in the early 1930s and in the recent crisis, the last two US panics. Both events were associated with major financing crunches. And of course both were associated with disastrous macroeconomic contractions. In his 1983 paper, Bernanke examines the behavior of these spreads in the 1930s and acknowledges that they are "not consistent with my story that bank borrowers are those whose liabilities are too few to be publicly traded." This appears to be a weakness of his theory—one that isn't shared by the panic crunch theory.

Some analysts, while recognizing that financing crunches happen during crises and that they can seriously hurt the broader economy, attribute them to causes other than panics. For example, consider the plausible-sounding idea that financial firm failures (cessation of operations and insolvency proceedings) are the key ingredient in producing financing crunches. One sees this claim all the time. A good example is Gregory Mankiw and Laurence Ball's textbook *Macroeconomics and the Financial System*.[17] They present a flowchart that depicts how a financial crisis affects the real economy. The flowchart does include a financing crunch ("reduced lending"). However, it doesn't mention runs or panics. Instead, the financing crunch arises from financial firm failures, combined with falling asset prices (which decrease *borrowers'* collateral values).[18] Similarly, Carmen Reinhart and Kenneth Rogoff remark that, in a "systemic banking crisis," the "decrease in credit creation" is a consequence of "bank failures."[19] Note that the panic crunch story said nothing whatever about financial firm failures. In principle it is possible to have a panic (and hence a panic crunch) with no financial firm failures at all.

Consider next the plausible-sounding argument that financing crunches are the product of impairments of the equity capital (or net worth) of financial intermediaries. Michael Woodford recently made this argument.[20] According to Woodford, losses "that might seem of only modest significance for the aggregate economy . . . can have substantial aggregate effects if the losses in question happen to be concentrated in highly leveraged intermediaries, who suffer significant reductions in their capital as a result." Woodford assumes that intermediaries have access to only a limited quantity of equity capital and that their leverage is constrained by regulators or the market. Under these assumptions, losses by intermediaries will reduce the supply of credit to the economy. Three other economists recently offered a similar analysis.[21] Their paper analyzes the incentives of a hypothetical bank that suffers losses, causing its equity capital ratio to decline. The bank needs to restore its capital ratio and must choose whether to do so by raising new equity capital (increasing the numerator) or by shedding assets (reducing the denominator). The authors give reasons to think that banks might favor the latter. In particular, they suggest that banks in this scenario face what economists call a "debt overhang" problem: the value from a new equity offering tends to get "siphoned off" to creditors—so the bank sheds assets instead. This leads to a damaging credit crunch as banks engage in "socially excessive balance-sheet shrinkage." Note that this story involves neither short-term debt redemptions nor financial institution failures.

The distinctions between these financing crunch stories might seem subtle, and the stories are not mutually exclusive. It is perfectly reasonable to think there may be truth in all of them; panics, financial firm failures, and equity capital impairments may all contribute to financing crunches. Nonetheless, when it comes to regulatory design, it is a mistake to ascribe equal importance to every mechanism. The goal should be to distinguish major channels of harm from minor ones.

Evidence from the Recent Crisis

It is worth looking at the events of the recent crisis through the lens of the panic crunch. Much of the information that follows will be familiar to experts. However, even familiar facts can take on a different light when viewed with a particular theory in mind.

Let's look first at the central phenomenon: the macroeconomic disaster. Figures 4.4 and 4.5 show the performance of US economic output and employment for the relevant period. The figures show meaningful but still moderate economic deterioration before the Lehman episode, with a drastic worsening immediately thereafter. Note the sharpness and severity of the event. This was not a drawn-out process but an acute contraction.

Figures 4.4 and 4.5 may give the misleading impression of a return to

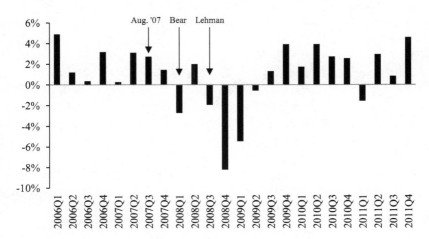

FIGURE 4.4. Change in US real GDP (quarterly)
Source: Federal Reserve Economic Database, series GDPC1. Compounded annual rate of change.

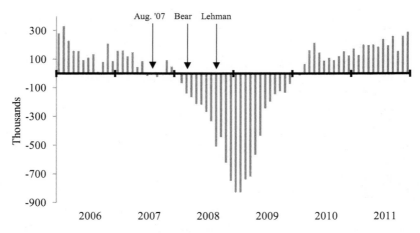

FIGURE 4.5. Change in US private employment (monthly)
Source: Federal Reserve Economic Database, series NPPTTL.

macroeconomic normalcy by 2010. However, what we do *not* see is "catch-up" growth in output or employment. In other words, the slump persisted after the shock. This can be seen more clearly in the next two figures. Figure 4.6 shows the performance of US real GDP compared with potential output. The difference between these two series is called the output gap. Clearly the output gap persisted long after the initial plunge.

Figure 4.6 might initially seem to contain some good news, in that the output gap has gradually narrowed since the initial plunge. But there is a more pessimistic interpretation: the deficiency of *actual* output could be eroding the economy's *potential* output. This phenomenon is called hysteresis.[22] As Larry Summers describes it, hysteresis is the idea that "lack of demand creates lack of potential supply."[23] The figure presents evidence that can be interpreted as hysteresis. It shows two series for potential output, one dating from 2007 and the other from 2015. The 2007 projection by the Congressional Budget Office continues along the economy's previous trend line, whereas the 2015 series bends downward significantly from the 2007 projection, consistent with hysteresis. According to Summers, "This might have been a theoretical notion some years ago. It is an empirical fact today. . . . Any reasonable reader of the data has to recognize that this financial crisis has confirmed the doctrine of hysteresis more strongly than anyone might have supposed."[24] If Summers is right, then figure 4.6 gives little reason for comfort. What we are seeing is an erosion in the economy's productive capacity rather than a return to where we

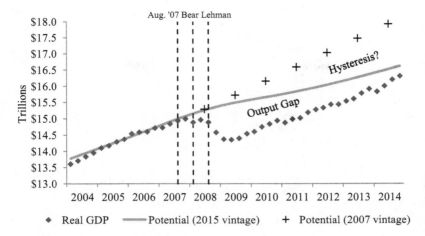

FIGURE 4.6. US real GDP versus potential
Source: Federal Reserve Economic Database, series GDPC1 and GDPPOT; Congressional Budget Office, "Revisions to CBO's Projection of Potential Output since 2007," February 2014.

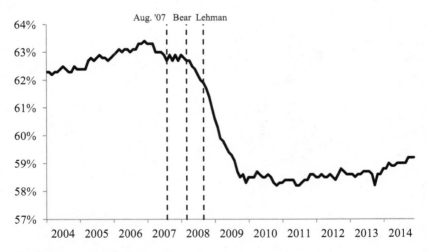

FIGURE 4.7. US civilian employment:population ratio
Source: Federal Reserve Economic Database, series EMRATIO.

otherwise would have been. Figure 4.7 underscores this point. It shows the US civilian employment-to-population ratio, a widely followed indicator of job market conditions. There has been very little tendency to recover to precrisis levels. These two figures show a protracted economic catastrophe.

I now want to make the case that a panic-induced financing crunch may

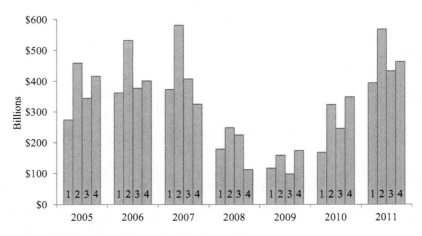

FIGURE 4.8. US syndicated loan origination (quarterly)
Source: WRDS-Reuters DealScan.

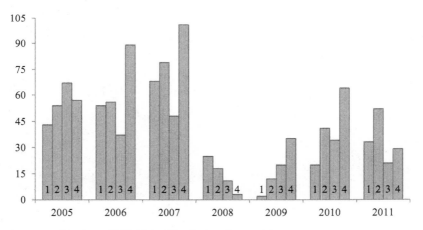

FIGURE 4.9. Number of US initial public offerings (quarterly)
Source: PricewaterhouseCoopers US IPO Watch: Analysis and Trends (2009 and 2011 editions).

bear substantial responsibility for the macroeconomic disaster. First, let's look at evidence that there was indeed a financing crunch. In any normal market, a sudden contraction in supply—a leftward supply curve shift—should generate both lower quantities and higher prices. Now look at figures 4.8 and 4.9. They show very large reductions in financing volumes in 2008 and 2009—specifically, in newly originated loans to big corporations and in US initial public offerings, respectively.

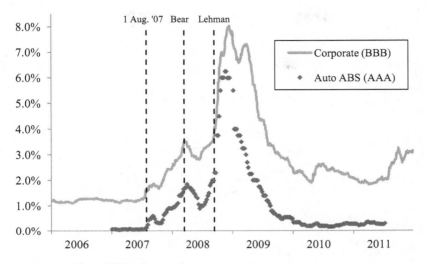

FIGURE 4.10. Selected US credit spreads
Source: Corporate spread is from Federal Reserve Economic Database, series BAML-CoA4CBBB. Auto ABS spread is from Financial Stability Oversight Council, *2011 Annual Report*.

So quantities of new financing collapsed for a period. What happened to prices? We have already seen the answer (fig. 4.3): corporate bond spreads spiked to levels not seen since the Great Depression. Figure 4.10 zooms in on the behavior of these same bond spreads in the recent crisis. It also shows spreads in the secondary market for *consumer* credit, exemplified by securitized auto loans. These spreads began to widen after the initial panic of August 2007, and they exploded with the Lehman episode. A similar phenomenon was evident in virtually every area of the consumer and business credit markets. Figure 4.11 shows a major tightening of bank lending standards in credit cards and in commercial and industrial lending during the same period.

The evidence, then, points to a sudden contraction in the supply of financing for consumers and businesses. Costs of financing shot up, while quantities collapsed. This is just what the panic crunch story predicts. There are, however, other possible explanations for collapsing quantities and rising prices in the financing markets. For instance, either a perception of deteriorating borrower credit quality or heightened aversion to risk could produce similar effects. How can we be certain these other factors weren't the main drivers?

There are at least two reasons to think the panic played a major role.

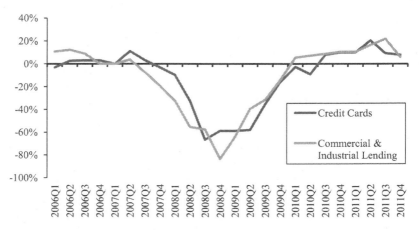

FIGURE 4.11. Net percentage of banks easing lending standards
Source: Federal Reserve Senior Loan Officer Survey.

The first comes from a recent study by Victoria Ivashina and David Scharfstein.[25] They examine US financial firms' syndicated lending to the corporate sector during 2007 and 2008.[26] They show that lenders with higher amounts of (uninsured) nondeposit financing reduced their syndicated lending in the second half of 2008 far more than did those with more stable deposit funding (much of which is FDIC insured). Simply put, financial firms that were more reliant on run-prone funding cut back much more sharply on new corporate lending.[27] The authors conclude that their findings are "consistent with a decline in the supply of funding as a result of the bank run." They further note that "the drop in supply puts upward pressure on interest rate spreads, and leads to a greater fall in lending than one might see in a typical recession."

There is a second, more direct piece of evidence that the panic bore substantial responsibility for the financing crunch. That evidence, the "CDS-bond basis," appears in figure 4.12.[28] This figure requires some explanation. The credit default swap (CDS) market is a derivative market in which investors make side bets on corporate and other credits. When two parties enter into a CDS contract with respect to a debtor and that debtor subsequently defaults, one party to the CDS contract (the "protection seller") pays the other party (the "protection buyer") an amount equal to the difference between the principal amount and the market price of the debtor's bonds. The purchase price of this protection is the CDS rate. The debtor itself is not a party to the contract.

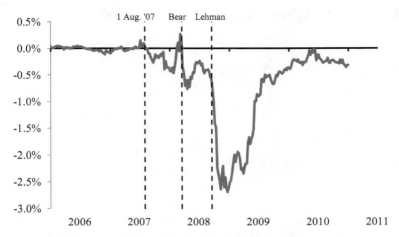

FIGURE 4.12. CDS-bond basis for US high-grade corporate issuers
Source: Mark Mitchell, CNH Partners, LLC.

Under normal conditions the CDS rate associated with an issuer should
track very closely the actual spread observed on the issuer's bonds. This
is because even a small divergence between the CDS rate and the bond
spread creates an arbitrage opportunity for investors. For example, if a
bond spread exceeds the corresponding CDS rate, an investor can buy
the bond, simultaneously buy CDS protection, and thereby create a "risk-
free" security with a yield that exceeds the risk-free rate. Bond yields and
CDS rates should therefore move in lockstep. Put differently, the *difference* between the CDS rate and the bond spread should normally stay
very close to zero. This difference is the CDS-bond basis, sometimes called
the cash-synthetic basis.

As figure 4.12 shows, before the crisis the CDS-bond basis did in fact
hover very close to zero. But in August 2007 the CDS-bond basis abruptly
went negative, which is to say that bond spreads widened in relation to
CDS rates. This negative basis exploded to shocking levels after Lehman
failed. Assuming CDS rates reflected the market's "true" view on fundamental credit risk, corporate bonds were extremely underpriced. In a research note that was released in the depths of the crisis, the elite hedge
fund D. E. Shaw opined, "We believe that [credit default] swap markets
have often priced in a 'truer' level of the market's fundamental view on a
particular issuer's credit risk than that implied by prices of cash bonds (although we don't believe this will necessarily always be the case)."[29]

Figure 4.12 thus shows an incredible failure of arbitrage. Under efficient market conditions this really shouldn't happen. If markets were functioning properly, this profit opportunity would never materialize; it would be immediately arbitraged away as investors snapped up the bonds (reducing bond spreads) and bought CDS protection (raising CDS rates), thereby causing the basis to collapse back to zero. So what we see here is the proverbial $100 bill lying on the sidewalk with nobody picking it up. How can we make sense of this?

The panic crunch explains this anomaly. The panic crunch story predicts that bond spreads will rise to artificially inflated levels during a panic. However, *it makes no such prediction regarding CDS rates*. Bond spreads rise because investors that fund themselves with runnable short-term debt must dump bonds to raise cash and meet redemptions. CDS contracts, however, are synthetic instruments, not cash instruments. This means that, unlike bond purchases, CDS positions don't need to be funded: protection sellers (who are taking long positions) part with little or no cash up front.[30] Hence the premium on cash during a panic would not necessarily affect CDS rates. Accordingly, in the event of a panic crunch, the CDS-bond basis should go negative—and that's just what happened.

This analysis turns out to provide an elegant test of competing claims. I noted above that collapsing quantities and spiking costs of financing could arise from sources other than a panic crunch, such as a perception of deteriorating borrower credit quality or heightened aversion to risk. But these other explanations would be expected to affect *both* CDS rates *and* bond spreads in equal measure. They would not affect the CDS-bond basis. The evidence thus suggests that bond yields (and hence financing rates in the primary markets) were unduly elevated for a time. When combined with the Ivashina-Scharfstein analysis, the evidence of a panic-induced financing crunch is powerful.

Now let's tie the foregoing analysis together. I argue that the CDS-bond basis provides dramatic visible evidence of a panic crunch. How well does the panic crunch match up with the macroeconomic disaster? Figure 4.13 overlays the change in US employment (fig. 4.5) with the CDS-bond basis (fig. 4.12). The correspondence between these two data series is remarkable in terms of both timing and acuity. If the CDS-bond basis is our best evidence of a panic crunch—inasmuch as it reflects artificially elevated costs of financing—then the panic crunch fits the jobs disaster like a glove.

Now, one might argue that lots of things were happening around the same time—the housing market collapse, for example. As we will see later

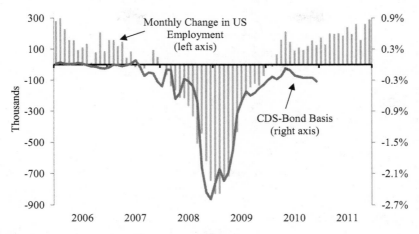

FIGURE 4.13. The panic crunch and the jobs disaster

in the chapter, some prominent analysts have argued that the 2007–9 col-lapse in US housing prices, coupled with large household debt loads, bears primary responsibility for the Great Recession. But I will show there that, from a timing and acuity standpoint, the housing collapse story provides a less compelling fit.

Econometric evidence corroborates the conclusion that disruptions in the supply of financing dealt a severe blow to US employment in 2008 and 2009. In a remarkable study,[31] Gabriel Chodorow-Reich finds that "firms that had precrisis relationships with less healthy lenders had a lower likeli-hood of obtaining a loan following the Lehman bankruptcy, paid a higher interest rate if they did borrow, and reduced employment by more com-pared to precrisis clients of healthier lenders." He further finds that "the withdrawal of credit accounts for between one-third and one-half of the employment decline at small and medium firms in the sample in the year following the Lehman bankruptcy." Because Chodorow-Reich looks only at differential impacts based on lender health, he likely understates the effect of credit supply disruptions on employment. Remember, the panic crunch story predicts a *generalized* contraction in the supply of financing.

To sum up: there appears to have been a severe financing crunch in the United States between 2007 and 2009. There are good reasons to think this crunch was largely a consequence of the shadow banking panics. And there are good reasons to think the financing crunch was a major driver of the macroeconomic disaster. Taken together, these conclusions offer sug-gestive evidence that a panic-induced financing crunch bore substantial responsibility for the Great Recession in the United States. When we consider this evidence in light of coincidence of panics and economic disasters in US history, it adds up to a strong case that panics should be viewed as *the* central problem for financial stability policy.

Some Competing Theories

Not everyone agrees that panics are a leading source of severe recessions. It is worthwhile to highlight some alternative viewpoints. We will look here at five categories of dissenters: Austrian business cycle theorists; advocates of what has been called a "spending hypothesis"; neoclassical theorists; market monetarists; and a class of theories that can be called debt cycle theories. Debt cycle theories will receive special attention because they have formed the conceptual basis for much of the financial reform theorizing of recent years.

To be clear, I am not purporting to offer an exhaustive overview of all economic thought on the subject of deep recessions—far from it. Thankfully, such an overview is not needed for our purposes. This section seeks to make only a modest point: that there are significant schools of economic thought whose proponents tend to downplay, or deny altogether, the causal role of panics in severe recessions. These schools stand in opposition to the views of Bagehot, Friedman and Schwartz, Gorton, and Bernanke reviewed above. To reduce the chances of mischaracterization, the discussion that follows will rely heavily on quotations from relevant theorists.

Austrian Business Cycle Theory

Austrian business cycle theory has been called the "original explanation" for the Great Depression.[32] This school of thought is perhaps not as influential as it used to be. Still, it is of more than merely historical interest. Several mainstream economists have recently found merit in parts of the Austrian theory.[33] Moreover, as others have pointed out before, the Austrian view actually has quite a bit of overlap with the debt cycle theories we will review shortly, which are very influential today. Austrian business cycle theory tends to be associated with the libertarian "right" while debt cycle theories have more of a "left" association—but on inspection they have a lot in common.

Ludwig von Mises gave the original formulation of the Austrian theory of business cycles.[34] Mises's story starts with the banking system. When banks issue "fiduciary media"—redeemable bank money consisting of bank notes or checkable deposits—they push down the "money rate of interest." And banks by their nature have the capacity to "extend their issue of fiduciary media arbitrarily." When they overextend, interest rates fall too low: there is a "divergence . . . between the money rate and the natural rate of interest." This divergence induces businesspeople to engage in "longer," more "roundabout" processes of production. This can't last forever: "The banks will ultimately be forced to cease their endeav- ours to underbid the natural rate of interest." But the damage has been done. "Economic goods which could have satisfied more important wants," Mises writes, "have been employed for the satisfaction of less important." Unsound investments are then liquidated. Workers lose their jobs as the economy goes through a necessary period of adjustment.

Under the Austrian theory of the business cycle, a recession is a nec- essary consequence of the excesses that preceded it. Panics do not play a central role in the theory. If anything, they are perhaps a symptom or manifestation of the "malinvestment" that has already occurred. Indeed, under the Austrian view, panics can be seen as an aspect of the needed liquidation that is a prerequisite to sustainable recovery. It follows from this theory that, once a crisis is under way, remedial policies are likely to prove counterproductive. Here is Austrian economist Friedrich Hayek on the subject:

> The thing which is needed to secure healthy conditions is the most speedy and complete adaptation possible of the structure of production. . . . The only way permanently to "mobilise" all available resources is, therefore, not to use arti- ficial stimulants—whether during a crisis or thereafter—but to leave it to time to effect a permanent cure by the slow process of adapting the structure of pro- duction to the means available for capital purposes.
>
> And so, at the end of our analysis, we arrive at results which only confirm the old truth that we may perhaps prevent a crisis by checking expansion in time, but that we can do nothing to get out of it before its natural end, once it has come.[35]

Lionel Robbins, another prominent economist in the Austrian tradition, made a similar point.[36] "When the extent of mal-investment and overin- debtedness has passed a certain limit, measures which postpone liquida- tion only tend to make matters worse," he wrote. "To prevent the depres- sion the only effective method is to prevent the boom."

Joseph Schumpeter is sometimes classified as an economist in the

Austrian tradition; he was in fact Austrian by nationality. His theory of business cycles was, however, rather distinctive, with a less central role for money and credit.[37] In any case, Schumpeter shared the Austrian school's distaste for remedial policies:

> Depressions are not simply evils, which we might attempt to suppress, but—perhaps undesirable—forms of something which has to be done, namely, adjustment to previous economic change. Most of what would be effective in remedying a depression would be equally effective in preventing this adjustment. . . .
>
> . . . Our analysis leads us to believe that recovery is sound only if it does come of itself. For any revival which is merely due to artificial stimulus leaves part of the work of depressions undone and adds, to an undigested remnant of maladjustment, new maladjustment of its own which has to be liquidated in turn, thus threatening business with another crisis ahead.[38]

Such views were not confined to the ivory tower. They echo Herbert Hoover's unhappy recollection of the advice he received from some of his advisers in the first years of the Depression:

> The "leave it alone liquidationists" headed by Secretary of the Treasury Mellon . . . felt that government must keep its hands off and let the slump liquidate itself. Mr. Mellon had only one formula: "Liquidate labor, liquidate stocks, liquidate the farmers, liquidate real estate." . . . He held that even a panic was not altogether a bad thing. He said: "It will purge the rottenness out of the system. High costs of living and high living will come down. People will work harder, live a more moral life. Values will be adjusted, and enterprising people will pick up the wrecks from less competent people."[39]

According to Austrian school economist Murray Rothbard, "While phrased somewhat luridly, this was the sound and proper course for the administration to follow."[40]

Unsurprisingly, John Maynard Keynes disagreed with these views. He condemned the liquidationist perspective in colorful terms:

> Some austere and puritanical souls regard [the current depression] both as an inevitable and a desirable nemesis on so much overexpansion, as they call it; a nemesis on man's speculative spirit. It would, they feel, be a victory for the mammon of unrighteousness if so much prosperity was not subsequently balanced by universal bankruptcy. We need, they say, what they politely call a

"prolonged liquidation" to put us right. The liquidation, they tell us, is not yet complete. But in time it will be. And when sufficient time has elapsed for the completion of the liquidation, all will be well with us again.

I do not take this view.... And I do not understand how universal bankruptcy can do any good or bring us nearer to prosperity.[41]

Friedman and Schwartz, too, found the Austrian theory untenable. They rejected the idea that the Great Depression was "a desirable and necessary economic development required to eliminate inefficiency and weakness."[42] As we saw above, they believed that the Depression was brought about by monetary forces—and that the banking panics played a pivotal role in the collapse of the money supply.

The Spending Hypothesis

Turn now to a second viewpoint that tends to relegate panics (or financial crises more generally) to an insignificant role in major economic disruptions. In his 1976 book *Did Monetary Forces Cause the Great Depression?* Peter Temin challenges the idea that the banking panics of the early 1930s played an important causal role in the Great Depression.[43] "The banking panics were a part of a larger process that started with the decline in autonomous spending," he writes. "Had they not taken place ... the overall story of the Depression would not have been much different."

Temin's book is styled as a rebuttal to the Friedman-Schwartz argument. He rejects their "money hypothesis" in favor of what he calls a "spending hypothesis." According to Temin, the Great Depression was most likely the product of an "autonomous" and "unexplained" fall in consumption spending in 1930. Temin says that "the spending hypothesis sees the banking panics as results of the Depression rather than as causes, while the money hypothesis sees them as primary causative events." Ben Bernanke characterized Temin's book as having suggested "totally nonfinancial sources of the Great Depression."[44]

Temin's analysis finds a counterpart in relation to the recent crisis. Economist Dean Baker has offered a variant of the spending hypothesis to explain the Great Recession. In Baker's view, the slump can be explained by losses of housing wealth, which reduced consumer spending through a wealth effect. "The problem is not first and foremost a financial crisis," Baker argues.[45] Indeed, the financial crisis and rescue were "all a sideshow." Baker wrote in 2012 that, while the financial crisis did hasten the downturn, "we would be in pretty much the same place today even if the financial crisis had not happened."[46] To Baker, the story of the recession "is the story of a collapsed bubble, not a financial crisis."

The views of Temin and Baker are similar enough that they can usefully be considered together. Neither Temin nor Baker ascribes much importance to financial crises or panics—at least when it comes to the Great Depression and Great Recession, respectively.

Neoclassical Theory

Economists of a neoclassical persuasion emphasize the role of "real" (as opposed to monetary or financial) disturbances and government policies in generating major contractions. They tend to downplay the role of panics, or of financial crises more generally, in severe recessions. Consider the following from Nobel Prize winner Edward Prescott, speaking in March 2009 as US output was plummeting: "Once the Fed stopped trying to stabilize the economy, the economy got a lot more stable. . . . I think the financial crisis has been greatly overstated as a problem. [It has] had virtually no consequences for the real economy. . . . With benign neglect the economy would have come roaring back quite quickly."[47]

A few months earlier, several other neoclassical economists questioned whether it is even *plausible* that a financial crisis might hurt business investment.[48] "It is difficult to see how disruptions in financial markets will directly affect investment decisions by a typical firm," they wrote. After all, "the typical firm can finance its capital expenditures entirely from retained earnings" without resorting to external finance. "Furthermore, to the extent that redirecting funds from firms that have excess resources to firms that need resources is important, such redirection can occur if firms are able to borrow and lend to each other directly or pursue joint ventures of various kinds." In other words, such redirection can happen without intermediation. Unsurprisingly, the authors were skeptics of the financial stabilization program then under way: "We feel that a trillion dollar intervention warrants a bit more serious analysis than we have seen."

Along similar lines, another neoclassical economist, Lee Ohanian, recently challenged the belief that financial crises cause large recessions and depressions.[49] In his view, "the Great Depression would have been 'Great' even in the absence of the banking and financial crises," and "the impact of banking crises on the Depression remains an open question." Ohanian raises similar questions about the Great Recession. Among other things, he notes that the "financial explanation" does not explain "why economic weakness continued for so long after the worst of the financial crisis passed." He concludes that more research is required before we can say that the financial crisis was a major factor behind the Great Recession.

Casey Mulligan, another economist in the neoclassical tradition, argues that redistributive policies in 2008 and 2009 are largely to blame for the Great Recession. Those policies reduced incentives to work, he says, and the result was lower employment and output. Mulligan advances this thesis in his 2012 book *The Redistribution Recession*.[50] "This book does not just add to the list of plausible though potentially minor impulses," he writes. Rather, the book contends that safety net expansions "were *enough by themselves* to generate changes in the major macro aggregates that resemble the actual changes in direction, amount, and timing" (emphasis added). Mulligan concludes that "the expanding social safety net may well be the largest single factor reducing labor during the 2008–09 recession."

Mulligan does not deny that the financial crisis played a role in the recession, but he offers a very unusual interpretation. He stresses *indirect* causation, claiming the financial crisis made the safety net expansion possible: "The 2008 financial crisis probably made it politically possible, if not politically inevitable, to expand other parts of the social safety net."[51] In a Q&A that is available online, he characterizes his book as having shown how the financial crisis and housing crash "affect the labor market through redistributive public policy rather than depressing the labor market through some other mechanism."[52]

Curiously, though, Mulligan also argues that causation went in the opposite direction: safety net expansions may have caused the financial crisis.[53] In particular, he notes that "the market value of capital *reacts to* labor market distortions, and declines before labor supply distortions actually appear—namely, when news of labor distortions becomes known in the market place." Mulligan argues that "the sharp drops in consumption, investment, and capital market values during 2008 . . . were, in significant part, a reaction to, and anticipation of, labor market contractions created by the expanding social safety net." He reiterates this point in the online Q&A: "Redistribution depresses the value of businesses, so the magnitude of the financial crisis may itself be a signal of the redistribution ahead." So, anticipated safety net expansion caused the financial crisis—and the financial crisis in turn made the safety net expansion possible! In any case, in Mulligan's telling it was the growing safety net, not the financial crisis per se, that bore most of the responsibility for the severe contraction.

It seems fair to say that economists of a neoclassical persuasion tend to doubt the (direct) role of financial crises, and hence of panics, in causing or amplifying major recessions.

Market Monetarism

The term market monetarism refers to a distinctive and idiosyncratic set of views about monetary policy and macroeconomics. Its leading exponent is Scott Sumner, whom Paul Krugman has described as "in a lot of ways, the heir to Milton Friedman."[54] Market monetarism is associated with a specific policy proposal. Sumner and other market monetarists propose that central banks set an explicit target path for nominal gross domestic product (NGDP). The idea is to target NGDP *levels*, not growth rates, which means the central bank should commit to correct for any deviations from the target NGDP path. The proposal is called NGDP level targeting, abbreviated NGDPLT.

Sumner contends that the Great Recession was a consequence of tight money. In particular, "extremely tight monetary policy in the US (and perhaps Europe and Japan) seems to have sharply depressed nominal spending after July 2008."[55] Those who have not followed Sumner's writings may find this claim perplexing. Figure 4.14 shows the US monetary base since 1990. It shows explosive growth immediately after July 2008. To most people this probably looks like *loose* money, but Sumner says exactly the opposite. He argues that the monetary base is not a reliable indicator of the stance of monetary policy. It's all about the path of NGDP—and this, he says, is under the Fed's control.

In Sumner's view the financial crisis was not a big factor in the recession. "Most economists simply assumed that a severe intensification of the financial crisis depressed spending," he says.[56] But "the proximate cause of the [economic] crash was not a financial crisis." In fact, "the reverse was more nearly true." That is, the fall in NGDP caused the severe financial crisis: "Tight money greatly intensified the financial crisis in late 2008."[57] Sumner makes a similar argument regarding the Great Depression: "The first financial crisis occurred more than a year into the Depression, and it was probably caused by the collapse in spending that was then already in progress."[58] To Sumner, "the problem was 100% tight money after September 1929."[59]

Sumner's brand of monetarism differs from Milton Friedman's in at

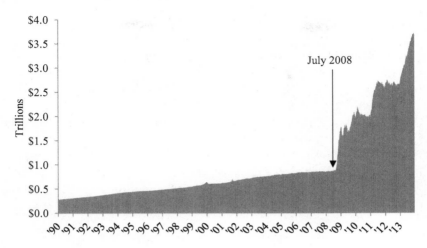

FIGURE 4.14. US monetary base
Source: Federal Reserve Economic Database, series BASE.

least one important respect. In Friedman's worldview, banks are important monetary institutions. Friedman and Schwartz focus on measures of the money supply that include bank-issued money—M2 is their preferred measure—and they identify banking panics as the key mechanism that caused the money supply to collapse in the early 1930s. Sumner sees things very differently. He admonishes economists to "keep banks out of macro" and argues that "macroeconomists grossly overrate the importance of banking."[60] According to Sumner, "Most economists put far too much weight on banking crises as a causal factor." Naturally Sumner does not ascribe much significance to panics. At the time of a severe recession, he says, "it always looks like the 'real problem' was some symptom of the monetary shock, such as financial panic."[61] Sumner refers to his own "obsession with currency" and "dismissal of banking."[62]

Sumner argues that good monetary policy would obviate the need for banking regulation. "I'm trying to get the Fed to target NGDP," he says. "And then we'll abolish [too big to fail], as we'll no longer fear that big bank failures will lead to recessions. And then we'll abolish [the] FDIC. And then we'll allow free banking."[63] If the central bank would only adopt the right policy rule, then we could do away with bank regulation entirely: "In a world of no Too-Big-to-Fail, no FDIC, and NGDPLT, the optimal bank regulatory regime is no regulation at all."[64]

Debt Cycle Theories

The final class of theories we will address can be grouped loosely under the heading "debt cycle theories." These theories focus on cycles of debt and deleveraging without attributing any particular significance to *short-term* debt. They emphasize how deleveraging hurts the broader economy, but they are not primarily about panics. Loosely speaking, this genre includes the "debt-deflation" theory of Irving Fisher, the "financial instability hypothesis" of Hyman Minsky, the "balance sheet recession" theory of Richard Koo, the "leverage cycle" view of John Geanakoplos, and the "financial accelerator" view of Ben Bernanke. We now look at these in turn.

Consider first the foundational version of this theory, that of Irving Fisher. In his classic 1933 article "The Debt-Deflation Theory of Great Depressions,"[65] Fisher argues that "great booms and depressions" are attributable to "two dominant factors, namely overindebtedness to start with and deflation following soon after." According to Fisher, "a state of overindebtedness . . . will tend to lead to liquidation, through the alarm either of debtors or creditors or both." Liquidation of debt leads to distressed selling and a fall in the price level, which in turn magnifies debt loads because "each dollar of debt still unpaid becomes a bigger dollar." This leads to a "paradox," namely that "the more the debtors pay, the more they owe." Under these conditions there occurs a "reduction in output, in trade and in employment of labor." To Fisher, neither overindebtedness nor deflation is much of a problem standing alone; it is their combination that is so pernicious. This is important, because it suggests a policy solution: "It is always economically possible to stop or prevent such a depression simply by reflating the price level." Thus major depressions are "curable and preventable."

Hyman Minsky is next in our line of debt cycle theorists.[66] Minsky writes that "something is fundamentally wrong with our economy": it is "inherently flawed because its investment and financing processes introduce endogenous destabilizing forces." Over the course of a boom, stable financial arrangements are supplanted by what he calls "speculative finance" and "Ponzi finance." Speculative finance consists of debt structures in which cash flows are sufficient to cover interest but not principal. Ponzi finance consists of debt structures in which cash flows are insufficient even to cover interest and that therefore rely on ever more borrowing. The shift toward these unstable structures is part of the internal dynamics of a capitalist economy: "Profit opportunities within a robust financial structure make the shift from robustness to fragility an endogenous phenomenon." In short, "serious business cycles are due to financial attributes that are essential to capitalism." (The latter point is a persistent theme in Minsky's work; he wrote elsewhere that "there are endogenous disequilibrating forces within a capitalist economy" and that "the internal workings of a capitalist economy generate financial relations that are conducive to instability.")[67] Minsky calls his theory the "financial instability hypothesis," and he acknowledges Fisher as an important precursor.

The third of our debt cycle theorists is Richard Koo, the originator of the "balance sheet recession" theory.[68] Koo argues that the bursting of asset-price bubbles is a leading cause of deep recessions. Such bubbles are "usually a result of private-sector overconfidence about future economic prospects." When the bubble bursts, "the private sector begins paying down debt en masse." Businesses become "obsessed with repairing damaged balance sheets" rather than with maximizing profits, and this leads to a severe recession. The good and bad phases of the economy are "linked in a cycle." Koo's theory emerged from his analysis of Japan's experience in the 1990s, but he argues that it explains the Great Depression and Great Recession too. Banking distress does not play an important role in Koo's theory. On the contrary, he insists that in Japan's recession "the problems at banks were a *result* of the recession, not a cause." Koo acknowledges that his theory resembles Fisher's debt-deflation theory, but he disagrees with Fisher's emphasis on deflation as a key driver.

Fourth in our line of debt cycle theories is the "leverage cycle" theory of John Geanakoplos.[69] Geanakoplos says that "the present crisis is the bottom of a leverage cycle." "There are times," he writes, when leverage is high, such that many assets can be acquired "with very little money down." At other times leverage is low, and buyers "must have all or nearly all of the money in hand to purchase those very same assets." The transition from high-leverage to low-leverage states starts with "bad news" that causes lenders to increase margins (lend at reduced leverage). Losses and bankruptcies follow, causing a feedback loop of more bad news and even higher margins, and so on. As a consequence, "in ebullient times asset prices are too high, and in crisis times they plummet too low. This is the leverage cycle." And the cycle is "bad for the economy" for a variety of reasons, including bankruptcy costs and the incentive effects of debt overhang. Geanakoplos cites Minsky as a "modern pioneer in calling attention to the dangers of leverage."

Finally, Ben Bernanke's "financial accelerator" theory can be placed in the debt cycle category. The seed of this theory was planted in Bernanke's classic 1983 article, discussed above. Recall that the article argued that banking distress in the early 1930s disrupted the supply of credit and worsened the Great Depression. This is probably the paper's most enduring takeaway. But the paper also made a second argument. Bernanke observed that declining income and falling prices reduced borrowers' net worth by eroding the value of their collateral relative to debt burdens. These developments increased the information problems that are associated with lending, making it harder for borrowers to get credit. In other words, credit allocation was impeded not just because of problems on the banking side but also because of the declining creditworthiness of borrowers. This disruption in the credit allocation process hurt overall economic output. In subsequent work, Bernanke and his coauthors refer to this effect as the "financial accelerator." Bernanke notes that the financial accelerator idea is closely related to Fisher's debt-deflation thesis.[70] The financial accelerator idea has been very influential. Robert Hall says that "the dominant view among macroeconomists today is that a financial crisis causes real economic activity to collapse by raising frictions," and he refers to the financial accelerator as "the canon of this line of thinking."[71]

There are important distinctions among the debt cycle theorists mentioned here, but their views do share a core logic. And note that these theories are not about panics; they have no necessary connection to *short-term* debt. These theorists view excessive debt as a potential source of severe economic damage whether or not a panic happens.

Of Debt-Fueled Bubbles, Prolonged Slumps, and Japan

Clearly, the role of panics in causing or amplifying severe recessions is a subject of disagreement. This book will have nothing more to say about the first four theories mentioned above: Austrian business cycle theory, the spending hypothesis, neoclassical theory, and market monetarism. Proponents of those theories generally deny that panics, or financial crises more generally, are important causes of major economic contractions (including the Great Recession). My reading of the evidence suggests otherwise.

For the rest of this chapter we will confine ourselves to the fifth category above: debt cycle theories. Debt cycle theories present a more difficult challenge to my argument. Proponents of these theories don't deny that panics matter, but they tend to place much more emphasis on debt-fueled bubbles (or credit booms and busts) as the more fundamental issue. In this regard, think back to the schematic in figure 4.2. Debt cycle theorists tend to see panel A as more nearly correct than panel B.

Debt cycle theorists will mount three main objections to my argument for panic primacy. First, they will point to Japan's "lost decade" in the 1990s. That episode, they say, shows how the collapse of a debt-fueled asset-price bubble can produce a severe, prolonged slump, even without a panic. Second, they will point to recent work by economists Atif Mian and Amir Sufi that suggests household leverage was the main driver of the Great Recession in the United States. Third, they will argue that panics, which are brief events, can't explain *protracted* slumps. I conclude this chapter by addressing these three objections in turn.

Japan's Lost Decade

It is widely believed that Japan's lost decade in the 1990s shows how the bursting of a debt-fueled bubble can sink an economy even without a panic. But I believe a short-term funding panic may very well have played a big and underappreciated role in Japan's slump.

Accounts of Japan's experience in the 1990s seldom mention a panic in the short-term wholesale funding markets. For instance, Charles Kindleberger's classic history of financial crises says Japan provides "a striking story of a mania and a crash—but without a panic."[72] Yet it turns out that Japan *did* experience a major panic in late 1997. In a recent paper, two Nomura analysts describe how the broader Asian financial crisis led to the failure of a fairly small Japanese securities firm on November 3, 1997.[73] Japan had a shadow banking system, and this firm was part of it. It funded its balance sheet with short-term (money market) debt. Its failure was "the first default ever in Japan's money market." The default prompted a loss of confidence in the money market and ignited a "serious financial crisis." A number of other financial firms were unable to roll over short-term yen funding and failed that month. The authors note that although the initial default "did not involve a large amount," it nonetheless "radically reduced the provision of credit to market participants and shrank liquidity throughout the financial system."

Hiroshi Nakaso of the Bank of Japan describes the same events, noting that this "small default paralysed the entire interbank market."[74] By late November "it was as though the financial system was starting to melt down." A panic was under way; short-term creditors were redeeming en masse. The central bank and finance ministry "issued an extraordinary joint statement . . . in which they reiterated their commitment to the stability of the financial system" and "confirmed that all deposits including interbank deposits were protected." November 26, 1997, he says, "was probably the day that Japan's financial system was closest to a systemic collapse." Financial sector short-term funding spreads spiked sharply, as did corporate bond spreads.[75] This all sounds quite a bit like the United States in the fall of 2008.

Sure enough, what followed was a severe financing crunch. That such a crunch emerged in Japan in late 1997 is well known, but its connection to the wholesale funding panic is routinely overlooked. Thus Richard Koo remarks that "by early 1998, the whole country was engulfed in a credit crunch."[76] But he says the crunch was caused by fiscal tightening coupled with "additional clarification of capital regulations announced by the government in October 1997." He makes no mention of a panic in the wholesale money markets. Similarly, in his famous paper on Japan's liquidity trap, Paul Krugman notes that "the reasons for the emergence of credit constraints in late 1997 [are] quite clear. The immediate forcing event was the announcement, in October 1997, of new capital adequacy standards, to be effective from April 1998."[77] Again, no mention here of a shadow bank run.

But didn't Japan's slump start in the early 1990s—years before the 1997 panic? Figure 4.15 offers one way of looking at this question. It replicates an analysis from Paul Krugman's blog.[78] Krugman plots Japan's real GDP per working-age resident from 1991 to 2007. Assume, he says, that the economy was operating at potential at the endpoints. Then draw a curve between the endpoints corresponding to a constant annualized growth rate (the dotted curve). This is the inferred path of "potential" GDP per working-age resident. The difference between potential and actual is the inferred output gap.

This is obviously a back of the envelope kind of analysis, but let's go with Krugman's setup here. The figure shows a mild slump in the early 1990s, in the aftermath of the central bank's monetary tightening (1989–91) and the collapse of Japan's asset-price bubble. Note that there was no outright recession in Japan in the early 1990s; despite staggering losses of stock and real estate wealth throughout the economy, GDP did not shrink. As Adam Posen has noted, Japan's economic problems in the early part of the decade were "far milder than is commonly recognised." The figure suggests that

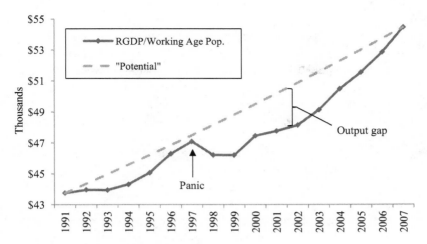

FIGURE 4.15. Japan's inferred output gap, 1991–2007
Source: Real GDP in Japan, in 2011 US dollars, from Federal Reserve Economic Database, series JPNRGDPR. Japan working age population (ages fifteen to sixty-four) from OECD.

by 1996 the economy was again operating close to potential. Then we see a huge contraction—an outright recession—in 1998. The picture is consistent with a big negative shock at the end of 1997, when the panic happened.

Narrative accounts seem to back up this story. Koo observes that "people felt no pain before October 1997." Before that time, he writes, "banks were very willing lenders" and "the banking problem had scarcely impacted on people's lives."[79] Likewise, an International Monetary Fund economist has noted that Japan's economy "was regaining its balance" in 1996 and 1997.[80] But the recovery was then derailed: "Rather than recovering, however, in 1997 the economy entered into its first recession since the early 1970s." Both Koo and Krugman argue that misguided fiscal policies bore primary responsibility for the sharp downturn in 1997.[81] I am suggesting that a shadow banking panic (and a resulting financing crunch) may shoulder much of the blame.[82] Japan's experience therefore does not refute my claim that, when it comes to financial stability policy, panics—not debt-fueled bubbles—are the main problem.

Mian and Sufi

A second objection to panic primacy comes from the influential work of Atif Mian and Amir Sufi. In a series of academic articles and their recent book *House of Debt*,[83] Mian and Sufi argue that the Great Recession in the United States was caused mostly by a combination of falling real estate prices and excessive household debt. In their "levered losses" framework, losses of housing wealth cause household spending to collapse, thereby hurting employment. Although they focus mostly on the Great Recession, they believe the pattern is more general: it applies to previous severe recessions too, including the Great Depression. They boldly contend that "the dramatic loss in wealth of indebted home owners is the key driver of severe recessions."[84]

Mian and Sufi doubt that financial system distress played a major role in the Great Recession. A core part of their argument has to do with timing. They stress the fact that the US economy entered recession well before the severe phase of the financial crisis struck in September 2008.[85] This isn't very informative, however. As we saw in chapter 3, the first wave of panics happened in August 2007, several months before the recession started. Further, the vast majority of the job losses came after the events of September 2008; it is reasonable to think that those events greatly amplified the contraction, turning an otherwise ordinary recession into a terrible one. Mian and Sufi also contend that problems in the financial system can't explain continued job losses in 2009, because "there is no evidence that banks were under any duress after 2008."[86] Having worked on financial stability policy at Treasury during the harrowing first half of 2009, I remember things differently. A broad set of indicators shows significant financial stress continuing into the second half of 2009.[87]

As a matter of fact, from a timing and acuity standpoint, the panic crunch story corresponds much better to the macroeconomic disaster than does the housing wealth story. We saw earlier in this chapter that the 2007 to 2009 financing crunch (as exemplified by the CDS-bond basis) matches up extremely well with the jobs disaster. By contrast, the housing collapse story fits rather awkwardly. The housing collapse started in earnest in March 2007 and ended in May 2009.[88] When employment peaked in January 2008, the housing collapse was already 35% over. Of course, it is quite possible that declining housing wealth affected employment with a time lag. But the housing wealth story can't explain the severe *intensification* of the jobs decline after the bankruptcy of Lehman, when the panic reached its acute phase. The housing collapse was already 67% over when Lehman failed (at which point the jobs collapse was only 16% over), and there was *no* discernible intensification in the housing collapse either before or after Lehman's failure. On the contrary, the housing decline continued at a remarkably steady pace from March 2007 to May 2009. Was it merely a random coincidence that the economy went into free fall right when the severe panic struck? (To be fair, Mian and Sufi do acknowledge that "what happened in the fall of 2008 no doubt exacerbated economic weakness" and that "some of the decline in the economy during the heart of the financial crisis was a result of problems in the banking sector."[89] But they clearly view this as ancillary to the main story.)

Not only are Mian and Sufi doubtful that a financing crunch bore primary responsibility for the Great Recession, they doubt that there even *was* a serious financing crunch in 2008 and 2009. They point out that total bank loans outstanding actually surged in the late 2008 as firms drew down on lines of credit.[90] This is true, but why did firms draw down existing credit lines? Such drawdowns were due to the unavailability of other sources of financing; they were yet another manifestation of the run on the financial sector.[91] In addition, Mian and Sufi cite survey data in which small businesses cited poor sales, rather than financing constraints, as their single most important concern throughout the crisis. But other survey data show a steep increase during the crisis in the net percentage of small businesses reporting that credit had become harder to obtain.[92] Besides, if financing crunches depress spending economywide, it stands to reason that small businesses would cite poor sales as their single biggest problem during such an episode. In any case, I refer readers back to the data presented earlier in this chapter, which suggest a major contraction in the supply of financing during the crisis.

Mian and Sufi's strongest evidence that households' levered losses caused the Great Recession consists of a zip code–level analysis of household leverage, spending, and employment. They find that in 2008 and 2009 spending fell more in counties with larger declines in housing net worth than in counties with smaller declines. Furthermore, the decline in jobs catering to *local* demand was larger in counties with larger declines in housing net worth; by contrast, the decline in jobs catering to *national* demand was spread evenly across counties. These are powerful findings, and they do suggest a significant role for household balance sheets. But they need to be interpreted carefully. A sharp contraction in the supply of financing should be expected to have a disproportionate impact on spending (and on jobs catering to local demand) in zip codes where consumers and local businesses have been relying more heavily on debt to finance expenditures. Mian and Sufi's findings therefore don't tell us what would have happened without the panic crunch.

Finally, stepping back from the Great Recession, Mian and Sufi suggest

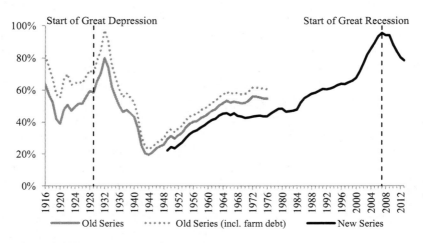

FIGURE 4.16. US household debt to GDP, 1916–2013
Source: Old series are from *Historical Statistics of the United States: Millennial Edition Online*, tables Cj882–889 and Ca10. New series is from Federal Reserve Economic Database, series CMDEBT and GDPA.

that household debt is the primary driver of other severe recessions, including the Great Depression. With respect to the Depression, they refer in general terms to a run-up in household debt in the 1920s.[93] I produce long-term data on US household debt to GDP in figure 4.16. Mian and Sufi are right: the Great Depression was preceded by a significant run-up in household debt, from about 40% to about 60% of GDP in the 1920s.[94] (The spike from 60% in 1929 to 80% in 1932 was entirely a function of collapsing GDP; it was a consequence, not a cause, of the Depression.) But it is important to keep in mind that other things were happening too. A substantial body of literature suggests that the banking panics of the early 1930s and the operation of the international gold standard—both of which are aspects of monetary system design—were key drivers of the Depression. Indeed, Ben Bernanke wrote in 2000 that "there is now overwhelming evidence that the main factor depressing aggregate demand was a worldwide contraction in world money supplies."[95] Household debt may very well have been a contributing cause of the Depression; whether it was a primary driver is far from clear. To sum up, Mian and Sufi's work does not refute my argument that, when it comes to preventing macroeconomic disasters, we should be much more concerned about panics than about debt-fueled bubbles per se.

Prolonged Slumps

This leads us to the final topic of this chapter: whether panics can explain *protracted* slumps. Panics are brief events, so why doesn't the economy just bounce right back once the panic is over? Paul Krugman, for one, thinks the panic can be only part of the story of the recent global slump. "A run on the shadow banking system . . . [was] clearly key to understanding the severity of the 2007–9 slump," he writes.[96] But he points out that "financial stress peaked in early 2009, then fell sharply." He then poses the question, "The economy didn't come roaring back. Why?" Krugman thinks the main answer is large debt loads. In particular, he points to "the sharp rise in household debt that accompanied the bubble." Krugman concludes: "I would argue that this debt overhang has held back spending even though financial markets are operating more or less normally again."

Is it possible that this argument starts from a flawed premise? Perhaps market economies have no automatic tendency to "come roaring back" after large negative shocks, even if postshock monetary policy is conducted optimally. That is to say, a severe negative shock (such as a panic) could knock the economy onto a lower track—a persistent high-unemployment equilibrium. In a 1935 article, John Maynard Keynes observed that, under the prevailing economic orthodoxy of the time, the economic system was viewed as having "an inherent tendency towards self-adjustment." But Keynes described himself as a "heretic" who believed that the system was *not* self-adjusting.[97] He elaborated on this point in his *General Theory*. "The economic system may find itself in stable equilibrium with [employment] at a level below full employment," he wrote. "This analysis supplies us with an explanation of the paradox of poverty in the midst of plenty. For the mere existence of an insufficiency of effective demand may, and often will, bring the increase of employment to a standstill *before* a level of full employment has been reached."[98]

Half a century later James Tobin—who basically agreed with Keynes on this score—characterized the debate as follows:[99]

> The big issue between Keynes and his "old classical" opponents was the efficacy of the economy's natural market adjustment mechanisms in restoring full employment equilibrium, once a negative real demand shock had pushed the economy off that equilibrium. Keynes and Keynesians said those mechanisms were weak, possibly nonexistent or perverse, and needed help from gov-

ernment policy. That is still the major question of macroeconomic theory and policy.

Tobin goes on to offer his own account of why an economy might not bounce right back after a big negative shock. Tobin conceives of the problem as a kind of economywide coordination failure. The problem he describes is circular: output is constrained by demand for goods and services; demand for goods and services is constrained by the level of employment; and the level of employment is constrained by output. And he insists that this has nothing to do with irrationality. "Individual rationality does not necessarily create the institutions that would guarantee 'invisible hand' results," he writes. "Keynes was not questioning the rationality of individual economic agents; he was arguing that their behavior would yield optimal results if and only if they as citizens organized the necessary collective institutions and government policies."

Tobin's basic point is that market economies can get stuck on a lower trajectory after a big negative shock. Most everyone might be better off if we could all agree to hold hands and "jump" back to precrisis levels of consumption and investment. But we can't reach such a deal, and no one has an incentive to move unilaterally. Nor can adjustments in interest rates or prices be expected to (or be made to) do the job. Tobin's story isn't about excessive debt loads or balance sheet repair.[100] In essence, it is a story about coordination failure. This is the stag hunt from chapter 2 writ large. (Tobin described the problem as one of *dis*equilibrium, but this doesn't seem to matter; he was agreeing with Keynes.)

Other economists have formalized the idea that coordination failures may prevent the economy from recovering after severe negative shocks. In one paper—part of a body of work for which he won a Nobel Prize—Peter Diamond suggests an analogy to a tropical island in which the only good is coconuts.[101] People get coconuts by climbing palm trees, which is costly. There is a taboo against consuming coconuts one has picked oneself, so people have to trade before they can consume. In this island economy, people will climb palm trees to pick coconuts only if they expect that enough other people will do the same. Thus individuals' beliefs about what other individuals will do affect aggregate "production," and the economy can get stuck at an inefficiently low level of output. Subsequent research has further developed the idea that the macroeconomy may sometimes be characterized by multiple equilibria owing to coordination failures.[102] If one buys this story (or some version of it), one needn't have recourse to high debt loads to explain sluggish postcrisis recoveries.

In a recent study, three Fed economists examine 149 recessions for twenty-three advanced economies from about 1970 to 2014.[103] They find that output usually does *not* return to prerecession trend following recessions, especially deep ones. It appears that economies generally don't come roaring back. "Economic models usually assume that recession-induced gaps will close over time, typically via a period of above trend growth," they write. "In our results, growth is not faster after the recession than before." This means that "economists may be too optimistic about the recovery path of output following recessions." They note that their findings "may imply that demand shocks have permanent effects." No doubt macroeconomic stimulus techniques can be improved, but perhaps the main focus should be on avoiding severe demand shocks in the first place. Panics appear to be a preeminent source of such trauma.

*   *   *

Thus neither the Japan experience, nor the evidence of Mian and Sufi, nor the prolonged nature of postcrisis slumps undermines my argument for panic primacy. To be clear, my claim is not that debt-fueled bubbles are insignificant or that debt cycle theorists are wrong to be concerned about them. Rather, my claim is that panics appear to pose a far graver threat to the broader economy—they appear to dwarf other financial phenomena in their destructiveness—and that, in a panic-proof system, we could probably worry much less about debt-fueled bubbles and the like. To be sure, the panic-centric view and the debt cycle view are not mutually exclusive. But it is important to prioritize. We are looking for the main arteries of damage, not capillaries.

Relatedly, it is worth highlighting here a critical point that will not be fully fleshed out until chapter 7. I argue there that our modern policy response to panics—basically a standing commitment of public support for the financial sector's short-term debt—may in fact be a major *source* of "debt-fueled bubbles," "credit booms," "overleverage," or whatever one chooses to call it. In other words, such excesses might be largely a product of our defective approach to fighting panics. If this is right, then a more sensible approach to the panic problem could go a long way toward reducing the incidence and severity of these excesses.

The conclusion that panics are the central problem for financial stability policy brings a great deal of clarity to the task at hand. It implies that the paramount objective should be not to prevent financial crises in some generic sense, but to prevent panics, which are a pathology of short-term debt. In other words, financial instability is mostly about private money. In fact it always has been.

*   *   *

This brings us to the end of part 1. A brief recap is in order. Chapter 1 made the case that the financial sector's short-term debt serves a monetary function. The chapter sought to give functional content to this idea. Chapters 2 and 3 examined the business model through which these monetary instruments are issued—the business model of banking (or shadow banking, as the case may be). We saw that, given the existence of some established medium of exchange, this business model can arise through the operation of background rules of property and contract. And we saw that this business model is unstable; it involves a coordination game with a bad expectational equilibrium. Finally, the present chapter made the case that the instability of this business model should be viewed as *the* central problem for financial stability policy—at least insofar as the goal is to prevent macroeconomic disasters.

Stated at this level of generality, these points are embarrassingly straightforward. Still, all of them are controversial. What is more, part 3 will show that the financial reform debates of recent years have been preoccupied with all sorts of other things. If we accept the arguments of part 1, then it is hard to escape the conclusion that financial instability is largely a problem of monetary system design. And this conclusion suggests a need to rethink, from first principles, the basic design of our monetary institutions. This is where we turn now.

PART II

Design Alternatives

CHAPTER FIVE

A Monetary Thought Experiment

We cannot say that the public interests to which we have adverted, and others, are not sufficient to warrant the State in taking the whole business of banking under its control. On the
contrary we are of opinion that it may go on from regulation to prohibition except upon such
conditions as it may prescribe.—Justice Oliver Wendell Holmes Jr., 1911[1]

The government hardly made an appearance in part 1. We just posited
the existence of some amount of state-issued fiat money and went
forward from there. That strategy was useful because it allowed us to isolate some crucial issues—but it will no longer do. The government now
moves to center stage. This may seem like an abrupt shift of gears, but
everything will come together in the next three chapters.

In this chapter we are state builders, undertaking a project of institutional engineering. The goal is to construct a well-functioning fiat monetary system. We will examine the problem through the device of a thought
experiment, one structured to clarify the key practical challenges of monetary system design. Surprisingly, many of these topics have never been systematically explored, at least not in an integrated way. Much of this chapter's discussion will concern the *operations* by which money is created and
destroyed. These operations will turn out to present some unavoidable
difficulties. We will also consider the administrative independence of the
monetary authority, as well as the topic of "seigniorage," or fiscal revenue
that comes from money creation.

The thought experiment relies on an important simplifying assumption:
we will assume that the business model of money creation does not exist.
Perhaps fractional reserve banking is outlawed; or perhaps the "good
equilibrium," in which money-claimants prefer to hold redeemable claims
on a bank instead of government-issued base money, simply never materi-
alizes. In any case, in this chapter all money is issued directly by the state.

The next three chapters will bring public and private together. In particular, we will examine three broad approaches to regulating "banking," understood as the business model of money creation. The first approach uses regulatory risk constraints, such as portfolio constraints and capital requirements, to deal with the instability of banking. The second approach adds public liquidity support through a lender of last resort. And the third approach is a public-private partnership, under which bank-issued money is sovereign and nondefaultable.

There is an analytical logic to this sequence, but also a historical one. Since its inception in the 1860s, US federal bank regulation has proceeded through three broad phases, corresponding to the three regulatory approaches just described. The present chapter ends with a brief review of this history, which will serve as a prelude to the chapters that follow.

A Simple Monetary System

Imagine an economy with a fiat money system. There is no paper currency. Instead, money consists of entries in an electronic database maintained by the government. The database has two columns. The left-hand column contains unique identifiers for each agent in the economy. The right-hand column contains nonnegative values—"money values"—one for each agent. To make a payment, an agent instructs the government to reduce (debit) his or her money value and increase (credit) the payee's money value by an equivalent amount. There is no such thing as a physical transfer of money; all payments are made through these bookkeeping entries.

The money values in the database do not merely "represent" or "stand for" money. They *are* money. They do not carry a redemption option of any kind. They do not default, at least not in any conventional legal sense. They are not contracts, any more than a dollar bill is a contract. They have no explicit terms and conditions. It might initially seem implausible that agents would ascribe value to these electronic book entries. But the proposed system is essentially no different from our existing fiat monetary system, in which people ascribe value to intrinsically valueless bits of paper. Our hypothetical system merely substitutes database entries for bits of paper.

If there is anything mysterious about this system, the mystery has to do with the phenomenon of fiat money itself. James Tobin, one of the preeminent monetary theorists of the past century, discussed the puzzling nature of fiat money in his Nobel Lecture:

> [The] quest for the microfoundations of monetary theory ... is still unfinished. The reason, I think, is the difficulty of explaining within the basic paradigms of economic theory why paper that makes no intrinsic contribution to utility or technology is held at all and has positive value in exchange for goods and services. I certainly have no solution to that deep question, nor do I regard one as prerequisite to pragmatic monetary theory.[2]

So far this book has had little to say about why fiat money is valued. Now is an opportune time to discuss this topic. In chapter 3 I made the cursory observation that we can view fiat money as a coordination game: people value it at least in part because they expect other people to value it. This is a perfectly mainstream thing to say. For example, the leading macro textbook says that "everyone values fiat money because they expect everyone else to value it."[3] Friedman and Schwartz said much the same. "Each accepts them because he is confident others will," they wrote. "The pieces of green paper have value because everybody thinks they have value, and everybody thinks they have value because in his experience they have had value."[4]

Some readers will object, however. They will say that the coordination game view is misleading or even wrong because it supposedly implies that the state is unnecessary or that money is a purely "social" rather than a "political" phenomenon. And they will put forward a supposedly contrary position, placing the government front and center. Specifically, they will stress that it is the taxing power of the state that imparts value to fiat money. Abba Lerner advanced this thesis in a well-known 1947 paper:

> The modern state can make anything it chooses generally acceptable as money and thus establish its value quite apart from any connection, even of the most formal kind, with gold or with backing of any kind. It is true that a simple declaration that such and such is money will not do. . . . But if the state is willing to accept the proposed money in payment of taxes and other obligations to itself the trick is done.[5]

Adam Smith made basically the same point in 1776: "A prince, who should enact that a certain proportion of his taxes should be paid in a paper money of a certain kind, might thereby give a certain value to this paper money."[6] By commanding that taxes be paid in fiat money, the argument goes, the government creates demand for it. In short, "taxes drive money."[7]

There is, I think, less at stake in this debate than meets the eye. Contrary to what some taxes-drive-money proponents may believe, nothing in the coordination game story implies that a well-functioning monetary system should be expected to arise spontaneously from "the market" or from "social" practices. Just because a good equilibrium is possible does not mean it will be stable or that it will be realized at all. Hence one can buy the coordination game story while still believing that government involvement in money is absolutely essential. What I do not believe—and what the taxes-drive-money position, at least in its strong form, seems to imply—is that the value of fiat money is somehow mechanically determined by expected future tax burdens. It seems far more plausible that the state's issuing a particular medium of exchange, and accepting that medium for tax purposes, serves to anchor agents in the good expectational equilibrium. At any rate, like Tobin, we will take it for granted that fiat money "works."

Recall from the introduction that, in describing the reformed monetary system, we imagined there was no physical currency. The point was to declutter the institutional environment; bits of paper have a way of being conceptually distracting. The motivation is the same here. It is worth pointing out that in the reformed system it was the member banks that maintained the "r-currency" ledgers. By contrast, in this chapter we haven't (yet) introduced any banks. The government maintains the ledger. This arrangement no doubt sets off civil libertarian alarm bells, but set those issues aside for now; just assume a benevolent government. Note that there is just one money ledger in the thought experiment, so no clearing and settlement apparatus is needed.

The successful management of this hypothetical monetary system requires a measure of government competence. The government must possess adequate recordkeeping capabilities, and it must reliably process debits and credits. Also, the government will need to establish payment authentication procedures to prevent fraud. These are routinized processing functions—"back office" functions, in business jargon. This is not to say they are trivial; they do require a real commitment of resources and technology. But this kind of administrative competence appears to be necessary in any monetary system the state might choose to establish. For example, in a fiat paper system, paper currency must be printed and physically distributed, and anticounterfeiting measures must be established and enforced.

Money Supply Adjustments

We have seen how transfers of money take place in our hypothetical economy, but we have neglected the question of money creation (and destruction). A permanently static money supply is unlikely to serve the public interest.[8] If prices in the economy are "sticky," then changes in the money supply will affect the real economy, at least in the short run. A benevolent government will want to adjust the money supply to serve its macroeconomic policy objectives. So how does new money come into existence in our hypothetical economy? In one sense the answer is obvious. Money is created ex nihilo, by increasing agents' aggregate money balances. Presumably, though, these increases do not happen at random. They arise in the context of some *operation*. It is these operations that pose the real challenge.

In one scenario, money might come into existence through government expenditures. When the government buys a battleship, compensates a postal worker, or makes a social welfare payment, the payee receives a credit to his or her money balance. So long as the government does not debit its own money balance correspondingly, it has augmented the money supply. Such government expenditures are financed through seigniorage: government "revenue" that arises from money creation.

A problem with this approach is that there is no necessary connection between the optimal path of the money supply and the desired level of government expenditure over any given period. What if optimal money growth over a given period were greater than the desired amount of government spending? The government might decide to just exceed its desired spending; but that would be wasteful. The very notion of a "desired" amount of spending implies that the government satisfies its policy objectives at that level. Buying more battleships for purely monetary purposes would divert resources from other uses. Making larger than desired social welfare payments could undermine incentives to work. Such wasteful expenditures would be socially counterproductive. (Further, spending the money supply into circulation would be incompatible with monetary policy independence, an issue I discuss below.)

Another possibility would be for the government to buy back some of its outstanding debt, offering newly issued money in exchange. In effect, this would mean issuing money to finance *past* government expenditures. But here I want to introduce an assumption that we will relax later: assume that the government runs a balanced budget every period. Revenues equal expenditures, so the government has no outstanding debt. This is obviously contrary to current practice, but the assumption will help us isolate some important issues. So we're ruling out money creation by way of sovereign debt repurchases.

Does the government have other ways to augment the money supply? Consider this option: a "money split" (analogous to a stock split in corporate finance). The government could declare that by a stroke on a computer keyboard it has increased everyone's money balance by some proportion, say 5%. Suddenly each agent would have a larger nominal money value than before. In theory, the money split should stimulate the economy.

Unfortunately, there appears to be a serious practical problem with the money split. To see why, suppose some agents, observing signs of a possible slowdown in economic activity, suspected that the government might announce a money split in the near future. At the margin, such agents would seek to accumulate money in order to profit from the split, thereby taking advantage of sticky prices. They would reduce spending and monetize assets. This behavior would tend to reduce economic activity and exert downward pressure on prices. These effects, in turn, would further raise expectations of a money split, thereby inducing more money hoarding throughout the economy. Thus the money split strategy generates a perverse expectational equilibrium in which the anticipation of a money split produces the very economic conditions that the money split is intended to counteract. This is a bad feature for a monetary system.

Other "keystroke" approaches to money creation give rise to similar incentive problems. Consider, for example, Milton Friedman's picturesque notion of a "helicopter drop" of money.[9] In our institutional setup, we can imagine doing a helicopter drop with a keystroke. When the government increases the money supply, everyone could just get a fixed amount. So, if the government issues D new dollars and the population is N, then each person gets D/N credited to his or her account. This approach doesn't generate the money split's perverse equilibrium, since payouts are not a function of existing balances. Still, the approach raises problems of its own. The (electronic) helicopter drop means that, over any given period, money supply growth per capita operates as gratuitous "income" per capita. We can't pretend that such a policy wouldn't affect incentives to work and save. It isn't "neutral" in this regard. Now, we might very well like the idea of gratuitous income as a matter of social welfare policy. But the optimal calibration of such a policy has no logical connection to optimal changes in the money supply over any given period.

The trouble with keystroke approaches comes through even more when we consider monetary *contractions*. In some circumstances our benevolent government may want to shrink the money supply in furtherance of its macro objectives. Whose account should the government debit? There is no "neutral" way to do this either. So keystroke strategies have major drawbacks.

The discussion above illustrates a more general point: when it comes to changes in the money supply, the mechanism matters. This is far from an original insight. In his Nobel Lecture, Robert Lucas made this point explicitly:

> From the beginnings of modern monetary theory, in David Hume's marvelous essays of 1752, *Of Money* and *Of Interest*, conclusions about the effect of changes in money have seemed to depend critically on the way in which the change is effected....
>
> ...There is something a little magical about the way that changes in money come about in Hume's examples. All the gold in England gets "annihilated." Elsewhere he asks us to "suppose that, by miracle, every man in Great Britain should have five pounds slipped into his pocket in one night." Money changes in reality do not occur by such means. Is this just a matter of exposition, or should we be concerned about it! This turns out to be a crucial question.[10]

Interestingly, Tobin touched on a similar theme in his own Nobel Lecture:

> Too often macro-economic models describe monetary policy as a stock M whose time path is chosen autonomously by a central authority, without clearly describing the operations that implement the policy. In fact money supplies are changed by government transactions with the public in which goods or non-monetary financial assets are exchanged for money, or by similar transactions between banks and the non-bank public. What transactions are the sources of variation of money stocks makes a difference.[11]

Lucas and Tobin are making similar points here—that monetary adjustments are undertaken within a particular institutional apparatus, and that the apparatus matters.

Continuing now with the thought experiment, what other options are available for monetary expansion? Consider this alternative: the government could start lending (or, equivalently, buying bonds). If the government is a competent underwriter of credit, this method of monetary expansion has attractive features. When it makes a loan, the government credits the borrower's money value in exchange for a promissory note or bond. It doesn't debit its own money value, so new money is now in circulation. Essentially the government has "rented out" new money instead of spending it. Interestingly, the emergence of this institutional technology—the shift from a spending channel to a lending channel—has a real historical basis. In the late seventeenth and early eighteenth centuries, American colonial governments began to issue paper money, called "bills of credit," in direct payment for goods and services. "When public expenses declined," notes legal historian Christine Desan, colonial governments "devised a second way of putting paper into circulation. They established public land banks that lent borrowers paper money on the security of their land."[12]

The lending approach to issuing money has big advantages over the spending approach. Under the lending approach the government never spends money wastefully on real goods and services. It buys financial assets instead. The lending approach also has advantages over the keystroke approaches described above. We saw that keystroke approaches raise unavoidable incentive problems—bad expectational equilibria (in the case of the money split) or poorly calibrated gratuitous income (in the case of helicopter drops). It should be obvious that the lending approach doesn't have these particular problems. Furthermore, the keystroke approaches ran into trouble when the state needed to conduct a monetary *contraction*. Some group of people needed to have their money balances debited at the push of a button. The lending approach doesn't have this problem either. The government can shrink the money supply by letting loans/bonds mature or by selling them in the secondary market.

But why should the government adjust the money supply by buying and selling *financial* assets as opposed to other types of investment assets? For instance, the government could buy real estate instead of loans/bonds; it could acquire a portfolio of rental properties. A moment's reflection suggests two reasons bonds are likely to be better. First, real estate purchases have much higher transaction costs than bond purchases. The government will want to keep transaction costs to a minimum. Second, managing a real estate portfolio is complicated. Facilities upkeep and tenant management are very resource-intensive. Clearly, a trillion-dollar real estate portfolio is much more "high maintenance" than a trillion-dollar bond portfolio.

This explains why the government should prefer financial assets over real assets. But why should those financial assets be *credit* assets instead of equities—why buy bonds rather than stocks? This question is harder to answer. We could just posit that the government is risk-averse (stocks are riskier than bonds) and leave it at that. But this is unsatisfying; it assumes the very thing we want to understand.

To see why the government might prefer bonds over stocks, we need to consider the topic of *fiscal smoothing*. Assume the government always earns a fair risk-adjusted return on its financial asset portfolio; it neither underpays nor overpays systematically. Such returns constitute seigniorage revenues to the government. The basic idea of fiscal smoothing is that the public is better off if seigniorage revenues are smooth rather than volatile, because volatile seigniorage revenues would complicate the government's fiscal management. If seigniorage revenues vary sharply and unpredictably from period to period, then the government will need to offset such swings with corresponding period-to-period adjustments in tax rates or borrowings (yes, we assumed above that the government doesn't borrow, but relax that assumption for just a moment). It is a well-established principle of public finance that optimal tax policy involves smoothing tax rates over time.[13] By the same token, large period-to-period swings in government borrowings may be undesirable—they may "crowd out" private borrowings and hurt the private economy.[14]

Fiscal smoothing considerations thus weigh in favor of a smoother seigniorage revenue stream. Credit returns are less volatile than equity returns, of course (see fig. 5.1). Accordingly, assuming the government earns a fair risk-adjusted return no matter what, it should stick with bonds rather than stocks. Moreover, the fiscal smoothing argument implies that the government should limit itself to the safer end of the credit spectrum; it should buy high-grade bonds rather than junk bonds.

To sum up: Our benevolent government has decided to effect changes in the money supply by buying and selling financial assets. It has opted for credit assets instead of equities. The return on its credit portfolio constitutes seigniorage. This basic structure should seem familiar—it sounds like central banking. The point I want to make is that there are, in fact, good reasons for doing money this way. Some readers won't need any convincing on this score, but it is important to lay out the case explicitly and from

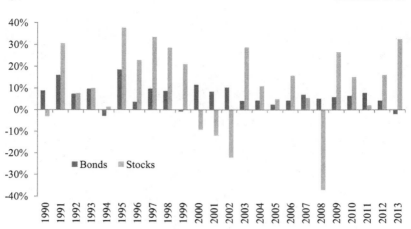

FIGURE 5.1. US bond versus stock returns, 1990–2013
Source: Bond returns are represented by the Barclays Capital US Aggregate Bond Index, available on the Barclays Indices website. Stock returns are represented by the S&P 500 Index, available on the S&P Dow Jones Indices website.

first principles. One will search the literature in vain for a clear exposition of these matters. Later, when we discuss banking regulation, this analysis will help us avoid some unproductive detours.

Administration and the Joint Venture

So far we have imagined the government as a single unified entity. In reality government structures are more complicated—and for good reason. Some organs of the US government are designed to be insulated from political influence, at least to some degree. The federal judiciary is the most obvious example. US Supreme Court justices and most federal appellate judges enjoy constitutionally mandated life tenure and salary protection.[15] These constitutional provisions—the cornerstones of judicial independence, part and parcel of the separation of powers—are designed to foster fair, impartial adjudication.

Looking beyond the judiciary to the administrative state, one finds analogous structures. Administrative agencies are creatures of Congress, not of the Constitution. But Congress has seen fit to grant many agency heads specified terms of tenure, coupled with immunity from removal by the president other than "for cause" (such as malfeasance). These protections are designed to insulate agencies from the shifting winds of politics, allowing them, at least in theory, to focus on the long-term public interest.

As government functions go, monetary policy seems to be a particularly good candidate for insulation from politics. Ben Bernanke has explained why.[16] Monetary policymakers who are "subject to short-term political influence may face pressures to overstimulate the economy to achieve short-term output and employment gains that exceed the economy's underlying potential," he says.

> Such gains may be popular at first, and thus helpful in an election campaign, but they are not sustainable and soon evaporate, leaving behind only inflationary pressures that worsen the economy's longer-term prospects. Thus, political interference in monetary policy can generate undesirable boom-bust cycles that ultimately lead to both a less stable economy and higher inflation.

In short, incumbent politicians often have an "inflation bias." If they were allowed to pull the levers of monetary policy, the likely result would be undesirable levels of inflation. Empirical studies generally support this conclusion: monetary policy independence is associated with greater price stability.[17]

It is therefore perhaps not surprising that, within the vast US administrative state, the Federal Reserve enjoys an unparalleled degree of formal independence. Members of the Fed's Board of Governors serve for fourteen-year staggered terms and may be removed only for cause.[18] By contrast, no other independent agency head (or governing body member, as the case may be) has a term longer than nine years, and the vast majority are in the three- to seven-year range.[19] Long terms and staggered appointments reduce the likelihood that the Fed board will be dominated by any one presidential administration or party. What is more, unlike most other agencies, the Fed is self-funding: its expenses are paid out of the interest it earns on its giant bond portfolio.[20] This arrangement frees the Fed from the appropriations process, insulating it not only from the president but also from Congress.[21] Legal scholars continue to debate whether US independent agencies are properly viewed as a "fourth branch" of government."[22] But if any single US government agency deserves that label, it has to be the Federal Reserve.[23] After all, the Fed chair is often described as the second most powerful person in the country!

Let's stipulate that Bernanke is right: it is important to insulate monetary policy from short-term political influence. So let's divide our hypothetical government into a monetary authority and a fiscal authority. The monetary authority is an independent agency (branch?) of government, relatively insulated from short-term political expediencies. Its leaders enjoy long terms of office and may be removed only for cause. The monetary authority issues money (consisting of ledger entries) in exchange for credit assets. It earns a stream of returns on its credit portfolio, which it hands over to the fiscal authority as seigniorage after deducting its own expenses. The monetary authority follows a legal (statutory or constitutional) mandate of prudent monetary management, perhaps along the lines of the Federal Reserve's dual mandate of full employment and price stability.[24]

Our imagined fiscal authority, on the other hand, has no operational control over the money supply or monetary policy. The fiscal authority spends money on public priorities: national defense, the social safety net, law enforcement, and so forth. It finances these expenditures with tax revenues and with the seigniorage revenues it gets from the monetary authority. (We are still assuming the government doesn't borrow.) For any given level of spending, seigniorage revenues reduce taxes dollar for dollar. Thus, even though the monetary authority is now administratively independent, the public still accrues a fiscal benefit from money creation, consisting of a relatively smooth and perpetual revenue stream.

At the beginning of the thought experiment we imagined the government to be spending money directly into circulation in exchange for goods and services. Note that such an arrangement would make it impossible to administratively separate monetary policy from fiscal affairs— they would be hopelessly entangled. This is yet another reason to prefer lending rather than spending the money supply into circulation; it makes monetary policy independence possible. Under our imagined institutional design, the path of the money supply need have no connection at all to the path of government spending. The system is compatible with a large government (vis-à-vis the size of the economy) or a small one. (This point will be highly relevant when we discuss "narrow banking" in chapter 6.)

Let's now relax the assumption that the government's fiscal arm never borrows. This makes the setting more realistic, and it raises some interesting questions about the relation between the monetary and fiscal authorities. Previously, the monetary authority issued money in exchange for private credit assets. Should it now include government bonds in its portfolio? Presumably the answer is yes, so long as government bonds are exceptionally safe. Indeed, we might be tempted to require that the monetary authority buy *only* government bonds.

The trouble with this strategy is that there may not be enough government bonds to accommodate the desired money supply. This might initially seem to be a purely theoretical concern; sovereign debts today are huge and growing, and they dwarf central bank balance sheets. Remember, though, that in our thought experiment there is no bank-issued money to supplement government-issued money. This monetary authority has to satisfy *all* of the economy's monetary needs. The comparison with existing central banks is therefore inapposite.

Even disregarding this point, it was not so long ago that Federal Reserve officials *were* in fact concerned about running out of Treasuries to buy. Marvin Goodfriend, who was a Fed economist during the relevant period, tells the story:

> The emergence of large federal budget surpluses in 2000 and 2001 led to a substantial paying down of federal government debt and the possibility that the stock of U.S. Treasury debt could be reduced substantially in subsequent years. Fed assets at the time, accumulated in providing currency and bank reserves to the economy, consisted almost entirely of roughly $500 billion of Treasury securities. At its March 2000 meeting, the FOMC authorized a subcommittee ... to consider a variety of options to study what assets it should acquire in place of Treasuries should they be retired.[25]

Federal Reserve official Don Kohn introduced the subcommittee's report by remarking that "the issue cannot be put off for much longer. Under a wide variety of assumptions about the growth of the economy and the political process, Treasury debt will be repaid over coming years." Kohn noted that "there are no easy, obvious solutions to the problem of what assets to hold under this circumstance." He proceeded with a penetrating analysis, one that sets the stage for the rest of our thought experiment:

> Of course, the alternative of taking on private obligations raises other issues, including those involved with potential effects on private credit allocation and the management of risk and liquidity in the System's portfolio.... A key tradeoff would be between minimizing the effects of System portfolio choices on relative asset prices on the one hand, and minimizing risk and maximizing liquidity on the other. A broadly diversified portfolio, which included credit to

financial intermediaries holding nonmarketable assets, would have the greatest chance of exerting as little influence as possible on private credit decisions.
With such a portfolio, the System would have a low profile in each market and
it would not be favoring one type of asset over another. But the System would
be acquiring riskier and less liquid assets. . . . At the other end of the spectrum,
if the Committee chose to concentrate operations in a small subset of markets that promised the least credit risk and the greatest liquidity . . . it would
increase the odds on eventually affecting relative asset prices.[26]

With the benefit of hindsight we know that the Fed needn't have worried. The 2001 recession and tax cuts sent the US public debt back on an
upward trajectory, one that steepened sharply with the onset of the Great
Recession some years later. Even so, this discussion shows that we are not
talking about a fanciful scenario.[27] When doing monetary system design,
we can't assume there will always be enough public debt to accommodate
the entire money supply—or even just the *base* money supply if such a
concept exists in one's institutional setup. Presumably we would want the
monetary system to work even if the government consistently balanced
its budget.

So let's assume that, even if the government does borrow, its outstanding debt isn't large enough to accommodate the desired money supply.
The monetary authority must therefore buy private credit assets. We are
then left with the problem Kohn was describing—the problem of credit
allocation. This is an issue we haven't yet grappled with in the thought experiment, and it is the last piece of the puzzle.

The basic problem can be summarized as follows. To the extent that it
needs to acquire private credit assets, the monetary authority would prefer
to limit itself to liquid, high-quality bonds with observable market prices.
Such bonds are easily bought and sold, and the government can rely on
the mechanisms of market efficiency to avoid systematically overpaying;
it just pays the market price. Unfortunately, such bonds may represent (in
Kohn's words) "a small subset of markets" with limited depth. The monetary authority has a very large balance sheet, and it could end up dominat-
ing these markets. Its activities would push asset prices around and distort
credit allocation.

To avoid this outcome the monetary authority would need to expand
into less liquid credit markets—perhaps even direct lending to private
borrowers. In illiquid markets, though, the monetary authority can't rely
on observable prices and market efficiency to protect it from overpay-

ing. Like other credit investors, it would need to engage in fundamental credit analysis. We assumed earlier that the government is proficient at "back office" tasks, but credit investing is a "front office" operation. It requires information gathering and analytical skills, local knowledge, and expert judgment. Characteristically, Walter Bagehot summed up the problem beautifully:

> A central bank, which is governed in the capital and descends on a country district, has much fewer modes of lending money safely than a bank of which the partners belong to that district, and know the men and things in it. . . . A banker who lives in the district, who has always lived there, whose whole mind is a history of the district and its changes, is easily able to lend money safely there. But a manager deputed by a single central establishment does so with difficulty. The worst people will come to him and ask for loans. His ignorance is a mark for all the shrewd and crafty people thereabouts.[28]

If the monetary authority is a bad credit investor, resources will be poorly allocated. Compounding this dilemma is another problem: whenever the monetary authority is investing in private credit, there is the potential for political controversy and the appearance (or reality) of favoritism. Such controversies, in turn, could end up undermining the cherished independence of the monetary authority.

So what should our hypothetical monetary authority do? There are no perfect answers, but with some thoughtful institutional engineering, it can mitigate these problems. What I have in mind is a joint venture system. The monetary authority could enter into joint venture agreements with private managers that have expertise in credit investing. Each manager would be required to put up some of its own resources as "skin in the game"—a first-loss equity position. The managers would be authorized to acquire credit assets on behalf of the state. The sellers (in the secondary markets) or issuers (in the primary markets) of these credit assets would receive newly created money, which still consists of entries in the government's ledger. The returns from each manager's credit portfolio would be split between the manager and the state, with the state holding a senior claim. The state's returns from the system would constitute its seigniorage revenues.

This joint venture system provides an answer—albeit an imperfect one—to the monetary authority's credit allocation problem. The monetary authority no longer has a balance sheet of its own; the investment function is now in the hands of the joint venture managers. The system is designed to harness market incentives to issue money in an efficient, non-distortive way. Furthermore, because the monetary authority no longer makes individual credit allocation decisions, the arrangement should help shield it from allegations of favoritism and threats to its independence. Obviously, the joint ventures would not be the only credit investors in the economy. They would exist alongside other investors, and their credit market share would depend on the size of the money supply in relation to the size of the entire credit market.

Of course, such a joint venture (or public-private partnership) system raises problems of its own. All joint ventures—indeed, all financing contracts—raise problems of incentive misalignment, and this one is no exception. How best to align the incentives of the managers with those of the monetary authority is an important question. There is no perfect way to do this, but I want to set these issues aside for now. They can await chapter 8, which delves more deeply into these structural issues.

A Brief History of US Bank Regulation

It may not have seemed like it, but the thought experiment above suggests the outlines of a concrete approach to real-world banking regulation—the third of three approaches we will examine in the next three chapters. To set the stage for those chapters, it will be useful to briefly review the history of US federal banking regulation. That history can be understood in terms of three phases, corresponding to the three regulatory approaches we will be considering.

Phase 1: Risk Constraints

US federal banking regulation started with the National Bank Acts of 1863 and 1864,[29] which established a federal Office of the Comptroller of the Currency and authorized it to create a new category of federally chartered banks. From the start, national banks were required to abide by a detailed and comprehensive array of regulatory risk constraints, including strict portfolio and activity limits, portfolio diversification requirements, cash reserve requirements, capital requirements, dividend restrictions, and tight limits on real estate ownership.[30] The acts also imposed quarterly and monthly financial reporting obligations and established a supervisory regime that gave the comptroller the "power to make a thorough examination into all the affairs" of national banks.[31] It is noteworthy that these provisions, established a century and a half ago, remain at the core of US banking regulation today, albeit in somewhat modified form.

Despite these risk constraints, banking panics were a recurring feature of the US financial landscape in the late nineteenth and early twentieth centuries. There were major banking panics in 1873, 1893, and 1907, with a number of minor panics in between.[32] Each major panic was accompanied by a severe disruption to the broader economy. Arguably the fault lay not with the risk constraint approach per se but rather with its incomplete coverage. State-chartered banks and trust companies existed alongside the national banking system, and they were subject to less stringent regulation. Perhaps a universally applicable system of banking risk constraints, as opposed to the fragmented system that emerged, would have been more conducive to stability. In any case, Congress ultimately decided that risk constraints alone weren't enough.

Phase 2: Lender of Last Resort

About fifty years after the National Bank Acts, Congress introduced a new tool: the lender of last resort. A key impetus for its creation was the panic of 1907, which brought the US banking system to the brink of collapse—a calamity averted only through a series of bold initiatives orchestrated by the era's most prominent investment banker, John Pierpont Morgan. Congress, appalled to find the nation's financial stability at the mercy of one powerful individual with no public responsibilities, decided another approach was needed. The eventual result was the Federal Reserve Act of 1913,[33] which established a central bank and authorized it to supply liquidity to the banking system in times of stress. (There was precedent for this approach abroad; the Bank of England, established in 1694, first assumed its role as lender of last resort in the second half of the eighteenth century.)

Having a power is one thing; using it is another. Despite the Federal Reserve's existence, waves of bank panics swept through the country in the early 1930s. Friedman and Schwartz attributed the Great Depression that followed to the Federal Reserve's failure to take action to avert the liquidity crisis.[34] Appropriate use of the lender of last resort "would have prevented the catastrophe," they wrote. Instead, despite "ample powers," the Federal Reserve followed a "passive, defensive, hesitant policy."

Note, however, that the Federal Reserve's powers were limited. Its architects had envisioned that support for the banking system would be subject to strict statutory constraints. In particular, the types of assets that could serve as collateral for central bank loans under the original Federal Reserve Act were quite narrow.[35] It is not entirely obvious that a more vigorous exercise of the Fed's limited powers would have succeeded in avoiding economic disaster.

Phase 3: The Public-Private Partnership

Either way, Congress responded in 1933 with the final major step in the development of modern bank regulation: it made the federal government the explicit guarantor of the bulk of the banking system's monetary liabilities.[36] The establishment of deposit insurance fundamentally altered the social contract between the banking system and the rest of society. The government's commitment to honor deposits was no longer contingent; it was guaranteed up front. Insured deposits were now sovereign money.

The creation of federal deposit insurance inaugurated what Gary Gorton has called the Quiet Period in US banking, one that lasted nearly three-quarters of a century:

> The period from 1934, when deposit insurance was enacted, until the current crisis is somewhat special in that there were no systemic banking crises in the United States. It is the "Quiet Period" in U.S. banking. . . . This Quiet Period led to the view that banking panics were a thing of the past. . . . From a longer historical perspective, however, banking panics are the norm in American history.[37]

The emergence of deposit insurance did not make regulatory risk constraints obsolete. To the contrary, it arguably made them even more important. But their economic purpose changed. They were no longer primarily a tool of panic prevention; that objective was accomplished by deposit insurance itself. Rather, risk constraints now were needed to address the incentive problems that were an unavoidable consequence of the public's guarantee.

The model of bank regulation that emerged was, in effect, a public-private partnership. The government recognized the money supply (insofar as it consisted of insured deposits) as a public good: within the insured banking system, money was established as a sovereign obligation, not a private one. But the government outsourced to private firms—firms with investment expertise and detailed knowledge of specific markets—the task of issuing these monetary instruments in exchange for credit assets. Naturally this outsourcing contract came with a set of terms and conditions, consisting of the risk constraints of traditional bank regulation. It also came with fees, as the government now occupied the senior-most position in the financing structure of insured banks, exposing it to potential losses. The resulting system was not altogether different from the one that emerged from the thought experiment above.

To summarize: the historical progression of US banking regulation has been one of increasingly affirmative measures to prevent defaults on banks' monetary liabilities. This historical evolution culminated in a public-private partnership approach, the establishment of which led to an unprecedented period of stable, panic-free conditions. It was only with the emergence of shadow banking—private money creation *outside* the insured banking system—that instability returned.

*   *   *

The history above provides a nice road map for the rest of part 2. Chapter 6 will analyze regulatory risk constraints as a tool of panic prevention. Chapter 7 adds the lender of last resort to the analysis. Finally, chapter 8 returns us to the public-private partnership system, with a particular focus on how to structure the joint venture arrangement. I aim to show that the public-private partnership compares favorably with the realistic design alternatives.

CHAPTER SIX

The Limits of Risk Constraints

There is a cardinal difference between banking and other kinds of commerce; you can afford to run much less risk in banking than in commerce, and you must take much greater precautions.—Walter Bagehot, 1873[1]

The previous chapter examined the key challenges the state faces in establishing a workable fiat monetary system. The thought experiment ruled out the business model of money creation; there were no banks issuing private, defaultable money. All money was sovereign and default-free, and the state was the exclusive issuer. Needless to say, that assumption was artificial. We saw in part 1 that, *given* the existence of some established medium of exchange—and in the absence of any special legal impediments—the banking business model can arise through the operation of background rules of property and contract. We now reintroduce this business model into the analysis.

How does the existence of the banking business model bear on the state's institutional design challenge? From the state's perspective, there is at least one major advantage: if private-sector banking "works," the state can scale back its own monetary endeavors. That is to say, the private sector can take some role, perhaps a very large one, in issuing money. Maybe the state can get away with issuing only a relatively modest amount of fiat "base" money, which the banking system can then augment with redeemable private money. A large proportion of money creation would then be in private hands.

In the extreme scenario the government could get out of money creation altogether. Perhaps it could simply define the unit of account—in a "weights and measures" sense—without issuing any monetary instruments at all. The private sector would then furnish the entire money supply. This may sound outlandish, but we will see later in this chapter that this laissez-faire approach has had some prominent advocates. For the reasons described there, I doubt that such an approach can be relied on to produce a workable monetary framework. This chapter is therefore mostly occupied with a more moderate and familiar approach: partial rather than complete privatization of money issuance. The banking system supplements, rather than replaces, the government's role in money creation.

There is no doubt that such a two-tiered system is feasible; it is just fractional reserve banking. The question is whether it is a *good* system, relative to the realistic institutional alternatives. The basic problem with such a system is the one we analyzed in part 1. The banking business model involves a coordination game with a self-fulfilling bad equilibrium. Banks are susceptible to runs, and a commonly observed run at one bank may serve as a Schelling focal point for runs at other banks. If the bad equilibrium is realized on a broad scale, the economy may be exposed to disaster.

Can the state somehow make this activity stable? One approach to doing so would be to require banks to abide by regulatory risk constraints. The present chapter evaluates this approach. In particular, it considers two forms of substantive risk constraint that are widely used in financial regulation: portfolio constraints and capital requirements. The primary aim of these tools is to reduce the likelihood that the value of a bank's assets will fall dangerously close to or below the value of its liabilities.

To facilitate the analysis in this chapter—as well as the next two—I will assume that there exists a single, identifiable set of money creation firms or "banks." There is no such thing as "shadow" banking; all nonbanks are assumed to finance themselves exclusively in the capital markets, with equity and long-term debt, and are therefore immune to runs and panics. This assumption obviously departs from current reality, but we need to simplify the setting to make analytical progress. (Moreover, I will argue in part 3 that legally *confining* money-claim issuance to the chartered banking system should be the starting point for real-world financial stability policy.)

This chapter also assumes that the government does not provide any support to the banking sector. There is no lender of last resort and no deposit insurance. Those institutional technologies will be introduced into the analysis in the next two chapters. For now, we are looking at regulatory risk constraints in isolation.

A Diagrammatic Model

To organize the analysis that follows, it will be useful to introduce the simplest of microeconomic models, which will prove surprisingly helpful in analyzing various regulatory responses to the instability of banking. It is a model of the firm—in this case, the money-claim issuer or bank. The firm finances itself with a large amount of money-claims (redeemable for fiat base money) and a smaller amount of common equity (a residual claim).[2] The common shareholders control the firm, and they seek profit maximization.

The firm earns a profit by investing in the capital markets. As we saw in chapter 3, there are good reasons to think that, even in the absence of government regulation, issuers of large quantities of money-claims will tend to hold portfolios that consist largely of financial assets—credit assets in particular. This does appear to be the historical pattern. So we will imagine that the bank's portfolio consists of loans and bonds. For simplicity, the firm is assumed to earn no fee income; all its earnings come from its "spread" business.

Figure 6.1 illustrates the firm's production under laissez-faire. The firm's marginal cost curve represents its total weighted average cost of fi-

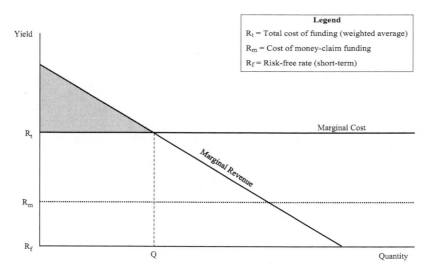

FIGURE 6.1. Simple model of the money creation firm

nancing (R_t)—that is, its all-in cost of financing, including the cost of equity. (Assume the firm has no other expenses.) The firm's cost of money-claim funding is also shown (R_m). Naturally this curve sits below the firm's weighted average cost of financing, but it sits above the short-term risk-free rate (R_f) since the firm has a positive probability of defaulting on its money-claims. The cost curves are horizontal, reflecting the simplifying assumption that the firm's financing costs do not change as it increases production, all else equal.

The marginal revenue curve represents the yield the firm earns on its asset portfolio. The profit-maximizing firm deploys its financing proceeds first toward higher-value business opportunities—those investments with the highest expected risk-adjusted returns—and then progressively toward lower-value opportunities. The downward slope implies that the credit markets in which the firm invests are not perfectly competitive. That is, the firm can identify and capitalize on "mispriced" assets within its field of specialization—through superior analysis, a well-developed distribution infrastructure (such as a branch network), a well-known brand that attracts customers seeking financing, or some combination of these sorts of advantages.

The intersection of the marginal cost and marginal revenue curves determines the profit-maximizing quantity of production. The bank "produces" its investment portfolio and issues money-claims in the process. It ceases further production at the point where the marginal revenue derived from additional investment equals the marginal cost of financing—in other words, when it can identify no further investments with positive net present value. The firm's economic profit is depicted by the shaded area, representing the difference between the returns on the firm's investment portfolio and its weighted average cost of financing. With this model in hand, we now consider the effects of regulatory risk constraints.

Portfolio Constraints—and "Narrow" Banking

As I noted above, even in the absence of government regulation, banks can be expected to hold portfolios consisting mostly of credit assets, or senior claims on other economic agents. Banks' portfolios will therefore tend to be fairly safe compared with the assets of most other types of firms. (This was Bagehot's point at the start of the chapter.) Nonetheless,

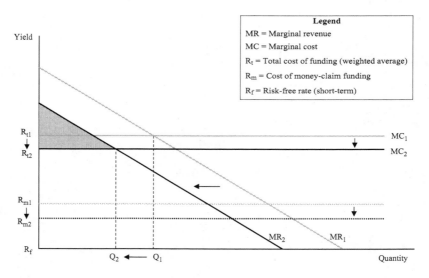

FIGURE 6.2. Portfolio constraints

there can be no assurance that the bad equilibrium will never be realized. The bank game is in effect, and self-fulfilling panics are possible.

To reduce the likelihood of damaging panics, the government might impose portfolio constraints on the banking system, requiring banks to hold even safer portfolios than they would hold under laissez-faire. More specifically, the government may seek to confine banks' asset portfolios to the safer end of the credit spectrum. It may also require portfolio diversification to further reduce risk. Those who are acquainted with US deposit banking regulation will find this approach quite familiar. Portfolio constraints have always been a core part of US federal banking law.[3]

Portfolio constraints should be expected to reduce the likelihood of damaging runs and panics, but they also require the bank to forgo its chosen revenue opportunities. The effects of portfolio constraints on the firm are illustrated in figure 6.2. With portfolio constraints, the marginal revenue curve shifts leftward: requiring the bank to forgo its chosen revenue opportunities reduces its portfolio returns. The marginal cost curve shifts downward: insofar as the portfolio constraints are effective in reducing risk, the firm's likelihood of default decreases, thereby reducing the firm's financing costs. It is evident that the shifts in these two curves have countervailing effects on firm profits. However, we should expect the firm's profits to be lower under portfolio constraints than they would be under laissez-faire. Otherwise a rational firm would self-impose such constraints.

Lower banking profits are not a good thing, but the state may judge that the social costs of portfolio constraints are outweighed by the social benefit; namely, a lower incidence of panics. This kind of cost-benefit analysis is difficult, to say the least. It requires the state to determine the effects of portfolio constraints on both the probability and the social cost of a panic. As to the former, if banking is characterized by a coordination game, then there is no formulaic way to determine the likelihood of a run/panic. Indeed, both the Diamond-Dybvig model and the bank game abstracted away from portfolio characteristics altogether. Agents run, at least in part, because they expect others to run. How agents' expectations are formed may depend on any number of things—the fundamental condition of the bank being only one of them—and what those things are may change over time. As to the latter, the state faces an equally daunting challenge. As shown in chapter 4, whether and how panics affect the broader economy is a subject of wide disagreement.[4] Thus, if portfolio constraints alone are being used to deal with the panic problem, their optimal calibration presents a very difficult policy challenge.

There is an even more fundamental problem with relying exclusively on portfolio constraints to stabilize banking: onerous portfolio constraints may compromise the banking system's ability to produce "enough" money. This is because the quantity of eligible banking assets serves as an upper bound on the quantity of money-claims that the banking system can issue. If the state wants the banking system to play a large role in money creation, then portfolio constraints need to be lenient enough to accommodate that role.

This brings us to "narrow banking." Narrow banking proposals have a distinguished lineage in the banking literature. The basic idea of narrow banking is to divorce the issuance of monetary instruments (checkable deposits in particular) from portfolios of risky assets. Under the original and purest version of narrow banking, called 100% reserve banking, entities with demand deposit liabilities would own nothing but base money. Fractional reserve banking would be abolished; deposit banks would resemble the currency warehouses described in chapter 2. Less stringent narrow banking proposals would give deposit banks slightly broader investment powers, allowing them to invest in ultrasafe assets like Treasury bills.

Narrow banking proposals have been very influential within the economics profession. Henry Simons, a founding father of the Chicago school of economics, was a leading advocate of 100% reserve banking in the early 1930s.[5] Irving Fisher, one of the greatest economists in US history, was a forceful proponent too.[6] So was Milton Friedman, another towering American economist.[7] Other proponents of versions of narrow banking have included Nobel Prize–winning economists Merton Miller, Robert Merton, and James Tobin.[8] More recently, Gregory Mankiw has expressed tentative support, and Laurence Kotlikoff has pushed for a variant of narrow banking that he calls limited purpose banking.[9]

What's the trouble with narrow banking? The main problem has to do with the question we encountered above: whether such a system can issue "enough" money. Suppose that both the central bank and deposit banks confine their asset portfolios to Treasury bills. In that case the quantity of T-bills outstanding serves as an upper bound on the money supply (assuming there is no "shadow" banking). If the supply of T-bills is too small, then the economy's demand for monetary instruments will not be satisfied. Thus Robert Merton and Zvi Bodie note that "the demand for highly liquid, riskless transaction deposits" may exceed "the supply of U.S. Treasury bills."[10] Along the same lines, Hyman Minsky noted that among the "institutional prerequisites" for a narrow banking system are "a large government debt that can be monetized" and "a Federal Government fiscal posture which can readily be adapted" to accommodate the economy's need for growing transaction account balances.[11] This issue should be familiar from chapter 5.

Some advocates of 100% reserve banking have acknowledged this problem, but they have not given a satisfactory answer. Irving Fisher posed the question this way: "If it should come to pass, some fine day, that the whole national debt had been paid off, what then?"[12] Fisher's answer was to produce more government debt through tax cuts. This answer is fine as a conceptual matter, but it has troubling practical implications. Monetary and fiscal functions would become deeply entangled. Monetary policy independence would be compromised; for example, in a divided government, a majority in one house of Congress could seek to inflict political damage on the president by declining to increase the public debt, thereby precluding monetary expansion. Moreover, a policy under which tax rates are adjusted for monetary purposes might have troubling incentive effects for individuals and businesses, since agents would seek to adjust their activities to realize income during low-tax periods. Finally, the benefits of tax smoothing (see chapter 5) would be forgone if tax policy were to become an instrument of monetary policy.

Milton Friedman saw the problem too.[13] While he favored 100% reserve banking, he had concerns about "the close connection between the 100% reserve plan and debt management." If the supply of government debt were exhausted, he wrote, then "subsequent increases in the stock of money" would come from either "the creation of additional debt to finance deficits" or the acquisition by the central bank of private credit assets. Friedman viewed neither option as "particularly appealing." In particular, he pointed out that purchases of private assets would mean "putting the government into the banking business"—in his view, a distinctly unwelcome outcome.

Bob Litan, whose 1987 book *What Should Banks Do?* remains the most fully formed narrow banking proposal, reaches a conclusion similar to Friedman's.[14] Litan suggests that narrow bank portfolios would ideally be limited to T-bills. But he acknowledges that "the total supply of privately held short-term Treasury securities (with maturities of up to one year) is limited." Litan discusses the possibility of letting narrow banks invest in private credit assets like commercial paper, but he finds this approach "problematic," noting that it would "undermine the case" for narrow banking. On the other hand, Litan seems more comfortable with letting the *central* bank invest in a broader range of assets. If narrow banks were to elbow the central bank out of the market for T-bills, he writes, then "strong consideration could be given to expanding the investment authority of the Federal Reserve."

These analyses by Friedman and Litan are fascinating: they represent a complete inversion of the logic described in chapter 5—the logic that underlies the reformed monetary system I sketched in the introduction. So committed are Friedman and Litan to restricting deposit banks to super-safe holdings that they are willing to entertain *central* bank investments in somewhat *riskier* assets. By contrast, in chapter 5 (and in the reformed system) the whole point of involving private firms in monetary affairs was to harness private incentives in the difficult task of credit allocation (the decision having been made to issue money in exchange for credit assets) and to insulate that investment process from politics. Friedman and Litan clearly do not see banking this way.

This discussion raises a fundamental question for narrow banking enthusiasts: if it makes sense to let the central bank (and not deposit banks) do private credit allocation, then why have any deposit banks at all—why not just let everyone hold an account at the central bank? After all, if the central bank can handle the front-office task of credit allocation, then surely it can handle the back-office task of transaction processing. The great corporate theorist Gardiner Means, who was a White House staffer in the Franklin Roosevelt administration, made this very point in a 1933 memo on banking reform.[15] "'Taking care' of deposits requires relatively little judgment and can be easily routinized and administered centrally," he wrote. By contrast "the making of loans requires very great judgment and cannot be easily routinized or centrally administered." Means went on to say that "it is in the making of loans that political favoritism or irresponsible judgment could play havoc in a banking system."

This analysis might seem academic in view of the huge supply of US Treasury debt that exists today. However, as we saw in chapter 5, it was not so long ago that Fed officials *were* in fact concerned about the declining public debt—and they needed only enough public debt to accommodate the *base* money supply. (Narrow banking would compound the problem, for obvious reasons.) Current trends may not last forever; the fiscal picture can change. Presumably we should aim to design a monetary system that is compatible with a variety of fiscal environments, including a balanced budget. More generally, this discussion illustrates why it is pointless to discuss banking regulation without considering the broader monetary context. Banking regulation must be considered as an aspect of monetary system design.

Before leaving the topic of narrow banking, it is worth touching on one other issue that narrow banking proponents have had to confront: how to prevent financial institutions from evading the system by developing close substitutes for bank accounts. Henry Simons became so preoccupied with this problem that he ultimately soured on the proposal he had spearheaded. Simons worried that the development of near monies "might render our drastic reform quite empty, nominal, and unsubstantial."[16] He remarked that "the whole problem which we now associate with commercial banking might easily reappear in other forms of financial arrangements."[17] That such near monies "cannot serve as a circulating medium is not decisively important," he wrote, "for they are an effective substitute medium for purposes of cash balances." Hence "the problem of runs would still be with us." In retrospect, Simons's concerns look remarkably prescient: he was describing shadow banking. By 1936 Simons had concluded that the 100% reserve plan, standing on its own, "would promise little but evasion."[18]

Unlike Simons, other narrow banking proponents have downplayed the evasion problem. Irving Fisher, for one, believed the problem was fairly minor; he thought transaction accounts were the main issue.[19] Milton Friedman thought the evasion problem could be handled by paying interest on reserves to 100% reserve banks.[20] Bob Litan suggested that the evasion problem was "a valid concern but one that should not be overstated."[21] In Litan's view, issuers of near monies would be likely to maintain capital ratios significantly higher than those of narrow banks.

Simons was clearly right. The problem of substitute forms of money is critical. Indeed, I argue that facing up to this problem—the shadow banking problem—is *the* central challenge of financial reform. But I don't share Simons's occasional defeatism on this score (see chapter 9).

Capital Requirements

We turn now to the second major category of risk constraint. Capital requirements are designed to ensure that banks maintain at least some specified proportion of residual (equity) claims in their financing structures. Figure 6.3 illustrates the effect of capital requirements on the bank. Capital requirements shift the marginal cost curve upward: the firm's weighted average cost of financing increases to the extent that it is required to increase the proportion of equity in its financing structure, and therefore reduce the proportion of money-claims. The firm's quantity of production decreases, and its profit shrinks.

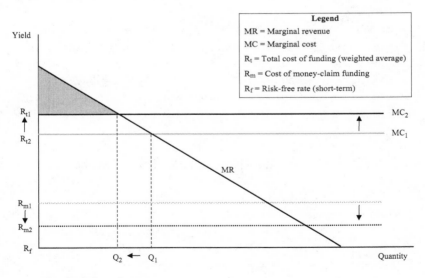

FIGURE 6.3. Capital requirements

These conclusions may appear to violate the Modigliani-Miller theorem from corporate finance, but recall from chapter 3 that the Modigliani-Miller theorem has to be seriously qualified when it comes to banks. Banks' money-claim liabilities offer their holders a nonpecuniary moneyness yield, so their pecuniary yields are very low. Decreasing banks' money-claim liabilities therefore increases their all-in cost of financing. Hence, in the model shown here, capital requirements increase banks' marginal costs, reduce their profits, and reduce the size of their balance sheets.

And therein lies the central problem with onerous capital requirements: like portfolio constraints, capital requirements may impair the banking system's ability to play a large role in issuing the money supply. If the capital requirement is k, expressed as a percentage of assets Q, then each bank must have capital financing of at least $k \times Q$. Money-claim liabilities are therefore capped at $(1 - k) \times Q$. For any given quantity of assets, higher k means a lower quantity of money-claims issuable. A 5% capital requirement would mean that a banking system with $10 trillion in assets could issue up to $9.5 trillion in money-claims. Increasing the capital requirement to 50% would mean that, holding assets constant, the banking system could issue no more than $5 trillion in money-claims. The problem is only magnified if the banking system shrinks its assets in response to higher capital requirements, as figure 6.3 suggests. If the state wants the banking system to play a large role in money creation, then capital requirements must be lenient enough to accommodate that role.

This analysis provides a nice vantage point from which to evaluate the influential work of economists Anat Admati and Martin Hellwig, which we encountered in chapter 3. Admati and Hellwig, together with their coauthors,[22] argue that "the social costs of *significantly* increasing equity requirements for large financial institutions would be, if there were any at all, very small." They tentatively suggest capital requirements of 20% to 30% —far higher than current requirements.

As I noted in chapter 3, Admati and Hellwig do acknowledge that deposit liabilities are special in the sense that they are bundled with transaction services. (They also dismiss the idea that nondeposit short-term debt has moneyness, but this issue has already been dealt with.) Yet they brush aside concerns that substantially higher capital requirements might compromise the banking system's ability to issue such instruments. In particular, they and their coauthors note that banks can comply with higher capital requirements without reducing their liabilities at all, because banks can use the proceeds from their new equity financing to acquire more assets. This strategy, they say, is "always viable" for solvent banks. Thus "banks need not change their deposit base or the amount of debt they have issued in response to an increase in equity requirements."

It is certainly true as a matter of logic that banks "need not" reduce their liabilities in response to higher capital requirements, because it is "always viable" for solvent banks to just increase their assets. But the more pertinent question is what we should *expect* banks to do. And the starting point for such an analysis should be that banks, like other firms, generally pursue investments with positive net present values. Equivalently stated, a bank should be expected to seek investments whose expected risk-adjusted returns exceed its weighted average cost of financing.[23] There is no reason to think higher capital requirements would *lower* banks' total cost of financing; the analysis above suggests the opposite. Nor does requiring a bank to maintain more equity financing in any way alter its investment opportunities. Consequently, one should not expect banks to increase their assets in response to higher capital requirements.

This analysis explains, I think, why practically no one would advocate 90% capital requirements for deposit banks. Most people have an intuitive sense that such a requirement would squeeze out banks' monetary liabilities and that that would be a bad thing. We *want* banks to have money-claim liabilities, yet those liabilities are the source of the panic problem. Capital requirements offer no escape from this dilemma. It's true that capital requirements should be expected to reduce the incidence of panics. Nonetheless, because banking is characterized by a coordination game, the extent of this benefit is uncertain. We have the same cost-benefit problem that was discussed above in the context of portfolio constraints. There can be no assurance that any system of capital requirements that is compatible with the state's monetary objectives will substantially mitigate the panic problem. (We are still assuming there is no lender of last resort; it will be introduced in the next chapter.) Capital requirements, then, are an indirect and imperfect response to the panic problem.

More than that, capital requirements are extremely difficult to implement. This point often gets lost in discussions of capital regulation, so it merits some attention. There is widespread enthusiasm today for "simple" capital regulation, but I want to suggest there are limits to how simple capital regulation can be if it is to be effective. Put differently, there is a degree of *irreducible* complexity in capital regulation, at least when it comes to complex financial institutions.

The point is fairly easy to illustrate. If you wanted to implement a "simple" system of capital regulation, how would you go about it? The most straightforward approach would go something like this. Every financial institution has a portfolio of assets, to which we can attach some notion of fair value. Subtract the institution's liabilities from its assets, and you have its equity capital. The ratio of equity capital to asset value is the capital ratio. Establish a regulatory minimum for this ratio, and you have a capital requirement. This basic approach, or variants of it, is often referred to as a "simple leverage ratio."

This approach is indeed simple, but it has two major problems. First, it is easy to game. (I borrow the following example from Matt Levine, a former derivatives specialist at Goldman Sachs who is now a financial writer.)[24] Suppose a financial firm's assets consist of $100 in fairly safe bonds, which it finances with $5 of equity and $95 of debt. Now suppose that our simple capital requirement is imposed, say at the 15% level. The firm needs to raise its capital ratio by ten percentage points. It might raise new equity to pay down debt, or it might shrink its balance sheet by selling assets and reducing liabilities while holding equity constant. But consider this alternative strategy: the firm could sell its entire bond portfolio to a third party for $100 and simultaneously buy a call option on the portfolio from the third party at a strike price of $70. If the bonds really are quite safe, the call option costs about $30. The firm uses the remaining $70 to pay down debt. It now has assets (the call option) worth $30 and equity of $5. Its capital ratio is 17%, so it now complies with our simple capital requirement. But the firm is no less likely to go insolvent than it was before; a 5% drop in the value of the original bond portfolio still renders the firm insolvent. To deal with this problem, we could modify the capital requirement by keying it to the riskiness of the firm's asset portfolio. This, however, would take us into the controversial realm of "risk weighting," and it would make capital regulation considerably less simple.[25]

The second problem with the simple approach described above is even more serious. It has to do with contingent claims on the firm. Suppose a financial firm writes $10 million of protection on Company X bonds under a credit default swap (CDS). The firm has added $10 million of potential loss exposure, but the value of its assets has not changed, since the CDS contract has a fair value of zero at inception. The simple capital requirement described above doesn't account for this kind of risk. If the point of capital is to absorb losses, then presumably capital requirements should be scaled to the firm's loss exposures—including those arising from contingent claims.

One might propose to deal with this second problem by changing the denominator of the capital requirement. Instead of aggregating the "value" of the firm's holdings, we could aggregate the maximum potential loss on each instrument. This modification wouldn't add much complexity—but it may not be such a good idea, either. Among other things, it would effectively prohibit many short positions. For example, suppose a financial firm enters into a $10 million total return swap (TRS) on Company X stock, under which the financial firm pays the total return in exchange for an interest rate stream. This is a standard equity derivative. The potential loss exposure under this contract is infinite, since there is no upper bound on Company X's stock price. So the financial firm can *never* comply with our modified "simple" capital requirement.

At this point the natural inclination might be to proceed taxonomically. We could specify the capital treatment of every category of position or contract at a high degree of granularity. This is a viable option, but it is far from simple. And it leaves us with another type of problem. By treating each instrument in isolation, we fail to take account of the relations among different positions. Consider the TRS example again, but now imagine that the financial firm already owned $10 million of Company X stock when it entered into the TRS. The TRS has *reduced* the firm's risk, since the long position offsets the short. It would be perverse if entering into such a hedging transaction meant the firm had to maintain *more* capital—if a matched book required more capital than a directional bet. Again, this problem is not insurmountable; we could establish criteria for what constitutes an offsetting position. Yet this adds still another layer of complexity.

Furthermore, if one chooses to proceed taxonomically, one must confront the issue of gross versus net exposures. Suppose two financial firms have entered into multiple derivative trades with each other. For each firm, some of the trades have positive value and others have negative value. Suppose the parties have agreed to settle their trades on a net basis pursuant to a master netting contract, as is the usual practice. The question is whether capital requirements should be keyed to the gross exposures (under each trade) or the net exposure (under the master contract). As an accounting matter, International Financial Reporting Standards (IFRS) generally disallow derivatives netting, whereas US Generally Accepted Accounting Principles (GAAP) generally allow it. From a balance sheet perspective the consequences are enormous. One recent analysis finds that five large US financial firms (Bank of America, Citigroup, Goldman Sachs, JPMorgan, and Morgan Stanley) would have $5.7 trillion in *additional* assets if reported on an IFRS basis—a 69% increase over their reported GAAP assets.[26] The implications for the denominator of the leverage ratio are obvious. There is no "right" answer—there are reasonable arguments on both sides—but this is an issue of great quantitative significance for capital regulation.[27]

Is there a better way to deal with these issues? Perhaps it is unwise to apply capital requirements taxonomically, instrument by instrument; maybe we should look at the portfolio as a whole instead. A sensible approach might be to adopt sophisticated risk measurement tools from modern finance—such as value at risk (VaR) methodologies—and use them as the basis for capital regulation. This approach has a great deal of intellectual appeal, but it takes us even further from simplicity.

All of what I have just described is well known to regulatory capital experts. But these points are often lost on self-styled experts on financial regulation, who tend to bemoan the supposedly needless complexity of capital regulation while failing to get close enough to perceive the very real difficulties. Much of the history of international capital regulation consists of efforts to grapple with the issues just described.[28] The original 1988 Basel Accord ("Basel I")[29] took account of the credit risk of contingent claims by converting them into "credit equivalent amounts" and including them in the denominator of capital ratio calculations. It also provided for special treatment of interest rate and foreign exchange swaps. The 1996 Market Risk Amendment to Basel I allowed banks to use sophisticated VaR methodologies to quantify risks from derivatives and other exposures in the "trading book."[30] The 2004 Basel II Accord let banks apply such models to the "banking book."[31]

The latest iteration of international capital standards, the Basel III Accord of 2010,[32] adds a new, purportedly "simple" leverage ratio to the Basel regime. The new Basel leverage ratio disallows the use of advanced models in measuring the denominator. Even so, no one should be fooled into thinking there is anything simple about the new Basel leverage ratio. The calculation is extremely complicated![33] Consider the treatment of derivatives, which uses what I referred to above as the taxonomic approach. Under the new Basel leverage ratio, derivative exposures are generally calculated as replacement cost plus an add-on for potential future exposure. Where an eligible bilateral netting contract is in effect with a given counterparty—and yes, the eligibility criteria must be specified (more complexity)—the replacement cost is the net (as opposed to gross) exposure. The add-on factors depend on the category of exposure—interest rates (0% to 1.5%), foreign exchange and gold (1% to 7.5%), equities (6% to 10%), precious metals except for gold (7% to 8%), and other commodities (10% to 15%)—with the precise add-on factor depending on the residual maturity of the contract. Written credit derivatives are subject to a special set of provisions under which the notional amount of the contract (plus an add-on factor) is included in the denominator, subject to reduction for offsetting purchased protection so long as the reference obligation of the purchased protection is "pari passu" or junior to the written protection and the remaining maturity of the purchased protection is equal to or greater than the remaining maturity of the written protection.

As Levine points out, this treatment of credit derivatives leads to an absurd outcome: a five-year total return swap (with the bank receiving the total return) on Company X stock requires only a small fraction of the capital of a five-year credit default swap (with the bank writing protection) on the same notional amount of Company X bonds. "I think it is self-evident that trade 1 is riskier than trade 2? Bonds tend to outrank equity, much of the time," Levine notes (tongue in cheek). "But Basel leverage counts trade 1 as 12x less risky because, basically, people don't like CDS, while no one really gets exercised about equity swaps."[34] If one is inclined to think of a "simple" leverage ratio as just equity divided by assets, one is in for a rude awakening here. Levine gets it right: "If you think of the leverage ratio as a pure, objective, simple, unbiased, non-risk-based thing, you are lost."[35]

My point is not to defend any particular approach to capital regulation but rather to point out that, despite decades of attention by very smart people, no simple (and effective) way of doing capital regulation for complex institutions has yet been devised. A high degree of complexity is unavoidable if capital regulation is to be effective for such firms. I emphasize this point for two reasons. First, it underscores the fact that *any* financial regulatory tool will necessarily incorporate some degree of complexity and will be susceptible to some degree of avoidance or "regulatory arbitrage." There are no magic solutions; a measure of imperfection and arbitrariness has to be tolerated. This conclusion will have direct relevance in chapter 9, when we discuss the feasibility of regulatory limitations on fragile short-term debt funding.

Second, this discussion gets to a final point that, as far as I know, has been missing from the capital regulation literature to date. It has to do with the essential complementarity between capital requirements and portfolio constraints. Simply put, these two regulatory tools "go together."

It isn't hard to write down and implement a capital requirement for an institution that owns nothing but relatively high-quality credit assets and that isn't in the derivatives business. Straightforward portfolios make capital regulation vastly easier. This fact has important implications for the feasibility of the reformed monetary system described in the introduction. That system does include capital requirements for member banks, but it also includes strict portfolio constraints. For these firms, capital regulation can indeed be quite simple.

It has become conventional wisdom that capital regulation failed dismally in the run-up to the recent crisis. But perhaps we have just been asking too much of it. In a panic-proof system, capital regulation could take on a smaller, more modest role—a weight it might conceivably bear (see chapter 8).

Floating Price Money?

The discussion so far has assumed that banks issue claims that have a stable nominal value. Does this need to be the case? Why shouldn't claims on banks float in price, like claims on mutual funds? Several prominent economists have advanced this idea, and it merits a brief response. I have doubts about the workability of such a system.

Robert Greenfield and Leland Yeager envisioned a system without any "government-issued or government-specified medium of exchange."[36] Instead, the government would "define the unit of account physically, in terms of many commodities." The defined unit of value would be analogous to a defined unit of length or weight; the government would merely "noncoercively [offer] a definition, just as it does with weights and measures." And that would be the government's only role in the monetary system. The authors speculate that, under this laissez-faire system, "financial intermediaries blending the characteristics of present-day banks and mutual funds would presumably develop." Shares in these funds would fluctuate in value relative to the unit of account. Customers would write checks drawn on these funds. Given that "there is no base money," the funds would "presumably agree" on "portfolio assets" that would be acceptable for settlement purposes.

Tyler Cowen and Randall Kroszner describe a similar system, which they call mutual fund banking.[37] In their system, agents would hold checkable interests in mutual funds, which "may fluctuate in nominal value," rather than deposit-type fixed claims. The authors observe that "the equity-nature of the liabilities eliminates the sources of instability associated with traditional banking institutions." Like Greenfield and Yeager, Cowen and Kroszner suggest that the government could significantly scale back its monetary activities. "We envisage mutual fund banking as a move toward currency competition and away from government control of high-powered money," they write. They describe the system as "a likely and viable scenario for the evolution of banking and financial institutions under laissez faire."

The Greenfield/Yeager and Cowen/Kroszner laissez-faire systems are so different from existing systems that it is difficult even to envision quite how they would work. The payment, clearing, and settlement arrangements seem to present difficulties, but perhaps they are surmountable. My larger concern with this class of ideas was articulated by James Tobin in 1984, and I will outsource the critique to him:

> Some discussions of "private money" in the literature seem to suggest that the government can define the "dollar" as the unit of account without printing and issuing any dollars. Private agents could issue promises to pay dollars, and these would circulate. But what are they promising to pay? ... The idea of a disembodied fiat unit of account, with embodiments of it freely and competitively supplied by private agents, seems to me to be a fairy tale. ...
>
> Some writers ... appeal to an analogy of the unit of account to a unit of measurement. ... It is not a good analogy. Those agents, private or public, who promise to pay on demand "dollars" so defined must have stocks on hand to enable them to fulfill their promises. That is the only way to assure the defined equivalence.
>
> I conclude that there must be store-of-value embodiments of a monetary unit of account, and that basically these will be and should be designated and supplied by the central government. ... I have an uneasy suspicion that in the general enthusiasm for deregulation we are in danger of reestablishing the conditions and problems which generated financial regulations in the first place.[38]

Milton Friedman, while less critical, was also skeptical of this class of ideas. "As yet," he wrote in 1985, "they seem too radical, too unsupported by evidence, to be regarded as a practical proposal for institutional reform."[39] This remains true today.

A rather different version of mutual fund banking comes from a recent paper by John Cochrane.[40] Cochrane argues that banks should be financed with "mostly common equity, though some long-term or other non-runnable debt can exist as well." Modern technological advances have made such a system possible. "With today's technology," he writes, "you could buy a cup of coffee by swiping a card or tapping a cell phone, selling two dollars and fifty cents of an S&P 500 fund, and crediting the coffee seller's two dollars and fifty cents mortgage-backed security fund." Accordingly, "'liquidity' no longer requires that people hold a large inventory of fixed-value, pay-on-demand, and hence run-prone securities." In Cochrane's system, financial institutions are penalized for issuing run-prone debt that is not backed by short-term Treasuries. Insofar as there is demand in the economy for fixed-nominal-value assets, today's large government debt "is enough to 100 percent back any imaginable fundamental economic need" for them. This is "a bright side to our government's fiscal profligacy."

Some of Cochrane's views align quite nicely with those advanced in this book.[41] He asserts that "short-term debt *is* money" (the argument of chapter 1). He asserts that the central task for financial stability policy "should be to eliminate runs" (the argument of chapter 4). And he asserts that limiting run-prone liabilities, while not a trivial regulatory task, is "an order of magnitude easier than" current forms of financial regulation, including capital regulation (an argument I will make in chapter 9, drawing on the present chapter).

Cochrane and I part ways, however, when it comes to institutional design. His vision is far more radical than my own. I argued in chapter 1 that, in a sticky price world, we should expect to see large demand for assets that have a very stable value in nominal terms. We do observe such demand in the real world. Its satisfaction is, in my view, a central function of the monetary system. In Cochrane's design, it is the *fiscal* authority that satiates this demand. As a matter of institutional engineering, this strikes me as a step backward. The reformed monetary system described in the introduction constitutes a freestanding, administratively independent monetary framework, compatible with any fiscal environment—high government debt or no government debt. For reasons already discussed, I believe there are considerable advantages to such an approach.

*   *   *

The core message of this chapter can be summarized as follows. If the banking system is to play a major role in money creation, then regulatory risk constraints—in particular, portfolio constraints and capital requirements—need to be lenient enough to accommodate that role. And because banking is characterized by a coordination game, there can be no assurance that any set of risk constraints that is compatible with the state's monetary objectives will successfully fend off panics. For this reason, risk constraints, standing alone, are not a sufficient answer to the panic problem. The next chapter considers another long-standing institutional technology for banking stabilization. We will find problems with it too.

CHAPTER SEVEN

Public Support and Subsidized Finance

Someday you guys are going to need to tell me how we ended up with a system like this. . . . We're not doing something right if we're stuck with these miserable choices.—President George W. Bush, September 16, 2008[1]

D on't we already have a good enough answer to the panic problem? Governments have long supported financial institutions during times of liquidity stress. Typically this support has been supplied by central banks, operating in their capacity as lender of last resort (LOLR). The patron saint of the lender of last resort is Walter Bagehot, who championed this function of central banks in his 1873 masterpiece *Lombard Street*.[2] "Theory suggests, and experience proves, that in a panic the holders of the ultimate Bank reserve (whether one bank or many) should lend to all that bring good securities quickly, freely, and readily," he wrote. "By that policy they allay a panic; by every other policy they intensify it." Bagehot argued that "the only safe plan for the [central bank] is the brave plan, to lend in a panic on every kind of current security, or every sort on which money is ordinarily and usually lent."

This advice has been influential. Charles Kindleberger's history of financial crises says that "the role of the lender of last resort was not respectable among theorists until Bagehot's *Lombard Street* appeared in 1873."[3] Friedman and Schwartz referred to *Lombard Street* as "the *locus classicus* of central bank policy."[4] More recently, a leading financial journalist has written that "to an astounding degree, Bagehot's description remains the basic guide for central bankers more than 125 years later. They cite it as an authoritative guide to behavior and refer to it with the same reverence that ministers and rabbis use when quoting from the Bible."[5]

This chapter argues that the LOLR is a flawed answer to panics. There are three problems. First, the very existence of the LOLR gives rise to a wealth transfer from the public to potential LOLR beneficiaries. This subsidy is independent of any "too big to fail" policy, although TBTF is certainly an aggravating factor. Second, the LOLR presents an unavoidable trade-off: in direct proportion to its effectiveness in arresting panics, the LOLR generates bad incentives for financial firms. Third, those bad incentives can reasonably be expected to introduce distortions—such as excessive credit and asset-price bubbles—into the financial system and the broader economy.

This third point has crucial implications for financial stability policy. A central claim of this book is that, insofar as financial stability policy is about avoiding macroeconomic disasters, it should concern itself mostly with panic-proofing, or stamping out run-prone funding structures. This position is decidedly unorthodox. Under the prevailing view (see chapter 10), financial stability policy should focus primarily on combating various financial "excesses": excessive credit, debt-fueled bubbles, excessive risk taking, "systemic risk," what have you. The prevailing view regards panic-proofing as far too narrow a strategy, because panic-proofing is not responsive to these (purportedly) more fundamental problems.

However, if the prospect of public support is a major *source* of the financial system's excesses, the picture starts to look rather different. This chapter makes the case that our existing monetary framework—in which money-claim issuance is neither confined nor capped, and in which the government implicitly commits to honor the financial sector's monetary liabilities—should be expected to produce or amplify various financial excesses. With a more sensible monetary framework, we might see fewer such excesses. Problems like "systemic risk" might then turn out to be, if not illusory, then at least more manageable than is commonly supposed.

I am far from the first to point to the dangers of public support for the financial sector. But it is important to make the three points noted above explicitly and to connect them up with the broader project of monetary system design. The LOLR is widely viewed as a sound and adequate response to the panic problem, at least if used judiciously. I aim to challenge this widespread view.

Funding Subsidies

The LOLR is a strange institution in a market economy. Here we have a standing commitment by the government to help certain private firms meet their obligations under certain conditions. Anyone with free market sensibilities should naturally be skeptical of such an institution.[6] What sorts of firms should be eligible for such extraordinary support, and in what circumstances?

We can examine the effects of the LOLR using the diagrammatic model from the previous chapter. Recall the institutional setting. The government issues fiat base money. Money creation firms (banks, in the functional sense) issue private money-claims that are redeemable for base money. In keeping with chapter 6, we are assuming that there exists a distinct and identifiable set of banks, and no shadow banking. Banks are susceptible to damaging runs and panics. Chapter 6 showed that regulatory risk constraints alone do not offer a satisfactory answer to the panic problem.

Now the government establishes a lender of last resort. This function might be performed by a central bank, though this need not be the case. For now, assume the LOLR credibly adheres to a "classical" policy: it lends only to *solvent banks*, against *good collateral*, and at a *high rate*. This is the usual distillation of Bagehot's advice, and it remains the lodestar for central bankers today. According to Brian Madigan, a key architect of the Federal Reserve's emergency policies during the recent crisis, "As Bagehot recommended, we should look to the restrictions of lending only to solvent firms, only against good collateral, and only at high rates."[7]

The LOLR's effect on an individual bank is shown in figure 7.1. Because the firm's likelihood of default has diminished, money-claimants accept lower yields ex ante. The firm's marginal cost curve shifts downward. Assuming the marginal revenue curve remains stationary, the quantity of production increases. The LOLR leaves intact the original profit (light gray area). It also creates a funding subsidy (dark gray area). The size of the funding subsidy depends on money-claimants' judgments about the likelihood that the government will intervene to support the firm in the event of a run. Note that I have said nothing here about any kind of "too big to fail" or bailout policy. Rather, I am arguing that the very existence of the LOLR—even one that adheres to the conservative, classical policy—increases banks' profits simply by reducing the likelihood of default. This is a wealth transfer from the public.

Quite apart from these subsidies, it is not obvious that the classical policy will succeed in shielding the economy from disaster. In particular, the requirement of good collateral poses a problem. What if banks lack

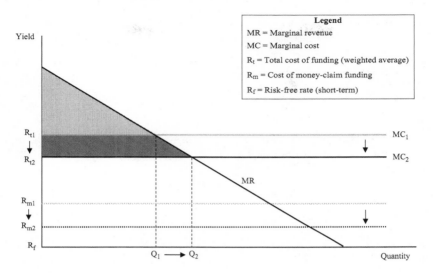

FIGURE 7.1. Funding subsidy

the requisite collateral to support an adequate emergency loan from the LOLR in a panic? Bear in mind that top Federal Reserve officials have said that Lehman Brothers had insufficient acceptable collateral in September 2008 to support a loan large enough to prevent default.[8] Even if one finds this questionable in Lehman's case, one must admit that such a situation is possible. The panic may then proceed, and the economy may sustain severe damage.

It might be argued that a credible commitment to the classical policy would induce banks to fully "back" their short-term funding with collateral acceptable to the LOLR. But experience suggests otherwise. When the Federal Reserve System was established in 1913, it was widely assumed that state-chartered banks would join the system to have access to LOLR support. Yet as of 1922 only 15% of eligible state banks had joined—and the trend was toward withdrawal.[9] Membership required state banks to abide by higher cash reserve requirements than mandated under most state laws. According to one contemporaneous study, "probably the reason most frequently [given] for giving up membership has been the loss of interest on the reserve balance which must be kept with the federal reserve bank.... Many [banks] regard the loss as payment for insurance, and cheap insurance at that. But many member banks ... claim that the protection given is charged for at too high a rate."[10] Insofar as banks must forgo their preferred investment opportunities in order to own collateral acceptable to the LOLR, they incur an opportunity cost. They will weigh this cost against the expected value of liquidity support, and the expected benefit will not necessarily exceed the cost.

The classical LOLR, then, is an unreliable solution to panics. But perhaps a modest liberalizing of the classical policy would make it more effective. In particular, the good-collateral condition could be dropped. After all, it arguably is redundant; the classical policy also has a *solvency* condition. So long as the borrower remains balance-sheet solvent, the government is protected against loss. Central banker Stanley Fischer describes the problem with this strategy:

> Why does Bagehot insist that the lender of last resort lend against collateral, and that the test be whether the collateral is good in normal times? The availability of collateral is a rough and robust test of whether the institution in trouble is likely to be solvent in normal times. By applying this test, the lender of last resort avoids the need to form a judgment on the solvency of the institution applying for liquidity, while retaining the capacity to operate at the speed necessary to stay a panic.[11]

Madigan agrees: "In a financial crisis, markets may be dysfunctional and price quotes volatile or even unavailable, adding to the uncertainty in assessing firms' solvency."[12] In short, solvency is not easily observable. To assess fundamental solvency, the LOLR must be capable of evaluating whatever asset portfolio the distressed financial firm happens to own. Is the LOLR capable of accurately valuing, on short notice, a large portfolio of illiquid commercial real estate loans? What about a large derivatives book? A private equity portfolio? A complex structured credit portfolio? (Lehman Brothers had all these things.) The good-collateral condition protects taxpayers against costly misjudgments by requiring that loans be secured by familiar, marketable instruments. Abandoning this condition could be expensive.

Once the classical policy is abandoned—once the LOLR is liberalized—other problems start to crop up. One of them is the "too big to fail" (TBTF) problem. It is obvious from the diagram above that the quantity of a bank's production is an increasing function of the likelihood of public support. (The more likely the support, the lower the marginal cost curve.) However, under the liberalized policy, the reverse should also be true: the likelihood of support should be an increasing function of the firm's production. This is because the default of a large bank is more likely to trigger or amplify a damaging panic than the default of a small one. Liberalization brings a measure of discretion and subjectivity into the LOLR's decision making. It stands to reason that authorities will err on the side of caution. Larger financial firms may therefore get favorable treatment—and official pronouncements to the contrary may not be credible. Note that Bagehot's classical policy does *not* contemplate taking into account the *consequences* of a firm's failure when deciding whether to lend. But central bankers sometimes admit they do so. For example, Madigan notes that "the decision as to whether to lend to a given firm" may entail judgments "about the possible market effects of the failure of the firm."[13]

This approach leads to a perverse result. The initial introduction of the liberalized LOLR shifts the marginal cost curve downward and increases the firm's size. This increased size, in turn, increases the likelihood of support, causing a further downward shift in the marginal cost curve. This downward shift results in further portfolio growth, and so on. The result is a vicious circle in which money-claim issuers have incentives to grow. The liberalized LOLR should therefore be expected to produce TBTF subsidies. A growing body of empirical evidence suggests that such subsidies do exist. For example, a recent IMF study finds TBTF subsidies in the 2011–12 period of $15 to $70 billion in the United States, $25 to $110 billion in Japan, $20 to $110 billion in the United Kingdom, and $90 to $300 billion in the Euro area.[14] If these figures are even in the right zip code, they are staggering.

A recent study by the US Government Accountability Office (GAO) finds mixed evidence on whether the largest US bank holding companies enjoy funding subsidies today.[15] It suggests that the creation of new regulatory powers to manage financial firm insolvencies—the Orderly Liquidation Authority (OLA), a key component of the Dodd-Frank Act of 2010—may have substantially reduced such subsidies. But the GAO study suffers from a hitherto unrecognized defect. As we will see in chapter 10, OLA offers a plausible mechanism to write down long-term unsecured debt of large financial firms while still honoring short-term liabilities and derivatives contracts. But the GAO analyzed subsidies by looking *solely* at spreads on unsecured bonds, whose average time to maturity was six years. Clearly, large financial firms may enjoy funding subsidies that are not reflected in long-term bond spreads.

Finally, I should emphasize that funding subsidies are not necessarily limited to institutions that are expected to be direct beneficiaries of public support. Like taxes, subsidies do not necessarily rest at their point of entry; their incidence can fall elsewhere. A likely major beneficiary of public support for Wall Street securities firms is their hedge fund customers. Hedge funds in effect "rent" dealer balance sheets through the dealers' prime brokerage operations. (Specifically, hedge funds hypothecate their securities to the dealers, which in turn rehypothecate them in the short-term repo markets.)[16] Consequently, implicit public support for Wall Street securities firms almost certainly produces significantly lower funding costs for hedge funds.[17]

Moral Hazard

The analysis above focused only on funding subsidies. Now we turn to incentives for risk taking. Once the government assumes a material risk of loss, we have the well-known problem of moral hazard, or a party's incentive to take greater risks when somebody else bears at least part of the downside. Robert Solow has written, "Does a serious problem of 'moral hazard' arise whenever there is an effective lender of last resort? . . . The answer . . . is pretty obviously 'Yes.'"[18]

Figure 7.2 shows the effects of moral hazard on the bank. Moral hazard shifts the marginal revenue curve rightward: the possibility that the government may bear losses means the firm can profit by investing in riskier assets.[19] The figure depicts both funding subsidy (dark gray area) and moral hazard subsidy (medium gray area). The light gray area is the firm's original profit under laissez-faire.

It is evident that the liberalized LOLR shifts the marginal cost curve downward and the marginal revenue curve rightward. Interestingly, regulatory risk constraints were shown in the previous chapter to have exactly the opposite effect: portfolio restrictions shift the marginal revenue curve leftward, and capital requirements shift the marginal cost curve upward. Our two panic-fighting strategies—risk constraints and liquidity support—have countervailing effects on the firm.

This analysis suggests an intriguing possibility: Can the *combination* of the liberalized LOLR and regulatory risk constraints make banking work well? Such a combination may very well improve on using either tool in isolation—and on the laissez-faire alternative—but there is a problem. Recall from chapter 6 that risk constraints may impair the banking

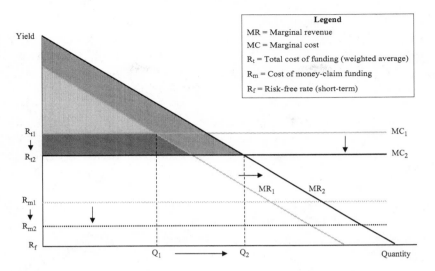

FIGURE 7.2. Moral hazard

system's ability to issue "enough" money. Thus, suppose the liberalized LOLR is introduced, but the government imposes portfolio constraints that keep each bank's marginal revenue curve stationary. The government then imposes capital requirements so as to return each bank to its laissez-faire level of profits (light gray area). Necessarily, each bank's capital level will need to be much higher than it was under laissez-faire. Money-claim issuance will therefore be correspondingly lower. If the government is relying on the banking system to help it satisfy money demand, the combined strategy may undermine that function.

One might argue that risk constraints should be relaxed to the extent necessary for the banking system to achieve the state's monetary goals—and if banks enjoy subsidies as a result, so be it. But this only raises the question whether other tools could produce better outcomes. In principle, the government could require banks to disgorge the value they receive from the prospect of LOLR support. By analogy, lenders in the private sector typically charge commitment fees for undrawn lines of credit. The LOLR can be viewed as an undrawn line of credit for which the government charges no commitment fee. The failure to charge such a fee constitutes a wealth transfer—at least if we start from the baseline assumption that the benefits of public facilities should accrue to the public.

More pointedly, if the government is capable of imposing approximately market financing costs on banks through administrative regulation, it is hard to see any useful social role for run-prone funding structures in the first place. Government insurance of money-claim funding plus an appropriate fee would lead to an optimal outcome, and it would do so without compromising the banking system's ability to issue "enough" money. The objection to such a system must be that the government's fee-setting abilities are imperfect. I deal with this objection in the next chapter. But note that the liberalized LOLR requires *precisely the same capacity*. The government writes the same put option on the bank's portfolio in either case; it must solve the same valuation problem. That's what it means to assess solvency.

In fact, the liberalized LOLR, owing to its conditional nature, requires the government to make even *more* difficult judgments than does the insurance approach. As we saw above, the modern LOLR attempts to accurately predict the consequences of a given firm's default. How much confidence should we have in this capacity? The case of Lehman Brothers is instructive. At the time of Lehman's failure, many experts thought the US financial system could withstand the firm's collapse. Journalist David Wessel describes a conference call of senior government officials just before Lehman's bankruptcy. "With Lehman clearly struggling for survival, Paulson and Bernanke assured each other—and others on the call—that all the companies and traders that did business with Lehman had been given time to protect themselves from a possible Lehman bankruptcy," Wessel writes.

> One Fed official confided later in September that he had acquiesced in the decision to let Lehman go. Why? "Because I thought people had anticipated it. They [Lehman Brothers] were still very big [but] they had shrunk a lot. It was time to find out what would happen if we didn't stand behind all these guys. It had been a long time coming." With hindsight, that tough-guy stance looked, at best, naïve.[20]

The tough-guy stance wasn't confined to the halls of government. The day after Lehman's bankruptcy, Ken Rogoff—among the world's leading experts on financial crises—wrote an op-ed titled "No More Creampuffs."[21] He applauded regulators for "forc[ing] some discipline onto the system" and expressed hope that "they hang tough for at least a little while longer." It would be a "mistake," he wrote, for the government to "get back into the game" before "a great deal more consolidation takes place." (To be fair, Rogoff acknowledged that "the risks are very real" and that "there really is no telling where the unprecedented failure of a big investment bank might lead"—but this is exactly my point.) Likewise, another well-known economist opined that same day that "Lehman did not cast a long enough shadow over markets to warrant support. And Treasury Secretary Henry Paulson and his colleagues are to be congratulated for the courage to make that determination."[22]

These expert judgments turned out to be questionable; Lehman's bankruptcy set off a devastating chain reaction. My point is not to criticize, but rather to note that such judgments are inherently speculative and error-prone—and that they are an unavoidable part of the modern, liberalized LOLR. An institutional design that obviated the need for such judgments would be preferable.

Backstops and Bubbles

As we saw in chapter 3, most of the Fed's lending during the recent crisis went to *nonbank* financial firms. The modern LOLR constitutes a standing commitment by the public sector to stand behind practically all of the financial sector's runnable debt. I believe the ex ante consequences of such a vast, open-ended commitment have gone underappreciated. More specifically, bad incentives arising from the liberalized LOLR can reasonably be expected to introduce distortions—such as excessive credit and asset-price bubbles—into the financial markets and the broader economy.

Paul Krugman is an excellent guide in this area, and I will quote him extensively. In an unpublished 1998 paper titled "What Happened to Asia?"[23] Krugman looked closely at the run-up to the severe financial crisis that struck Thailand, Indonesia, Malaysia, and South Korea in 1997. He observed that many financial firms in the relevant Asian economies "borrowed short-term money" and were "perceived as having an implicit government guarantee." Those beliefs were "validated by experience," as many Asian financial institutions "did in fact turn out to have guaranteed liabilities." According to Krugman, "the excessive risky lending of these institutions created inflation—not of goods but of asset prices." Krugman develops a model in which "the problem of moral hazard in financial intermediaries ... can lead to over-investment at the aggregate level" as well as "over-pricing of assets." In his model, real estate and other assets take on "Pangloss values"—values that far exceed what they would be "in an undistorted economy." In subsequent writings, Krugman has expanded on this analysis.[24] "The claim that Asian borrowing represented free private-sector decisions was not quite the truth," he writes. "For Southeast Asia . . . had a moral hazard problem." Krugman remarks that "throughout the region . . . implicit government guarantees were helping underwrite invest-ments that were both riskier and less promising than would have been un-dertaken without those guarantees, adding fuel to what would probably anyway have been an overheated speculative boom."

Krugman applies the same analysis to Japan's gigantic debt-fueled bubble in stocks and real estate in the 1980s. Here is his account of its causes:

> Japan's bubble was only one of several outbreaks of speculative fever around the world during the 1980s. . . . The most famous case was that of America's savings and loan associations. . . . But similar outbreaks of dubious lending occurred elsewhere, notably in Sweden, another country not usually associated with speculative fever. And economists have long argued that behind all such episodes lies the same economic principle. . . . The principle is known as moral hazard. . . .
>
> . . . In the 1980s there was a sort of global epidemic of moral hazard. Few countries can be proud of their handling of the situation—surely not the United States, whose mishandling of the savings and loan affair was a classic case of imprudent, short-sighted, and occasionally corrupt policymaking. But Japan, where all the usual lines—between government and business, between banks and their clients, between what was and what was not subject to gov-ernment guarantee—were especially blurry, was peculiarly ill suited to a loos-ened financial regime. Japan's banks lent more, with less regard for quality of the borrower, than anyone else's. In so doing they helped inflate the bubble economy to grotesque proportions.[25]

With Krugman's analysis as a backdrop, let's turn our attention back to the recent financial crisis. The parallel is all too obvious. The recent crisis was preceded in the United States by a wave of dubious lending and in-flated asset prices, in real estate and other areas. The causes of this credit boom and asset-price bubble have been extensively debated. Commonly cited culprits include predatory lending and other abuses; fraud; global imbalances of savings; loose monetary policy; flawed credit ratings; flawed risk management models; securitization and the "originate-to-distribute" model for lending; flawed compensation structures; "irrational exuber-

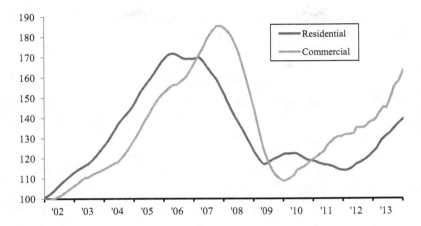

FIGURE 7.3. US real estate prices
Sources: Residential price data, represented by the S&P/Case-Shiller composite twenty-city home price index (seasonally adjusted), is from Federal Reserve Economic Database, series SPCS20RSA. Commercial real estate price data, represented by the Moody's/RCA CPPI "Core Commercial" index (which excludes apartment buildings), is from the RCA Analytics website. November 2001 (business cycle trough) = 100.

ance" or "animal spirits"; various types of regulatory failure; the list could go on. The liberalized LOLR, however, is seldom mentioned as a proximate cause of the precrisis bubble.[26]

To be sure, many analysts have pointed to implicit public support for Fannie Mae and Freddie Mac—the government-sponsored enterprises that have long been major players in US housing finance—as a cause of the debt binge and bubble. Yet Fannie and Freddie, and US housing policy more generally, can't possibly be the whole story. The precrisis period witnessed a *broad-based* credit boom that affected all leveraged asset classes in the United States, including commercial real estate and leveraged buyouts. Indeed, as shown in figure 7.3, the commercial real estate boom and bust was comparable in magnitude to the residential real estate boom and bust. This generalized credit and asset-price boom can't be plausibly explained by residential housing policies alone.

I suggest we look at the precrisis period through the lens Krugman used above. Arguably an "epidemic of moral hazard" preceded the recent financial crisis. After all, the crisis *did* witness massive government interventions in support of the financial system. Market participants presumably anticipated that, in the event of a crisis, such a rescue was possible. Krugman's model therefore applies. While it is certainly possible that these three debt-fueled bubbles—Japan's in the 1980s, Southeast Asia's in the 1990s, and the United States' in the 2000s—had idiosyncratic causes, there is a plausible case that these episodes shared important commonalities.

This analysis adds a new dimension to the infamous "Greenspan put"—the long-standing belief among many US investors that the Federal Reserve will cut interest rates in order to prop up securities prices if they fall too much. The notion that such an interest-rate policy may generate moral hazard and inflated asset prices is well understood.[27] I would only add that a (sufficiently liberalized) LOLR should be expected to have similar ex ante effects on financial markets. The central bank "put," then, is two-pronged, involving both interest-rate policy and LOLR policy. Both components distort asset prices.

An intriguing question is whether liberalized LOLR policies might bear at least partial responsibility for other credit and asset-price booms in US history. In chapter 4 we looked at the growth of household debt in the United States in the 1920s. That decade also included (famously) a stock market boom and bust and (less famously) a real estate boom and bust. A recent study by Gary Gorton and Andrew Metrick examines the Federal Reserve's LOLR policies in the 1920s. In the early part of the decade, hundreds of banks borrowed continuously from the Federal Reserve for extended periods and at interest rates below the market rate. According to Gorton and Metrick, "By the latter part of the 1920s, the Fed became concerned with trying to distinguish between 'speculative security loans' and loans for 'legitimate business.' In other words, was discount window credit being used to pump up stock market values? Was it leading to high growth in real estate prices, labeled a 'bubble' by some?"[28] It is not unreasonable to think that the generous LOLR policies of the 1920s may have played a role in that decade's debt buildup and asset-price boom.

The policy implications of this analysis are significant. As I noted at the start of this chapter, the prevailing view holds, or at least implies, that a panic-proofing approach to financial stability policy is much too narrow because it fails to address the more "fundamental" excesses (such as debt-fueled bubbles) that precede panics. Such debt-fueled bubbles are usually seen as emerging from the internal workings of finance; they are viewed, in Minskian fashion, as endemic to financial capitalism. But if debt-fueled bubbles are induced, to a substantial degree, by carelessly designed public support facilities—the liberalized LOLR in particular—then perhaps we should reconsider what the "fundamental" problem really is.

The Precrisis World Revisited

Let me conclude this chapter with a little-known story about a 1991 change in US law that may shed some light on the precrisis years. The story relates to the Federal Reserve's LOLR powers. It is widely known that since 1932 the Fed has had the power to lend to nonbanks (entities lacking a deposit banking charter) under "unusual and exigent circumstances."[29] This power is embodied in section 13(3) of the Federal Reserve Act.[30] Section 13(3) was the main legal authority the Fed relied on in its emergency interventions in 2008 and 2009.

What is not widely known—even among experts—is that the Fed's power to lend to nonbanks was highly circumscribed before 1991.[31] The reason was collateral limits. Before 1991, US law specifically enjoined the Fed from lending to nonbanks against collateral consisting of "notes, drafts, or bills covering merely investments or issued or drawn for the purpose of carrying or trading in stocks, bonds, or other investment securities" apart from US government securities.[32] (Fed loans to deposit banks, by contrast, were free from such limitations; such loans only needed to be "secured to the satisfaction" of the Fed.)[33] For the big Wall Street securities firms, these collateral limits meant that Fed liquidity support was not available as a practical matter. Their balance sheets consisted mostly of ineligible collateral. According to a 1991 Senate Banking Committee report, "Stocks, bonds and investment securities not eligible for discount are the greatest share of the assets of the nation's securities firms. Because these assets are not eligible for discount, the Federal Reserve is limited in its ability to make discount advances to securities firms in emergency situations."[34]

The securities industry lobbied to do away with the collateral limits. Robert N. Downey, a Goldman Sachs partner and chair of the Securities Industry Association, testified in a Senate committee hearing in April 1990.[35] "We are requesting access to the lender of last resort, if you will, only in times of generalized liquidity crises," he said. Downey argued that the very existence of this power would make its use unlikely: "Frankly, if the banks note that the Fed has the power to do that, we don't expect it would ever be used because, with proper collateral, they will answer the phone and make the loan if they know the Fed is going to do it if they don't." Needless to say, the prediction that it would never be used turned out to be wrong.

The industry's argument prevailed. In 1991 Congress did away with the long-standing collateral limits on Fed loans to nonbanks. The change was tucked into the Federal Deposit Insurance Corporation Improvement Act,[36] where it was barely noticed. (One person who did notice was Anna Schwartz, who criticized the change: "As interpreted by Sullivan & Cromwell, a New York law firm, for its clients in a memorandum of December 2, 1991, this provision enables the Fed to lend directly to security firms in emergency situations. . . . In my view, the provision in the FDIC Improvement Act of 1991 portends expanded misuse of the discount window.")[37] The amendment provided that Fed loans to securities firms and other nonbanks needed only to be "secured to the satisfaction" of the Fed. This was the same collateral standard that had long applied to deposit banks.

Senator Christopher Dodd championed the amendment. "My provision," he said in the Senate debate in 1991, "allows the Fed more power to provide liquidity, by enabling it to make fully-secured loans to securities firms" in an emergency.[38] There is a historical irony here that I can't resist recounting. On September 16, 2008, two days after Lehman filed for bankruptcy, Ben Bernanke and Hank Paulson visited Capitol Hill to brief congressional leaders on the Fed's $85 billion emergency loan to AIG, the giant insurance firm. Because AIG was not a bank, the loan was effected under section 13(3). According to one report of the meeting, "Senator Christopher Dodd twice asked how the Fed had the authority to lend to, and take control of, an insurance company. Bernanke . . . gave a brief tutorial on a little-known section of the Fed's authorizing statute."[39] Somebody might have informed the senator that the power came from the amendment he had sponsored seventeen years before!

How should we think about the likely unintended consequences of the 1991 amendment to section 13(3), in light of the analysis of this chapter? I suggested above that firms eligible for liberalized LOLR support may have incentives to grow. According to a recent study, US "securities industry output" accelerated sharply in the early 1990s.[40] The nondeposit short-term debt markets might also be expected to grow rapidly. Chapter 1 showed that this has certainly been true since the early 1990s. Hedge fund growth might also be expected; as described above, hedge funds "rent" securities firm balance sheets through prime brokerage relationships. Explosive hedge fund growth has also been a notable feature of the US financial landscape over the past twenty years. In addition, subsidies arising from the liberalized LOLR might be expected to lead to bloated financial sector compensation. According to a recent study, "Workers in finance earn[ed] the same education-adjusted wages as other workers until 1990, but by 2006 the premium [was] 50% on average. Top executive compensation in finance follows the same pattern and timing, where the premium reache[d] 250%."[41]

This analysis is only suggestive, of course. All the phenomena just described were undoubtedly the product of a number of factors, including technological change and financial market globalization. Still, it is not unreasonable to think that the 1991 liberalization of the US LOLR may have played a meaningful role. Indeed, there is a case to be made that the 1991 amendment to section 13(3) was just as consequential, in terms of the subsequent trajectory of the US financial industry, as the far more controversial repeal of Glass-Steagall later in the decade. Tyler Cowen recently wrote that "it's as if the major banks have tapped a hole in the social till and they are drinking from it with a straw."[42] The liberalized LOLR may be a big part of the story.

*　　*　　*

In recent years, some analysts have shown enthusiasm for vastly expanded central bank interventions in financial markets. Under one variant, the central bank would assume the mantle of "*dealer* of last resort," intervening directly even in the derivative markets if need be to manage asset prices.[43] Along these lines, the governor of the Bank of England recently announced a liberalization of its LOLR policies—in particular, widening the range of collateral the bank will accept; expressing openness to giving some nonbanks access to its "regular facilities"; and even suggesting that it may sometimes act as a dealer (market maker) during periods of market disruption.[44]

I have deep misgivings about this policy direction. Public liquidity backstops are not benign. They generate subsidies and troubling incentive effects. These problems are not solved by layering on more regulation, nor can they be adequately managed by creating special resolution tools for complex financial firms (see chapter 10). Other institutional designs need to be considered. The next chapter examines a more promising alternative.

CHAPTER EIGHT

The Public-Private Partnership

We have regulation about the government having monopoly over currency, but we allow these very close substitutes, we think it's good, but maybe . . . it's not so good.—Ken Rogoff, 2013[1]

The previous two chapters examined two distinct strategies for stabilizing private money creation by the banking system: regulatory risk constraints and public liquidity support. Both strategies were shown to have big problems, whether used individually or in combination. Onerous risk constraints may compromise the banking system's ability to create "enough" money. Public liquidity support gives rise to subsidies and bad incentives; it may also produce or amplify debt-fueled bubbles and other financial excesses. Just as important, unless implemented in their most extreme forms, both strategies leave open the possibility of damaging panics.

This chapter returns us to a panic-proof system of the type that emerged from the analysis of chapter 5 and that appeared in the introduction as the reformed monetary system. In chapter 5 we *started* from the presumption that the entire money supply was sovereign and nondefaultable. Run-prone funding structures did not exist, at least not on any meaningful scale. The analysis was concerned with how to construct a workable monetary framework in such a setting. What emerged was a type of joint venture or public-private partnership (PPP).

We now look again at the PPP system, but this time we get under the hood. This chapter discusses the structuring of the joint venture arrangement. First we will look at the economics of the deal, in particular the revenue split between banks and the government. Then we will look at incentive problems. All joint ventures—indeed, all financing arrangements—raise problems of incentive misalignment. A central concern will be how to deal with this issue. I will suggest that a well-structured PPP system should mimic standard features of private financial arrangements.

Of necessity, the PPP system lacks "market discipline" by short-term debt claimants. I will argue that such discipline is overrated. When it comes to money-claims, market discipline is just another name for runs and panics.[2] Further, as we will see, real-world money-claimants don't do much in the way of fundamental credit analysis—raising questions about what their discipline is good for.

The chapter ends with a brief analysis of the US deposit insurance system, which can be understood as a rough form of PPP system. I conclude that, despite its flaws, on balance this system has worked remarkably well. Unfortunately, we have allowed money creation to bypass this system on a massive scale through the emergence of shadow banking.

Economics of the Joint Venture

In keeping with the previous two chapters, we will envision an economy with a distinct and identifiable set of money creation firms or "banks." In the PPP system, bank-issued money-claims are sovereign and nondefaultable. Run-prone funding structures are therefore nonexistent. Holders of money-claims receive the short-term risk-free rate. You can think of this as government insurance of private obligations, or you can just imagine banks to be licensed issuers of sovereign instruments. These two perspectives amount to the same thing. In the PPP system, the government in effect owns a senior claim on each bank's asset portfolio. This claim entitles the government to an income stream, so the government charges ongoing fees. The fees are risk-based, meaning the government requires higher fees from riskier issuers, much as the FDIC does in the current US deposit insurance system.

We can look at this system using the diagrammatic model from the previous two chapters. To begin with, suppose the government can price the fee perfectly (an assumption that will be relaxed in the next section). The effect is shown in figure 8.1. Although money-claimants receive the risk-free rate, the optimal fee pins down the firm's cost of money-claim funding at its actuarially fair level. The firm's marginal cost curve is therefore also fair. "Fairness" in this context just means that the bank's cost of financing approximates what it would be if the bank financed itself exclusively in the

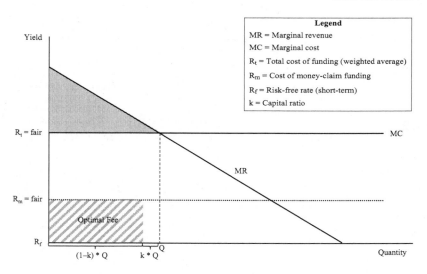

FIGURE 8.1. Optimal fee

private capital markets, with equity and longer-term debt. From the firm's perspective, the all-in cost of financing is unsubsidized. The quantity of production is realized at its unsubsidized level, and so is the bank's profit. A perfectly calibrated fee thus achieves an optimal result. Damaging panics are eliminated, and resource allocation is undistorted.

The government receives an income stream from this arrangement, but it also assumes a risk. A bank that becomes insolvent will be unable to honor its obligations. Money-claimants are fully protected, so the government is exposed to losses. One might be tempted to conclude that, if the government truly charges a fair fee, its losses will exactly offset its gains over time. The government's net revenues from the PPP system would then be zero in the long run.

This conclusion, however, isn't quite right—and this brings us to an important point about the economics of the joint venture. It turns out that the government will earn a positive return. To see why, imagine a bank whose money-claim liabilities consist entirely of demandable (zero maturity) instruments. These are transaction account balances; in the PPP system they constitute fiat money.[3] Observe that the state must reduce its fee stream by one dollar for each dollar of interest the bank pays on such transaction balances. This must be the case if the state wants the bank's *all-in* cost of financing to remain actuarially fair. (The government's fee thus consists of the *difference* between the actuarially fair rate and any interest the bank pays on its money-claims.) The bank therefore bears none of the cost of paying interest on transaction account balances; the government bears all of it. Accordingly, the determination of how much (if any) interest is to be paid on such balances is a *policy* question, to be determined by the monetary authority. It is not a matter to be left to banks and their account holders.

Some may hear echoes here of an old-fashioned idea. Under the famous Regulation Q, US banks were subject to regulatory controls on the interest they paid on deposits.[4] These constraints were phased out in the 1980s for most deposits, and the remaining vestiges were repealed in the Dodd-Frank Act of 2010.[5] The PPP system described here would reinstate administrative controls over interest payments on the banking system's monetary liabilities. Such interest payments would have fiscal revenue implications as well as potential macroeconomic implications. They are properly a policy matter.

Now let's consider what this means for the government's net revenues from the system. Suppose the government opts for zero interest on transaction account balances, just as zero interest is paid on fiat physical currency today. Suppose also that banks' administrative costs in maintaining transaction accounts are negligible. Under these conditions, the state's optimal fee is just the yield on a (fairly priced) bond issued by the bank. This means that, so long as the government charges a fair fee, it will earn a profit over time. Net fiscal revenues from the system are not zero; they are positive.

Such returns constitute seigniorage, or government revenue from money creation. On reflection, this is perfectly natural. If the government had licensed no private-sector banks at all—if it had retained a monopoly on money creation, say through a state-owned central bank—then it would have accrued all of the revenue from money creation. The state's decision to enlist private managers in no way obligates it to forfeit the entirety of the associated revenue stream. On the contrary, it should forfeit no more revenue than is necessary to induce the managers to do a good job. In the PPP system, as in all joint venture arrangements, the returns are split between the partners—in this case between bank shareholders and the government. The fair fee thus causes banks to disgorge what would otherwise amount to private seigniorage.[6]

The discussion so far has focused on transaction accounts, but what about banks' cash equivalent liabilities? (Recall that cash equivalents are money-claims that are not demandable and therefore do not function as an exchange medium.) Banks in the PPP system issue these instruments too, and they are sovereign and nondefaultable. Cash equivalents must offer a positive nominal return if anyone is to be induced to hold them.[7] Even so, the government will still earn a seigniorage profit in relation to the system's cash equivalents. Recall from chapter 1 that high-quality short-term debt offers a nonpecuniary moneyness yield, sometimes called a "convenience yield." Equivalently stated, the pecuniary yield on such instruments is extraordinarily low—much lower than an extrapolation of longer-term rates would predict. Issuers of such instruments (in this case, the banks of the PPP system) thus enjoy a pecuniary benefit. The optimal fee—designed to cause banks to incur the financing cost they would face in the longer-term private capital markets—will need to offset this pecuniary benefit. The pecuniary benefit therefore accrues to the government. Hence cash equivalents do generate seigniorage revenues to the state, albeit at a lower rate than transaction accounts. This is only logical, since cash equivalents have less "moneyness" than cash itself.

Stepping back, this analysis shows why it may be misleading to think of banks in the PPP system as financial "intermediaries" that are in the business of "taking funds" from savers and then investing those "funds." It is more useful to think of these firms as chartered *issuers* of sovereign "funds." Money-claims in this system do not represent claims on pools of assets, any more than a dollar bill today represents a claim on the Federal Reserve's asset portfolio. The terms and conditions of sovereign money are a matter to be determined by the state.

Incentive Alignment

We assumed above that the government could perfectly price the risk-based fee, but this was unrealistic. The government's fee-pricing capabilities are imperfect. Banks therefore have an opportunity to extract value from the government. This is the moral hazard problem, which we analyzed in chapter 7. When the government can't gauge risk perfectly, banks will seek to expand into riskier asset classes. This incentive problem can be understood in terms of options theory. In the PPP system the government writes a put option on the bank's assets, struck at the face amount of the bank's outstanding money-claims.[8] The value of such an option is an increasing function of the volatility of the bank's asset portfolio. Banks will try to increase the value of the option by increasing portfolio risk. In addition, if the government underprices the fee, banks will seek to replace equity financing with money-claim funding, thereby compressing their capital ratios.

This moral hazard problem furnishes a policy rationale for regulatory risk constraints—portfolio restrictions and capital requirements—in the PPP system. Moral hazard causes banks to want to increase portfolio risk. Portfolio constraints are designed to prevent this. And equity capital requirements serve a loss-absorption and incentive-alignment function. Bank owners will take more care if they bear more of the downside risk.

Importantly, these regulatory techniques mirror private sector practices. Insurance firms—which are in the business of writing put options—use these very techniques. They charge premiums tailored to the degree of risk underwritten; impose deductibles to align incentives and absorb "first loss"; and impose covenants to constrain risk taking. These techniques are precise analogues to the PPP system's risk-based fees, capital requirements, and portfolio constraints, respectively. In other words, the PPP system embodies the standard private-sector techniques for optimizing insurance and debt contracts (lenders are put writers too). The ubiquity of these techniques in the private sector highlights the underlying economic logic of the PPP system.

I have argued that the US system of insured banking that exists today can be understood as a rough form of PPP system. And it is noteworthy that the current system uses precisely the techniques just described. Fischer Black, Merton Miller, and Richard Posner have remarked on "the similarity between the requirements the government imposes on banks and the requirements a lender imposes on a borrower."[9] Miller has separately written that banking regulations "should resemble the measures adopted by freely-contracting private lenders in similar circumstances. And, at least in a broad-brush way, they really do."[10] This insight is extraordinarily powerful—it gives us a way to understand the structure of banking law—but it is has yet to be internalized in the broader banking literature.

Lest this insight seem obvious, consider the arguments of a seminal article from the legal literature in this area: Robert Clark's "The Soundness of Financial Intermediaries."[11] Clark conducts an extended inquiry into the rationale for regulating banks' asset portfolios and capital. But he fails to consider the idea that such constraints might serve an important function in counteracting the incentive problems that arise from deposit insurance. Clark expresses "grave doubts about the wisdom of continuing many existing techniques of portfolio regulation," finding them "arbitrary and unduly restrictive." He goes on to say that "there is more than enough doubt to warrant further research into what, if anything, is being accomplished by the nation's several thousand bank examiners." Remarkably, he is also skeptical of "the belief that capital cushions . . . have something to do with bank soundness," at least "in situations [that] are present to a significant degree in the real world." Clark sees deposit insurance and soundness regulation not as complements but as alternatives. Under a deposit insurance system with risk-based premiums, he argues, portfolio constraints and capital requirements "might be dispensed with, in whole or in significant part." He suggests that an "ideal mix" of strategies would probably include "*substantially* curtailing" such risk constraints. Clark concludes by referring to the "addictive charms" of portfolio regulation, and he suggests that "radical changes are called for." He remarks that "even the experiment of permitting banks . . . to invest in any kinds of financial assets in any proportions should be seriously considered." Let's just say I find Clark's analysis unconvincing. He clearly does not see bank portfolio constraints, capital requirements, and risk-based fees as components of an integrated and logical system, one that mirrors private sector practices for dealing with moral hazard.

Each of the PPP regime's three distinct regulatory tools—portfolio restrictions, capital requirements, and ongoing fees—requires calibration. Let's look now at how the government (or an agency or branch thereof, which we can call the "monetary authority") might go about this task.

Portfolio Constraints

Consider first the calibration of the PPP system's portfolio constraints. Here the monetary authority faces a trade-off. On one hand, allowing banks to invest in riskier assets exacerbates the moral hazard problem.[12] This consideration tends to favor the safest assets available, such as Treasuries. On the other hand, portfolio constraints need to be lenient enough to accommodate the desired money supply (see chapters 5 and 6). The optimal supply of money-claims might far exceed the available supply of government securities. This consideration favors a wider range of permissible investments, encompassing riskier assets.

The PPP system's portfolio restrictions will therefore be a function of both the desired money supply and the available categories of credit assets. The monetary authority starts by making the safest assets eligible. It then admits assets of increasing risk—presumably, various types of consumer and business credit (loans and bonds)—until an adequate supply of investment opportunities exists. Naturally stocks and other subordinated instruments are excluded. The monetary authority also imposes diversification requirements to limit concentration risks.

The techniques just described are part of the standard tool kit of US deposit banking regulation as it exists today. Much of banking law is about *confining deposit banks to diversified portfolios of safe-ish credit assets.* This point will be obvious enough to banking lawyers, but for some reason it seems to be lost on much of the academic literature. So let me be explicit.[13] US deposit banks can make loans and buy investment-grade bonds, but they generally can't buy stocks or junk bonds.[14] They can lend against real estate, but they can't engage as equity investors in real estate development or related activities.[15] They generally can't run commercial enterprises directly; for example, a deposit bank can't run a travel agency.[16] They are generally prohibited from engaging in securities dealing and underwriting as well as insurance underwriting.[17] They can lease personal property to customers only if the lease is functionally equivalent to a loan secured by the property—in other words, only if the bank does not bear the residual risk of the leased asset.[18] The same goes for leases of real estate.[19] The point of all of this is to keep bank portfolios relatively safe—to keep banks away from residual (equity) interests in assets. In addition, US deposit banks are subject to strict portfolio diversification standards. A bank's investment in the securities of any one issuer can't exceed 10% of the bank's regulatory capital, and loans to one borrower generally can't exceed 15% of regulatory capital.[20] It is an axiom of finance theory and practice that portfolio diversification reduces risk.

Thus, when it comes to portfolio constraints, US deposit banking law roughly corresponds to our theory of what a PPP regime should look like. There is, however, one major exception—an area in which bank regulatory practice has diverged sharply from the theory sketched above. That area is derivatives. This is a big issue for banking regulation today, and it merits a brief analysis.

Let's start with the theory. It should be fairly obvious that if we understand banks first and foremost as monetary institutions, then allowing banks to take on risk in the derivative markets would be inimical to the system's underlying purposes. This has nothing to do with any prejudice against derivatives. Derivatives are an extremely important part of modern finance, and there is nothing inherently dangerous about them. But derivatives are a singularly ineffective way of issuing money. Chapter 2 described the mechanics by which banks issue money in the process of acquiring financial assets such as loans and bonds. With derivatives, however, the amount of cash exchanged up front is almost always very small in relation to the risk taken. (This is why, in finance jargon, stocks and bonds are called "cash instruments" while derivatives are "synthetic instruments.") Indeed, often *no* cash is exchanged up front.

Take a concrete example. Suppose a bank wanted to write protection in the credit default swap (CDS) markets. This activity might be profitable; banks are experts in credit analysis, after all. But it would do nothing to advance the banking system's monetary function. A bank creates no money when it writes CDS protection; the trade does not augment its balance sheet. The bank merely accepts an income stream in exchange for a contingent payment. It takes on risk without issuing any monetary instruments. This is the opposite of what we want banks to do, which is to *minimize* the amount of risk taken in relation to the quantity of money issued (or, equivalently, to *maximize* the money issued in relation to the risk taken).

What if, instead of taking directional or speculative bets in the derivatives markets, the bank maintains a "matched book"—it hedges its derivatives exposures through offsetting positions? For example, when the bank writes CDS protection, it can simultaneously buy protection on the same reference asset from a third party. The bank would then be functioning as a dealer or market maker. This is safer than outright speculation—but it's still quite risky. Derivatives dealers face the risk of counterparty default; they face "basis risk," or the risk that a hedge will not move perfectly in tandem with the offsetting position; and they inevitably face some market risk. The risk taken in derivatives dealing is very large in relation to the amount of cash that changes hands. Our monetary theory of banking therefore suggests that derivatives dealing is properly the domain of *nonbank* financial firms.

This argument from theory is, I think, pretty straightforward. Yet US deposit bank regulation has gone in a very different direction in recent decades, in what legal scholar Saule Omarova has described as a "quiet metamorphosis."[21] Before 1987, national banks' derivatives activities were limited to hedging the interest-rate risk of their existing banking books[22]—unquestionably a good idea. In 1987, however, the Office of the Comptroller of the Currency (OCC) began allowing national banks to enter into commodity derivatives on a matched book basis.[23] This was not hedging of existing risks; it was derivatives *dealing*. The OCC explicitly stated that it was moving beyond the "textbook sense" of banking and toward a "modern concept of banking as funds intermediation."

With this conceptual abstraction the floodgates were open. In 1988 the OCC allowed national banks to issue "deposits" with returns linked to stock market indexes and to hedge the associated risks in the equity swaps markets.[24] Claims on banks were now competing with investment company shares. In the early 1990s the OCC dropped the matched book requirement for national banks' derivatives positions and allowed them to hedge on a portfolio basis.[25] In 1993 the OCC allowed national banks to take *physical* delivery of commodities to hedge derivatives risks— arguably departing from one of the most venerable of banking doctrines, the separation of banking and commerce.[26] In 2000 the OCC even allowed national banks to purchase equity securities to hedge derivatives exposures—this despite the *specific statutory prohibition* on purchases of stock by national banks.[27]

The Dodd-Frank Act sought to partially turn back the clock on these developments. Dodd-Frank's "swaps push-out rule" would have required insured banks to cease some, though not all, of their derivatives dealing.[28] These activities were to be "pushed out" into nonbank affiliates. The provision was very controversial, prompting criticism and ambivalence even from otherwise staunch defenders of financial regulation. For example, during the Dodd-Frank legislative process, Sheila Bair, then chair of the FDIC, expressed concerns about an early draft of the push-out, noting that "insured banks play an essential role in providing market-making functions" for certain derivatives.[29] Paul Volcker, usually known as a traditionalist on banking matters, criticized the rule too.[30] Ben Bernanke likewise criticized the provision for "essentially prohibit[ing] all insured depository institutions from acting as a swap dealer."[31] (As if that were a bad thing!) The swaps push-out was later substantially repealed.[32]

Once we accept that deposit banks should be required to abide by portfolio and activity constraints, it is hard to see why they should be in the business of derivatives dealing. Again, the issue is not whether derivatives dealing is good or bad (it is good) but whether it is appropriate for insured banks. The handful of giant US financial firms that dominate today's derivatives markets prefer to book these trades in their insured bank subsidiaries only because it is especially cheap, presumably owing to especially robust public backstops. But why shouldn't derivatives be subject to market pricing? Is there any reason to think they would become unduly expensive if they were booked in these firms' broker-dealer or other non-bank subsidiaries?

A more general lesson emerges from this discussion. In allowing insured banks to get into derivatives dealing, the OCC explicitly relied on a generic conception of banking as financial intermediation. But this generic conception imposes no meaningful limiting principle on bank activities and portfolios. If derivatives dealing within deposit banks is acceptable, then why not repeal the existing statutory prohibition on securities dealing by deposit banks? What about insurance underwriting, which is also prohibited by statute? For that matter, why not let deposit banks own large private equity portfolios? All these activities constitute "financial intermediation." Without an actual theory of banking regulation—without some way to organize our thinking about these matters—we are left with nothing but ad hoc judgments and gut feelings. The notion that banking is synonymous with financial intermediation may sound sophisticated and modern, but it ends up unmooring banking law from its logical foundations and depriving it of internal coherence.

The theory sketched here suggests a clear way of thinking about bank portfolio constraints in the PPP system. Simply put, we want the banking system to maximize its ratio of monetary liabilities to portfolio risk. This means owning a diversified portfolio of relatively high-quality credit, consistent with the accommodation of the desired money supply. Under this view, other financial activities—including derivatives dealing—should take place outside licensed banking entities.

Capital Requirements

Next, consider the calibration of capital requirements in the PPP system. Capital requirements serve a function of loss absorption and incentive alignment, thereby counteracting the effects of moral hazard. But there is a trade-off here too. Suppose the monetary authority wants the banking system to generate $9 trillion of monetary instruments. A capital requirement of 10% would mean the banking system must own at least $10 trillion of assets. Increasing the capital requirement to 50% would translate into an asset portfolio of at least $18 trillion—an increase of 80%. Portfolio constraints would need to be relaxed to accommodate the larger asset size; riskier assets would need to be made admissible. Capital requirements and portfolio constraints would be working at cross-purposes. Capital requirements must therefore be calibrated in conjunction with portfolio constraints. The monetary authority optimizes the PPP system, in theory at least, by selecting the *combination* of portfolio constraints and capital requirements that maximizes the safety of the government's senior claim.

Chapter 6 argued that portfolio constraints and capital requirements are ineffective tools for preventing runs and panics. It is important to stress that, while the PPP system incorporates both of these tools, they are *not* being relied on for this purpose. All money-claims are sovereign and nondefaultable in this system; panics are ruled out completely. Portfolio constraints and capital requirements are being used here to neutralize, or at least mitigate, the incentive problems that arise as a consequence of the government's commitment. This is a very different role, and a far more modest one.

In chapter 6 I remarked on the widespread enthusiasm for making capital regulation "simple." My argument was that, when it comes to devising capital requirements for complex institutions like Wall Street securities firms, simplicity is incompatible with effectiveness. Derivatives portfolios in particular pose a huge challenge for capital regulation. The relevance of this point for the PPP system is obvious. Banks within this system are confined to diversified portfolios of fairly high-quality credit assets, and they can't get into the derivatives business. The capital regime for the PPP system can therefore be quite simple.

Ongoing Fees

Finally, the monetary authority calibrates the PPP system's risk-based fees. As I described above, the government seeks to charge each issuer a fair premium for a put option written on the issuer's asset portfolio, struck at the face value of the issuer's outstanding money-claims. (More specifically, it charges the fair put premium plus the difference between the risk-free rate corresponding to the average duration of the bank's portfolio and the interest paid by the bank on its money-claim liabilities.)[33] The value of this option is a function of the issuer's portfolio volatility (asset quality) and its level of capital (the difference between the fair value of the firm's assets and the face value of its money-claim liabilities).

To estimate portfolio volatility, the monetary authority would take into account such factors as the historical financial performance of the firm; the historical loss experience of the asset categories on the firm's balance sheet; secondary-market benchmarks for those asset categories; standard asset quality metrics (such as loan delinquencies); the pricing of the firm's capital market instruments, if actively traded; publicly available credit ratings; assessments by brokerage research analysts; the quality of management; the adequacy of risk management practices; the firm's loan underwriting standards and practices; reviews of loan files during the supervisory process; and geographic and sectoral concentrations. These are the types of factors US banking regulators rely on today in prudential regulation and in setting deposit insurance fees.

Once portfolio volatility has been estimated, the government can avail itself of widely used pricing models to value the put option. Because issuers' asset portfolios are dynamic, each firm's risk-based fee would be adjusted periodically (perhaps quarterly). As I noted in the sketch of the reformed monetary system in the introduction, such fees bear some resemblance to today's deposit insurance fees. But there is an important difference: in the system described here, risk-based fees are a source of seigniorage revenue to the government. This is not true of deposit insurance fees today.

The pricing of these fees will not be perfect, but perfection is not the relevant standard. As Black, Miller, and Posner point out, "The ability of the government to estimate the risk of a bank . . . is sometimes called into question. Some observers doubt that there is any way to estimate this risk. But private lenders estimate this sort of risk all the time."[34] They further note that "any system of estimating risk will have arbitrary elements in it." To be sure, the PPP system requires the monetary authority to make difficult appraisals of value, and inaccurate appraisals are costly. But challenges of this nature appear to be inescapable in any monetary system the state might choose to establish. For that matter, valuation problems arise in every government activity—from national defense, to antitrust enforcement, to environmental protection, to social insurance, to the provision of infrastructure, and so on. All these activities require the government to make difficult appraisals of value, and inaccurate appraisals are costly. Establishing a well-functioning monetary system turns out to be no different. As always, the aim is to select the best design from among the realistic alternatives.

Money and Market Discipline

A standard critique of deposit insurance is that it undermines market discipline by holders of insured balances. Insured claimants have no incentive to monitor the bank's activities or deny funding to unsound banks. They are indifferent to the bank's fundamental condition. The PPP system, which can be viewed as a form of deposit insurance, is vulnerable to this critique. How much does this matter?

Needless to say, market discipline is not an end in itself but rather a means to efficient resource allocation. Extensive information gathering and expert analysis are essential preconditions to financial market efficiency. Holders of private money-claims, however, do very little in the way of fundamental analysis. Because they are involved in a coordination game, their orientation is largely *horizontal*—focused on what other money-claimants are likely to do. Fundamental credit analysis is expensive, but money-claimants can get an approximate sense of an issuer's fundamental condition without much effort. They can outsource credit analysis by observing credit ratings, for example, or they can compile cursory credit metrics. Anything more than an approximate sense of fundamental condition is not very useful, because the degree of fundamental deterioration that will trigger a run can't be ascertained in advance.

That money-claimants don't do much fundamental investment research is widely known. Consider these observations from the leading money market reference work, *Stigum's Money Market*.[35] "One might expect most institutional [short-term] portfolios to be managed with considerable sophistication," the authors say. But "many short-term portfolios are not managed as well as they could be, and some are not managed at all." They remark that "some of the ablest [short-term] portfolio managers tend to steer clear of credit analysis." In fact, "a good portfolio manager can, as many do, refuse to get into credit analysis." What is more, investors in these markets rely heavily on credit ratings. According to a JPMorgan research report issued during the crisis, "nearly all of these liquidity-focused [short-term] investors are credit rating sensitive and are more attuned to the opinions of S&P and Moody's than they are of the other rating agencies."[36] None of this is any secret. A newspaper report on the 2008 unraveling of the auction-rate securities market (a short-term debt market) notes that "it had never occurred to [securities holders] to get [prospectuses] on what they thought was a cash equivalent investment. . . . Only after disaster struck did people start to find out what they had bought."[37] For those accustomed to thinking of financial markets as quite efficient, these statements may be jarring. Money market investors adopt a fundamentally different approach from, say, high-yield bond investors (who do extensive investment research).

It is sometimes argued that *secured* money-claimants decline to do fundamental analysis on their counterparties only because they look to the collateral, not the counterparty, for protection. This view is mistaken. A 2010 report by a task force of repo market participants underscores this point: "Discussions in the Task Force emphasized repeatedly that many [repo investors] focus primarily if not almost exclusively on *counterparty* concerns and that they will withdraw secured funding on the same or very similar timeframes as they would withdraw unsecured funding" (emphasis added).[38] The report further observed that, during the recent crisis, borrowers in the repo market "did not sufficiently appreciate the sensitivity of many [repo investors] to counterparty concerns even in the presence of high-quality collateral." The experience of Bear Stearns is a case in point. In the aftermath of the firm's collapse, Securities and Exchange Commission chair Christopher Cox noted that the agency had failed to appreciate "the possibility that secured funding, even that backed by high-quality collateral such as US Treasury and agency securities, could become unavailable."[39] The CEO of Bear Stearns likewise remarked that in March 2008 "counterparties increasingly refused to lend against even high-quality collateral."[40] And Bear's head of funding told investigators from the Financial Crisis Inquiry Commission that some repo lenders stopped lending to the firm even against Treasuries.[41]

The notion that there would be a run on fully secured Treasury repo might initially seem puzzling, but it is perfectly consonant with the analysis of part 1 of this book. This is a crucial point: secured money-claimants are *not indifferent* between holding the money-claim and holding the underlying collateral. They chose to hold the money-claim (instead of an asset like the collateral) precisely because of its monetary attributes; they chose to sacrifice yield for moneyness. Even if the collateral can be seized immediately upon default,[42] the collateral lacks the moneyness property that was the very reason for holding a money-claim in the first place. (Recall from figure 1.6 that even Treasuries maturing in as little as six months have only modest moneyness.) Repo creditors don't want the collateral. It's all downside—collateral value in excess of the repo face amount must be returned to the defaulting borrower—and besides it's an operational hassle. Accordingly, repo creditors and other secured money-claimants *do* care about whether the issuer will default, which means they care about what other money-claimants will do. The coordination game is in full force.

Gary Gorton and other economists use the term "informationally insensitive" to describe financial instruments, such as money-claims, on which detailed credit analysis is generally not worthwhile. According to Gorton:

Broadly speaking, [informationally insensitive] debt does not really correspond to the textbook descriptions of "efficient markets," a notion that is basically about stock markets.... [It] is sold based almost exclusively on its rating.... Intuitively, information-insensitive debt is debt that no one need devote a lot of resources to investigating. It is designed to avoid exactly that.[43]

Bengt Holmstrom makes a similar observation.[44] "Money markets are fundamentally different from stock markets," he writes. "Stock markets are about price discovery for the purpose of allocating risk efficiently. Money markets are about obviating the need for price discovery.... A state of 'No Questions Asked' is the hallmark of money market liquidity." There are reasons to question whether this odd variety of market "discipline" is conducive to efficient resource allocation.

The Success of US Federal Deposit Insurance

Chapter 5 noted that the advent of deposit insurance marked a revolutionary change in the design of the US monetary system. In one fell swoop, the bulk of the money supply went from private to sovereign, inaugurating seventy-plus years of panic-free conditions. Not until the emergence on a huge scale of shadow banking—money creation *outside* the insured deposit banking sector—did instability return. The shadow banking panic, I have argued, bore substantial responsibility for the Great Recession.

A persistent theme in the postcrisis literature has been that the financial crisis was due to insufficient "regulation." The image that suggests itself is of a kind of financial regulatory dial that can be turned up and down. The dial evidently got turned down too far, leading to disaster. This conception is, I think, far too general to be useful. The Quiet Period was mostly attributable not to "regulation" in some generic sense but rather to a very specific intervention: the deposit insurance system. Today the drive to use regulation to reduce "systemic risk"—a vague concept that can mean practically anything—has been counterproductive. I expand on these issues in chapter 10.

Deposit insurance is sometimes mistakenly viewed primarily as a tool for protecting small, unsophisticated account holders. For example, Robert Clark is critical of the idea that bank regulation serves "some vitally important economic function beyond protection of [small account holders]." He is skeptical of the "alleged special economic function" that banks perform.[45] Here again I find little to agree with in Clark's analysis of banking. The consumer protection perspective is at best incomplete; at worst it misses the point. Former Federal Reserve vice chair Alan Blinder has remarked that "the U.S. government is in the deposit insurance business mainly to enhance macroeconomic and financial stability" and that "protecting the small depositor is an incidental benefit, not the main social purpose of deposit insurance."[46] Other banking experts have reached similar conclusions. One historical study notes that

> it is clear from both the statements and actions of many proponents and administrators of bank-obligation insurance systems that the primary object has not been to guard the individual depositor or noteholder against loss but, instead, to restore to the community, as quickly as possible, circulating medium destroyed or made unavailable as a consequence of bank failures. In this view, bank-obligation insurance has a monetary function, and the protection of the small creditor against loss is incidental to the achievement of the primary objective.[47]

Friedman and Schwartz agreed. "Protection of the circulating medium," they wrote, "rather than protection of the small depositor against loss was the overriding concern of the legislators in establishing [US federal] deposit insurance."[48]

The idea that deposit insurance is (or ought to be) mostly about protecting small account holders represents a mindless application of concepts from securities and investment company regulation. In those areas the idea is that "big boys" (believe it or not, this is a term of art for corporate lawyers) can fend for themselves; it is the small, unsophisticated investor who needs legal protection. This just isn't a useful prism through which to understand banking regulation. Widespread bank runs expose the economy to catastrophe—and the big boys are *precisely* the ones *most* likely to run. In the recent financial crisis, institutional (as opposed to retail) money-claimants were the source of the vast majority of redemptions. The economy promptly tanked. Thus, when it comes to banking, it is a mistake to indiscriminately graft concepts from securities law. Monetary institutions raise an entirely distinct set of problems.

Notably, in the heat of the recent crisis, the cap on deposit insurance coverage was removed: US transaction account balances were insured to an unlimited amount on an emergency basis.[49] And the Treasury Department's emergency guarantee of money market mutual funds had no coverage caps. The objective of these measures was of course to arrest the panic. Some prominent analysts have called for abolishing caps on deposit insurance coverage. For example, Black, Miller, and Posner note that "the nature of government regulation has been such that most deposits are 100% insured in fact.... There is no obvious reason why this should not be made official by instituting unlimited insurance of deposits."[50] In particular, they observe that "with 100% deposit insurance, the government could stop worrying about the macroeconomic effects of bank failures." The PPP system described in this chapter adopts this very strategy, and there are good reasons for it.

To be sure, deposit insurance systems can be costly, especially if they are poorly designed.[51] The history of US federal deposit insurance has not been one of unqualified success. The bank and thrift debacle of the 1980s led to a costly $124 billion taxpayer bailout.[52] But it is important to understand that, in the years preceding the debacle, US bank and thrift regulation was characterized by glaring design defects. First, Congress gutted bank and thrift portfolio constraints in the early 1980s, allowing insured institutions to massively increase exposures to risky asset classes (e.g., high-risk construction loans and junk bonds).[53] Second, regulators lacked a robust and consistent approach to capital regulation; the approach was haphazard and failed to account for off-balance-sheet exposures. Third, deposit insurance fees were "one size fits all"—they weren't scaled to the risk of the institution. Fourth, regulatory accounting standards were extremely lax, allowing insured institutions to overstate their net worth and setting the stage for outright looting by owners and managers.[54] Fifth, penalties were too weak to deter misconduct by bad actors, and enforcement was abysmal. Finally, regulators in the 1980s were under no statutory obligation to promptly shut down critically undercapitalized banks and thrifts, so problems were left to fester for years.

In response to the debacle of the 1980s, huge improvements were made to the design of insured bank and thrift regulation in the United States. Portfolio constraints were tightened back up considerably (albeit not in the derivatives area, as we have seen).[55] A coherent capital regime was put in place; the first Basel Accord, adopted in 1988, was implemented in the United States in the early 1990s.[56] Risk-based deposit insurance fees were established.[57] (Evidence from the stock market suggests that the introduction of risk-based fees penalized risky banks and rewarded safer banks—exactly the desired incentive effect.)[58] Regulatory accounting standards were made much more stringent.[59] Civil and criminal penalties were stiffened and regulatory enforcement powers bolstered.[60] And prompt regulatory resolution of insolvent insured institutions was mandated.[61]

The cumulative impact of these measures was immense. And it is noteworthy that, despite the staggering magnitude of credit losses in the United States from 2007 to 2010, no taxpayer support of the deposit insurance system was required—not even close. Total bank and thrift failure costs to the FDIC's deposit insurance fund as a result of the recent crisis are estimated to be about $90 billion.[62] These losses are being fully recouped from insured banks and thrifts, whose reported equity capital currently stands at $1.7 trillion.[63] The fiscal cost to taxpayers is zero. In short, the deposit insurance system has done more or less what it was designed to do.

Not all banking experts favor deposit insurance. Raghuram Rajan has argued for phasing out deposit insurance, calling it an "archaic privilege."[64] Given his advocacy of the commitment device theory of banking (see chapter 3), this should not be surprising. Charles Calomiris and Stephen Haber, in their recent book *Fragile by Design*, cast deposit insurance as an undesirable product of "populist" political forces.[65] Because I see well-structured deposit insurance as a quantum leap forward in monetary system design, I can't share their interpretation. On balance, deposit insurance in the United States has been a resounding policy success.

*   *   *

This brings us to the end of part 2. The goal has been to offer a way of organizing our thinking about monetary system design and, in particular, the role of the banking system. In chapter 5 we considered the problem of monetary system design from the state's perspective, in a system in which all money was sovereign and nondefaultable. The analysis led to a type of public-private partnership. Chapters 6 and 7 examined two approaches to stabilizing private (defaultable) money creation by the banking system. Both were found to pose problems. Chapter 8 looked again at the PPP system, this time from a structural perspective.

The PPP system embodies an intelligible logic, and its advantages over the alternatives are substantial. Chapter 6 showed that onerous regulatory risk constraints may compromise the banking system's ability to create "enough" money. The PPP system doesn't have this problem; the calibration of its components *is determined by* the state's monetary objectives. Chapter 7 showed that, as a practical matter, public liquidity support generates unavoidable subsidies and bad incentives. The PPP system's risk-based fees are an essential tool in addressing these problems; the PPP system can, at least in theory, accomplish the state's monetary objectives without producing subsidies and other distortions. Most important, the PPP system simply rules out panics. The other designs do not, unless administered in their most extreme and questionable forms.

Part 3 returns us to the reformed monetary system from the introduction, which is a particular instantiation of the PPP approach. My argument is that the problem of financial instability has been widely misunderstood; financial instability is mostly a problem of monetary system design. This recognition is liberating—it brings a great deal of clarity to the task at hand. For it suggests that what we are facing is a manageable project of institutional engineering rather than an open-ended battle against an amorphous enemy like "systemic risk." As we will see, the reformed system represents an approach to financial stability regulation that is very different from the one being pursued today. At its core, it would recognize money creation as a sovereign prerogative.

PART III

Money and Sovereignty

CHAPTER NINE

A More Detailed Blueprint

Sovereign and unified control of the monetary system is needed in any economy, whatever freedoms may be proper otherwise.—Bray Hammond, 1957[1]

Throughout part 2 we posited the existence of a single system of licensed money creation firms—"banks"—and assumed that run-prone funding structures were nonexistent outside that system. The real world obviously looks quite different. Run-prone funding structures do exist outside the chartered banking system; indeed, this is precisely what we have called "shadow" banking. And we saw in part 1 that shadow banking was at the center of the recent financial crisis.

Does this mean the preceding chapters hold little relevance for current problems? Not at all. We needed to organize our thinking about banking regulation before turning to shadow banking. The rest of the book argues that parts 1 and 2 point the way toward a concrete and workable approach to financial stability policy in the real world. I aim to drive home my central claim: that financial instability is, at bottom, a problem of monetary system design.

This part proceeds in two steps. The first step—the task of this chapter—is to flesh out the reformed monetary system that I sketched in the introduction. The reformed system is a particular implementation of the more generic public-private partnership system of money creation that emerged from part 2. The preceding chapters laid the foundations; we're now ready to finish the institutional engineering. A central topic will be how to *confine* money creation to the chartered banking system. This means implementing a general prohibition on a particular funding model. This is less radical than it sounds: keep in mind that we already prohibit "deposit" funding in the absence of a special charter. I also discuss international dimensions of the reformed system, as well as transition issues.

The second step—the task of chapter 10—is criticism. Having engineered our system, we will turn a critical eye toward prevailing opinion on the problem of financial instability. We will also review recent and pending US financial stability reforms. Those reforms, I contend, have been based on vague and superficial notions about the nature of the underlying problem. And the failure has been mostly one of ideas, not of politics.

Structure and Operations

Let's start by fleshing out the reformed monetary system. Features that were discussed in the introduction will only be touched on briefly here.

Medium of Exchange

Record currency or "r-currency," which has no *physical* existence, serves as the primary medium of exchange. It is issued by member banks of the system. R-currency is sovereign, fiat money, and it does not bear interest. It is denominated in the standard unit of account (e.g., dollars in the United States). The government accepts r-currency in payment of taxes and declares it to be legal tender.[2] R-currency works just like a fully insured checkable deposit. Agents in the economy hold r-currency accounts, and transfers of r-currency are done through ledger entries.

The reformed system may or may not include physical currency. If physical currency is included, it is legally and economically equivalent to r-currency. (Physical currency is r-currency in bearer form; r-currency is physical currency in registered form.) Introducing physical currency into the system is a trivial matter—it raises no conceptual or significant practical difficulties. Purely for ease of exposition, the discussion that follows will assume that physical currency does not exist.

Payment Mechanics/Clearing and Settlement

Payments are made as follows. If the payer and payee hold r-currency accounts with the same member bank, nothing more than an electronic ledger entry is required. If they hold accounts with different member banks, then clearing and settlement are needed. Here is how they work. The payer's member bank debits the payer's account and simultaneously books an equivalent liability, called a "sovereign debit." The payee's member bank credits the payee's account and simultaneously books an equivalent asset, called a "sovereign credit." As payments are processed, each member bank continuously nets its sovereign credits against its sovereign debits. So, at any given moment each member bank's balance sheet has either a sovereign credit balance or a sovereign debit balance—or neither—but never both.[3]

Sovereign debits and credits have real functional significance: they play a role in determining each bank's seigniorage fees (see below). Also, sovereign credits are not counted as assets in the denominator of capital requirements. The system works "as if" there were just a single member bank effecting payments through ledger entries.

Member Banks

Member banks are chartered by the government and owned by private shareholders.[4] They issue r-currency in exchange for loans and bonds, subject to the risk constraints described below. When a member bank buys a bond or makes a loan, it augments the money supply and puts downward pressure on market interest rates. When it sells bonds or loans—or lets them mature—it shrinks the money supply and puts upward pressure on market interest rates. Member banks' business models are quite simple; they are credit investors. Their function is to invest the money supply into circulation and to manage the payments system (as described above). Obviously, member banks are not the only credit investors in the economy. They exist alongside all sorts of other financial firms.

Risk Constraints

Member banks are subject to portfolio restrictions and capital requirements.[5] These regulatory risk constraints are calibrated along the lines described in chapter 8. Regulators will aim to keep member banks confined to diversified portfolios of relatively safe credit assets. At the same time, risk constraints need to be lenient enough to accommodate the desired money supply (see the discussion of monetary policy below). Member banks are disallowed from participating in derivatives markets (apart from risk-reducing hedging) because such activities do not advance the system's monetary function.[6] Capital regulation for member banks can be quite straightforward, since member bank portfolios are fairly simple. Capital requirements may or may not be risk-based; there are reasonable arguments both pro and con. A supervisory regime monitors compliance with the risk constraints.

Unauthorized Banking

The reformed system aims to confine money creation to member banks. This means establishing and enforcing a general prohibition on the issuance of money-claims—essentially, short-term debt instruments, excluding trade credit—by entities that are not member banks.[7] In the reformed system, the use of this distinctive funding model is *the very legal privilege that a member banking charter conveys*. Operationalizing this restriction is a crucial feature of the reformed monetary system. Because of its importance, I treat this topic in detail in the next section.

As a result of this prohibition, member banks in the reformed system are the exclusive issuers not only of r-currency but also of cash equivalents. Furthermore, cash equivalents, like r-currency, are sovereign and nondefaultable; member banks' cash equivalent liabilities simply become r-currency at maturity.[8] Note that there are no money market mutual funds or other nonbank monetary institutions in the reformed system. Member banks are the exclusive issuers of the broad money supply.

Affiliations

The reformed system may or may not include restrictions on affiliations between member banks and other types of financial firms—securities dealers, insurance companies, and so forth. (Basically, "affiliation" means ownership within the same corporate group.) If such affiliations are allowed, then limitations on affiliate transactions will be needed.[9] In the broader scheme of things, the question of affiliations is not very important.

Risk-Based Fees

Member banks pay risk-based fees to the government, called seigniorage fees.[10] A member bank's seigniorage fees are keyed off the sum of its r-currency liabilities, cash equivalent liabilities, and sovereign debits less sovereign credits. From the government's standpoint, seigniorage fees are a fiscal revenue item. To a first approximation, seigniorage fees should be calibrated to cause each member bank to incur the financing cost it would incur if it financed itself entirely in the longer-term private capital markets.[11] Seigniorage fee rates are therefore lower in relation to cash equivalents (which bear interest) than in relation to r-currency (which does not). The relative outstanding quantities of r-currency and cash equivalents are a function of monetary policy, as described below.

In practice, seigniorage fees need to be low enough to induce private managers to participate. If member banking isn't profitable enough to attract talented managers, then the government is ipso facto doing it wrong. (This is related to what Gary Gorton has called "charter value.")[12] Moreover, to incent member banks to provide good customer service to account holders, member banks receive partial fee rebates based on their outstanding r-currency balances. In effect, the government gives up some seigniorage revenue to compensate member banks for operating the payments system.

Insolvency System

When a member bank becomes critically undercapitalized, it enters a special insolvency system under which the bank's monetary liabilities (r-currency and cash equivalents) are seamlessly honored while other claims on the bank are subject to impairment or extinguishment.[13] The insolvency system aims to return the member bank to private hands, presumably under new management, as expeditiously as possible. Typically this will be accomplished by selling the recapitalized bank's equity, either to a private buyer (most likely another member bank) or into the public equity markets.

An insolvent member bank must be recapitalized before it is sold. To the extent that this can't be achieved from within the member bank's existing capital structure—through conversion of long-term/nonmonetary debt into equity—recapitalization is accomplished by adding sovereign credits to the member bank's balance sheet. This is not mere accounting magic. Remember, sovereign credits are netted against monetary liabilities in determining seigniorage fees. Hence, for a member bank, a sovereign credit represents the forgiveness of an economic obligation. The loser here is the taxpayer: when member banks go insolvent and must be recapitalized with sovereign credits, future seigniorage revenues are forgone. Member bank failures are therefore costly to the public; there is no free lunch. Note that there is no need for any kind of insurance fund to support member banks' monetary liabilities, any more than today's Federal Reserve needs a fund to support its monetary liabilities.

Administration

The reformed monetary system is administered by a monetary authority—an independent government agency. Its board members have relatively long tenures and may be removed only for cause.[14] It is also self-funding; the monetary authority deducts its expenses from seigniorage revenues before remitting them to the fiscal authority.[15] The monetary authority is governed by a statutory macroeconomic policy mandate, perhaps a dual mandate of full employment and price stability.[16]

Certain specific regulatory functions might be allocated to other agencies. For example, regulation and supervision of member banks could be handled by a separate banking agency. The same goes for the special insolvency system. These questions of administrative structure are secondary issues. For present purposes, we will assume that all of the system's functions are handled by the monetary authority.

Monetary Policy Operations

Member banks operate within a "cap and trade" system, which places an adjustable cap on the broad money supply. A member bank must possess permit capacity greater than or equal to the sum of its r-currency liabilities, cash equivalent liabilities, and sovereign debits less sovereign credits. Permit capacity is tradable among member banks. The monetary authority may increase or decrease permit capacity in the conduct of monetary policy, thereby influencing interest rates, the price level, and overall economic activity.[17] For diversification and competition purposes, no member bank is permitted to hold more than 10% of outstanding permit capacity.[18] Note that there is no upper bound on the amount of money the system can create; the monetary authority can always raise the cap.

In practice, cap adjustments may be a rather blunt monetary policy tool. But the monetary authority has a second tool: it can adjust the relative quantities of r-currency and cash equivalents outstanding. The auction of cash equivalents by the member banking system extinguishes a corresponding quantity of r-currency and increases short-term interest rates. Such auctions can be analogized to open-market sales of Treasury bills by the Federal Reserve; the public relinquishes cash in exchange for near money, and the effect is contractionary. Reverse auctions have the opposite effect. In a reverse auction, member banks bid for cash equivalents— issuing r-currency in exchange—and the effect is expansionary.

The monetary authority might manage daily (or even more frequent) auctions or reverse auctions of cash equivalents by the member banking system. Such operations can be used to fine-tune monetary policy. Pricing in these operations, and in secondary market trading of cash equivalents, establishes the short-term yield curve. The monetary authority may choose to adopt one or more short-term interest rates as policy target(s). Monetary policy thus determines the relative quantities of r-currency and cash equivalents outstanding. Seigniorage fees, if implemented correctly, should make member banks more or less indifferent to this split, since they incur basically the same funding costs in any case.

"Extraordinary" Monetary Policy

What if member banks decline to augment the money supply despite having unused permit capacity? This situation, which some macroeconomists would call a "liquidity trap," presents a potential impediment to the monetary authority's ability to satisfy its macroeconomic policy mandate. If this situation were to arise, the monetary authority might consider taking extraordinary action. Specifically, it could temporarily reduce member banks' seigniorage fee rates below their actuarially fair levels. This measure would reduce member banks' funding costs and thereby reduce their required rate of return on new investments. At the margin, they would grow their balance sheets, and the result would be expansionary.

This extraordinary measure would come at a fiscal cost to the government in the form of lower seigniorage. (We might therefore think of it as a form of *fiscal* policy.) But the government presumably would incur this fiscal cost even if it were operating the entire monetary system by itself. After all, if member banks can't find credit investments with positive net present values, the monetary authority acting alone is unlikely to find them either.

The Central Bank

In theory the reformed monetary system could get along fine without a central bank. We have just seen that the monetary authority can conduct monetary policy without managing a balance sheet of its own.[19] In addition, other key functions of modern central banks should be rendered unnecessary. For example, clearing and settlement in the reformed system are effectuated through the sovereign credit/debit mechanism, with no need for a central bank. And member banks never need liquidity support from a central bank; they are *issuers* of fiat money.

Nonetheless, it would probably be wise to include a central bank in the system—certainly in the first instance. A central bank would help fine-tune monetary policy in ordinary times. It could also assist in the conduct of extraordinary monetary policy should the need arise. Note, however, that such a central bank would differ from today's central banks in a crucial respect. In the reformed system there is no base money/bank money distinction; central bank money has precisely the same legal and economic status as member bank money. A central bank in the reformed system, then, is just another member bank—one whose equity happens to be owned by the government.

Confining Money Creation (Herein of Unauthorized Banking)

We turn now to a discussion of what may be the most controversial aspect of the reformed monetary system: the general prohibition on money-claim issuance by entities other than member banks. In the introduction I referred to this species of restriction as the "first law of banking." If we're going to have a system of specially chartered banks, we need to answer a threshold question: Precisely what privilege does a banking charter convey?

This, I would argue, has been *the* central question of bank regulatory history. It is instructive to review some highlights from that history. Chapter 5 described the launch of US federal bank regulation with the National Bank Acts of 1863 and 1864. The National Bank Acts created a new class of federally chartered "national" banks that were authorized to issue a new form of paper money (national bank notes). With the creation of this system, Congress sought to federalize money creation; the system was intended to supplant, rather than supplement, money creation by state-chartered banks. Fatefully, though, Congress's chosen device to drive state banks out of existence was to impose a prohibitive tax on the *issuance of bank notes* by entities other than national banks.[20]

This story is well known to students of US banking history—a classic instance of financial regulatory arbitrage. Once the tax was enacted, state banks swiftly responded by changing the form of their monetary liabilities: they shifted from bank notes to checkable deposits. The significance of this shift was not appreciated at the time. Not until the turn of the twentieth century was there widespread recognition that deposit liabilities might

pose more or less the same policy problem as bank notes. According to a
US National Monetary Commission study in 1911,

> The increasing attention paid in recent years by the state legislatures to the
> regulation of the state banks . . . is to be accounted for primarily by a change
> of view as to the purpose of banking regulation. The antebellum state-bank
> regulations were intended to secure the safety of the bank note. Although the
> depositor was protected by many of the regulations, this protection was purely
> incidental. The view that note-issuing banks alone required governmental regu-
> lation persisted for a considerable time after the passage of the national-bank
> act [of 1864]. Since the national banks had a monopoly of the issue of bank
> notes, the regulation of state banks was considered needless. As the impor-
> tance of note issue as a banking function decreased, banking regulation, as seen
> in the national-bank act, began to be considered desirable as a protection to
> depositors.[21]

Amazingly, a similar sequence of events had already unfolded in
England. Soon after the founding of the Bank of England in 1694,
Parliament forbade any other entity in England, apart from small partnership banks consisting of six or fewer persons, to issue "bills or notes
payable at demand or at any less time than six months" from issuance.[22]
Subsequent acts of Parliament, such as the Banking Act of 1742, reaffirmed the prohibition:

> And to prevent any doubts that may arise concerning the privilege or power
> given by former acts of Parliament to [the Bank of England] of exclusive bank-
> ing, . . . it is hereby further enacted and declared . . . that it is the true intent and
> meaning of this act . . . that it shall not be lawful for any body politick or corpo-
> rate whatsoever, erected or to be erected, or for any other persons whatsoever,
> united or to be united in covenants or partnership, exceeding the number of six
> persons, in the part of Great Britain called England, to borrow, owe, or take up,
> any sum or sums of money on their bills or notes payable at demand, or at any
> less time than six months from the borrowing thereof.[23]

The practical effect of this prohibition was to confer on the Bank of
England a monopoly on issuing bank notes in London. Small partnership banks in London, while technically allowed to issue bank notes, could
not realistically compete with the Bank of England. (By contrast, *outside*
London—where the Bank of England had no branches—small partnership banks continued to issue bank notes.)[24] Deposit banks (as opposed to

note-issuing banks) did survive in London, but this was still a niche business in the eighteenth century. As Walter Bagehot observed many decades
later, "Our present system of deposit banking, in which no bills or promissory notes are issued, was not then known on a great scale, and was not
called banking."[25]

In the early nineteenth century, however, deposit banking began to
develop rapidly in London. Checkable deposits became more and more
popular as a means of payment, gradually supplanting bank notes. At that
point, Bagehot reports, "people began to inquire" why deposit banking in
London should be confined to small partnerships. Why not allow corporate (or "joint stock") deposit banks to operate in London, so long as they
did not issue bank notes? "And then it was seen," writes Bagehot, that the
law "only forb[ade] the issue of negotiable instruments, and not the receiving of money when no such instrument is given. Upon this construction . . . all our older joint stock banks were founded." This interpretation
was codified in 1833, when Parliament confirmed that joint-stock deposit
banks could be established in London and its vicinity so long as they did
not issue bank notes:

> Whereas doubts have arisen as to the construction of [previous] Acts, and as
> to the extent of [the Bank of England's] exclusive privilege; and it is expedient
> that all such doubts should be removed; be it therefore declared and enacted,
> that any body politic or corporate, or society, or company, or partnership,
> although consisting of more than six persons, may carry on the trade or busi-
> ness of banking in London . . . provided that such [entities] do not borrow, owe,
> or take up in England any sum or sums of money on their bills or notes payable
> on demand, or at any less time than six months from the borrowing thereof.[26]

The famous Peel's Act of 1844 reaffirmed the long-standing dichotomy
in English law between bank notes and deposits.[27] Peel's Act gave the
Bank of England an effective monopoly on bank note issuance throughout England; it provided for the eventual extinguishment of note issuance
by other banks. In keeping with long-standing English law, however, Peel's
Act imposed no similar limitation on deposit liabilities. Unsurprisingly, deposit banking flourished. According to one historical study, written in 1905,

> It is not easy nowadays to realize the position of the early joint stock banks. At
> the present time many of them overshadow the Bank of England itself in the
> amount of their deposits and the magnitude of their transactions. . . .

... Deposit banking, with its great facilities for economizing capital, has developed to a greater extent in England than in any other country, and this is to a large extent due to the fact that the London joint stock banks have been forbidden to issue notes, and have therefore exerted all their energies in fostering deposit banking, and that therefore cheques have to a large extent superseded notes in circulation.[28]

Thus, in both England and the United States, a formalistic distinction between bank notes and deposits had a pivotal influence on banking history. As economist Charles Dunbar wrote in 1917,

That governments have so frequently felt it their duty to take measures for the protection of the holders of bank-notes against the insolvency of the bank, but have so seldom legislated for the protection of depositors, is due to several reasons. Legislators have generally failed to perceive the similarity of the two kinds of liability, and the claim for equal consideration which can be made, with some show of reason, on behalf of depositors.[29]

To modern sensibilities, the policy failure Dunbar describes may seem like an elementary mistake. Checkable deposits are the *quintessential* monetary instrument in the modern world. Look at any modern textbook on money and banking or macroeconomics, and you will see bank money creation depicted as deposit creation. How could our predecessors have failed to recognize the functional equivalence of bank notes and checkable deposits? Why were they so caught up in bits of paper? Surely we have surpassed them in our understanding—surely modern thinking on money and banking is far more sophisticated.

But it really isn't. The rise of shadow banking represents yet another iteration of the same historical pattern. Yet again, a substitute form of money, pyramiding off existing money, came to prominence. Yet again, lawmakers and scholars only dimly perceived what was happening if they perceived it at all. In one conspicuous instance, money substitutes arose with regulators' blessing. The emergence of money market mutual funds (MMFs) in the 1970s and 1980s represented a deliberate end-run around the US deposit banking system, one that the Securities and Exchange Commission abetted by granting MMFs special exemptions from its standard investment company rules on portfolio valuation and redemptions.[30] In most cases, though, the emergence of money substitutes escaped attention. As we saw in chapter 1, the 1990s and 2000s witnessed explosive growth in all manner of cash equivalents. The phenomenon went virtually unnoticed in both academic and policy circles; the stability implications simply were not appreciated.

The emergence of shadow banking thus represents the continuation of a centuries-old problem. One might be tempted to conclude from this history that circumvention is inevitable—that the creation of money substitutes will always sidestep whatever legal rules are put in place. But I see no basis for such a sweeping and defeatist conclusion. The fact is that there has never been any *attempt* to devise a functional legal definition of what constitutes a monetary instrument. The history in this area is one of exasperating formalism. Lawmakers and scholars alike have shown a pervasive tendency to blindly follow existing institutional forms.

The challenge is to define what constitutes "money" for legal-institutional purposes. It is worth pointing out that this is a standard type of regulatory problem. By way of analogy, the first step of securities law is to define "security."[31] This is not exactly a straightforward matter. Students of securities regulation spend multiple class periods with this question; they learn that, according to the US Supreme Court, "in searching for the meaning and scope of the word 'security' in the [federal securities laws], form should be disregarded for substance and the emphasis should be on economic reality."[32] Similar problems of definition crop up in just about every area of economic regulation. In investment company regulation, "investment company" must be defined.[33] How to do so isn't obvious; lawyers refer to a gray zone in which a commercial firm can become an "inadvertent" investment company.[34] In insurance law, defining the "business of insurance" for regulatory purposes is notoriously tricky—yet we seem to do it tolerably well. Swaps regulation requires a definition of "swap";[35] proprietary trading regulation requires a definition of "proprietary trading";[36] antitrust law requires some notion of contracts "in restraint of trade."[37] In every case there are difficult questions of line drawing and interpretation, and there is always room for a certain amount of circumvention by market participants. Yet few would argue that such circumvention, in itself, calls into question the whole enterprise of economic regulation. If we allowed ourselves to be immobilized by these sorts of definitional problems, no economic regulation would ever get off the ground.

In the interest of concreteness, the appendix to this chapter offers draft statutory text for an "unauthorized banking" provision in the reformed monetary system. It is written in the style of US federal statutory law.

The provision is concise; it is only a few pages long. It lays out a general prohibition on a particular funding model. The provision specifies that only member banks may issue "money-claims" in meaningful quantities. Money-claims are defined as, basically, short-term debt instruments and their functional equivalents, subject to certain exclusions (such as trade credit). The maturity cutoff is one year. The provision also proscribes the issuance of "drawable facilities"—revolving credit facilities and their equivalents—by entities that are not member banks. Such facilities are functional substitutes for money-claims,[38] and they are susceptible to self-fulfilling runs.

The statutory text provides for certain de minimis exceptions, and it gives the monetary authority rulemaking powers for clarification and for preventing evasion. Like any legal text, the provision should be interpreted in light of its underlying purposes. In essence, it aims to prohibit the large-scale issuance, by anyone other than a member bank, of instruments that have the moneyness property described in chapter 1 (checkable deposits and their close substitutes). This moneyness property is an essential predicate to the coordination game described in chapter 2. And this coordination game, I argued in chapter 4, is a major source of macroeconomic disasters. The appendix discusses how the draft provision would treat several specific types of financial transactions that may be of interest to specialists, but these are just details. What I hope to illustrate is that confining money creation is neither conceptually nor practically different from other types of economic regulation.

The provision can be criticized as arbitrary—in particular, the one-year maturity cutoff. True enough, but all sorts of arbitrary lines must be drawn in any legal or regulatory system. As I noted in chapter 1, voting ages and statutes of limitation are arbitrary. The accounting definition of "cash equivalent" selects an arbitrary maturity cutoff of three months.[39] The exemption from registration under the federal securities laws for short-term debt selects an arbitrary maturity cutoff of nine months.[40] The Basel Committee has selected an arbitrary maturity cutoff of one year for its definition of "stable funding."[41] MMF portfolio securities are subject to an arbitrary maturity cutoff of 397 days.[42] In short, some arbitrariness has to be tolerated in the design of legal and regulatory systems. And bear in mind that arbitrary does not mean random. Chapter 1 offered reason to think that the moneyness of even the highest-quality debt securities is negligible at maturities above one year.

The provision also presents problems of detection and enforcement.

But again, this is no different from any other area of economic regulation. Enforcement against currency counterfeiters is challenging too. The same goes for insider traders, money launderers, price fixers, and tax evaders. In fact, when it comes to detection and enforcement, the unauthorized banking provision has a major advantage over these other areas. Banking is inherently a "law of large numbers" business, which makes it much more difficult for violators to operate secretly and thereby escape detection.

It may be useful to compare the practical difficulty of implementing the unauthorized banking statute with the practical difficulty of implementing capital regulation. The inherent challenges of capital regulation for complex institutions, particularly those with large derivatives businesses, were discussed in chapter 6. A prohibition on money-claim issuance is exponentially easier. Unlike capital regulation, the unauthorized banking statute does not rely on any *quantification* of risk exposures to feed into a ratio calculation. The quantification of such exposures is what makes capital regulation so vexing. As I noted in chapter 6, University of Chicago economist John Cochrane recently wrote that "detecting hidden run-prone financing . . . is an order of magnitude easier" than current forms of financial regulation, including capital regulation.[43] While I don't share Cochrane's overall prescriptions for financial reform, I wholeheartedly agree with him on this score.

During the Great Depression, another University of Chicago economist wrote about these very issues. Henry Simons—whose views on banking we also encountered in chapter 6—wrote in 1934 that "a major source of instability is . . . to be found in the widespread practice of borrowing at short term."[44] Two years later he wrote that "the economy becomes exposed to catastrophic disturbances as soon as short-term borrowing develops on a large scale."[45] Simons continued:

> Banking is a pervasive phenomenon, not something to be dealt with merely by legislation directed at what we call banks. The experience with the control of note issue is likely to be repeated in the future; many expedients for controlling similar practices may prove ineffective and disappointing because of the reappearance of prohibited practices in new and unprohibited forms. . . . But we perhaps approach insight when we conceive the problem broadly as that of achieving a financial structure in which the volume of short-term borrowing would be minimized, and in which only the government would be able to create (and destroy) either effective circulating media or [near monies].

Simons's insight on these matters was nothing short of astounding. Unfortunately, as we will see in the next chapter, modern financial regulation has been preoccupied with all sorts of other things.

The unauthorized banking provision discussed here is not conceptually radical. A banking license must convey *some* privilege; otherwise it is a meaningless scrap of paper. And a legal privilege logically entails a prohibition. Current law prohibits nonbanks from incurring "deposit" liabilities, but I hope it is apparent by now that the category "deposit" is formalistic and obsolete. The failure to specify a *functional* legal definition of what constitutes a monetary instrument is the original sin of banking law, and it is the main source of our current regulatory troubles.

International Dimensions

Suppose the US government were to implement the unauthorized banking statute just described. US domestic entities, apart from member banks, would be disallowed from issuing dollar-denominated money-claims in meaningful quantities. But what is to stop overseas entities from issuing such instruments outside the jurisdiction of US law? Couldn't the activity just migrate abroad?

This problem is not merely hypothetical. Today, overseas financial entities do in fact issue huge amounts of dollar-denominated cash equivalents. We encountered these instruments in chapter 1. They are called Eurodollars. They are often issued to US-based institutions, and the bulk of the proceeds is typically invested back into the US credit markets. This is classic fractional reserve banking—it is money creation. It involves issuing cash equivalents that are denominated in dollars, but it takes place outside the reach of US monetary and banking authorities.

This point may seem straightforward enough, but Milton Friedman thought it was sufficiently misunderstood that he devoted an entire article to explaining it.[46] "This point—that Euro-dollar institutions, like Chicago banks, are part of a fractional reserve banking system—is the key to understanding the Euro-dollar market," he wrote. "The failure to recognize it is the chief source of misunderstanding about the Euro-dollar market." According to Friedman, "the existence of the Euro-dollar market increases the total amount of dollar balances available to be held by nonbanks throughout the world for any given amount of money (currency plus deposits at Federal Reserve Banks) created by the Federal Reserve

System. It does so by permitting a greater pyramiding on this base by the use of deposits at U.S. banks as prudential reserves for Euro-dollar deposits."

The Eurodollar market is enormous. By my estimates (see figs. 1.1 and 1.2) it reached a peak size of $4.9 trillion in 2007, making Eurodollars the single largest category of dollar money-claims on the eve of the financial crisis—bigger even than insured deposits ($4.3 trillion) and short-term repo ($4.1 trillion). Like the rest of the private money markets, the Eurodollar market saw severe stress during the financial crisis. In response, the Federal Reserve provided a staggering $583 billion (peak level) in US dollar loans to *foreign* institutions to support their short-term dollar funding. It provided this support indirectly, through liquidity swaps with foreign central banks. These liquidity swaps were the single largest Fed facility in the crisis, as measured by peak levels.

It might be tempting to dismiss fragile Eurodollar funding as other countries' problem. This conclusion would be wrong. Recall the mechanics of the "panic crunch" from chapter 4. Financial institutions suddenly lose short-term dollar funding, and they dump dollar-denominated assets to meet redemptions. Prices of those assets fall; equivalently stated, their yields rise. These elevated yields then serve as the hurdle rate for new originations in the primary financing markets. The result is a sharp contraction in the supply of dollar financing. This mechanism does not respect national boundaries.

We saw an illustration of this dynamic in the second half of 2011, when Europe's sovereign debt crisis erupted. European banks experienced sudden large withdrawals of short-term dollar funding during that period. (A major source of redemptions was US MMFs, which were heavily exposed to Eurodollars.)[47] According to a recent study, in response to these dollar funding pressures, European banks sharply curtailed their *dollar* lending relative to their euro lending in the second half of 2011.[48] This might initially seem puzzling. Why didn't the affected banks just borrow euros instead, sell those euros for dollars in the spot market, make the same dollar loans as before, and simultaneously hedge the resulting foreign exchange risk in the forward market? (This combined spot/forward transaction is called an FX swap.) As the authors explain, this synthetic dollar funding strategy won't work if there is limited capital on the other side of the FX trade. And this appeared to be the case: synthetic dollar borrowing became strikingly expensive during the relevant period. So European banks abruptly cut back on dollar lending. The authors note that these overseas funding markets could pose a risk to "purely domestic U.S. borrowers" and hence to the US economy.

This issue, as much as any other, highlights the need for a basic reorientation of our thinking about financial stability regulation. Simply put, the Eurodollar markets—and the Eurocurrency markets more generally— are incompatible with financial stability. They present a serious risk of economic harm, but this risk has gone largely unrecognized. To a remarkable extent, the existence of these markets is taken for granted. They are widely seen as somehow essential to modern finance—as though foreign banks couldn't function properly without issuing enormous quantities of dollar-denominated cash equivalents.

Traditionally, money creation has been viewed as a matter of national sovereignty.[49] For reasons that are too obvious to mention, governments have a compelling interest in preventing the counterfeiting of their currencies beyond their borders. The US Treasury Department, working through the Secret Service, maintains significant overseas anticounterfeiting operations, in conjunction with local authorities.[50] And US law forbids the domestic creation or use of counterfeit *foreign* money.[51] It is self-evident, then, that a measure of international cooperation is required if monetary sovereignty is to be realized. But once it is accepted that money creation is a sovereign prerogative, why shouldn't the Eurocurrency markets be viewed as an abrogation of sovereignty? So ensconced are the Eurocurrency markets in modern finance that this question is virtually never asked. It is viewed as outside the range of acceptable discourse.

Let's address the topic head-on. Suppose a country (say, the United States) wanted to prevent foreign financial institutions from creating substitutes for its domestic currency. How might it go about it? There are two basic avenues. The first route would be for the United States to deny dollar clearing services to foreign institutions that are known issuers of dollar-denominated money-claims. To meet redemptions, a Eurodollar issuer must have a fractional reserve of "dollars," which will generally consist of a deposit account with a US correspondent bank that has access to the US payments system. Hence domestic law can have extraterritorial reach: foreign issuers of dollar-denominated money-claims could be denied access to such correspondent accounts. Essentially, they would be blacklisted from the dollar clearing system. The strategy I am describing here resembles existing US regulatory techniques for enforcing sanctions against foreign nations.

The second, more desirable route would be cooperative and multilat-

eral. Countries (or currency areas) would mutually agree to prohibit domestic financial institutions from issuing money-claims denominated in
nondomestic currencies. Money creation would be recognized as a sovereign prerogative; each country or currency area would have jurisdiction
over its own broad money supply. Lest this kind of international financial coordination seem unrealistic, keep in mind that the Basel capital
standards have been adopted by about 120 countries.[52] In principle, the
money-claim accord I am describing is no less feasible than a capital accord. Governments arguably have a far more compelling interest in establishing jurisdiction over their broad money supplies than in aligning
capital regulation across borders.[53]

To avoid any misunderstanding, let me emphasize that the step I am
describing here is really quite narrow. I am not saying that overseas financial institutions should be restricted in any way from owning or dealing in
dollar-denominated securities—far from it. This has nothing to do with
capital controls. Nor am I saying that foreign institutions should be restricted in any way from accessing dollar financing in the longer-term
debt and equity capital markets. Nor am I saying that foreign central
banks should be restricted or discouraged in any way from owning dollar-
denominated assets. Nor, for that matter, am I expressing any objection to
foreign institutions' owning equity interests in chartered US banks. Such
ownership is entirely compatible with monetary sovereignty, and it would
pose no problem in the reformed monetary system. The step I am describing is far more modest and narrowly tailored. It relates to the activity of
overseas money *creation*—money-claim issuance—and nothing else.

Getting There from Here

I have emphasized that the reformed system bears a close resemblance
to our existing US system of money and banking. Consider the following parallels (citations to relevant existing law were given in the notes
above). Today, deposit banks have special charters that permit them to
issue monetary instruments styled as "deposits." Other entities are legally
prohibited from issuing such instruments. Most deposits are federally insured; they are sovereign money. Deposit banks are subject to strict portfolio constraints that mostly confine them to diversified portfolios of
credit assets. They must abide by equity capital requirements. They must
submit to a supervisory regime. They are subject to strict limitations on

affiliate transactions. They pay risk-based fees to the state through the deposit insurance system. When a deposit bank's capital is impaired, the government places it into a special insolvency system under which insured deposits are seamlessly honored while the entity's portfolio is monetized in satisfaction of the government's senior claim. Current law prohibits any one deposit bank from gaining control (through acquisitions) of more than 10% of outstanding insured deposits. The monetary authority enjoys a high degree of administrative independence. All these features are present in the reformed system. Even the reformed system's most seemingly exotic feature—the cap and trade approach to managing the money supply—finds a direct analogue in the current deposit banking system. Cash reserve requirements (not to be confused with capital requirements) play a very similar role, at least when they are binding. As Jeremy Stein has written, under a system of reserve requirements, central bank reserves function as "tradable permits" for "private money creation."[54]

The reformed system thus embodies many of the core features of our familiar deposit banking regime. It relies on institutional technologies that have been in active use for many decades, and it could be implemented through a series of incremental reforms. Specifically, the following measures would get us to a pretty close approximation of the reformed system:

- Enact the unauthorized banking law described above, or something like it.
- Apply reserve requirements to all the money-claims (inclusive of deposits) issued by the deposit bank sector, thereby placing an adjustable cap on the broad money supply.
- Fully insure (with no coverage caps) all of deposit banks' outstanding money-claims (and *only* their money-claims—terminate insurance of long-term certificates of deposit).
- Charge risk-based fees to the deposit banking sector for this public backstop, and keep charging such fees even if the FDIC's insurance fund is fully funded (at which point the fees would become a fiscal revenue item).
- Reinstate administrative controls over interest on deposit banks' monetary liabilities.
- Tighten up existing deposit bank portfolio constraints—most important, implement a swaps push-out rule (see chapter 8).
- Supplement the existing Basel accord with an international accord that prohibits financial institutions from issuing money-claims denominated in nondomestic currencies.

These steps are far from revolutionary. The reformed system is essentially conservative in its basic design. It would modernize the current US system along functional lines.

Today's chartered deposit banks would be grandfathered into the reformed monetary system as member banks. They would find the reformed system quite familiar and largely congenial. Nonbank financial firms are another matter; they would have to comply with the new unauthorized banking statute. Again, this requirement should not be viewed as radical. Nonbanks are already prohibited from financing themselves with "deposit" liabilities. The proposed unauthorized banking statute merely updates this traditional prohibition. That the provision would mean big changes for Wall Street's current funding model only goes to show how far money creation has bypassed our system of sovereign control.

At this time, the major Wall Street firms have meaningfully extended the duration of their liabilities relative to the precrisis years. While this shift is welcome, it should not be seen as a permanent institutional change. Rather, as Stein has pointed out, this shift is largely a consequence of the availability today of historically cheap long-term debt financing—cheapness that he attributes in significant measure to the Federal Reserve's unconventional monetary policies of recent years.[55] This financing shift should not be expected to persist when interest rates return to a more typical configuration. It would obviously be a mistake to interpret a temporary fluctuation as a permanent structural change.

It is sometimes suggested that securities firms and other nonbank financial firms "need" to fund themselves with short-term debt—that they somehow can't conduct their businesses otherwise. This argument needs to be put to rest. There is nothing about these firms' business models that requires unstable short-term funding. Securities firms could conduct all their current activities while financing themselves entirely in the capital markets, with equity and longer-term debt. Naturally their cost of financing would go up to some degree, reducing their profits; but so what? Nothing fundamental need change. Short-term wholesale funding is prevalent in the financial sector not because it is "necessary" or even "important," but merely because it is relatively cheap.

To be sure, the unauthorized banking statute would have costs. Bid-ask spreads in at least some segments of the financial markets would probably go up, and trading would therefore get somewhat more expensive. Hedge funds would see higher prime brokerage borrowing rates, lowering their returns. And it is possible, though by no means assured, that consumers and nonfinancial businesses would see higher overall financing rates. But all these costs are a natural incident to removing distortive subsidies from the financial sector. Removing a subsidy is always costly to its ultimate beneficiaries, but this is hardly a reason to keep the subsidy. Finally, costs must be weighed against benefits. If panics are a preeminent source of deep recessions, the benefits of panic-proofing would be immense.

*   *   *

There may at first seem to be a tension between my claim that our existing system of money and banking has serious flaws and my claim that no radical reform is needed. But these positions are easily reconciled. By way of analogy, an otherwise sound computer program may be rendered crash-prone by a few lines of corrupt code. I believe we are tantalizingly close to a *good* system of money and banking. As we are about to see, though, recent reforms are taking us in a different direction.

Appendix to Chapter 9: Proposed "Unauthorized Banking" Statute

This appendix offers statutory text for the unauthorized banking statute in the reformed monetary system. The draft is intended as a starting point for discussion. I discuss some implications below.

SECTION IOI. UNAUTHORIZED BANKING.

(a) DEFINITIONS.—In this section, the following definitions shall apply:

    (1) MONEY-CLAIM.—The term "money-claim" means:

        (A) any debt instrument that is payable in cash or its equivalent and that has a maturity of less than one year, including any such instrument that is styled as a "deposit";

        (B) any sale and repurchase agreement that functionally resembles the instruments described in paragraph (A);

        (C) any equity instrument that functionally resembles the instruments described in paragraph (A); and

        (D) any other financial instrument or arrangement, regardless of form, that functionally resembles the instruments described in paragraph (A), provided that in no instance shall the term "money-claim" include:

(i)   trade credit; or

(ii) any obligation to deliver cash or its equivalent that is held on a custodial basis.

(2) DRAWABLE FACILITY.—The term "drawable facility" means:

(A) any instrument, including any revolving credit facility, pursuant to which one party has an effective option to borrow cash or its equivalent from another party (the issuer of the facility) on an ongoing basis; and

(B) any other financial instrument or arrangement, regardless of form, that functionally resembles those described in paragraph (A).

(3) TRADE CREDIT.—The term "trade credit" means:

(A) any payment obligation that is incurred as an incident to the purchase of bona fide goods or services, including any such obligation that is classifiable as "accounts payable" under generally accepted accounting principles as in effect on the date of enactment of this section; and

(B) any ordinary settlement obligation that is incurred as an incident to the purchase of one or more financial or nonfinancial assets.

(4) MATURITY.—The term "maturity" means the length of the period from the original issuance of an instrument until earliest to occur of:

(A) the original stated date on which the principal amount is to be repaid, provided that if the principal is to be amortized or otherwise paid in installments, then the weighted average of the principal repayment dates shall be deemed to be the date on which the principal amount is to be repaid;

(B) in the case of an instrument with an embedded put option or other demand feature, the earliest date on which any substantial portion of the principal amount can be recovered through demand;

(C) in the case of an instrument that is designed to provide investor liquidity through a periodic auction process, the date of the earliest auction; and

(D) in the case of an instrument that has been called for redemption or prepayment, in whole or in part, the date on which the earliest redemption payment or prepayment is to be made, provided that the maturity of such an instrument shall continue to be determined in accordance with paragraph (A) if the issuer did not intend as of the issuance date to exercise such early redemption or prepayment.

(5) PERSON.—The term "person" means any person, firm, corporation, association, or other similar organization.

(b) PROHIBITION.—Except as hereinafter provided, it shall be unlawful for any
     person to issue or have outstanding any (1) money-claims or (2) drawable
     facilities.

(c) EXEMPTIONS.—The restrictions under subsection (b) shall not apply to:

     (1) any member bank;

     (2) any person (A) whose issued and outstanding money-claims are held by
          not more than five other persons and (B) whose issued and outstanding
          drawable facilities are held by not more than five other persons; or

     (3) any person whose issued and outstanding money-claims, when combined
          with drawn amounts under the person's issued and outstanding draw-
          able facilities, do not exceed $1,000,000 in the aggregate.

(d) RULEMAKING.—The monetary authority may prescribe such rules and regu-
     lations, including definitions of terms, as it deems necessary to effectuate the
     purposes and to prevent evasions of this section.

(e) PENALTIES.—Any person who willfully violates any of the provisions of this
     section shall upon conviction be fined not more than $250,000 or imprisoned
     not more than five years, or both, and any officer, director, employee, or agent
     of any person who knowingly participates in any such violation shall be pun-
     ished by a like fine or imprisonment or both.

*   *   *

How would the provisions above affect existing financial arrangements?
Here I briefly address some specific applications.

Puttable Bonds

The money-claim definition encompasses bonds with embedded put options that are exercisable within one year of original issuance. The definition does not encompass bonds with issuer prepayment options (callable
bonds), which generally are of no concern unless the issuer uses the call
feature in such a way as to create functional equivalents for money-claims
(paragraph (a)(4)(D) addresses this possibility).

Money Market Mutual Funds

The money-claim definition encompasses shares of MMFs whose net asset
values (NAVs) are "fixed" (see paragraph (a)(1)(C)). Whether MMFs
with *floating* NAVs would fly would depend on whether their shares were

deemed to "functionally resemble" short-term debt instruments. This is an area in which rulemaking by the monetary authority would probably be appropriate. Note that, in any case, the universe of permissible investments for such MMFs would consist exclusively of *sovereign* instruments, since the private instruments that MMFs invest in today would no longer exist.

Commercial Paper

The money-claim definition encompasses commercial paper. So, under the provision above, neither financial nor commercial/industrial firms would be allowed to finance themselves with commercial paper, subject to the exemptions set forth in the statute. It is important to keep in mind that, contrary to widespread belief, nonfinancial commercial paper is a trivial market. It is not an important source of financing for corporate America today (see chapter 1). Commercial paper issued by midsize companies could be accommodated under a de minimis exception.

Prime Brokerage

Prime brokerage credit consists of loans from Wall Street securities firms to hedge funds. The money-claim definition encompasses prime brokerage credit in which the lender has the option to withdraw funding within one year of inception, as is usually the case. Even so, the provision would allow a hedge fund—or anyone else for that matter—to borrow unlimited amounts on a short-term basis from up to five lenders.[56] This exemption means that most hedge funds' current borrowing practices need not change in any material respect. Note that prime brokers *themselves* would no longer enjoy money market funding in this system. For this reason, hedge funds' borrowing costs should be expected to increase. Free credit balances (demandable debt that securities firms owe to hedge funds) would not be permissible under the statute, but securities firms can always hold cash for customers on a custodial basis.

Securities Lending

The money-claim definition does *not* encompass securities lending transactions, because securities loans are not "payable in cash or its equivalent." The unauthorized banking provision therefore has no direct implications for loans of securities. It does, however, have implications for collateral management practices in securities lending transactions. A securities borrower typically posts cash collateral with the securities lender. The securities lender invests the collateral and is obligated to return cash to the securities borrower when the security is returned. The securities *lender* is therefore the *issuer* of a money-claim, and such transactions fall within the prohibition. The unauthorized banking provision would therefore require changes in current collateral practices in securities lending. Specifically, securities lenders would be required to hold cash collateral on a custodial basis rather than investing it. As a result, costs of securities borrowing (and therefore of nonsynthetic shorting) should be expected to increase somewhat.

Derivatives

Generally speaking, the money-claim definition does *not* encompass derivatives. Forwards, futures, options, swaps, and related instruments are contingent claims and therefore do not typically resemble debt instruments. That said, derivatives can obviously be used as building blocks to create functional equivalents for debt instruments. A sale and repurchase agreement (repo) is precisely such an instrument: it is the sale of a security coupled with a forward purchase of the same security. The money-claim definition above specifically covers repos (see paragraph (a)(1)(B)). But other types of circumvention are possible, and it may be necessary for the monetary authority to adopt rules to prevent avoidance through derivative transactions. The monetary authority should be on high alert whenever market participants begin to lobby accounting authorities to classify any given class of instruments as "cash equivalents" for accounting purposes (as was the case with auction-rate securities and variable-rate demand notes in the mid-2000s).

CHAPTER TEN

Financial Reform Revisited

We have involved ourselves in a colossal muddle, having blundered in the control of a delicate machine, the working of which we do not understand.—John Maynard Keynes, 1930[1]

At the start of this book, and several times thereafter, I referred to a prevailing view on financial instability. The prevailing view sees instability as an intrinsic feature of financial capitalism. It views panics— widespread redemptions of defaultable monetary instruments—as just one part of a much broader set of problems, often grouped under a generic label like "systemic risk." The prevailing view does not see a close connection between financial stability policy and monetary system design. Indeed, it seldom recognizes any connection at all.[2]

Recent US reforms have been a product of the prevailing view. And it is easy to see how that view might lend itself to a sprawling regulatory apparatus. After all, if systemic risk can arise in unexpected places—including (perhaps even especially) the outer reaches of modern finance—then our regulatory structure needs to measure up to the challenge. Perceived risks multiply, and regulations multiply alongside. In the wake of the recent crisis, we have created a financial regulatory system of staggering scale and complexity.

Yet, despite this regulatory proliferation, unstable funding structures have remained largely unscathed. Indeed, it is no exaggeration to say that "free banking" remains official policy in the United States today. That is to say, even after the reforms of recent years, money creation remains a right, not a privilege. The distinctive, fragile funding model of banking still requires no special license; the activity of money-claim issuance is characterized by free entry.

This concluding chapter offers a critique of the current direction of US financial stability policy and of the prevailing view that underlies it. The focus is on the United States, but the thrust of the critique applies to other jurisdictions too. I argue that modern financial regulation is trying to do far too much, and there is a very real danger that it will fail in its central mission of fending off future economic disasters. I also make the (provocative) case that implementing the reformed monetary system could pave the way for a substantial reduction in *other* forms of financial stability regulation. I end the book with some final thoughts on the legal engineering of monetary institutions.

"Systemic Risk" and Regulatory Complexity

This book has defended the position that, when it comes to financial stability policy, panics are the main problem—at least insofar as financial stability policy is about preventing macroeconomic disasters. Even if one accepts this position, one might not favor panic-proofing as a regulatory solution. We might instead leave run-prone funding structures intact while taking aim at the sorts of things that *trigger* panics. For example, if panics are virtually always precipitated by one or more financial "excesses"— say, debt-fueled bubbles that burst—then panics can be avoided by preventing such excesses from emerging.

The trouble with this indirect strategy can be illustrated with an analogy. A village sits at the base of a hill that is prone to damaging landslides. Landslides are triggered only by rainstorms. What might the villagers do to limit future landslide damage? One option would be to try somehow to prevent rainstorms, the triggering event. But this option might be unaffordable or impossible, and it might also have terrible side effects. A better option would be to target the hillside directly, by removing soil, erecting barriers, and so on. The seemingly obvious point is that focusing on triggering events can lead to bad policies. There is a natural human tendency to trace causal chains backward in search of more "fundamental" causes. In policy analysis, though, this instinct needs to be resisted. Intervening earlier in the causal chain isn't necessarily better.

Much of recent financial stability policy has been akin to preventing rainstorms. Instead of taking dead aim at fragile funding structures, policy has been mostly preoccupied with issues that are widely thought to be more "fundamental." Various excesses that are supposedly endemic to finance—excessive leverage, excessive risk taking, "overheating" markets, and other "systemic" risks—are widely seen as the primary evils. The result has been a tsunami of new legal requirements dealing with derivatives, securitization, proprietary trading, capital buffers, stress tests, credit ratings, and on and on.

Historically, major US banking legislation has been admirably concise. In chapter 5 we looked at what I called the three major phases in US banking history, corresponding to three landmark banking laws. The first of these, the National Bank Act of 1864,[3] was 19 pages long. The second, the Federal Reserve Act of 1913,[4] went to 24 pages. The third, the Banking Act of 1933[5]—which established the famous Glass-Steagall separation as well as deposit insurance—clocked in at 33 pages. The Dodd-Frank Act of 2010[6] is of a different order of magnitude. It consists of 848 pages of statutory text, the bulk of them dealing with financial stability regulation. And this is only the tip of the iceberg. Dodd-Frank includes 390 total rulemaking requirements for financial regulators, most relating to financial stability.[7] As of the five-year anniversary of Dodd-Frank's enactment, only 63% of these rulemakings had been met with finalized rules. The delays have not been for lack of effort; the burden on regulators has been extreme. By my calculations, final rule releases under Dodd-Frank are on track to occupy over 15,000 pages in the *Federal Register*.

Admittedly, page counts and numbers of rulemakings are imperfect measures of regulatory scope and complexity. However, more impressionistic assessments tell the same story. Legal practitioners who specialize in financial regulation will tell you the situation has gotten completely out of hand. Some regulators will tell you they are overworked, discouraged, and unsure of the value being produced. Law teachers (like me) will tell you financial regulation has become nearly impossible to teach in a comprehensive and rigorous way. The volume and technical complexity of the material is stunning, and it grows by the month. Financial regulation has suddenly morphed into a hyperspecialized field.

The very concept of systemic risk invites this kind of regulatory proliferation. The concept is inherently vague. For several years now, a great deal of effort has gone into devising ways to measure and monitor systemic risk. Such initiatives garner excitement in some corners of the regulatory and academic worlds. For now, though, no such measure has caught on, and systemic risk remains in the eye of the beholder. The specter of systemic risk thus operates as a kind of freestanding justification for more regulation. It offers no limiting principle and no way to prioritize among perceived problems.

But hasn't financial stability policy taken some meaningful steps toward "hillside stabilization"—dealing *directly* with unstable short-term debt structures? Two such regulatory initiatives deserve special mention. First, the Securities and Exchange Commission has enacted new regulations for money market mutual funds, including enhanced portfolio constraints as well as a requirement that institutional (as opposed to retail) prime MMFs "float" their share prices.[8] Second, US bank regulators have promulgated new Basel liquidity regulations for the largest financial institutions, which will require such firms to hold enough "high-quality liquid assets" to meet expected outflows under a thirty-day stress scenario.[9]

These and related initiatives are commendable, but they need to be kept in perspective: they do not come close to solving the panic problem. Take the MMF reforms first. Enhanced portfolio constraints are all well and good, but we saw in chapter 6 that portfolio constraints are an unreliable safeguard against panics. This is particularly true for institutions like MMFs that maintain virtually no equity capital. As for floating share prices, they are no panacea either; European MMFs with floating share prices have proved susceptible to runs.[10] In spite of recent reforms, then, the MMF sector remains a serious threat to the US economy. And the Treasury Department's authority to provide a blanket guarantee to the MMF industry—arguably the single most important emergency policy measure in the recent crisis—no longer exists. The legal basis for the program has been revoked.[11]

The new Basel liquidity rules for big financial firms have similar shortcomings. These rules are technical and complicated. They presuppose that it is possible to specify in advance what sorts of assets can be easily liquidated in a panic. How confident should we be in this capacity? Apart from the highest-quality sovereign securities, it isn't clear that *any* assets can be reliably sold at little or no discount in a severe panic. (This brings to mind Keynes's remark: "Of the maxims of orthodox finance none, surely, is more anti-social than the fetish of liquidity, the doctrine that it is a positive virtue on the part of investment institutions to concentrate their resources upon the holding of 'liquid' securities. It forgets that there is no such thing as liquidity of investment for the community as a whole.")[12] In addition, the new liquidity rules have a gaping exception: they treat "matched book" repo—short-term debt funding that securities firms provide to hedge funds—as "high-quality liquid assets."[13] Calling these loans in a panic will mean suddenly withdrawing financing from hedge funds on a large scale. Hedge funds will have to dump assets to meet these prime brokerage calls. The result will be a damaging financing crunch—the very thing we want to avoid.

More generally, by dealing with particular institutional forms in piece-meal fashion, we run a very real danger of repeating the classic mistake of banking history, discussed in the previous chapter. Recall that, in centuries past, lawmakers in both the United States and England focused on confining the issuance of *bank notes* to a special set of chartered banks. They failed to recognize the functional equivalence of bank notes and checkable deposits. Today we are again failing to deal with money creation comprehensively and functionally. Both issuers and holders of cash equivalents should be expected to adjust to the new rules in all sorts of ways. For example, according to one report, Boeing Inc. "has already moved cash into separately managed accounts in anticipation of the new [MMF] rules."[14] If cash parkers respond to the new MMF rules by disintermediating MMFs and going directly to the (runnable) private money markets, we aren't making much progress from a stability standpoint. If you squeeze the balloon in just one or two places, it will expand elsewhere.[15]

But isn't there still a case for using a lighter touch to fragile funding than I have proposed? Perhaps the financial sector's short-term debt can be fine-tuned to some optimal level through taxation or regulation. To be sure, fine-tuning approaches are attractive in some domains—those in which risks can be gauged with relatively high precision and in which outcomes fall along a fairly smooth continuum. But this setting isn't like that. The risk of a panic can't be gauged with any precision; this is *inherently* true if panics have a self-fulfilling dimension. And outcomes are discontinuous—a panic is a discrete and extremely costly event. In such settings, fine-tuning isn't realistic, and structural approaches hold more appeal. The idea that skilled technocrats can somehow manage systemic risks to an acceptable level, as if turning dials on a complex machine, is a persistent one in the recent financial reform literature. This mindset diverts energy from structural solutions.

In a 2013 speech, William Dudley, president of the Federal Reserve Bank of New York, asked, "How comfortable should we be with a system in which critical financial activities continue to be financed with short-term wholesale funding without the safeguards necessary to reduce the risk of runs and the fire sales of assets that can threaten the stability of the entire financial system?" His answer: "I don't think we should be comfortable" with such a system. Yet, he noted, that is the system we have—

even after the financial reforms of recent years. "We have not come close to fixing all the institutional flaws in our wholesale funding markets," Dudley remarked.[16] Three months later, Federal Reserve governor Daniel Tarullo addressed the same topic. Tarullo did not mince words. "I strongly believe that we would do the American public a fundamental disservice were we to declare victory [over financial instability] without tackling the structural weaknesses of short-term wholesale funding markets, both in general and as they affect the too-big-to-fail problem," Tarullo said. "This is the major problem that remains, and I would suggest that additional reform measures be evaluated by reference to how effective they could be in solving it." While he noted that "there is not yet a blueprint" for dealing with these markets, Tarullo emphasized the need for policy measures that "appl[y] more or less comprehensively to all uses of short-term wholesale funding, without regard to the form of the transactions or whether the borrower was a prudentially regulated institution."[17] Not much has changed since these two speeches. No one can plausibly claim we have addressed run-prone funding in a comprehensive and structural way.

Resolution Authority and Its Limitations

In the fall of 2008, systemically important nonbank financial institutions (nonbank SIFIs) that were on the verge of failure faced a binary situation: bankruptcy or bailout. From a policy standpoint, neither option was attractive. On the one hand, the bankruptcy of Lehman Brothers set off a devastating chain reaction. On the other hand, the bailout of AIG, the giant insurance company, was appalling: it both exemplified and reinforced too big to fail.

An alternative was needed. Specifically, most experts agreed on the need for a "resolution authority," or special insolvency system, for nonbank SIFIs. Dodd-Frank created such a resolution authority, called the Orderly Liquidation Authority (OLA). Its goal is ambitious. As set forth in the statute, OLA is designed "to provide the necessary authority to liquidate failing financial companies that pose a significant risk to the financial stability of the United States in a manner that mitigates such risk and minimizes moral hazard."[18] OLA is probably the single most important financial stability component of Dodd-Frank. It holds significant promise in certain respects, as I explain below. Nonetheless, it is important to understand OLA's limitations. OLA does not offer a plausible answer to the panic problem, nor does it address the other problems associated with our current system of private money creation (shadow banking).

To appreciate OLA's promise—as well as its limits—it is useful to look briefly at the system OLA was patterned on: the FDIC's long-standing resolution system for insured deposit banks. The FDIC's "Resolutions Handbook" describes the origins of the latter system this way:

> To understand why the U.S. Congress gave the FDIC the powers it has, it is nec-essary to look at the structure of the banking industry and the conditions of the 1930s. The FDIC was created in 1933 to halt a banking crisis. Nine thousand banks—a third of the banking industry in the United States at that time—failed in the four years before the FDIC was established....
>
> In general practice, between 1865 and 1933, depositors of national and state banks were treated in the same way as other creditors—they received funds from the liquidation of the bank's assets *after* those assets were liquidated. On average, it took about six years at the federal level to liquidate a failed bank's assets, to pay the depositors, and to close the bank's books—although in at least one instance this process took 21 years. Even when depositors did ultimately receive their funds, the amounts were significantly less than they had originally deposited into the banks.... Given the long delays in receiving any money and the significant risk in getting their deposits back, it was understandable why anxious depositors withdrew their savings at any hint of problems. With the wave of banking failures that began in 1929, it became widely recognized that the lack of liquidity that resulted from the process for resolving bank failures contributed significantly to the economic depression in the United States.[19]

As the Handbook notes, Congress responded to these problems by, among other things, creating deposit insurance and granting the FDIC special powers to resolve failed banks.

This policy response was broadly successful. With the FDIC's creation, deposit bank failures became much less disruptive. But the starring role in this story clearly belongs not to the bank resolution/receivership system per se, *but to deposit insurance*. Resolution plays only a supporting role. Bear in mind that corporate bankruptcy is fundamentally incompatible with deposit insurance. Bankruptcy imposes an automatic stay on creditor claims and impairs them if there isn't enough value to go around. Deposit insurance requires exactly the opposite—insured deposits must be hon-ored seamlessly and in full. Special resolution machinery is therefore essential if deposit insurance is to fulfill its purpose. But it would be a mistake to conflate these two distinct functions. To quote the Handbook, "The FDIC as receiver is functionally and legally separate from the FDIC acting ... as deposit insurer, and the FDIC as receiver has separate rights, duties, and obligations from those of the FDIC as insurer. Courts have long recognized these dual and separate capacities."[20]

With this discussion as a backdrop, consider OLA. OLA is a complex tool, and how it will work in practice remains uncertain. But we can gain some clarity by asking a basic question: How will OLA treat the money-claim liabilities of nonbank financial firms? Are they in the position of insured deposits, certain to be honored in full and on time? The answer is clearly no. OLA does not create a liability insurance system. Money-claims of firms that go into OLA remain susceptible to default.

It is true that money-claims *may* be honored fully and seamlessly within OLA. The FDIC intends to pursue an OLA implementation strategy called "single point of entry" (SPOE).[21] Under SPOE, the FDIC will take into receivership only the top-tier holding company of a failing financial institution. The firm will be recapitalized by wiping out equity and writing down debt at the parent company level. The subsidiaries will remain open and operating and will continue to honor all their obligations, presumably with public liquidity support. As a result, under SPOE, money-claim liabilities that reside at the operating subsidiary level are to be honored in accordance with their terms.

But what if the failing financial institution doesn't have enough loss-absorbing capacity at the holding company level? In that case SPOE won't work, and losses must be borne by operating subsidiaries. "If there are circumstances under which the losses cannot be fully absorbed by the holding company's shareholders and creditors, then the subsidiaries with the greatest losses would have to be placed into receivership, exposing those subsidiar[ies'] creditors ... to loss," notes the FDIC. "Creditors, including uninsured depositors, of operating subsidiaries therefore should not expect with certainty that they would be protected from loss in the event of financial difficulties."[22] Top practitioners share this understanding. Rodgin Cohen of Sullivan & Cromwell recently said that, if losses are substantial enough, "there will be multiple points of entry."[23]

So what happens to money-claimants of operating subsidiaries in the *multiple* point of entry scenario? Notably, the OLA legislation gives the FDIC the power to make "additional payments" to third parties if certain conditions are met.[24] In theory this power could be used to promptly honor the money-claim liabilities of insolvent operating subsidiaries in OLA receivership—in effect, prioritizing money-claimants over long-term creditors. However, even if short-term claims are seamlessly honored with additional payments, the FDIC is required to claw back such additional payments if it can't recoup its outlays in any given resolution.[25] This creates a strong incentive for money-claimants to run before OLA receivership is initiated. What's more, the FDIC has indicated that short-term creditors will practically never be eligible for such payments in the first place:

> Short-term debt holders ... are highly unlikely to meet the criteria set forth in the statute for permitting payment of additional amounts. In virtually all cases, creditors with shorter-term claims on the covered financial company will receive the same pro rata share of their claim that is being provided to the long-term debt holders. Accordingly, a potential credit provider to a company subject to the Dodd-Frank resolution process should have no expectation of treatment that differs depending upon whether it lends for a period of over 360 days or for a shorter term.[26]

To drive home the point, the FDIC asked for public comment on the following question: "Are there additional ways to counteract any impression that shorter term debt is not at risk?" This is obviously a far cry from the FDIC's posture toward insured deposits. FDIC officials are fond of emphasizing that no depositor has ever lost a penny of insured deposits since the FDIC's creation in 1933.

Even if the FDIC decides it *wants* to seamlessly honor money-claim liabilities of operating subsidiaries under the multiple point of entry scenario, it still faces a problem: the mechanics of liquidity support present significant execution risks. Day-one funding needs for a failing SIFI in OLA could be in the hundreds of billions of dollars. The Federal Reserve is explicitly prohibited by statute from lending to an institution that is in insolvency proceedings, including OLA.[27] The Dodd-Frank statutory scheme contemplates that the FDIC will borrow the necessary funds from Treasury, which in turn must borrow them from the bond market.[28] But Treasury's borrowing capacity is limited by the statutory debt ceiling, and lifting it requires congressional action.[29] This risk is hardly trivial; the debt ceiling needed to be increased in *both* of the major pieces of crisis-response legislation enacted in the second half of 2008.[30] To get around this problem, the FDIC might guarantee bond offerings by the failing institution itself. This would sidestep debt ceiling issues, but note that such bonds wouldn't be "full faith and credit" securities. Market appetite may therefore be limited—and we are talking here about a bond offering of potentially unprecedented size, to be executed on an absurdly compressed time frame and under presumably distressed market conditions. Nothing like this has ever been done before.

Thus, whether money-claims will be honored under OLA may depend crucially on whether the SPOE strategy is pursued in any given case. And the viability of SPOE, in turn, depends on the failing institution's corporate structure. As the FDIC has stressed, for the strategy to work, "it is critical that the top-tier holding company maintain a sufficient amount of equity and unsecured debt."[31] Similarly, Daniel Tarullo has said that, for SPOE to work, the holding company must be kept "non-operational and otherwise 'clean' through limits on the issuance of short-term debt and on the conduct of material business operations in the parent holding company."[32] Tarullo indicated that the Federal Reserve intends to require that SIFIs maintain "a minimum amount of long-term, unsecured debt at the parent holding company" to facilitate SPOE.[33] Keep in mind, though, that no one contemplates that any such requirement will be made coextensive with the set of firms that issue money-claims. Rather, the requirement will apply exclusively to SIFIs. (The panic phenomenon bears no necessary connection to SIFIs; there were no SIFIs in the United States in the early 1930s.)

And here we reach the critical limitation of OLA—and of resolution more generally—as a panic-avoidance device. Recall again why deposit insurance works so well. Insured depositors know with certainty that their claims will be seamlessly honored no matter what. By contrast, notwithstanding OLA, money-claimants of nonbanks can have no such assurance ex ante. There is no way to be sure that any given nonbank financial institution will enter OLA if it fails. Bankruptcy is the default option, and activating OLA requires the approval of not only supermajorities of the boards of the FDIC and the Fed but also the Treasury secretary in consultation with the president.[34] This is an extraordinary procedural hurdle, one that bears no resemblance to deposit bank resolution. (FDIC resolution is the *exclusive* insolvency system for deposit banks, and its operation requires no executive branch approval.) Moreover, even if a firm does enter OLA, whether SPOE will be followed is determined case by case. Money-claimants have little to gain from sticking around to find out the answer. We have seen that they are informationally insensitive; they generally do not conduct significant fundamental analysis. When they detect anything more than a minuscule probability of default, their incentives are to withdraw first and ask questions later. The bank game is therefore in effect, and the bad equilibrium can be realized on a broad scale. To sum up: notwithstanding OLA, the US financial system's short-term debt remains defaultable and therefore susceptible to catastrophic panics.

Some financial policy experts are fond of "constructive ambiguity," or leaving financial markets uncertain about what claims (if any) will be honored in a crisis. The idea seems to be that we can have it both ways—we can achieve systemic protection ex post while allowing market discipline to operate ex ante. This is a dubious policy strategy. If the market perceives a meaningful risk of money-claim defaults, it is probably because that risk actually exists. By the same token, a policy of honoring money-claims may be self-defeating if the market doesn't have confidence that it will materialize. As usual, Walter Bagehot said it best: "To lend a great deal, and yet not give the public confidence that you will lend sufficiently and effectually, is the worst of all policies; but it is the policy now pursued."[35] With constructive ambiguity, policymakers risk fooling only themselves.[36]

OLA does offer something important that we lacked before. In some circumstances it may offer a way to extinguish equity and impair long-term unsecured debt of SIFIs without triggering disastrous consequences. The SPOE strategy is particularly promising in this regard; it permits decoupling long-term financing at the holding company level from operating liabilities. Before OLA that wasn't realistically possible, and this contribution should not be minimized. Even so, this accomplishment needs to be kept in perspective. To the extent that short-term creditors are protected in OLA, we have the same problems discussed in chapter 7 in the context of the lender of last resort: implicit public support, subsidies, and the associated distorting effects on financial markets. OLA thus reinforces financial institutions' incentives to rely on unstable short-term funding (a point David Skeel has emphasized).[37] At the same time, OLA is subject to very serious execution risks. Insofar as panics are the problem, this is an indirect and unreliable way of dealing with them.

Scaling Back

Is US financial stability policy moving in a sensible direction? It will be some time before a verdict can be rendered. What seems clear is that regulation of run-prone funding structures has been timid at best. We still live in a system of "free banking," or free entry into the business model of money creation. Regulatory energies have mostly been focused elsewhere.

The reformed monetary system represents a fundamentally different approach to run-prone funding structures. Broad money creation is confined and capped; the broad money supply is made sovereign and nondefaultable; shadow banking, as I have defined it, ceases to exist. And here I take my argument to its logical conclusion. Implementing the reformed monetary system, I contend, could very well obviate the need for most *other* forms of financial stability regulation. That is to say, the reformed system could set the stage for a major scaling back of our current financial regulatory apparatus.

This conclusion is admittedly provocative; it cuts strongly against the prevailing view. I address key objections below. First, though, let's consider what such a scaling back would look like. Member banks themselves would of course be heavily regulated, as I described in the previous chapter. And nonbanks would be required to abide by the unauthorized banking statute. Apart from that, however, nonbank financial firms would be more or less completely released from stability-oriented financial regulation. (I will add some important qualifications in the next few paragraphs, so please bear with me.) So nonbank financial firms would not be subject to regulatory constraints on risk taking or capital levels—at least not for financial stability purposes. These matters would be left to the operation of market forces; the ordinary rules of capitalism would apply. Nonbanks would not have access to public liquidity support; their costs of financing would be unsubsidized. (The reformed system thus clarifies the boundary between private and sovereign claims—the opposite of constructive ambiguity.) Specific markets, such as the securitization and derivatives markets, would also be free from stability-focused regulation.

What are the key objections to such a system? Clearly, it leaves unaddressed a number of issues that are commonly associated with the problem of financial instability. These include excessive size and interconnectedness of financial firms; collateral damage and domino effects from failure; related disruptions for customers and counterparties; correlated risk exposures; the "melting ice cube" problem (the tendency for the enterprise value of financial firms to erode quickly during insolvency proceedings); excessive risk taking; excessive leverage in the financial system; opaque and risky derivatives markets; misaligned incentives in securitization; proprietary trading risks; flawed credit ratings; the list could go on. The reformed monetary system does not *directly* address any of these issues.

My response is simple: I concede all these points. For example, there is no doubt that, even if the reformed system were implemented, the bankruptcy of a major nonbank financial institution—say, a securities firm like Lehman Brothers—would be disruptive. Customers and counterparties would face real problems, and other financial institutions would sustain collateral damage. But the key question is not whether such disruptions would happen, but whether they would pose a serious risk of *plunging the economy into a deep slump*. We have very good reasons to think that panics are a major source of macroeconomic catastrophes; they are like a dagger to the gut of the economy (see chapter 4). Whether other financial phenomena realistically pose a similarly grave threat in the absence of a panic is far from obvious.

What is more, there are good reasons to think the reformed monetary system would *indirectly* address some of the issues cited above. We saw in chapter 7 that the existence of an implicit public backstop of the financial sector's monetary liabilities creates incentives for financial firms to grow and thereby exacerbates the too big to fail problem. We also saw that such public support may contribute significantly to debt-fueled bubbles and the like. If public support could credibly be withheld from nonbank financial firms, these two problems might be lessened.

I mention these two pathologies—too big to fail and debt-fueled bubbles—because a number of prominent analysts favor placing them at or near the center of financial stability policy. For example, FDIC vice chair Thomas Hoenig has advocated regulatory steps that would force a breakup of the largest US financial institutions, thereby addressing the too big to fail problem.[38] Other policy experts have promoted similar measures.[39] Likewise, it should come as no surprise that the "debt cycle" theorists we encountered in chapter 4 tend to favor systemwide limits on debt and leverage. Thus Hyman Minsky has argued that central banks should "continuously 'lean against' the use of speculative and Ponzi finance."[40] John Geanakoplos suggests "empowering a 'leverage supervisor' who could simply forbid loans at too high leverage in ebullient times."[41] Reinhart and Rogoff, who also lean toward the debt cycle view at times, advocate creating "a new independent international institution" that would "enforc[e] regulations relating to leverage."[42] Mian and Sufi call for increased use of equitylike contracts rather than debt.[43] And Paul Krugman argues for "higher capital ratios for banks, limits on risky lending, but also perhaps limits for borrowers too, such as maximum loan-to-value ratios on housing and restrictions on second mortgages." This, he says, "would guard against bubbles and excessive leverage."[44] My argument is that we probably should *not* do these things—at least not in the first instance. A more sensible approach to money creation might very well alleviate these other pathologies.

Now let me add some important caveats to the scaling back scenario just described. First, I am talking here only about financial *stability* regulation, by which I mean financial regulation whose purpose is to counter grave threats to the broader economy. It goes without saying that the financial system raises policy problems apart from instability. Regulation is warranted for other purposes: consumer protection, investor protection, dealing with certain conflicts of interest, ensuring disclosure, combating fraud, promoting competition, establishing orderly and efficient market structures, and so forth. Such regulations are justifiable on their own terms, irrespective of any connection to macroeconomic disasters. I am in no way suggesting they be carved back.

Second, there are pockets of nonbank financial activity where "risk" or "solvency" regulation would still be warranted, even after implementation of the reformed system. Specifically, there are good reasons why *retail*-facing insurance and securities firms should continue to be subject to portfolio constraints, capital requirements, and special insolvency systems. Note that the core rationale for these regulatory systems is not the prevention of severe recessions but rather the protection of financially unsophisticated retail consumers. It is similar to the rationale for regulating retail-facing investment companies (mutual funds). Protecting unsophisticated consumers is unquestionably an important policy objective, but it is not properly classified as a systemic stability issue.

Third, what about complex financial conglomerates that *own* member banks? Should they be subject to *firmwide* stability-type regulation, such as consolidated capital requirements and supervision? We can get at this question by considering what happens to a member bank in the reformed system when its affiliates fail. Upon their bankruptcy, the member bank is yanked into the special receivership system. The member bank's corporate form partitions its assets (the collateral for the government's senior claim) from those of its affiliates. And member banks are subject to strict limitations on affiliate transactions. In theory, then, affiliate distress shouldn't produce significant losses for a member bank. In practice, things may be more complicated and disruptive. If member banks can't realistically be adequately shielded from the effects of affiliate distress, then regulation and supervision of the consolidated enterprise may be in order. Unfortunately, this would involve regulators in the very difficult business of regulating and supervising complex institutional securities firms. A simpler alternative would be to prohibit such affiliations in the first place—in other words, impose a Glass-Steagall type of separation. There are reasonable arguments for both approaches. Given that the system is panic-proof in either case, the stakes here are not all that high.

Fourth, note that, while the reformed monetary system (including the unauthorized banking law) does render the financial sector panic-proof, it does *not* eliminate all potential sources of liquidity stress for financial firms. For example, financial firms that are heavily involved in the derivatives business are vulnerable to collateral calls, which can drain cash and lead to default. But it is critical to distinguish this scenario from a panic. A panic involves claimants with a more or less continuous and unconditional option to redeem. A derivative counterparty has no such option. A derivative collateral call is *contingent*—it happens when the trade moves against you. There is no coordination game, no significant self-fulfilling dimension. In short, not all sources of liquidity stress are created equal. The reformed system does not prevent all forms of cash drains, nor does it prevent nonbank financial firms from failing. It is not designed to do these things. It is designed to prevent panics.

Fifth, what if I'm wrong? My argument for scaling back depends on the proposition that, when it comes to financial stability policy, panics are "the problem" (or the main one, anyway). Admittedly, the case for this proposition is not open-and-shut. It is possible that other types of financial disruption could plunge the macroeconomy into a deep slump, even in a panic-proof system. But it is all too easy in this area to get caught up in a parade of horribles. All sorts of plausible-sounding dangers can be cited. I am making the case for prioritizing—for focusing our regulatory energies on known, grave threats to the broader economy rather than speculative ones. In any case, the reformed monetary system is certainly *compatible* with other forms of financial stability regulation. It comes down to a judgment call.

History does offer some evidence to support my case for scaling back. Recall that, with the advent of deposit insurance in 1933, the United States entered an unprecedented Quiet Period of seventy-plus years with no panics and no serious economic disasters. Only with the emergence of shadow banking—private money creation on a large scale *outside* the chartered banking system—did financial instability return; and with it came the Great Recession. Lawmakers did not erect a massive "systemic risk" apparatus in 1933. Rather, they brought money creation under the public umbrella. This seemed to work quite well.

A final objection to the reformed monetary system has to do with supposedly insurmountable political obstacles. This objection doesn't bother me much. The political winds can always shift. Besides, the reformed monetary system might win support from large segments of the financial industry if it were accompanied by a major scaling back of existing financial stability regulation, as just described. More broadly, the reformed system holds the prospect of removing large public subsidies from certain privileged segments of the financial sector. The distributional implications would be decidedly egalitarian. This is a political plus in a world where disparities of wealth and income seem to be gaining political traction. Practically no one wants a system in which certain big financial firms are parasitic on the state, which, notwithstanding recent reforms, is what we have today.

Final Thoughts

The core thesis of this book has been that financial instability is mostly a problem of monetary system design. If this is right, the problem is considerably narrower than is commonly supposed. We can stop thinking of financial instability as an endlessly complex and shape-shifting adversary. And we can reject the defeatist notion—usually stated with an air of worldly wisdom—that financial crises and their economic consequences are inevitable, that they are the price we must pay for financial capitalism. We are dealing instead with a discrete and well-defined project of institutional engineering.

As I noted at the start of the book, my argument reflects the traditional wisdom. In a remarkable 1939 memorandum titled "A Program for Monetary Reform,"[45] six distinguished US economists observed, "Throughout our history no economic problem has been more passionately discussed than the money problem." The authors described the existing monetary framework as "wholly inadequate." Chief among its defects was private money creation by the banking system. "The banks thus exercise what has always, and justly, been considered a prerogative of sovereign power," they wrote. "This situation is a most important factor in booms and depressions." With a better-designed monetary framework, "the disastrous effects of depressions would be lessened." The authors happened to favor 100% reserve banking, a proposal I have criticized in this book. But it is their *diagnosis* of the problem that really interests me. They viewed the banking problem in distinctly monetary terms. Today we have moved away from this insight. As a result, recent debates over financial reform have been hampered by conceptual blinders.

What explains this drift away from the traditional wisdom? Part of the answer may have to do with disciplinary boundaries and priorities. Within academia, money falls squarely within the domain of macroeconomics. And I think it is fair to say that, at least in recent decades, macroeconomists have been far more focused on model building than institution building. One often hears that modern macroeconomic models have tended to omit the institutional details of banking and finance. "To me," says Joseph Stiglitz, "the strangest aspect of modern macroeconomics [during the Great Recession] was that central banks were using a model in which banks and financial markets played no role."[46] Simon Wren-Lewis says that "everyone admits that mainstream macro analysis took finance for granted before the crash."[47] Charles Plosser says that "macroeconomists need to consider how to integrate the institutional design of central banks into our macroeconomic models."[48] Olivier Blanchard says that "our benchmark [macroeconomic] models ... should be expanded to better recognize the role of the financial system."[49] And Tobias Adrian and Hyun Song Shin say that "in conventional models of monetary economics commonly used in central banks, the banking sector has not played a prominent role."[50]

By all accounts, macroeconomists are now hard at work incorporating "financial frictions" into their models. I must confess that the very term friction gives me some pause; is the instability of private money creation really a "financial friction"? If unstable private money is in fact a major source of deep recessions—and if it is true that standard macro models omit this feature of institutional reality—then it is little wonder such models have been found wanting. In any case, rather than improving models to better match institutional reality, perhaps it is institutional reality that needs improving.

Adam Smith described bank money creation as "a sort of wagon-way through the air."[51] I like this metaphor, which evokes an image of infrastructure. The system of money and banking is, after all, a kind of institutional infrastructure. Like property and contract, the monetary framework is an essential component of a well-functioning market economy. And it matters very much *how* this infrastructure is built. Monetary institutions, like all legal institutions, stand in need of design, and some designs are better than others.

Notes

Preface

1. Ben S. Bernanke, "Reflections on a Year of Crisis," remarks at the Federal Reserve Bank of Kansas City's Annual Economic Symposium, Jackson Hole, Wyoming, August 21, 2009.

2. For example, see Paul Krugman, "Six Doctrines in Search of a Policy Regime," *The Conscience of a Liberal* (blog), *New York Times*, April 18, 2010. "Rather oddly," wrote Krugman, "there hasn't been much discussion of formally extending something like deposit insurance to the short-term liabilities of shadow banks." See also Edward Conard, *Unintended Consequences: Why Everything You've Been Told about the Economy Is Wrong* (New York: Portfolio/Penguin, 2012), chap. 7.

3. I borrow "thingify" from a classic work of legal realism: Felix Cohen, "Transcendental Nonsense and the Functional Approach," *Columbia Law Review* 35, no. 6 (1935): 811. The legal realists were influenced by William James, who remarked on "our inveterate human trick of turning names into things." William James, *Pragmatism* (1907), in *Pragmatism* and *The Meaning of Truth* (Cambridge, MA: Harvard University Press, 1978), 46.

4. "The only simplicity for which I would give a straw," Holmes wrote, "is that which is on the other side of the complex—not that which never has divined it." Letter from Oliver Wendell Holmes Jr. to Georgina Harriet Pollock, October 24, 1902, in *Holmes-Pollock Letters: The Correspondence of Mr. Justice Holmes and Sir Frederick Pollock, 1874–1932*, ed. Mark DeWolfe Howe (Cambridge, MA: Harvard University Press, 1941), 1:109.

5. Quoted in Walter Isaacson, "How Steve Jobs' Love of Simplicity Fueled a Design Revolution," *Smithsonian Magazine*, September 2012.

Introduction

1. Alexis de Tocqueville, "Paris on the Morrow of the 24th of February and the Next Days" (1850), in *The Recollections of Alexis de Tocqueville* (1893), trans. Alexander Teixeira de Mattos (New York: Macmillan, 1896), 101.

2. For example, see Henry C. Simons, "A Positive Program for Laissez Faire: Some Proposals for a Liberal Economic Policy" (1934), in *Economic Policy for a Free Society* (Chicago: University of Chicago Press, 1948); Lauchlin Currie, "A Proposed Revision of the Monetary System of the United States: Submitted to Secretary of the Treasury Henry Morgenthau" (1934), in *The Supply and Control of Money in the United States* (1935; repr., New York: Russell and Russell, 1968); Irving Fisher, *100% Money* (1935), 3rd ed. (New Haven, CT: City Printing, 1945).

3. Hyman P. Minsky, *Stabilizing an Unstable Economy*, rev. ed. (New York: McGraw-Hill, 2008), 194.

4. "Shadow banking" was coined in the early stages of the recent crisis by Paul McCulley, who used the term in reference to a class of investment conduits that funded themselves with short-term debt. See Paul McCulley, "Teton Reflections," *PIMCO Global Central Bank Focus*, August/September 2007.

5. Gary B. Gorton, *Slapped by the Invisible Hand: The Panic of 2007* (New York: Oxford University Press, 2010), 15.

6. Some readers may be unaccustomed to thinking of a deposit as an "instrument" that a bank "issues," but that's what it is. See chapter 2.

7. Milton Friedman and Anna J. Schwartz, *A Monetary History of the United States, 1867–1960* (Princeton, NJ: Princeton University Press, 1963), 351, 300.

8. See Barry Eichengreen, *Golden Fetters: The Gold Standard and the Great Depression, 1919–1939* (New York: Oxford University Press, 1992), 18.

9. Ben S. Bernanke, "On Milton Friedman's Ninetieth Birthday," address at the Conference to Honor Milton Friedman, University of Chicago, November 8, 2002.

10. See 12 U.S.C. § 378(a)(2).

11. If a deposit bank were to replace its deposit obligations with bond financing, it would be transformed into an ordinary finance company—a business model requiring no special charter.

12. See chapter 8 for a description of US deposit bank portfolio constraints.

13. See 12 U.S.C. § 24(Seventh).

14. See 12 U.S.C. § 1813(l).

15. Douglas W. Diamond, remarks at the Panel Discussion on Financial Regulation, Becker Friedman Institute, University of Chicago, November 6, 2010 (comment appears at the eight-minute mark).

16. The concept of "intrinsic" value is admittedly rather slippery. I'm just making the self-evident point that a twenty-dollar bill is worth more than the paper it's printed on. This book does not address the merits of commodity-based money. The difficulties with a commodity standard have been dealt with extensively elsewhere.

For example, see Milton Friedman, "Should There Be an Independent Monetary Authority?" in *In Search of a Monetary Constitution*, ed. Leland B. Yeager (Cambridge, MA: Harvard University Press, 1962), 220–24; Paul Krugman, "The Gold Bug Variations," *Slate*, November 22, 1996; Ben S. Bernanke, *The Federal Reserve and the Financial Crisis* (Princeton, NJ: Princeton University Press, 2013), 10–14.

17. See 18 U.S.C. §§ 470–477.

18. There are exceptions; for example, see Friedrich A. Hayek, *Denationalisation of Money*, 3rd ed. (London: Institute of Economic Affairs, 1990). Other laissez-faire perspectives include George A. Selgin, *The Theory of Free Banking: Money Supply under Competitive Note Issue* (Lanham, MD: Rowman and Littlefield, 1988), and Lawrence H. White, *The Theory of Monetary Institutions* (Malden, MA: Blackwell, 1999).

19. Milton Friedman, *A Program for Monetary Stability* (New York: Fordham University Press, 1960), 8. Friedman and his coauthor Anna Schwartz later revisited these comments and reached a somewhat ambiguous conclusion. See Milton Friedman and Anna J. Schwartz, "Has Government Any Role in Money?" in *Money in Historical Perspective*, ed. Anna J. Schwartz (Chicago: University of Chicago Press, 1987). The authors expressed openness to the idea that a *commodity*-based currency might arise through market forces alone. Nonetheless, they concluded on a note of pragmatic conservatism, declining to advocate government withdrawal from monetary affairs.

20. James M. Buchanan, "The Constitutionalization of Money," *Cato Journal* 30, no. 2 (2010): 251, 256.

21. The period from 1836 to 1863 is called the Free Banking Era in US banking history, but as many others have pointed out, this is a misnomer. Banks during that period were subject to strict portfolio constraints and other regulatory requirements at the state level.

22. Proponents have included Irving Fisher and Milton Friedman. See chapter 6 for a discussion.

23. I believe this insight is attributable to Wesley Newcomb Hohfeld, *Fundamental Legal Conceptions as Applied in Judicial Reasoning* (New Haven, CT: Yale University Press, 1919), 36.

24. 12 U.S.C. § 1821.

25. In the midst of the recent crisis, the Federal Deposit Insurance Corporation insured noninterest-bearing transaction accounts to an *unlimited* amount on an emergency basis. This was the FDIC's "Transaction Account Guarantee." See 12 C.F.R. § 370.4.

26. Article-length treatments have understandably addressed selected topics in isolation rather than approaching the monetary framework holistically, as an integrated design project. Notable entries in this literature include Christina D. Romer and David H. Romer, "Institutions for Monetary Stability," in *Reducing Inflation: Motivation and Strategy*, ed. Christina D. Romer and David H. Romer (Chicago:

University of Chicago Press, 1997); Alan S. Blinder, "Monetary Policy Today: Sixteen Questions and About Twelve Answers," in *Central Banks in the 21st Century*, ed. Santiago Fernández de Lis and Fernando Restoy (Madrid: Banco de España, 2006); Ricardo Reis, "Central Bank Design," *Journal of Economic Perspectives* 27, no. 4 (2013): 17–44.

27. By "deposit banks" I mean all chartered depository institutions—banks, thrifts, and credit unions—whether chartered at the state or the federal level.

28. The world may be moving in this direction anyway. For example, see Associated Press, "Sweden Moving towards Cashless Economy," CBSNews.com, March 18, 2012. See also Kenneth S. Rogoff, "Costs and Benefits to Phasing Out Paper Currency," *NBER Macroeconomics Annual* 29, no. 1 (2014).

29. Friedman and Schwartz make a similar observation, noting that the word "deposit" is "misleading" because it "connotes the placing of something in safekeeping, as in a 100 per cent reserve banking system." Milton Friedman and Anna J. Schwartz, *Monetary Statistics of the United States: Estimates, Sources, Methods* (New York: National Bureau of Economic Research, 1970), 59n4.

30. See chapter 5.

31. Nick Rowe aptly describes this structure as one of "asymmetric redeemability." Nick Rowe, "What Makes a Bank a Central Bank?" *Worthwhile Canadian Initiative* (blog), October 29, 2009.

32. Along similar lines, a leading commercial law scholar writes that "underlying much of the oddity of negotiable instruments law is our unthinking assumption that paper matters." James Steven Rogers, *The End of Negotiable Instruments: Bringing Payment Systems Law Out of the Past* (New York: Oxford University Press, 2012), 64.

33. Of course, member banks would need to own some real and personal property to conduct their business. They would also be allowed to enter into derivative contracts for hedging purposes.

34. When I refer in this book to the "desired" money supply, I am not advocating anything like money supply targeting. I just mean that any approach to monetary policy will result in some positive quantity of money outstanding. The (endogenous) quantity of money that emerges from "good" monetary policy—whatever one's conception of good monetary policy might be—is all I mean by the desired money supply.

35. "Trade credit" refers to IOUs issued in exchange for bona fide goods or services. For accounting purposes, trade credit generally appears as "accounts payable" (for the obligor) or "accounts receivable" (for the creditor) rather than as "borrowings" or "loans."

36. See 15 U.S.C. § 1.

37. I am referring to the US Bankruptcy Code's automatic stay. See 11 U.S.C. § 362. As a formal matter the automatic stay applies to contractual remedies as opposed to rights, but surely everyone agrees that rights without remedies are illu-

sory. The classic statement of this point is Oliver Wendell Holmes Jr., "The Path of the Law," *Harvard Law Review* 10, no. 8 (1897): 457–78.

38. Consequently there would be no such thing as, for example, a money market mutual fund (MMF). Instead there would be a single system of money creation firms (member banks) operating under a single set of terms and conditions and within a single regulatory and supervisory apparatus. The reformed monetary system would get the Securities and Exchange Commission (which regulates MMFs) out of the monetary business, which falls outside its expertise and core competency.

39. See Banking Act of 1933, Pub. L. No. 73-66, §§ 20–21, 48 Stat. 162, 188–89.

40. See Gramm-Leach-Bliley Act, Pub. L. No. 106-102, § 101, 113 Stat. 1338, 1341 (1999).

41. See Federal Reserve Act §§ 23A–23B, 12 U.S.C. §§ 371c–371c-1.

42. The proper calibration of these fees is an important question and is addressed in future chapters. Essentially, the fees are designed to replicate the financing costs that member banks would incur were they to replace their monetary liabilities with longer-term borrowings in the private markets.

43. Before the enactment of the Dodd-Frank Wall Street Reform and Consumer Protection Act, Pub. L. No. 111-203, 124 Stat. 1376 (2010), the FDIC was required to declare "dividends" from the deposit insurance fund to participating deposit banks once the fund reached a certain size in relation to outstanding insured deposits. Dodd-Frank gave the FDIC discretion to suspend or limit the declaration of dividends. See Dodd-Frank Act § 332, 12 U.S.C. § 1817(e). Even as modified, though, the deposit insurance system does not function as a source of government revenue.

44. Chapter 5 will qualify this conclusion; we will see that "fiscal smoothing" considerations may provide an independent rationale for imposing risk constraints on member banks in this system.

45. Cap adjustments are just one tool of monetary policy in the reformed system, analogous to reserve requirement adjustments in the current setup. Other tools exist, particularly for fine-tuning. See chapter 9.

46. To be clear, this book is agnostic on monetary policy *rules* and *operating targets*. I assume that the monetary authority operates under a broad macroeconomic policy mandate, such as the Federal Reserve's current dual mandate of full employment and price stability. See Federal Reserve Act § 2A, 12 U.S.C. § 225a.

47. Intraday credit is institutionally distinct from the discount window. For a technical overview, see Federal Reserve System, "Guide to the Federal Reserve's Payment System Risk Policy on Intraday Credit," July 2012.

48. In practice, sovereign debits would need to be slightly more expensive than r-currency liabilities to give member banks an incentive to service accounts. See chapter 9.

49. In bank regulatory parlance, they have a "0% risk weight."

50. Friedman, *Program for Monetary Stability*, 38.

51. For a good description of this funding structure, see Darrell Duffie, "The Failure Mechanics of Dealer Banks," *Journal of Economic Perspectives* 24, no. 1 (2010): 51–72.

Chapter One

1. John Hicks, *Value and Capital*, 2nd ed. (1946; repr., Oxford: Clarendon Press, 2001), 168, 163.

2. James Hamilton, "M3 or Not M3?" *Econbrowser* (blog), May 30, 2006.

3. Nick Rowe, "Money, Barter, and Recalculation," *Worthwhile Canadian Initiative* (blog), December 13, 2010.

4. Nick Rowe, "The Return of Monetarism," *Worthwhile Canadian Initiative* (blog), March 3, 2009.

5. Anat R. Admati and Martin F. Hellwig, "The Parade of Bankers' New Clothes Continues: 23 Flawed Claims Debunked," Rock Center for Corporate Governance at Stanford University Working Paper 143, June 23, 2013, 6.

6. Milton Friedman and Anna J. Schwartz, *Monetary Statistics of the United States: Estimates, Sources, Methods* (New York: National Bureau of Economic Research, 1970), 90, 137, 104.

7. Milton Friedman, *The Optimum Quantity of Money* (1969; repr., New Brunswick, NJ: Transaction, 2006), 3.

8. David Laidler makes a seemingly similar argument about the relation between precautionary money holdings and price stickiness, though his argument is not easy to decipher. See David Laidler, *Taking Money Seriously and Other Essays* (Cambridge, MA: MIT Press, 1990), 9–14.

9. For a prescient analysis of this institutional dichotomy, see Jonathan R. Macey and Geoffrey P. Miller, "Nondeposit Deposits and the Future of Bank Regulation," *Michigan Law Review* 91, no. 2 (1992): 237–73.

10. I will elaborate on this definition in chapter 9 for purposes of establishing an operative legal category.

11. Omitted categories include interests in enhanced cash funds and cash plus funds; prime brokerage free credit balances; federal funds purchased; auction-rate securities; and variable-rate demand notes.

12. This increased coverage was attributable to two policy measures: first, the statutory increase in the deposit insurance cap from $100,000 to $250,000 (see Emergency Economic Stabilization Act of 2008 § 136, 12 U.S.C. § 5241; Dodd-Frank Wall Street Reform and Consumer Protection Act, Pub. L. No. 111-203, § 335, 124 Stat. 1376, 1540 (2010)); and second, the Federal Deposit Insurance Corporation's Transaction Account Guarantee, which temporarily removed the deposit insurance cap for noninterest-bearing demand deposit obligations (see 12

C.F.R. § 370.4). The termination of the latter program is responsible for the uptick in uninsured deposits and the corresponding downtick in insured deposits after 2012.

13. One expert notes that only about 3% of prime MMF assets are invested in paper issued by nonfinancial firms. See David S. Scharfstein, "Perspectives on Money Market Mutual Fund Reforms," testimony before the Committee on Banking, Housing, and Urban Affairs, US Senate, June 21, 2012.

14. Similarly, Scharfstein calculates that commercial paper represented only 1.6% of the liabilities of nonfinancial firms as of early 2012. Ibid.

15. For a nuanced discussion of this issue, see Zoltan Pozsar, "Institutional Cash Pools and the Triffin Dilemma of the U.S. Banking System," IMF Working Paper 11/190, August 2011.

16. Financial Accounting Standards Board, "Statement of Cash Flows," Statement of Financial Accounting Standards 95, §§ 8–9.

17. International Accounting Standards Board, "Statement of Cash Flows," International Accounting Standard 7, § 7.

18. This book uses "cash equivalents" slightly more loosely than the accountants would have it, inasmuch as I am not adhering to a three-month cutoff.

19. The "Euro" prefix is misleading, since the issuer need not be European. See chapter 9 for an analysis of this market.

20. See Securities Act of 1933 § 3(a)(3), 15 U.S.C. § 77c(a)(3).

21. Securities issued by deposit banks are exempt from registration. See Securities Act of 1933 § 3(a)(2), 15 U.S.C. § 77c(a)(2).

22. See Securities Exchange Act of 1934 § 3(a)(10), 15 U.S.C. § 78c(a)(10).

23. See Investment Company Act of 1940 §§ 3(c)(1) & 2(a)(38), 15 U.S.C. §§ 80a-3(c)(1) & 80a-2(a)(38).

24. Securities and Exchange Commission, No-Action Letter, Willkie Farr & Gallagher, October 23, 2000.

25. European Central Bank website.

26. Letter from Henry Simons to Irving Fisher, July 4, 1934, quoted in Ronnie J. Phillips, *The Chicago Plan and New Deal Banking Reform* (New York: M. E. Sharpe, 1995), 90.

27. Henry C. Simons, "A Positive Program for Laissez Faire: Some Proposals for a Liberal Economic Policy" (1934), in *Economic Policy for a Free Society* (Chicago: University of Chicago Press, 1948), 320n7.

28. Robert E. Lucas Jr. and Nancy L. Stokey, "Liquidity Crises: Understanding Sources and Limiting Consequences; A Theoretical Framework," *Region*, June 2011, 2, 12.

29. Paul Krugman, "The Amnesiac Economy," *The Conscience of a Liberal* (blog), *New York Times*, October 26, 2011.

30. Gary B. Gorton, *Misunderstanding Financial Crises: Why We Don't See Them Coming* (New York: Oxford University Press, 2012), 5; Gary B. Gorton and

Guillermo Ordoñez, "Collateral Crises," *American Economic Review* 104, no. 2 (2014): 343.

31. Jeremy C. Stein, "Monetary Policy as Financial Stability Regulation," *Quarterly Journal of Economics* 127, no. 1 (2012): 58.

32. Marvin Goodfriend, "Money Markets," *Annual Review of Financial Economics*, no. 3 (2011): 120.

33. John H. Cochrane, "Toward a Run-Free Financial System," in *Across the Great Divide: New Perspectives on the Financial Crisis*, ed. Martin Neil Baily and John B. Taylor (Stanford, CA: Hoover Institution Press, 2014), 224.

34. Notable recent contributions to this literature include Pozsar, "Institutional Cash Pools"; Zoltan Pozsar and Manmohan Singh, "The Nonbank-Bank Nexus and the Shadow Banking System," IMF Working Paper 11/289, December 2011; Adi Sunderam, "Money Creation and the Shadow Banking System," *Review of Financial Studies* 28, no. 4 (2015): 939–77.

35. N. Gregory Mankiw, *Macroeconomics*, 8th ed. (New York: Worth, 2013), 85–86.

36. Frederic S. Mishkin, *The Economics of Money, Banking, and Financial Markets*, 10th ed. (Boston: Pearson, 2012), 59, 60, 104n4.

37. James Tobin, "The Interest-Elasticity of Transactions Demand for Cash," *Review of Economics and Statistics* 38, no. 3 (1956): 241.

38. This is a standard account of cash management practices; see Stephen A. Ross, Randolph W. Westerfield, and Jeffrey Jaffe, *Corporate Finance*, 8th ed. (Boston: McGraw-Hill/Irwin, 2008), 752–54.

39. See Mankiw, *Macroeconomics*, 12–13.

40. Marcia Stigum and Anthony Crescenzi, *Stigum's Money Market*, 4th ed. (New York: McGraw-Hill, 2007), 479.

41. Timothy Q. Cook and Robert K. Laroche, eds., *Instruments of the Money Market*, 7th ed. (Richmond, VA: Federal Reserve Bank of Richmond, 1998), 1.

42. Robin Greenwood, Samuel G. Hanson, and Jeremy C. Stein, "A Comparative-Advantage Approach to Government Debt Maturity," *Journal of Finance* 70, no. 4 (2015): 1718, 1687.

43. Specifically, the figure shows "the average spread, over the period 1983–2009, between actual Treasury-bill yields ('on-cycle' Treasury bills with maturities from 1 to 26 weeks) and fitted yields, based on a flexible extrapolation of the Treasury yield curve." Ibid., 1688.

44. John Maynard Keynes, *The General Theory of Employment, Interest, and Money* (1936; repr., San Diego, CA: First Harvest/Harcourt, 1964), 167. This quotation commits a small act of poetic license; Keynes actually defined the interest rate as the reward for parting with "liquidity." As we are about to see, though, Keynes used "liquidity"—at least in this context—to refer to assets with negligible price risk.

45. Stigum and Crescenzi, *Stigum's Money Market*, 456.

46. J. P. Morgan Securities Inc., "Short-Term Fixed Income Research Note," *U.S. Fixed Income Markets Weekly*, June 6, 2008.

47. Mishkin, *Economics of Money, Banking, and Financial Markets*, 55.

48. N. Gregory Mankiw, *Principles of Economics*, 7th ed. (Stamford, CT: Cengage Learning, 2014), 551.

49. Nick Rowe, "Medium of Account vs. Medium of Exchange," *Worthwhile Canadian Initiative* (blog), October 30, 2012.

50. See Basel Committee on Banking Supervision, "Basel III: The Net Stable Funding Ratio," October 2014, 2.

51. See Ricardo J. Caballero, "The 'Other' Imbalance and the Financial Crisis," NBER Working Paper 15636, January 2010; Gary B. Gorton, Stefan Lewellen, and Andrew Metrick, "The Safe-Asset Share," *American Economic Review: Papers and Proceedings* 102, no. 3 (2012): 101–6; International Monetary Fund, "Safe Assets: Financial System Cornerstone?" in *Global Financial Stability Report: The Quest for Lasting Stability* (Washington, DC: International Monetary Fund, 2012), 81–121; Gary B. Gorton and Guillermo Ordoñez, "The Supply and Demand for Safe Assets," working paper, August 2013.

52. Keynes, *General Theory*, 166–70.

53. Axel Leijonhufvud, *On Keynesian Economics and the Economics of Keynes: A Study in Monetary Theory* (New York: Oxford University Press, 1968), 149.

54. Friedman and Schwartz, *Monetary Statistics*, 133n65.

55. See William J. Baumol, "The Transactions Demand for Cash: An Inventory Theoretic Approach," *Quarterly Journal of Economics* 66, no. 4 (1952): 545–56; Tobin, "Interest-Elasticity of Transactions Demand for Cash."

56. Relatedly, Gorton remarks that when banks historically have suspended convertibility of deposits, those deposits "ceased being 'money' altogether." Gary B. Gorton, *Slapped by the Invisible Hand: The Panic of 2007* (New York: Oxford University Press, 2010), 178. And Hugh Rockoff argues that the "quality" of the US money stock declined in the early 1930s as a consequence of restrictions on withdrawals and the threat thereof. See Hugh Rockoff, "The Meaning of Money in the Great Depression," NBER Working Paper Series on Historical Factors in Long Run Growth, Historical Paper 52, December 1993.

57. Walter Bagehot, *Lombard Street: A Description of the Money Market* (1873; repr., New York: John Wiley, 1999), 39–40.

58. Ludwig Wittgenstein, *Philosophical Investigations* (1953), trans. G. E. M. Anscombe (Oxford: Basil Blackwell, 1958), 31.

59. See Dong He and Robert N. McCauley, "Offshore Markets for the Domestic Currency: Monetary and Financial Stability Issues," Hong Kong Monetary Authority Working Paper 02/2010, 6.

60. Robert J. Carbaugh, *International Economics*, 15th ed. (Boston: Cengage Learning, 2013), 510.

61. Joseph D. Smallman and Michael J. P. Selby, "Non-traditional Asset Se-

curitization for European Markets," in *Issuer Perspectives on Securitization*, ed. Frank J. Fabozzi (New Hope, PA: Frank J. Fabozzi Associates, 1998), 47.

Chapter Two

1. Quoted in Lauren T. LaCapra, "Goldman Names Schwartz CFO as Viniar Retires," *Reuters*, September 18, 2012.

2. In the case of demand deposits, it may at first seem unnatural to imagine them as being continuously rolled over, but that is what is happening. Demand deposits are IOUs that mature instantaneously and are rolled over by account holders each instant that they are not redeemed.

3. Richard A. Posner, *A Failure of Capitalism: The Crisis of '08 and the Descent into Depression* (Cambridge, MA: Harvard University Press, 2009), 46, xvi.

4. Walter Bagehot, *Lombard Street: A Description of the Money Market* (1873; repr., New York: John Wiley, 1999), 212–13.

5. This discussion of currency warehouses draws on Meir Kohn, *Financial Institutions and Markets*, 2nd ed. (New York: Oxford University Press, 2004), 21–24. This business model is sometimes called "100% reserve banking"; see chapter 6.

6. See L. Randall Wray, *Money and Credit in Capitalist Economies: The Endogenous Money Approach* (Aldershot, UK: Edward Elgar, 1990), esp. chaps. 3 and 4.

7. Uniform Commercial Code § 8-102.

8. As we will see in chapter 9, lawmakers' failure to appreciate the economic equivalence of bank notes and deposits was, from a bank regulatory standpoint, a consequential mistake in both England and the United States in the nineteenth century. This presumably is what Friedman and Schwartz had in mind when they referred to "the inappropriate differentiation of deposits from notes that has played so large a part in monetary history." Milton Friedman and Anna J. Schwartz, *A Monetary History of the United States, 1867–1960* (Princeton, NJ: Princeton University Press, 1963), 195.

9. N. Gregory Mankiw, *Macroeconomics*, 8th ed. (New York: Worth, 2013), 88–90.

10. John Maynard Keynes, *A Treatise on Money* (New York: Harcourt, Brace, 1930), 1:23–30.

11. James Tobin, "Commercial Banks as Creators of 'Money,'" in *Banking and Monetary Studies*, ed. Deane Carson (Homewood, IL: Richard D. Irwin, 1963), 412–13.

12. Paul Krugman, "Banking Mysticism, Continued," *The Conscience of a Liberal* (blog), *New York Times*, March 30, 2012.

13. See Nick Rowe, "Banking 'Mysticism' and the Hot Potato," *Worthwhile Canadian Initiative* (blog), March 31, 2012; L. Randall Wray, "Krugman versus Minsky," *EconoMonitor* (blog), April 2, 2012; David Glasner, "Endogenous Money," *Uneasy Money* (blog), April 11, 2012.

14. Michael McLeay, Amar Radia, and Ryland Thomas, "Money Creation in the Modern Economy," *Bank of England Quarterly Bulletin*, no. 1 (2014): 2–3.

15. Stephen Williamson, "Money Creation: Propagating Confusion," *New Monetarist Economics* (blog), March 27, 2014.

16. Robert K. Merton, "The Self-Fulfilling Prophecy," *Antioch Review* 8, no. 2 (1948): 194–95.

17. Douglas W. Diamond and Philip H. Dybvig, "Bank Runs, Deposit Insurance, and Liquidity," *Journal of Political Economy* 91, no. 3 (1983): 410. As of 2006, this paper was among the one hundred most-cited economics papers published since 1970. See E. Han Kim, Adair Morse, and Luigi Zingales, "What Has Mattered to Economics since 1970," *Journal of Economic Perspectives* 20, no. 4 (2006): 196.

18. Bagehot described a panic as "a species of neuralgia"—unwarranted pain. Bagehot, *Lombard Street*, 51.

19. Paul Krugman, "If Banks Are Outlawed, Only Outlaws Will Have Banks," *The Conscience of a Liberal* (blog), *New York Times*, October 10, 2011.

20. Ken Binmore, *Playing for Real: A Text on Game Theory* (Oxford: Oxford University Press, 2007), 4.

21. For example, the leading textbook on financial regulation says that "depositors face a collective action problem of the sort game theorists call the *prisoner's dilemma*." Richard S. Carnell, Jonathan R. Macey, and Geoffrey P. Miller, *The Law of Financial Institutions*, 5th ed. (New York: Wolters Kluwer, 2013), 271. Likewise, a well-known article in the banking literature says that "bank depositors face a form of the prisoner's dilemma." Daniel R. Fischel, Andrew M. Rosenfield, and Robert S. Stillman, "The Regulation of Banks and Bank Holding Companies," *Virginia Law Review* 73, no. 2 (1987): 307.

22. See Jean-Jacques Rousseau, *Discourse on the Origin of Inequality* (1754), trans. Donald A. Cress (Indianapolis: Hackett, 1992), 47.

23. See, respectively, Robert Jervis, "Cooperation under the Security Dilemma," *World Politics* 30, no. 2 (1978): 167–68; Russell Hardin, *Liberalism, Constitutionalism, and Democracy* (New York: Oxford University Press, 1999), 90–102; Ken Binmore, *Natural Justice* (Oxford: Oxford University Press, 2005), 66–68.

24. I am not the first to analogize bank runs to a stag hunt, though others have tended to be rather vague about how the payout structure works. See Richard H. McAdams, "Beyond the Prisoners' Dilemma: Coordination, Game Theory, and Law," *Southern California Law Review* 82, no. 2 (2009): 221; Charles K. Whitehead, "Destructive Coordination," *Cornell Law Review* 96, no. 2 (2013): 332.

25. Drew Fudenberg and Jean Tirole, *Game Theory* (Cambridge, MA: MIT Press, 1991), 3.

26. Binmore, *Playing for Real*, 268.

27. Thomas C. Schelling, *The Strategy of Conflict* (1960; repr., Cambridge, MA: Harvard University Press, 1980), 57, 98.

28. Ibid., 91.

29. Ibid., 208. Bagehot understood this multiplier effect. "At first, incipient

panic amounts to a kind of vague conversation," he wrote. But then "this floating suspicion becomes both more intense and more diffused; it attacks more persons, and attacks them all more virulently than at first." Bagehot, *Lombard Street*, 49.

30. I borrow the fishing example from Thomas H. Jackson, *The Logic and Limits of Bankruptcy Law* (Cambridge, MA: Harvard University Press, 1986), 11–12.

31. Ronald H. Coase, "The Problem of Social Cost," *Journal of Law and Economics* 3 (October 1960): 15, 18.

32. Alexander Hamilton, *The Report of the Secretary of the Treasury on the Subject of a National Bank* (1790; repr., New York: S. Whiting, 1811), 5–6.

33. Albert Gallatin, "Considerations on the Currency and Banking System of the United States" (1831), in *The Writings of Albert Gallatin*, ed. Henry Adams (Philadelphia: J. B. Lippincott, 1879), 3:267–68.

34. Henry Dunning MacLeod, *The Theory and Practice of Banking*, 4th ed. (London: Longmans, Green, Reader and Dyer, 1883), 1:330–31.

35. Charles F. Dunbar, "Deposits as Currency," *Quarterly Journal of Economics* 1, no. 4 (1887): 402–3.

36. J. Laurence Laughlin, *The Principles of Money* (New York: Charles Scribner's Sons, 1903), 119.

37. Frank A. Vanderlip, "The Modern Bank," in *The Currency Problem and the Present Financial Situation: A Series of Addresses Delivered at Columbia University, 1907–1908* (New York: Columbia University Press, 1908), 5–6.

38. Ludwig von Mises, *The Theory of Money and Credit* (1912), trans. H. E. Batson (1934; repr., New Haven, CT: Yale University Press, 1953), 53.

39. Irving Fisher, *The Purchasing Power of Money*, rev. ed. (New York: Macmillan, 1913), 37–39.

40. Joseph A. Schumpeter, "The Explanation of the Business Cycle" (1927), in *Essays: On Entrepreneurs, Innovations, Business Cycles, and the Evolution of Capitalism*, ed. Richard V. Clemence (1951; repr., New Brunswick, NJ: Transaction, 1989), 36n1, 36.

Chapter Three

1. 468 Parl. Deb., H.C. (5th ser.) (1949) 160 (U.K.).

2. Chapter 5 discusses this topic more fully.

3. Relatedly, we will see in chapter 8 that money market "investors" are notoriously light on fundamental credit analysis.

4. I borrow this terminology from Perry Mehrling, *The New Lombard Street: How the Fed Became the Dealer of Last Resort* (Princeton, NJ: Princeton University Press, 2011), 2–6.

5. For a comprehensive review, see Gary B. Gorton and Andrew Winton, "Financial Intermediation," in *Handbook of the Economics of Finance*, ed. George

M. Constantinides, Milton Harris, and René M. Stulz (Amsterdam: Elsevier/North Holland, 2003), 1A:431–552.

6. Charles W. Calomiris and Charles M. Kahn, "The Role of Demandable Debt in Structuring Optimal Banking Arrangements," *American Economic Review* 81, no. 3 (1991).

7. Ibid., 498.

8. Douglas W. Diamond and Raghuram G. Rajan, "Liquidity Risk, Liquidity Creation, and Financial Fragility: A Theory of Banking," *Journal of Political Economy* 109, no. 2 (2001): 321.

9. Mark J. Flannery, "Debt Maturity and the Deadweight Cost of Leverage: Optimally Financing Banking Firms," *American Economic Review* 84, no. 1 (1994): 321, 320, 325.

10. Diamond and Rajan, "Liquidity Risk," 287–88.

11. Calomiris and Kahn, "The Role of Demandable Debt," 500n8, 508, 509.

12. Another example is the explosive growth in the past few years of repo-funded agency REITs, which issue short-term IOUs to fund portfolios of agency mortgage-backed securities—about as far from an illiquid "relationship loan" as one could imagine. For data on the explosive growth of this industry in recent years, see Jeremy C. Stein, "Overheating in Credit Markets: Origins, Measurement, and Policy Responses," remarks at the Federal Reserve Bank of St. Louis, February 7, 2013.

13. Ben S. Bernanke, "Reflections on a Year of Crisis," remarks at the Federal Reserve Bank of Kansas City's Annual Economic Symposium, Jackson Hole, Wyoming, August 21, 2009.

14. Kenneth R. French et al., *The Squam Lake Report: Fixing the Financial System* (Princeton, NJ: Princeton University Press, 2010), 69.

15. For a similarly critical take on these models, see Anat R. Admati and Martin F. Hellwig, "Does Debt Discipline Bankers? An Academic Myth about Bank Indebtedness," Rock Center for Corporate Governance at Stanford University Working Paper 132, February 18, 2013.

16. Gary B. Gorton and George Pennacchi, "Financial Intermediaries and Liquidity Creation," *Journal of Finance* 45, no. 1 (1990).

17. I discuss information insensitivity in more detail in chapter 8.

18. Admati and Hellwig, "Does Debt Discipline Bankers?" 4–5.

19. Diamond and Rajan, "Liquidity Risk," 288, 287.

20. Flannery, "Debt Maturity," 321–22.

21. Gorton's views on these matters are considered in more detail below, in the discussion of the Diamond-Dybvig model.

22. See Gary B. Gorton and Andrew Metrick, "Regulating the Shadow Banking System," *Brookings Papers on Economic Activity*, Fall 2010, 261–97.

23. Douglas W. Diamond and Philip H. Dybvig, "Bank Runs, Deposit Insurance, and Liquidity," *Journal of Political Economy* 91, no. 3 (1983): 401–19.

24. Diamond and Dybvig, "Bank Runs," 405.

25. By assumption, the return earned on loans exceeds the discount rate that consumers apply to future consumption.

26. Diamond and Dybvig, "Bank Runs," 407.

27. Charles W. Calomiris and Gary B. Gorton, "The Origins of Banking Panics: Models, Facts, and Bank Regulation," in *Financial Markets and Financial Crises*, ed. R. Glenn Hubbard (Chicago: University of Chicago Press, 1991), 128.

28. Gorton and Winton, "Financial Intermediation," 453.

29. One might think the bank should just turn away type 2 consumers who try to redeem at T = 1, but Diamond and Dybvig stipulate that consumers' types are not publicly observable.

30. Diamond and Dybvig, "Bank Runs," 409–10.

31. Gary B. Gorton, "Some Reflections on the Recent Financial Crisis," NBER Working Paper 18397, September 2012, 14.

32. I elaborate on this point in chapter 8, where I discuss "market discipline" by money-claimants.

33. See Franco Modigliani and Merton H. Miller, "The Cost of Capital, Corporation Finance and the Theory of Investment," *American Economic Review* 48, no. 3 (1958): 261–97.

34. Merton H. Miller, "Do the M&M Propositions Apply to Banks?" *Journal of Banking and Finance* 19 (June 1995): 485.

35. See, respectively, N. Gregory Mankiw, "Comments on Alan Greenspan's 'The Crisis,'" *Greg Mankiw's Blog*, March 19, 2010, and Raghuram G. Rajan, "Love the Bank, Hate the Banker," *Project Syndicate*, March 27, 2013.

36. See Anat R. Admati and Martin F. Hellwig, *The Bankers' New Clothes: What's Wrong with Banking and What to Do about It* (Princeton, NJ: Princeton University Press, 2013), 110–12.

37. See Anat R. Admati and Martin F. Hellwig, "The Parade of Bankers' New Clothes Continues: 23 Flawed Claims Debunked," Rock Center for Corporate Governance at Stanford University Working Paper 143, June 23, 2013, 5–7.

38. For previous articulations of this argument, see Morgan Ricks, "Regulating Money Creation after the Crisis," *Harvard Business Law Review* 1, no. 1 (2011), 101–3; Samuel G. Hanson, Anil K. Kashyap, and Jeremy C. Stein, "A Macroprudential Approach to Financial Regulation," *Journal of Economic Perspectives* 25, no. 1 (2011), 17–18.

39. See Ricks, "Regulating Money Creation after the Crisis," 89–94. Relatedly, Joseph Sommer argues that certain financial firm liabilities, such as deposits, repo, and insurance policy reserves, have an independent value as products. Joseph H. Sommer, "Why Bail-In? And How!" *FRBNY Economic Policy Review* 20, no. 2 (2014): 209–12.

40. Bernanke, "Reflections on a Year of Crisis."

41. For example, see Franklin Allen and Douglas Gale, "Financial Contagion," *Journal of Political Economy* 108, no. 1 (2000): 1–33. Cf. Tobias Adrian and Hyun

Song Shin, "Liquidity and Financial Contagion," *Banque de France Financial Stability Review*, no. 11 (February 2008): 1–7. Adrian and Shin are skeptical of what they call the "domino model" of contagion, in which direct exposures among defaulting banks are responsible for contagion. Hal Scott is similarly skeptical of the domino model, at least as applied to the recent financial crisis. See Hal S. Scott, "Interconnectedness and Contagion," Committee on Capital Markets Regulation, November 20, 2012.

42. Charles W. Calomiris and Joseph R. Mason, "Fundamentals, Panics, and Bank Distress during the Depression," *American Economic Review* 93, no. 5 (2003): 1639.

43. Gary Richardson and William Troost, "Monetary Intervention Mitigated Banking Panics during the Great Depression: Quasi-Experimental Evidence from a Federal Reserve District Border, 1929–1933," *Journal of Political Economy* 117, no. 6 (2009): 1070.

44. Calomiris and Gorton, "Origins of Banking Panics," 120. See also Gary B. Gorton, "Banking Panics and Business Cycles," *Oxford Economic Papers* 40, no. 4 (1988): 106–19; Charles W. Calomiris, "Bank Failures, the Great Depression, and Other 'Contagious' Events," in *The Oxford Handbook of Banking*, 2nd ed., ed. Allen N. Berger, Philip Molyneux, and John O. S. Wilson (New York: Oxford University Press, 2015).

45. The Scottish banking system before 1810 was dominated by three chartered ("public") banks. The two oldest—the Bank of Scotland and the Royal Bank of Scotland—had names suggesting official status. The former in fact had a legal monopoly on bank note issuance for its first twenty-one years (1695–1716). Alone among Scottish banks, the three public banks enjoyed the legal privilege of limited shareholder liability, and the government would accept their bank notes—but *not* those of nonchartered banks—in payment of customs duties. Briones and Rockoff conclude that "certainly the Public banks were given privileges often associated with central banks." Ignacio Briones and Hugh Rockoff, "Do Economists Reach a Conclusion on Free-Banking Episodes?" *Econ Journal Watch* 2, no. 2 (2005): 295. Cowen and Kroszner note that they had "the appearance of official sanction." Tyler Cowen and Randall Kroszner, "Scottish Banking before 1845: A Model for Laissez-Faire?" *Journal of Money, Credit and Banking* 21, no. 2 (1989): 226. Lawrence White counters that, with the emergence of large joint-stock banks starting in 1810, the public banks no longer enjoyed an "advantaged position." Lawrence H. White, *Free Banking in Britain: Theory, Experience and Debate, 1800–1845*, 2nd ed., revised and extended (London: Institute for Economic Affairs, 1995), 51–52. However, Cowen and Kroszner direct us to S. G. Checkland's authoritative history of Scottish banking, which says that by 1810 "the principal and ultimate source of liquidity [in Britain] lay in London, and, in particular, the Bank of England. This was especially so for the Scottish banks. ... The pattern, by 1810, was in a real sense a centralised one." Sydney G. Checkland, *Scottish Banking: A His-*

tory, 1695–1973 (Glasgow: Collins, 1975), 432. White acknowledges that "in a few cases the Bank [of England] provided loans to Scottish banks" but stresses that it sometimes refused to lend. White, *Free Banking*, 58. He further contends that because the Bank of England lacked an announced ex ante *policy* of liquidity support, it was not acting "in the standard sense" as lender of last resort (59). White insists "this is not just a terminological point," but I am not so sure. The prospect of support, even if conditional, may well have reassured bank claimants and enhanced stability. Finally, the dramatic collapse of the (nonchartered) Ayr bank in Scotland in 1772—an event that convinced no less a free market advocate than Adam Smith of the need for banking regulation—raises questions about just how stable the Scottish system was. The Ayr collapse appeared to do significant damage to the Scottish economy, contributing to "a real decline in economic activity and high unemployment" (even if "the recovery was relatively rapid"). Hugh Rockoff, "Parallel Journeys: Adam Smith and Milton Friedman on the Regulation of Banking," *Journal of Cultural Economy* 4, no. 3 (2011): 264. In spite of all this, White makes a convincing case that Scotland offers an example of a relatively free banking system functioning relatively well for a relatively long period. And it would be hard to dispute his conclusion that "neither the case for nor the case against a free-banking policy depends exclusively on how well the Scottish experience exemplifies free banking." White, *Free Banking*, 46.

46. The two dominant Canadian banks of the colonial period, the Bank of Montreal (est. 1817) and the Bank of Upper Canada (est. 1822), had "close ties to the state." Michael D. Bordo, Angela Redish, and Hugh Rockoff, "Why Didn't Canada Have a Banking Crisis in 2008 (or in 1930, or 1907, or . . .)?" *Economic History Review* 68, no. 1 (2015): 223. Entry into banking was limited in Canada, and banks were subject to portfolio constraints and limits on bank note issuance. From the start the system was "oligopolistic" (228), a "cartel backed by the federal government" (224). The Bank of Upper Canada was dominated by the ruling clique of the province; after its founding, nine of its fifteen directors "had important stations in the government." Bray Hammond, *Banks and Politics in America from the Revolution to the Civil War* (Princeton, NJ: Princeton University Press, 1957), 652. It acted "rather as an organ of financial administration than as an institution for the assistance of agriculture and commerce." Roeliff Morton Breckenridge, *The Canadian Banking System, 1817–1890* (Toronto, 1894), 78. Likewise, the Bank of Montreal "very early became the government's bank and performed many central bank functions." Michael D. Bordo, "The Lender of Last Resort: Alternative Views and Historical Experience," *Federal Reserve Bank of Richmond Economic Review* 76, no. 1 (1990): 26. Although Canada had no official central bank until 1935, the government apparently acted as a lender of last resort before then; according to Bordo, "on two occasions, 1907 and 1914, [Canadian banks'] reserves proved inadequate to prevent a liquidity crisis and the Government of Canada had to step in to supplement the reserves" (26). And while Canada didn't have explicit deposit

insurance until 1967, Kryzanowski and Roberts uncover statements by government officials in the 1920s suggesting that deposits were implicitly 100% insured. This may explain why no banks failed in Canada during the Great Depression despite evidence that much of the banking system was fundamentally insolvent. See Lawrence Kryzanowski and Gordon S. Roberts, "Canadian Banking Solvency, 1922–1940," *Journal of Money, Credit and Banking* 25, no. 3 (1993): 361–76.

47. For a detailed description of the anatomy of the shadow banking system, a useful resource is Zoltan Pozsar et al., "Shadow Banking," *FRBNY Economic Policy Review*, December 2013, 1–16. See also Tobias Adrian and Adam B. Ashcraft, "Shadow Banking: A Review of the Literature," Federal Reserve Bank of New York Staff Report 580, October 2012; Markus K. Brunnermeier, "Deciphering the Liquidity and Credit Crunch 2007–2008," *Journal of Economic Perspectives* 23, no. 1 (2009): 77–100.

48. Financial Stability Board, "Strengthening Oversight and Regulation of Shadow Banking," Consultative Document, November 18, 2012, ii.

49. Walter Bagehot, *Lombard Street: A Description of the Money Market* (1873; repr., New York: John Wiley, 1999), 292, 28, 295, 290.

50. For a detailed account, see Daniel Covitz, Nellie Liang, and Gustavo A. Suarez, "The Evolution of a Financial Crisis: Collapse of the Asset-Backed Commercial Paper Market," *Journal of Finance* 68, no. 3 (2013): 815–48.

51. For a detailed account, see Gary B. Gorton and Andrew Metrick, "Securitized Banking and the Run on Repo," *Journal of Financial Economics* 104, no. 3 (2012): 425–51.

52. That this policy response also touched regulated bank holding companies does not contradict this conclusion. The most urgent problems for the big bank holding companies were in their broker-dealer operations—which are housed in separate subsidiaries from their deposit banking operations—and in their off-balance-sheet conduits.

Chapter Four

1. Quoted in David M. Herszenhorn, Carl Huse, and Sheryl Gay Stolberg, "Talks Implode during a Day of Chaos," *New York Times*, September 25, 2008.

2. In their sweeping history of financial crises, Reinhart and Rogoff define "banking crisis" in such a way as to *not* require that there be any bank run or panic; they include the US savings and loan debacle, for example. See Carmen M. Reinhart and Kenneth S. Rogoff, *This Time Is Different: Eight Centuries of Financial Folly* (Princeton, NJ: Princeton University Press, 2009), 10, 390. There is certainly nothing "wrong" with their classification scheme, but it does mean their study is of limited utility for this chapter's purposes.

3. Anna J. Schwartz, "Real and Pseudo-Financial Crises," in *Money in His-*

torical Perspective, ed. Anna J. Schwartz (Chicago: University of Chicago Press, 1987), 271–72.

4. Information on major panics and output contractions before World War I is from Andrew J. Jalil, "A New History of Banking Panics in the United States, 1825–1929: Construction and Implications," *American Economic Journal: Macroeconomics* 7, no. 3 (2015): 323, table 8.

5. Bank failure data are from George Hanc, "The Banking Crises of the 1980s and Early 1990s: Summary and Implications," in *History of the Eighties: Lessons for the Future* (Washington, DC: Federal Deposit Insurance Corporation, 1997), 1:14–15. Thrift failure data are from Timothy Curry and Lynn Shibut, "The Cost of the Savings and Loan Crisis: Truth and Consequences," *FDIC Banking Review* 13, no. 2 (2000): 27.

6. For evidence on the protracted nature of postcrisis recoveries, see Carmen M. Reinhart and Kenneth S. Rogoff, "Recovery from Financial Crises: Evidence from 100 Episodes," *American Economic Review: Papers and Proceedings*, May 2014, 50–55. They examine one hundred systemic banking crises worldwide since 1800 and find that recoveries tend to be "protracted and halting," with an average time of about 8 years, and a median time of about 6.5 years, to recover to the pre-crisis level of real per capita GDP.

7. Walter Bagehot, *Lombard Street: A Description of the Money Market* (1873; repr., New York: John Wiley, 1999), 17, 52, 122–23, 131, 159, 187.

8. Milton Friedman and Anna J. Schwartz, *A Monetary History of the United States, 1867–1960* (Princeton, NJ: Princeton University Press, 1963), 441–42, 355, 357, 358, 407, 441.

9. Gary B. Gorton, *Slapped by the Invisible Hand: The Panic of 2007* (New York: Oxford University Press, 2010), 62, 13–15, 186n6.

10. See Gary B. Gorton, *Misunderstanding Financial Crises: Why We Don't See Them Coming* (New York: Oxford University Press, 2012), 43.

11. Ben S. Bernanke, "Some Reflections on the Crisis and the Policy Response," remarks at the Russell Sage Foundation and the Century Foundation Conference on Rethinking Finance, New York, April 13, 2012.

12. Friedman and Schwartz, *Monetary History*, 346.

13. See Charles W. Calomiris and Joseph R. Mason, "Consequences of Bank Distress during the Great Depression," *American Economic Review* 93, no. 3 (2003): 937–47.

14. Ben S. Bernanke, "Nonmonetary Effects of the Financial Crisis in the Propagation of the Great Depression," *American Economic Review* 73, no. 3 (1983): 263, 264, 268, 260.

15. The elements of this theory appear in Jeremy C. Stein, "Monetary Policy as Financial Stability Regulation," *Quarterly Journal of Economics* 127, no. 1 (2012): 57–95, and Andrei Shleifer and Robert Vishny, "Fire Sales in Finance and Macroeconomics," *Journal of Economic Perspectives* 25, no. 1 (2011): 29–48.

16. Bagehot again put it best: "According to the saying, you 'can sell Consols on a Sunday.' . . . But not so in a general panic. . . . All ordinary bankers are wanting to sell, or thinking they may have to sell." Bagehot, *Lombard Street*, 60–61.

17. N. Gregory Mankiw and Laurence M. Ball, *Macroeconomics and the Financial System* (New York: Worth, 2011), 540.

18. The text does note in passing that financial firms may "reduce loans in order to increase their liquid assets and guard against runs" (ibid., 539), but this mechanism did not make it into the summary flowchart.

19. Reinhart and Rogoff, *This Time Is Different*, 172.

20. Michael Woodford, "Financial Intermediation and Macroeconomic Analysis," *Journal of Economic Perspectives* 24, no. 4 (2010): 35.

21. Samuel G. Hanson, Anil K. Kashyap, and Jeremy C. Stein, "A Macroprudential Approach to Financial Regulation," *Journal of Economic Perspectives* 25, no. 1 (2011): 6–7.

22. See Laurence Ball, J. Bradford DeLong, and Larry Summers, "Fiscal Policy and Full Employment," Center on Budget and Policy Priorities, Full Employment Project, April 2, 2014.

23. Larry Summers on Twitter, tweet of February 24, 2014, 12:26 p.m.

24. Larry Summers, "Fiscal Policy and Full Employment," remarks at the Center on Budget and Policy Priorities, April 2, 2014, available on Youtube.com (comments appear between the seventeen- and nineteen-minute marks).

25. Victoria Ivashina and David S. Scharfstein, "Bank Lending during the Financial Crisis of 2008," *Journal of Financial Economics* 97, no. 3 (2010): 320, 337. Another study similarly finds that "banks that relied more heavily on core deposit and equity capital financing, which are stable sources of financing, continued to lend relative to other banks" during the crisis. Marcia M. Cornett, Jamie J. McNutt, Philip E. Strahan, and Hassan Tehranian, "Liquidity Risk Management and Credit Supply in the Financial Crisis," *Journal of Financial Economics* 101, no. 2 (2011): 297.

26. A syndicated loan is a large corporate loan provided by multiple financing sources. The authors focus on this market because a robust dataset of new originations is available.

27. Yes, the panic-crunch theory predicts a *generalized* withdrawal of financing, but it is to be expected that run-prone institutions would cut back more severely.

28. The data series originally appeared in Mark Mitchell and Todd Pulvino, "Arbitrage Crashes and the Speed of Capital," *Journal of Financial Economics* 104, no. 3 (2012): 469–90.

29. D. E. Shaw Group, "The Basis Monster That Ate Wall Street," *D. E. Shaw Group Market Insights*, March 2009, 7. It is sometimes suggested that counterparty credit risk might explain the behavior of the CDS-bond basis during the crisis, but this is doubtful. Darrell Duffie concludes that the deviation was "far too large to

be realistically explained by CDS counterparty risk." Darrell Duffie, "Presidential Address: Asset Price Dynamics with Slow-Moving Capital," *Journal of Finance* 65, no. 4 (2010): 1246.

30. Technically, the writer of CDS protection usually parts with a small amount of cash up front in the form of "initial margin," but this is only a tiny fraction of the notional amount of the contract.

31. Gabriel Chodorow-Reich, "The Employment Effects of Credit Market Disruptions: Firm-Level Evidence from the 2008-9 Financial Crisis," *Quarterly Journal of Economics* 129, no. 1 (2014): 1. Cf. Kathleen M. Kahle and René M. Stulz, "Access to Capital, Investment, and the Financial Crisis," *Journal of Financial Economics* 110, no. 2 (2013): 280-99. Kahle and Stulz argue that firm behavior during the crisis suggests a shock to demand rather than impaired access to capital. However, as they acknowledge, a shock to the financing of businesses' *customers* would affect demand for firms' products.

32. Michael D. Bordo, "Comment on 'The Great Depression and the Friedman-Schwartz Hypothesis' by Lawrence Christiano, Roberto Motto, and Massimo Rostagno," *Journal of Money, Credit and Banking* 35, no. 6 (2003): 1199.

33. For example, see David Laidler, "The Price Level, Relative Prices and Economic Stability: Aspects of the Interwar Debate," BIS Working Paper 136, September 2003; Barry Eichengreen and Kris J. Mitchener, "The Great Depression as a Credit Boom Gone Wrong," in *Research in Economic History*, vol. 22, ed. Alexander J. Field (Oxford: Elsevier, 2004), 183-237; Guillermo Calvo, "Puzzling Over the Anatomy of Crises: Liquidity and the Veil of Finance," background paper for the Mayekawa Lecture at the Bank of Japan, Tokyo, June 2013.

34. Ludwig von Mises, *The Theory of Money and Credit* (1912), trans. H. E. Batson (1934; repr., New Haven, CT: Yale University Press, 1953), 263, 354-64.

35. Friedrich A. Hayek, *Prices and Production*, 2nd ed. (London: Routledge and Kegan Paul, 1935), 98-99. Whether Hayek opposed using monetary policy to counteract a sharp deflation is a subject of debate; Lawrence White says he did not. See Lawrence H. White, "Did Hayek and Robbins Deepen the Great Depression?" *Journal of Money, Credit and Banking* 40, no. 4 (2008): 751-68. But even White acknowledges that Hayek failed to push antideflationary monetary policy "in the early 1930s when it mattered most" (754).

36. Lionel Robbins, *The Great Depression* (New York: Macmillan, 1935), 75, 171. Robbins later disclaimed these views, at least as applied to the Great Depression. See Lionel Robbins, *Autobiography of an Economist* (London: Macmillan, 1971), 154.

37. Schumpeter is probably better viewed as a precursor to modern neoclassical economics, which we will look at below. See J. Bradford DeLong, "'Liquidation' Cycles: Old-Fashioned Real Business Cycle Theory and the Great Depression," NBER Working Paper 3546, December 1990.

38. Joseph A. Schumpeter, "Depressions: Can We Learn from Past Experi-

ence?" (1934), in *Essays: On Entrepreneurs, Innovations, Business Cycles, and the Evolution of Capitalism*, ed. Richard V. Clemence (1951; repr., New Brunswick, NJ: Transaction, 1989), 115, 117. Schumpeter's views appear to have moderated over time. He later expressed openness to remedial measures in some circumstances. See Joseph A. Schumpeter, "The Historical Approach to the Analysis of Business Cycles" (1949), in *Essays*, 323.

39. Herbert Hoover, *The Memoirs of Herbert Hoover*, vol. 3, *The Great Depression, 1929–1941* (New York: Macmillan, 1952), 30.

40. Murray N. Rothbard, *America's Great Depression*, 5th ed. (Auburn, AL: Mises Institute, 2000), 210. Rothbard's remark came to my attention from Charles P. Kindleberger and Robert Aliber, *Manias, Panics, and Crashes: A History of Financial Crises*, 6th ed. (New York: Palgrave Macmillan, 2011), 196.

41. John Maynard Keynes, "An Economic Analysis of Unemployment" (1931), in *The Collected Writings of John Maynard Keynes*, ed. Donald Moggridge, vol. 13 (London: Macmillan, 1973), 349. This passage came to my attention from Brad DeLong's blog.

42. Friedman and Schwartz, *Monetary History*, 409.

43. Peter Temin, *Did Monetary Forces Cause the Great Depression?* (New York: W. W. Norton, 1976), 9–10, 83, 11.

44. Bernanke, "Nonmonetary Effects," 268. Temin's later work put greater emphasis on the role of the international gold standard. See Peter Temin, *Lessons from the Great Depression* (Cambridge, MA: MIT Press, 1989).

45. Dean Baker, "Blame It on the Bubble," *Guardian*, March 8, 2010.

46. Dean Baker, "What Krugman Said, with a Not So Small Addendum," *Beat the Press* (blog), Center for Economic and Policy Research, October 20, 2012.

47. Edward C. Prescott, interview, "On the Economy with Tom Keene," *Bloomberg*, March 30, 2009 (comments appear between the nineteen- and twenty-one-minute marks).

48. V. V. Chari, Lawrence Christiano, and Patrick J. Kehoe, "Facts and Myths about the Financial Crisis of 2008," Federal Reserve Bank of Minneapolis Working Paper 666, October 2008, 4, 11.

49. Lee E. Ohanian, "The Economic Crisis from a Neoclassical Perspective," *Journal of Economic Perspectives* 24, no. 4 (2010): 57, 59.

50. Casey B. Mulligan, *The Redistribution Recession: How Labor Market Distortions Contracted the Economy* (New York: Oxford University Press, 2012), 8, 121, 109.

51. Ibid., 270.

52. Casey B. Mulligan, "Questions and Answers about the Book," n.d.

53. Mulligan, *Redistribution Recession*, 270, 121.

54. Paul Krugman, "End This Depression Now! A Politics and Prose Event," remarks at Politics and Prose, Washington, DC, May 1, 2012, available on Youtube .com (comment appears at the sixty-six-minute mark).

55. Scott Sumner, "Misdiagnosing the Crisis: The Real Problem Was Not Real, It Was Nominal," *Vox*, September 10, 2009.

56. Scott Sumner, "The Real Problem Was Nominal," *Cato Unbound*, September 14, 2009.

57. Scott Sumner, "Where I've Failed (So Far)," *TheMoneyIllusion* (blog), December 6, 2012.

58. Scott Sumner, "The Case for Nominal GDP Targeting," Mercatus Research, Mercatus Center at George Mason University, October 23, 2012, 14.

59. Scott Sumner, "FAQs," *TheMoneyIllusion* (blog), n.d.

60. Scott Sumner, "Keep Banks Out of Macro," *TheMoneyIllusion* (blog), January 22, 2013.

61. Sumner, "FAQs."

62. Scott Sumner, "Eugene Fama Makes Me Look Like an MMTer," *TheMoneyIllusion* (blog), March 9, 2012.

63. Scott Sumner, "An Idealistic Defense of Pragmatism," *TheMoneyIllusion* (blog), August 16, 2011.

64. Scott Sumner, "Miron and Rigol on Bank Failures and Output," *TheMoneyIllusion* (blog), September 17, 2013.

65. Irving Fisher, "The Debt-Deflation Theory of Great Depressions," *Econometrica* 1, no. 4 (1933): 341–42, 344, 342, 346, 350. Emphasis has been removed.

66. Hyman P. Minsky, *Stabilizing an Unstable Economy*, rev. ed. (New York: McGraw-Hill, 2008), 320, 230–31, 234, 194.

67. Hyman P. Minsky, "The Financial-Instability Hypothesis: Capitalist Processes and the Behavior of the Economy," in *Financial Crises: Theory, History, and Policy*, ed. Charles P. Kindleberger and Jean-Pierre Laffargue (London: Cambridge University Press, 1982), 16, 36. See also Hyman P. Minsky, "The Financial Instability Hypothesis," Jerome Levy Economics Institute of Bard College Working Paper 74, May 1992.

68. Richard C. Koo, *The Holy Grail of Macroeconomics: Lessons from Japan's Great Recession*, rev. ed. (Singapore: John Wiley, 2009), 157, 17, xiv, 147, 181.

69. John Geanakoplos, "Solving the Present Crisis and Managing the Leverage Cycle," *FRBNY Economic Policy Review* 16, no. 1 (2010): 101, 102, 103, 106, 105n7.

70. See Ben S. Bernanke, "The Financial Accelerator and the Credit Channel," remarks at the conference on the Credit Channel of Monetary Policy in the Twenty-First Century, Federal Reserve Bank of Atlanta, June 15, 2007.

71. Robert E. Hall, "Why Does the Economy Fall to Pieces after a Financial Crisis?" *Journal of Economic Perspectives* 24, no. 4 (2010): 6.

72. Kindleberger and Aliber, *Manias, Panics, and Crashes*, 5.

73. Yasuyuki Fuchita and Kei Kodachi, "Managing Systemwide Financial Crises: Some Lessons from Japan since 1990," in *Rocky Times: New Perspectives on Financial Stability*, ed. Yasuyuki Fuchita, Richard Herring, and Robert Litan (Washington, DC: Brookings Institution Press, 2012), 28–29.

74. Hiroshi Nakaso, "The Financial Crisis in Japan during the 1990s: How the Bank of Japan Responded and the Lessons Learnt," Bank for International Settlements Paper 6, October 2001, 9, 11.

75. See Masazumi Hattori, Koji Koyama, and Tatsuya Yonetani, "Analysis of Credit Spread in Japan's Corporate Bond Market," Bank for International Settlements Papers 5, October 2001.

76. Richard C. Koo, *Balance Sheet Recession: Japan's Struggle with Uncharted Economics and Its Global Implications* (Singapore: John Wiley, 2003), 43, 146.

77. Paul Krugman, "It's Baaack: Japan's Slump and the Return of the Liquidity Trap," *Brookings Papers on Economic Activity*, no. 2 (1998): 177.

78. Paul Krugman, "More on Japan (Wonkish)," *The Conscience of a Liberal* (blog), *New York Times*, January 10, 2012.

79. Koo, *Balance Sheet Recession*, 145–46.

80. Tamim Bayoumi, "The Morning After: Explaining the Slowdown in Japanese Growth in the 1990s," *Journal of International Economics* 53, no. 2 (2001): 242.

81. Paul Krugman, *The Return of Depression Economics and the Crisis of 2008* (New York: W. W. Norton, 2009), 72; Koo, *Holy Grail of Macroeconomics*, 152.

82. To be clear, I am not suggesting that fiscal policy—in particular, the consumption tax increase in April 1997—didn't hurt Japan's economy. But the sharp economic decline appears to have happened later in the year, coinciding with the panic. See Hideo Hayakawa and Eiji Maeda, "Understanding Japan's Financial and Economic Developments since Autumn 1997," Bank of Japan Working Paper 00-1 (January 2000).

83. Atif Mian and Amir Sufi, *House of Debt: How They (and You) Caused the Great Recession, and How We Can Prevent It from Happening Again* (Chicago: University of Chicago Press, 2014). See also Atif Mian and Amir Sufi, "What Explains the 2007–2009 Drop in Employment?" *Econometrica* 82, no. 6 (2014): 2197–223.

84. Mian and Sufi, *House of Debt*, 133.

85. Ibid., 31–33.

86. Ibid., 130.

87. For example, see the St. Louis Fed Financial Stress Index, available from the Federal Reserve Economic Database. See also the short-term funding spreads in figure 3.5 of this book. One can also look at CDS spreads for large US financial firms during the crisis; these can be found in Federal Reserve Board, "Monetary Policy Report to the Congress," February 24, 2010, 22 (fig. 33).

88. I am using the seasonally adjusted S&P Case-Shiller 20-City Composite Home Price Index. A graph of this series appears in figure 7.3.

89. Mian and Sufi, *House of Debt*, 32, 133.

90. Ibid., 130.

91. See Ivashina and Scharfstein, "Bank Lending during the Financial Crisis of 2008."

92. See Financial Stability Oversight Council, *2014 Annual Report*, 19 (chart 4.2.8).

93. Mian and Sufi, *House of Debt*, 4–6, 44. See also Atif Mian and Amir Sufi, "Household Debt and the Great Depression," *House of Debt* (blog), March 15, 2014.

94. The ratios are higher if one includes farm debt, but in that case the pre-Depression run-up is less pronounced.

95. Ben S. Bernanke, *Essays on the Great Depression* (Princeton, NJ: Princeton University Press, 2000), viii.

96. Paul Krugman, "What Janet Yellen—and Everyone Else—Got Wrong," *The Conscience of a Liberal* (blog), *New York Times*, August 8, 2013. See also Paul Krugman, "Worthwhile Canadian Comparison," *The Conscience of a Liberal* (blog), *New York Times*, June 15, 2013.

97. John Maynard Keynes, "A Self-Adjusting Economic System?" *New Republic*, February 20, 1935, 35–36. I was alerted to this piece by Mike Konczal, "Why Keynes Wouldn't Have Too Rosy a View of Our Economic Future," *Wonkblog*, *Washington Post*, September 7, 2013.

98. John Maynard Keynes, *The General Theory of Employment, Interest, and Money* (1936; repr., San Diego, CA: First Harvest/Harcourt, 1964), 30–31.

99. James Tobin, "Price Flexibility and Output Stability: An Old Keynesian View," *Journal of Economic Perspectives* 7, no. 1 (1993): 47–48. For a more recent take, see John Quiggin, "New Old Keynesianism," *Crooked Timber* (blog), January 22, 2014.

100. Tobin does refer approvingly to Fisher's debt-deflation theory, but this is clearly ancillary to his overall argument; it is not a core part of his story. Rather, Tobin says that debt deflation acts as a countervailing force against the "Pigou effect" or "real balance effect," which asserts that falling prices lead to higher real money balances, thereby stimulating demand. Tobin argues that the Pigou effect is "of dubious strength." Tobin, "Price Flexibility," 59–60.

101. See Peter A. Diamond, "Aggregate Demand Management in Search Equilibrium," *Journal of Political Economy* 90, no. 5 (1982): 892–94.

102. For a review of such models as of the late 1980s, see Russell Cooper and Andrew John, "Coordinating Coordination Failures in Keynesian Models," *Quarterly Journal of Economics* 103, no. 3 (1988): 441–63. The authors describe models that exhibit "underemployment equilibria" owing to "the inability of agents to coordinate their actions successfully in a many-person, decentralized economy" rather than to "the usual Keynesian assumptions" of wage or price rigidities (442). See also Roger E. A. Farmer, *How the Economy Works: Confidence, Crashes and Self-Fulfilling Prophecies* (New York: Oxford University Press, 2010).

103. Robert F. Martin, Teyanna Munyan, and Beth Anne Wilson, "Potential Output and Recessions: Are We Fooling Ourselves?" *IFDP Notes*, November 12, 2014.

Chapter Five

1. Noble State Bank v. Haskell, 219 U.S. 104, 113 (1911).

2. James Tobin, "Money and Finance in the Macro-economic Process," Nobel Lecture, December 8, 1981.

3. N. Gregory Mankiw, *Macroeconomics*, 8th ed. (New York: Worth, 2013), 84.

4. Milton Friedman and Anna J. Schwartz, *A Monetary History of the United States, 1867–1960* (Princeton, NJ: Princeton University Press, 1963), 696.

5. Abba P. Lerner, "Money as a Creature of the State," *American Economic Review* 37, no. 2 (1947): 313.

6. Adam Smith, *An Inquiry into the Nature and Causes of the Wealth of Nations* (1776), ed. R. H. Campbell and A. S. Skinner (Oxford: Clarendon Press, 1976), 1:328.

7. L. Randall Wray, *Modern Money Theory: A Primer on Macroeconomics for Sovereign Monetary Systems* (London: Palgrave Macmillan, 2012), 50.

8. A notable dissenter from this view was Milton Friedman, who eventually came to favor a permanently frozen monetary base. See Milton Friedman, "Monetary Policy for the 1980s," in *To Promote Prosperity: U.S. Domestic Policy in the Mid-1980s*, ed. John H. Moore (Stanford, CA: Hoover Institution Press, 1984), 48–52.

9. See Milton Friedman, *The Optimum Quantity of Money* (1969; repr., New Brunswick, NJ: Transaction, 2006), 4.

10. Robert E. Lucas Jr., "Monetary Neutrality," Nobel Lecture, December 7, 1995.

11. Tobin, "Money and Finance in the Macro-economic Process."

12. Christine Desan, "From Blood to Profit: Making Money in the Practice and Imagery of Early America," *Journal of Policy History* 20, no. 1 (2008): 28.

13. See Jonathan Gruber, *Public Finance and Public Policy*, 2nd ed. (New York: Worth, 2007), 585.

14. Ibid., 114.

15. U.S. Const. art. III, § 1.

16. Ben S. Bernanke, "Central Bank Independence, Transparency, and Accountability," remarks at the Institute for Monetary and Economic Studies International Conference, Bank of Japan, Tokyo, May 26, 2010.

17. For example, see Jeroen Klomp and Jakob de Haan, "Inflation and Central Bank Independence: A Meta-Regression Analysis," *Journal of Economic Surveys* 24, no. 4 (2010): 593–621.

18. 12 U.S.C. §§ 241–242.

19. See Kirti Datla and Richard L. Revesz, "Deconstructing Independent Agencies (and Executive Agencies)," *Cornell Law Review* 98, no. 4 (2013): 789–91.

20. 12 U.S.C. § 243.

21. Peter Conti-Brown stresses the nonlegal and informal aspects of Fed inde-

pendence while also suggesting that the Fed is less independent from politics than is often presumed. See Peter Conti-Brown, "The Institutions of Federal Reserve Independence," *Yale Journal on Regulation* 32, no. 2 (2015). Of course, independence is not binary; it is a matter of degree.

22. See Datla and Revesz, "Deconstructing Independent Agencies."

23. For an argument that the Fed has become a "fourth branch of government," see David Wessel, *In Fed We Trust: Ben Bernanke's War on the Great Panic* (New York: Three Rivers Press, 2009), 3–4.

24. See Federal Reserve Act § 2A, 12 U.S.C. § 225a.

25. Marvin Goodfriend, "Policy Debates at the Federal Open Market Committee: 1993–2002," in *The Origins, History, and Future of the Federal Reserve: A Return to Jekyll Island*, ed. Michael D. Bordo and William Roberds (New York: Cambridge University Press, 2013), 355–56.

26. Ibid.

27. History supplies another example. Under the original National Bank Acts (described below), national bank notes had to be collateralized by federal bonds. "After the Civil War, when the federal government gradually reduced its level of outstanding debt, the supply of Treasury securities fell," writes Bob Litan. "The low supply of Treasury securities forced a contraction in national bank note circulation." Robert E. Litan, *What Should Banks Do?* (Washington, DC: Brookings Institution Press, 1987), 21.

28. Walter Bagehot, *Lombard Street: A Description of the Money Market* (1873; repr., New York: John Wiley, 1999), 88–89.

29. National Bank Act of 1864, ch. 106, 13 Stat. 99 (superseding the National Currency Act of 1863, ch. 58, 12 Stat. 665). I am disregarding the ill-fated first and second Banks of the United States, which were not designed to implement broad-based banking regulation.

30. See National Bank Act § 8, 13 Stat. at 101 (portfolio and activity restrictions); § 29, 13 Stat. at 108 (diversification requirements); § 31, 13 Stat. at 108 (cash reserve requirements); § 7, 13 Stat. at 101 (capital requirements); § 38, 13 Stat. at 110 (dividend restrictions); § 28, 13 Stat. at 107 (limits on real estate ownership).

31. See National Bank Act § 34, 13 Stat. at 109 (reporting requirements); § 54, 13 Stat. at 116 (supervision).

32. See Andrew J. Jalil, "A New History of Banking Panics in the United States, 1825–1929: Construction and Implications," *American Economic Journal: Macroeconomics* 7, no. 3 (2015): 305, table 2.

33. Federal Reserve Act, Pub. L. No. 63-43, 38 Stat. 251 (1913).

34. Friedman and Schwartz, *Monetary History*, 407, 408, 411.

35. See Federal Reserve Act § 13, 38 Stat. at 263–64.

36. See Banking Act of 1933, Pub. L. No. 73-66, § 8, 48 Stat. 162, 168–80 (establishing deposit insurance effective January 1, 1934).

37. Gary B. Gorton, *Slapped by the Invisible Hand: The Panic of 2007* (New York: Oxford University Press, 2010), 13–14.

Chapter Six

1. Walter Bagehot, *Lombard Street: A Description of the Money Market* (1873; repr., New York: John Wiley, 1999), 231–32.

2. The introduction of long-term debt into the capital structure would complicate the exposition without materially altering the conclusions.

3. See National Bank Act of 1864, ch. 106, § 8, 13 Stat. 99, 101–2. Chapter 8 offers an overview of US bank portfolio constraints as they exist today.

4. For a nuanced analysis, see John C. Coates IV, "Cost-Benefit Analysis of Financial Regulation: Case Studies and Implications," *Yale Law Journal* 124, no. 4 (2015): 882–1011.

5. The 100% reserve proposal was then sometimes called the "Chicago Plan." For a fascinating history, see Ronnie J. Phillips, *The Chicago Plan and New Deal Banking Reform* (New York: M. E. Sharpe, 1995).

6. See Irving Fisher, *100% Money* (1935), 3rd ed. (New Haven, CT: City Printing, 1945). While his debt-deflation theory (see chapter 4), published in 1933, tends to get more attention today, Fisher in *100% Money* identified "the instability of demand deposits" as "the chief cause of both booms and depressions" (xviii).

7. See Milton Friedman, *A Program for Monetary Stability* (New York: Fordham University Press, 1960), chap. 3.

8. See, respectively, Merton H. Miller, "Do the M&M Propositions Apply to Banks?" *Journal of Banking and Finance* 19 (June 1995): 488–89; Robert C. Merton and Zvi Bodie, "Deposit Insurance Reform: A Functional Approach," *Carnegie-Rochester Conference Series on Public Policy* 38 (June 1993): 1–34; James Tobin, "The Case for Preserving Regulatory Distinctions," in *Restructuring the Financial System* (Kansas City: Federal Reserve Bank of Kansas City, 1987), 167–83.

9. See N. Gregory Mankiw, "Comments on Alan Greenspan's 'The Crisis,'" *Greg Mankiw's Blog*, March 19, 2010; Laurence J. Kotlikoff, *Jimmy Stewart Is Dead: Ending the World's Ongoing Financial Plague with Limited Purpose Banking* (Hoboken, NJ: John Wiley, 2010).

10. Merton and Bodie, "Deposit Insurance Reform," 21.

11. Hyman P. Minsky, foreword to Phillips, *Chicago Plan and New Deal Banking Reform*, xiii.

12. Fisher, *100% Money*, 207.

13. Friedman, *Program for Monetary Stability*, 71, 109n11.

14. Robert E. Litan, *What Should Banks Do?* (Washington, DC: Brookings Institution Press, 1987), 169, 171, 187. Litan's proposal called for allowing financial holding companies to engage in a broad range of financial activities (including in-

vestment banking) only if their deposit bank subsidiaries were narrow banks. This specific proposal was rendered moot by the Gramm-Leach-Bliley Act, Pub. L. No. 106-102, 113 Stat. 1338 (1999). Nonetheless, Litan's analysis of narrow banking remains highly relevant.

15. Gardiner Means, "Reorganization of the Banking System," memorandum (1933), quoted in Phillips, *Chicago Plan and New Deal Banking Reform*, 69 (emphasis removed).

16. Letter from Simons to Irving Fisher, January 19, 1934, quoted in Phillips, *Chicago Plan and New Deal Banking Reform*, 68.

17. Letter from Simons to Irving Fisher, July 4, 1934, quoted in Phillips, *Chicago Plan and New Deal Banking Reform*, 90.

18. Henry C. Simons, "Rules versus Authorities in Monetary Policy" (1936), in *Economic Policy for a Free Society* (Chicago: University of Chicago Press, 1948), 331n17.

19. See William R. Allen, "Irving Fisher and the 100 Percent Reserve Proposal," *Journal of Law and Economics* 36, no. 2 (1993): 708n21.

20. Friedman, *Program for Monetary Stability*, 73-74.

21. Litan, *What Should Banks Do?*, 185.

22. Anat R. Admati et al., "Fallacies, Irrelevant Facts, and Myths in the Discussion of Capital Regulation: Why Bank Equity Is Not Socially Expensive," Rock Center for Corporate Governance at Stanford University Working Paper 161, October 22, 2013, i, 55, 11, 40.

23. There is a theoretical argument that overleveraged institutions might decline to pursue positive NPV investments. This is the "debt overhang" argument, which I addressed briefly in chapter 4. Even if we accept that debt overhang affects bank incentives, the magnitude of the effect is uncertain, and there is no reason to suppose that banks would choose to maintain their liabilities at a constant level if they were required to maintain more equity financing.

24. See Matt Levine, "Bill to Make Banking Boring Actually Might Be Kind of Fun," *Dealbreaker* (blog), May 1, 2013. For a similar example, see David Jones, "Emerging Problems with the Basel Capital Accord: Regulatory Capital Arbitrage and Related Issues," *Journal of Banking and Finance* 24 (January 2000): 40. Relatedly, Robert C. Merton observed two decades ago that financial innovation had rendered the leverage ratio "less meaningful." Robert C. Merton, "Financial Innovation and the Management and Regulation of Financial Institutions," *Journal of Banking and Finance* 19 (June 1995): 461-81.

25. For criticisms of risk weighting, see, for example, Thomas M. Hoenig, "Basel III Capital: A Well-Intended Illusion," remarks to the International Association of Deposit Insurers 2013 Research Conference, Basel, April 9, 2013; Simon Johnson, "Bank Leverage Is the Defining Debate of Our Time," *Bloomberg*, September 3, 2013. The latter describes risk weighting as "a dangerous fantasy."

26. See Hoenig, "Basel III Capital," table 1.

27. For an analysis of the issues, with a focus on financial reporting implications,

see International Swaps and Derivatives Association, "Netting and Offsetting: Reporting Derivatives under U.S. GAAP and under IFRS," May 2012.

28. For a nice summary of the history of international capital regulation, see Hal S. Scott and Anna Gelpern, *International Finance: Transactions, Policy, and Regulation*, 19th ed. (New York: Foundation Press, 2012), chap. 7.

29. Basel Committee on Banking Supervision (BCBS), "International Convergence of Capital Measurement and Capital Standards," July 1988.

30. BCBS, "Amendment to the Capital Accord to Incorporate Market Risks," January 1996.

31. BCBS, "International Convergence of Capital Measurement and Capital Standards: A Revised Framework," June 2004.

32. BCBS, "Basel III: A Global Regulatory Framework for More Resilient Banks and Banking Systems," December 2010 (revised June 2011).

33. See BCBS, "Basel III Leverage Ratio Framework and Disclosure Requirements," January 2014. The US implementation of the leverage ratio for large banking organizations is roughly consistent with the Basel III methodology.

34. Matt Levine, "Relatively Simple Basel Leverage Rules Still Pretty Complicated," *Dealbreaker* (blog), June 26, 2013.

35. Matt Levine, "Basel Makes Its Simple Leverage Rules . . . Simpler?" *Bloomberg View* (blog), January 13, 2014.

36. Robert L. Greenfield and Leland B. Yeager, "A Laissez-Faire Approach to Monetary Stability," *Journal of Money, Credit and Banking* 15, no. 3 (1983): 304, 303, 305, 307.

37. Tyler Cowen and Randall Kroszner, "Mutual Fund Banking: A Market Approach," *Cato Journal* 10, no. 1 (1990): 225, 227, 230n13, 223.

38. James Tobin, "Financial Innovation and Deregulation in Perspective," *Bank of Japan Monetary and Economic Studies* 3, no. 2 (1985): 21–22.

39. Milton Friedman, "Monetary Policy for the 1980s," in *To Promote Prosperity: U.S. Domestic Policy in the Mid-1980s*, ed. John H. Moore (Stanford, CA: Hoover Institution Press, 1984), 48.

40. John H. Cochrane, "Toward a Run-Free Financial System," in *Across the Great Divide: New Perspectives on the Financial Crisis*, ed. Martin Neil Baily and John B. Taylor (Stanford, CA: Hoover Institution Press, 2014), 198, 199, 223.

41. Ibid., 224, 197, 216.

Chapter Seven

1. Quoted in James B. Stewart, "Eight Days: The Battle to Save the American Financial System," *New Yorker*, September 21, 2009, 72. Bush was speaking to Treasury secretary Henry Paulson and Federal Reserve chair Ben Bernanke.

2. Walter Bagehot, *Lombard Street: A Description of the Money Market* (1873; repr., New York: John Wiley, 1999), 173, 199.

3. Charles P. Kindleberger and Robert Aliber, *Manias, Panics, and Crashes: A History of Financial Crises*, 6th ed. (New York: Palgrave Macmillan, 2011), 214.

4. Milton Friedman and Anna J. Schwartz, *A Monetary History of the United States, 1867–1960* (Princeton, NJ: Princeton University Press, 1963), 395.

5. David Wessel, *In Fed We Trust: Ben Bernanke's War on the Great Panic* (New York: Three Rivers Press, 2009), 34.

6. Some economists of a laissez-faire persuasion have in fact been quite skeptical. For example, see George A. Selgin, "Legal Restrictions, Financial Weakening, and the Lender of Last Resort," *Cato Journal* 9, no. 2 (1989): 429–69; Anna J. Schwartz, "The Misuse of the Fed's Discount Window," Homer Jones Memorial Lecture, St. Louis University, April 9, 1992.

7. Brian F. Madigan, "Bagehot's Dictum in Practice: Formulating and Implementing Policies to Combat the Financial Crisis," remarks at the Federal Reserve Bank of Kansas City's Annual Economic Symposium, Jackson Hole, WY, August 21, 2009.

8. For example, see Ben S. Bernanke, "Current Economic and Financial Conditions," remarks at the National Association for Business Economics 50th Annual Meeting, Washington, DC, October 7, 2008.

9. See Charles S. Tippetts, "State Bank Withdrawals from the Federal Reserve System," *American Economic Review* 13, no. 3 (1923): 402n6.

10. Ibid., 404–5.

11. Stanley Fischer, "On the Need for an International Lender of Last Resort," Essays in International Economics, Princeton University, no. 220 (November 2000), 9.

12. Madigan, "Bagehot's Dictum in Practice."

13. Ibid. Traditionalists have criticized this approach. For example, see Thomas M. Humphrey, "Lender of Last Resort: What It Is, Whence It Came, and Why the Fed Isn't It," *Cato Journal* 30, no. 2 (2010): 333–64.

14. See International Monetary Fund, "How Big Is the Implicit Subsidy for Banks Considered Too Important to Fail?" in *Global Financial Stability Report: Moving from Liquidity- to Growth-Driven Markets* (Washington, DC: International Monetary Fund, 2014), 104.

15. Government Accountability Office, "Large Bank Holding Companies: Expectations of Government Support," Report to Congressional Requesters, July 2014.

16. For a discussion of rehypothecation practices, see Manmohan Singh and James Aitken, "The (Sizable) Role of Rehypothecation in the Shadow Banking System," IMF Working Paper 10/172, July 2010; see also Mark Mitchell and Todd Pulvino, "Arbitrage Crashes and the Speed of Capital," *Journal of Financial Economics* 104, no. 3 (2012): 469–90.

17. Thus one recent paper notes that dealer customers (such as hedge funds) may have "indirect" access to the lender of last resort. Viral V. Acharya and Bruce

Tuckman, "Unintended Consequences of LOLR Facilities: The Case of Illiquid Leverage," *IMF Economic Review* 62, no. 4 (2014): 645–46.

18. Robert M. Solow, "On the Lender of Last Resort," in *Financial Crises: Theory, History, and Policy*, ed. Charles P. Kindleberger and Jean-Pierre Laffargue (Cambridge: Cambridge University Press, 1982), 237–38.

19. Moral hazard also shifts the (subsidized) marginal cost curve back upward somewhat, since riskier firms are more likely to default. The upward shift reduces the funding subsidy; however, any such reduction must be more than offset by the new moral hazard subsidy. Otherwise the firm would not derive value from increasing risk.

20. Wessel, *In Fed We Trust*, 11, 21.

21. Kenneth S. Rogoff, "No More Creampuffs," *Washington Post*, September 16, 2008.

22. Vincent Reinhart, "Secretary Paulson Makes the Right Call," *Wall Street Journal*, September 16, 2008. I was reminded of these two op-eds by Paul Krugman, "Letting Lehman Fail," *The Conscience of a Liberal* (blog), *New York Times*, February 19, 2014.

23. Paul Krugman, "What Happened to Asia?" unpublished manuscript, January 1998, 3, 4, 2, 5–7.

24. Paul Krugman, *The Return of Depression Economics and the Crisis of 2008* (New York: W. W. Norton, 2009), 82, 84.

25. Ibid., 62, 65–66.

26. This is not to say it is never addressed. One recent study notes that "it is an open question to what extent implicit government insurance and the prospect of rescue operations have . . . contributed to the spectacular growth of finance and leverage within the system, creating more of the very hazards they were intended to solve." Moritz Schularick and Alan M. Taylor, "Credit Booms Gone Bust: Monetary Policy, Leverage Cycles, and Financial Crises, 1870–2008," *American Economic Review* 102, no. 2 (2012): 1042. However, I think it is fair to say this point has not been a central part of the bubble narrative.

27. For example, see Marcus Miller, Paul Weller, and Lei Zhang, "Moral Hazard and the US Stock Market: Analysing the 'Greenspan Put,'" *Economic Journal* 112 (March 2002): C171–86.

28. Gary B. Gorton and Andrew Metrick, "The Federal Reserve and Panic Prevention: The Roles of Financial Regulation and Lender of Last Resort," *Journal of Economic Perspectives* 27, no. 4 (2013): 52.

29. Emergency Relief and Construction Act of 1932, ch. 520, § 210, 47 Stat. 709, 715 (adding section 13(3) to the Federal Reserve Act).

30. 12 U.S.C. § 343.

31. Some journalists have taken note. For example, see Wessel, *In Fed We Trust*, 159–61; Binyamin Appelbaum and Neil Irwin, "Congress's Afterthought, Wall Street's Trillion Dollars," *Washington Post*, May 30, 2009.

32. 12 U.S.C. § 343 (1988). The 1988 version of the United States Code was the last edition preceding the 1991 amendment to section 13(3).

33. Federal Reserve Act § 10B, 12 U.S.C. § 347b.

34. Committee on Banking, Housing, and Urban Affairs, US Senate, "Comprehensive Deposit Insurance Reform and Taxpayer Protection Act of 1991," S. Rep. No. 102-67, at 203 (1991).

35. Deposit Insurance Reform and Financial Modernization: Hearings before the Committee on Banking, Housing, and Urban Affairs, US Senate, 101st Cong. 1:101 (April 3, 1990).

36. Federal Deposit Insurance Corporation Improvement Act of 1991, Pub. L. No. 102-242, § 473, 105 Stat. 2236, 2386.

37. See Schwartz, "Misuse of the Fed's Discount Window," 63. See also Walker F. Todd, "FDICIA's Emergency Liquidity Provisions," *Federal Reserve Bank of Cleveland Economic Review* 29, no. 3 (1993): 16–23.

38. Remarks by Senator Christopher Dodd on Comprehensive Deposit Insurance Reform and Taxpayer Protection Act of 1991, US Senate Floor, *Congressional Record* 137, Part 24, November 27, 1991: 36131–32.

39. Stewart, "Eight Days," 73.

40. Robin Greenwood and David S. Scharfstein, "The Growth of Finance," *Journal of Economic Perspectives* 27, no. 2 (2013): 9.

41. Thomas Philippon and Ariell Reshef, "Wages and Human Capital in the U.S. Finance Industry: 1909–2006," *Quarterly Journal of Economics* 127, no. 4 (2012): 1551.

42. Tyler Cowen, "The Inequality That Matters," *American Interest* 6, no. 3 (January/February 2011).

43. See Perry Mehrling, *The New Lombard Street: How the Fed Became the Dealer of Last Resort* (Princeton, NJ: Princeton University Press, 2011).

44. Mark Carney, "The U.K. at the Heart of a Renewed Globalisation," remarks at the 125th Anniversary of the *Financial Times*, London, October 24, 2013.

Chapter Eight

1. Remarks at the 14th Jacques Polak Annual Research Conference, International Monetary Fund, Washington, DC, November 8, 2013, final session (comment appears between the forty-three and forty-four minute marks).

2. I am echoing Lowell Bryan, who wrote that "market discipline by depositors is merely another name for bank panics." Lowell L. Bryan, "A Blueprint for Financial Reconstruction," *Harvard Business Review*, May/June 1991, 83.

3. In the reformed monetary system from the introduction, these instruments were called record currency or r-currency.

4. See Banking Act of 1933, Pub. L. No. 73-66, § 11, 48 Stat. 162, 181–82.

5. See, respectively, Depository Institutions Deregulation and Monetary Control Act of 1980, Pub. L. No. 96-221, §§ 201–210, 94 Stat. 132, 142–45; Dodd-Frank Wall Street Reform and Consumer Protection Act, Pub. L. No. 111-203, § 627, 124 Stat. 1376, 1640 (2010).

6. During the Great Depression, Princeton economist Frank Graham wrote that deposit banks earn "seigniorage profits in the nature of a tax on the community at large." He argued that "the government should get the seigniorage on the new issues of money" rather than "divesting itself of its prerogative in favor of the banks," and he lamented that "we have become inured to the present practice." Frank D. Graham, "Partial Reserve Money and the 100 Per Cent Proposal," *American Economic Review* 26, no. 3 (1936): 430, 434, 440. Along similar lines, Irving Fisher asked, "Why continue virtually to farm out to the banks for nothing a prerogative of Government?" Irving Fisher, *100% Money*, 3rd ed. (New Haven, CT: City Printing, 1945), 19. For a legal-historical take on private seigniorage, see Christine Desan, *Making Money: Coin, Currency, and the Coming of Capitalism* (New York: Oxford University Press, 2014), esp. 414–21.

7. As we will see in the next chapter, this (risk-free) return is determined by market forces. How the relative quantities of transaction accounts and cash equivalents are determined is deferred until the next chapter; it turns out to be a function of monetary policy.

8. I believe this point was first stated explicitly (in relation to deposit insurance) by Robert C. Merton, "An Analytic Derivation of the Cost of Deposit Insurance and Loan Guarantees: An Application of Modern Option Pricing Theory," *Journal of Banking and Finance* 1 (June 1977): 3–11.

9. Fischer Black, Merton H. Miller, and Richard A. Posner, "An Approach to the Regulation of Bank Holding Companies," *Journal of Business* 51, no. 3 (1978): 386n16.

10. Merton H. Miller, "Do the M&M Propositions Apply to Banks?" *Journal of Banking and Finance* 19 (June 1995): 487.

11. Robert C. Clark, "The Soundness of Financial Intermediaries," *Yale Law Journal* 86, no. 1 (1976): 58, 62, 63, 98, 101–2.

12. It also makes seigniorage revenues choppier, which is undesirable from a fiscal smoothing standpoint (see chapter 5).

13. The restrictions described in this paragraph are directly applicable to national banks; however, generally speaking, analogous restrictions apply to state-chartered banks. For a detailed overview of national bank powers, see Office of the Comptroller of the Currency (OCC), "Activities Permissible for a National Bank, Cumulative," 2011 annual edition.

14. See 12 U.S.C. § 24(Seventh); 12 C.F.R. § 1.3.

15. See 12 U.S.C. § 29.

16. See Arnold Tours Inc. v. Camp, 472 F.2d 427 (1st Cir. 1972).

17. See 12 U.S.C. § 24(Seventh) (securities dealing and underwriting); 15 U.S.C. § 6712(a) (insurance underwriting).

18. See M&M Leasing Corp. v. Seattle First National Bank, 563 F.2d 1377 (9th Cir. 1977).

19. See OCC Interpretive Letter 806 (October 17, 1997).

20. See, respectively, 12 U.S.C. § 24(Seventh); 12 U.S.C. § 84(a).

21. Saule T. Omarova, "The Quiet Metamorphosis: How Derivatives Changed the 'Business of Banking,'" *University of Miami Law Review* 63, no. 4 (2009): 1041–110.

22. See OCC Banking Circular 79 (November 2, 1976).

23. See OCC No Objection Letter 87-5 (July 20, 1987).

24. See OCC Interpretive Letter re: Chase Market Index Investment Deposit Account (August 8, 1988).

25. See OCC No Objection Letter 90-1 (February 16, 1990); OCC Interpretive Letter to First National Bank of Chicago (March 2, 1992).

26. See OCC Interpretive Letter 632 (June 30, 1993); OCC Interpretive Letter 684 (August 4, 1995).

27. See OCC Interpretive Letter 892 (September 13, 2000).

28. See Dodd-Frank Act § 716, 124 Stat. at 1648–51.

29. Letter from Sheila Bair to Senators Christopher Dodd and Blanche Lincoln (April 30, 2010), *Congressional Record* 156, May 4, 2010 (daily ed.): S3069–70. Bair subsequently opposed the repeal of the enacted version of the push-out. See Mike Konczal, "Sheila Bair: Dodd-Frank Really Did End Taxpayer Bailouts," *Wonkblog, Washington Post*, May 18, 2013.

30. See Letter from Paul Volcker to Senator Christopher Dodd (May 6, 2010), *Congressional Record* 159, October 30, 2013 (daily ed.): H6922.

31. Letter from Ben S. Bernanke to Senator Christopher Dodd (May 12, 2010), *Congressional Record* 159, October 30, 2013 (daily ed.): H6922.

32. See Consolidated and Further Continuing Appropriations Act, 2015, H.R. 83, 113th Cong. § 630 (2014).

33. Realistically, fees need to be low enough to induce participation; they may need to be slightly lower than "fair." I discuss this practical issue in chapter 9. For now the goal is to lay out the basic theory.

34. Black, Miller, and Posner, "Approach to the Regulation of Bank Holding Companies," 387.

35. Marcia Stigum and Anthony Crescenzi, *Stigum's Money Market*, 4th ed. (New York: McGraw-Hill, 2007), 455, 461, 462.

36. J. P. Morgan Securities Inc., "Short-Term Fixed Income Research Note," *U.S. Fixed Income Markets Weekly*, June 6, 2008, 3.

37. Floyd Norris, "Financial Perversions Sold during Credit Boom," *New York Times*, February 12, 2010.

38. Task Force on Tri-party Repo Infrastructure, Payments Risk Committee, "Task Force Report," May 17, 2010, 19.

66

39. Christopher Cox, testimony before the Committee on Banking, Housing, and Urban Affairs, US Senate, April 3, 2008.

40. Alan Schwartz, testimony before the Committee on Banking, Housing, and Urban Affairs, US Senate, April 3, 2008.

41. See Financial Crisis Inquiry Commission, *The Financial Crisis Inquiry Report: Final Report of the National Commission on the Causes of the Financial and Economic Crisis in the United States* (Washington, DC: Government Printing Office, 2011), 288.

42. Repo creditors and derivatives counterparties are the beneficiaries of a special exemption from the automatic stay in bankruptcy. They may seize and liquidate their collateral immediately. See 11 U.S.C. §§ 559–560. For a critical analysis, see Mark J. Roe, "The Derivatives Market's Payment Priorities as Financial Crisis Accelerator," *Stanford Law Review* 63, no. 3 (2011): 539–90.

43. Gary B. Gorton, *Slapped by the Invisible Hand: The Panic of 2007* (New York: Oxford University Press, 2010), 22–23.

44. Bengt Holmstrom, "Understanding the Role of Debt in the Financial System," Bank for International Settlements Working Paper 479, January 2015, 1–2.

45. Clark, "Soundness of Financial Intermediaries," 11, 23.

46. Alan S. Blinder and Robert F. Wescott, "Reform of Deposit Insurance: A Report to the FDIC," 2001.

47. Carter H. Golembe, "The Deposit Insurance Legislation of 1933: An Examination of its Antecedents and its Purposes," *Political Science Quarterly* 75, no. 2 (1960): 189.

48. Friedman and Schwartz, *Monetary History*, 435n14.

49. See Transaction Account Guarantee Program, 12 C.F.R. § 370.4.

50. Black, Miller, and Posner, "Approach to the Regulation of Bank Holding Companies," 391–92. See also Amar Bhidé, *A Call for Judgment: Sensible Finance for a Dynamic Economy* (Oxford: Oxford University Press, 2010), chap. 14.

51. Empirical evidence confirms that the institutional setting is a crucial determinant of deposit insurance outcomes. See Asli Demirgüç-Kunt and Edward J. Kane, "Deposit Insurance around the Globe: Where Does It Work?" *Journal of Economic Perspectives* 16, no. 2 (2002): 175–95.

52. For a tally of the fiscal costs, see Timothy Curry and Lynn Shibut, "The Cost of the Savings and Loan Crisis: Truth and Consequences," *FDIC Banking Review* 13, no. 2 (2000): 31.

53. See Depository Institutions Deregulation and Monetary Control Act of 1980, Pub. L. No. 96-221, §§ 401–402, 94 Stat. 132, 151–56; Garn-St. Germain Depository Institutions Act of 1982, Pub. L. No. 97-320, §§ 321–330 & 403, 96 Stat. 1469, 1499–1502 & 1510–11.

54. See George A. Akerlof and Paul M. Romer, "Looting: The Economic Underworld of Bankruptcy for Profit," *Brookings Papers on Economic Activity*, no. 2 (1993): 1–73.

55. See Financial Institutions Reform, Recovery, and Enforcement Act of 1989 (FIRREA), Pub. L. No. 101-73, §§ 222 & 301, 103 Stat. 183, 269–73 & 284–88.

56. See Basel Committee on Banking Supervision, "International Convergence of Capital Measurement and Capital Standards," July 1988; OCC, Final Rule, "Risk-Based Capital Guidelines," *Federal Register* 54, no. 17 (January 27, 1989): 4168–84; Federal Reserve System, Final Rule, "Risk-Based Capital Guidelines," *Federal Register* 54, no. 17 (January 27, 1989): 4186–221; Federal Deposit Insurance Corporation, Final Rule, "Final Statement of Policy on Risk-Based Capital," *Federal Register* 54, no. 53 (March 21, 1989): 11500–18.

57. See Federal Deposit Insurance Corporation Improvement Act of 1991 (FDICIA), Pub. L. No. 102-242, § 302(a)–(b), 105 Stat. 2236, 2345–49 (codified as amended at 12 U.S.C. §§ 1817(b)–(c)).

58. See Marcia M. Cornett, Hamid Mehran, and Hassan Tehranian, "The Impact of Risk-Based Premiums on FDIC-Insured Institutions," *Journal of Financial Services Research* 13, no. 2 (1998): 153–69.

59. See FIRREA § 301, 103 Stat. at 280; FDICIA § 121, 105 Stat. at 2250–52.

60. See FIRREA §§ 901–968, 103 Stat. at 446–506.

61. See FDICIA §§ 131–133, 105 Stat. at 2253–73 (codified as amended at 12 U.S.C. § 1831o).

62. See Diane Ellis, Memorandum to the FDIC Board of Directors from the Director of the Division of Insurance and Research: "Update of Projected Deposit Insurance Fund Losses, Income, and Reserve Ratios for the Restoration Plan," October 2, 2014, 3 (available on the FDIC website).

63. See FDIC, "Quarterly Banking Profile: Fourth Quarter 2014," *FDIC Quarterly* 9, no. 1 (2015): 5.

64. Raghuram G. Rajan, *Fault Lines: How Hidden Fractures Still Threaten the World Economy* (Princeton, NJ: Princeton University Press, 2010), 178–80.

65. Charles W. Calomiris and Stephen H. Haber, *Fragile by Design: The Political Origins of Banking Crises and Scarce Credit* (Princeton, NJ: Princeton University Press, 2014).

Chapter Nine

1. Bray Hammond, *Banks and Politics in America from the Revolution to the Civil War* (Princeton, NJ: Princeton University Press, 1957), 741.

2. Analogous to existing legal tender laws. See 31 U.S.C. § 5103.

3. If physical currency is included in the reformed system, an account holder's "withdrawal" of currency from a member bank results in a debit of the customer's account and the simultaneous booking of an equivalent sovereign debit. A customer's "deposit" of currency has the reverse effect: the member bank credits the

customer's account and simultaneously books a sovereign credit. Physical currency never appears on the balance sheet of a member bank. Instead, physical currency in the possession of member banks is deemed to be held for the monetary authority on a custodial basis.

4. Analogous to existing national bank charters. See 12 C.F.R. § 5.20.

5. Analogous to existing portfolio constraints and capital requirements for deposit banks. See 12 U.S.C. § 24 (Seventh) (core portfolio constraints); 12 U.S.C. § 18310(c)(1) (capital requirements).

6. Analogous to the swaps push-out provision of Dodd-Frank. See Dodd-Frank Wall Street Reform and Consumer Protection Act, Pub. L. No. 111-203, § 716, 124 Stat. 1376, 1648–51 (2010). As I noted in the previous chapter, this provision was later substantially repealed.

7. Analogous to existing restrictions on the maintenance of "deposit" liabilities in the absence of special authorization. See 12 U.S.C. § 378(a)(2).

8. Analogous to existing "term deposits" issued by the Federal Reserve. See Federal Reserve Board, Final Rule, "Reserve Requirements of Depository Institutions Policy on Payment System Risk," *Federal Register* 75, no. 86 (May 5, 2010): 24384–89 (amending Regulation D to allow the Fed to offer term deposits).

9. Analogous to existing restrictions on affiliate transactions by deposit banks. See Federal Reserve Act §§ 23A–23B, 12 U.S.C. §§ 371c–371c-1.

10. Analogous to existing risk-based deposit insurance premiums. See 12 U.S.C. § 1817(b).

11. Ideally, seigniorage fees are calibrated to align the duration of the firm's liabilities with that of its assets. Incidentally, this would practically eliminate the need for member banks to engage in interest-rate hedging.

12. See Gary B. Gorton, "Bank Regulation When 'Banks' and 'Banking' Are Not the Same," *Oxford Review of Economic Policy* 10, no. 4 (1994): 107.

13. Analogous to the existing deposit bank insolvency system. See 12 U.S.C. § 1821.

14. Analogous to the Federal Reserve's administrative structure. See 12 U.S.C. §§ 241–242.

15. Analogous to the Federal Reserve's funding provisions. See 12 U.S.C. § 243.

16. Analogous to the Federal Reserve's dual mandate. See Federal Reserve Act § 2A, 12 U.S.C. § 225a.

17. Analogous to existing reserve requirements, which place a legal cap on the quantity of reservable deposits outstanding. See 12 U.S.C. § 461.

18. Analogous to the existing nationwide deposit concentration limit for US banks. See 12 U.S.C. § 1842(d)(2)(A). The current limit applies only to acquisitions, not organic growth.

19. It is sometimes said that if bearer currency did not exist—if all money were record money—then expansionary monetary policy could take the form of "negative interest" on money. For reasons that aren't worth getting into, I have doubts

about the wisdom of this strategy. In any case, the reformed monetary system, if implemented without physical currency, would make this strategy possible.

20. See Act of March 3, 1865, ch. 78, § 6, 13 Stat. 469, 484 (as amended by Act of February 8, 1875, ch. 36, § 19, 18 Stat. 307, 311).

21. George E. Barnett, "State Banks and Trust Companies since the Passage of the National-Bank Act," in *Publications of the National Monetary Commission*, vol. 7 (Washington, DC: Government Printing Office, 1911), 11–12.

22. Bank of England Act, 1708, 7 Anne, c. 30, § 66.

23. Banking Act, 1742, 15 George II, c. 13, § 5.

24. Starting in 1826, note-issuing banks were allowed to operate in England on a *joint stock* basis so long as they stayed out of London and its vicinity. See Country Bankers Act, 1826, 7 George IV, c. 46, § 1. This situation was short-lived on account of Peel's Act (see below).

25. Walter Bagehot, *Lombard Street: A Description of the Money Market* (1873; repr., New York: John Wiley, 1999), 97–99.

26. Bank of England Act, 1833, 3 & 4 William IV, c. 98, § 3.

27. Act of 1844 (Peel's Act), 7 & 8 Victoria, c. 32.

28. Ernest Sykes, *Banking and Currency* (London: Butterworth, 1905), 95–96.

29. Charles F. Dunbar, *The Theory and History of Banking*, 3rd ed. (New York: G. P. Putnam's Sons, 1917), 63.

30. See Securities and Exchange Commission (SEC), Final Rule, "Valuation of Debt Instruments and Computation of Current Price per Share by Certain Open-End Investment Companies (Money Market Funds)," *Federal Register* 48, no. 138 (July 18, 1983): 32555–67. The final rule codified exemptions that had been granted since 1978. The Department of Justice appears to have played a role here too; it evidently opined in 1979 that claims on MMFs were not deposits as a legal matter. See Harvey L. Pitt and Julie L. Williams, "The Convergence of Commercial and Investment Banking: New Directions in the Financial Services Industry," *Journal of Comparative Business and Capital Market Law* 5, no. 2 (1983), 173–74.

31. See Securities Act of 1933 § 2(1), 15 U.S.C. § 77b(a)(1).

32. Tcherepnin v. Knight, 389 U.S. 332, 336 (1967).

33. See Investment Company Act of 1940 § 3(a)(1), 15 U.S.C. § 80a-3(a)(1).

34. See Edmund H. Kerr, "The Inadvertent Investment Company: Section 3(a)(3) of the Investment Company Act," *Stanford Law Review* 12, no. 1 (1959): 29–70.

35. See 7 U.S.C. § 1a(47).

36. See Dodd-Frank Act § 619, 12 U.S.C. § 1851(h)(4).

37. See Sherman Antitrust Act § 1, 15 U.S.C. § 1.

38. A drawable loan commitment "behaves *just like a demand deposit*" and offers "a very similar service." Anil K. Kashyap, Raghuram Rajan, and Jeremy C. Stein, "Banks as Liquidity Providers: An Explanation for the Coexistence of Lending and Deposit-Taking," *Journal of Finance* 57, no. 1 (2002): 35.

39. See Financial Accounting Standards Board, "Statement of Cash Flows," Statement of Financial Accounting Standards 95, §§ 8–9.

40. See Securities Exchange Act of 1934 § 3(a)(10), 15 U.S.C. § 78c(a)(10).

41. See Basel Committee on Banking Supervision, "Basel III: The Net Stable Funding Ratio," October 2014, 2.

42. See 17 C.F.R. § 270.2a-7(d)(1)(i).

43. John H. Cochrane, "Toward a Run-Free Financial System," in *Across the Great Divide: New Perspectives on the Financial Crisis*, ed. Martin Neil Baily and John B. Taylor (Stanford, CA: Hoover Institution Press, 2014), 216.

44. Henry C. Simons, "A Positive Program for Laissez Faire: Some Proposals for a Liberal Economic Policy" (1934), in *Economic Policy for a Free Society* (Chicago: University of Chicago Press, 1948), 320n7.

45. Henry C. Simons, "Rules versus Authorities in Monetary Policy" (1936), in *Economic Policy for a Free Society*, 166, 172.

46. Milton Friedman, "The Euro-Dollar Market: Some First Principles," *Federal Reserve Bank of St. Louis Review*, July 1971, 18, 21.

47. These events are described in Sergey Chernenko and Adi Sunderam, "Frictions in Shadow Banking: Evidence from the Lending Behavior of Money Market Mutual Funds," *Review of Financial Studies* 27, no. 6 (2014): 1717–50.

48. Victoria Ivashina, David S. Scharfstein, and Jeremy C. Stein, "Dollar Funding and the Lending Behavior of Global Banks," *Quarterly Journal of Economics* 130, no. 3 (2015): 1278.

49. See Francis A. Mann, *The Legal Aspect of Money*, 5th ed. (Oxford: Clarendon Press, 1992), chap. 16; Rosa M. Lastra, *International Financial and Monetary Law*, 2nd ed. (New York: Oxford University Press, 2015), chap. 1; Robert A. Mundell, "Monetary Unions and the Problem of Sovereignty," *Annals of the American Academy of Political and Social Science* 579 (January 2002): 123–52.

50. An overview can be found in US Treasury Department, "The Use and Counterfeiting of United States Currency Abroad," Report to the US Congress, Part 3, 2006, chap. 6.

51. See 18 U.S.C. §§ 478–483.

52. The Basel capital standards have spread "to the far corners of the world." Hal S. Scott and Anna Gelpern, *International Finance: Transactions, Policy, and Regulation*, 19th ed. (New York: Foundation Press, 2012), 559.

53. Incidentally, I suspect that many problems that are often associated with "international capital flows" or "global imbalances" are better understood as Eurocurrency problems, or more generally as problems of monetary system design. This is a topic for another day.

54. Jeremy C. Stein, "Monetary Policy as Financial Stability Regulation," *Quarterly Journal of Economics* 127, no. 1 (2012): 59.

55. Jeremy C. Stein, "Evaluating Large-Scale Asset Purchases," remarks at the Brookings Institution, Washington, DC, October 11, 2012.

56. Recall that the banking business model relies on the law of large numbers. Entities that borrow from five or fewer lenders are not engaged in money creation, even if the debt is demandable. Put differently, prime brokers do not characterize their callable loans to hedge funds as cash equivalents.

Chapter Ten

1. John Maynard Keynes, "The Great Slump of 1930" (1930), in *Essays in Persuasion* (1931; repr., New York: Palgrave Macmillan, 2010), 126.

2. The existence of this prevailing view is, I think, obvious. I see no need to document it. Citing a few adherents would unfairly single them out, and it would be impossible to cite them all.

3. Ch. 106, 13 Stat. 99.

4. Pub. L. No. 63-43, 38 Stat. 251.

5. Pub. L. No. 73-66, 48 Stat. 162.

6. Pub. L. No. 111-203, 124 Stat. 1376.

7. Rulemaking statistics in this paragraph are from Davis Polk and Wardwell LLP, "Dodd-Frank Progress Report: Five Year Anniversary Report," July 16, 2015.

8. See Securities and Exchange Commission (SEC), Final Rule, "Money Market Fund Reform," *Federal Register* 75, no. 42 (March 4, 2010): 10060–120; SEC, Final Rule, "Money Market Fund Reform; Amendments to Form PF," *Federal Register* 79, no. 157 (August 14, 2014): 47736–983.

9. Office of the Comptroller of the Currency, Federal Reserve Board, and Federal Deposit Insurance Corporation (FDIC), Final Rule, "Liquidity Coverage Ratio: Liquidity Risk Measurement Standards," *Federal Register* 79, no. 197 (October 10, 2014): 61440–541. The US rule is based on the new Basel liquidity standards. See Basel Committee on Banking Supervision, "Basel III: The Liquidity Coverage Ratio and Liquidity Risk Monitoring Tools," January 2013.

10. See Jeffrey N. Gordon and Christopher M. Gandia, "Money Market Funds Run Risk: Will Floating Net Asset Value Fix the Problem?" *Columbia Business Law Review*, no. 2 (2014): 313–69. See also Samuel G. Hanson, David S. Scharfstein, and Adi Sunderam, "An Evaluation of Money Market Fund Reform Proposals," working paper, May 2014.

11. See Emergency Economic Stabilization Act of 2008 § 131(b), 12 U.S.C. § 5236(b).

12. John Maynard Keynes, *The General Theory of Employment, Interest, and Money* (1936; repr., San Diego, CA: First Harvest/Harcourt, 1964), 155.

13. For a discussion, see Jeremy C. Stein, "The Fire-Sales Problem and Securities Financing Transactions," remarks at the Federal Reserve Bank of New York's Workshop on Fire Sales as a Driver of Systemic Risk in Triparty Repo and Other Secured Funding Markets, New York, October 4, 2013.

14. Andrew Ackerman, "Some Asset Managers Avoid Brunt of New Money-Fund Rules," *Wall Street Journal*, July 23, 2014.

15. This critique applies equally to other recent regulatory measures pertaining to short-term funding, including triparty repo initiatives (see Federal Reserve Bank of New York, Statement, "Update on Tri-party Repo Infrastructure Reform," February 13, 2014) and the decision to key capital surcharges for large institutions to levels of short-term wholesale funding (see Federal Reserve system, Final Rules, "Regulatory Capital Rules: Implementation of Risk-Based Capital Surcharges for Global Systemically Important Bank Holding Companies," *Federal Register* 80, no. 157 [August 14, 2015]: 49082–116.

16. William C. Dudley, "Fixing Wholesale Funding to Build a More Stable Financial System," remarks at the New York Bankers Association's Annual Meeting and Economic Forum, New York, February 1, 2013.

17. Daniel K. Tarullo, "Evaluating Progress in Regulatory Reforms to Promote Financial Stability," remarks at the Peterson Institute for International Economics, Washington, DC, May 3, 2013.

18. Dodd-Frank Act § 204(a), 12 U.S.C. § 5384(a).

19. FDIC, "Resolutions Handbook," 2003, 68–69, 70.

20. Ibid., 70.

21. FDIC, Notice and Request for Comments, "Resolution of Systemically Important Financial Institutions: The Single Point of Entry Strategy," *Federal Register* 78, no. 243 (December 18, 2013): 76614–24; FDIC and Bank of England, "Resolving Globally Active, Systemically Important, Financial Institutions," joint paper, December 10, 2012.

22. FDIC, "Single Point of Entry Strategy," 76623. Once a parent company has entered OLA receivership, the FDIC has built-in power to appoint itself receiver of the subsidiaries. See Dodd-Frank Act § 210(a)(1)(E), 12 U.S.C. § 5390(a)(1)(E).

23. Quoted in Barbara A. Rehm, "FDIC's Own Experts Skeptical of Resolution Plan," *American Banker*, December 12, 2013.

24. See Dodd-Frank Act §§ 210(b)(4), (d)(4) & (h)(5)(E), 12 U.S.C. §§ 5390(b)(4), (d)(4) & (h)(5)(E).

25. See Dodd-Frank Act § 210(o)(1)(D), 12 U.S.C. § 5390(o)(1)(D).

26. FDIC, Interim Final Rule, "Orderly Liquidation Authority Provisions of the Dodd-Frank Wall Street Reform and Consumer Protection Act," *Federal Register* 76, no. 16 (January 25, 2011): 4207, 4212, 4214.

27. See Dodd-Frank Act § 1101, 12 U.S.C. § 343.

28. See Dodd-Frank Act § 210(n), 12 U.S.C. § 5390(n).

29. See 31 U.S.C. § 3101.

30. See Housing and Economic Recovery Act of 2008, Pub. L. No. 110-289, § 3083, 122 Stat. 2654, 2908; Emergency Economic Stabilization Act of 2008, Pub. L. No. 110-343, § 122, 122 Stat. 3765, 3790.

31. FDIC, "Single Point of Entry Strategy," 76623.

32. Daniel K. Tarullo, "Toward Building a More Effective Resolution Regime: Progress and Challenges," remarks at the Federal Reserve Board and Federal Reserve Bank of Richmond Conference on Planning for the Orderly Resolution of a Global Systemically Important Bank, Washington, DC, October 18, 2013.

33. Note that calibrating the appropriate amount of long-term unsecured debt presents basically the same challenge as calibrating capital requirements. For firms with significant derivative operations, this is extremely difficult; see chapter 6. Incidentally, one could be forgiven for wondering why, if we know how much loss-absorbency is needed, we don't just set the equity capital requirement to that level and be done with it.

34. See Dodd-Frank Act § 203, 12 U.S.C. § 5383.

35. Walter Bagehot, *Lombard Street: A Description of the Money Market* (1873; repr., New York: John Wiley, 1999), 65.

36. For a similarly critical analysis of constructive ambiguity, see David A. Skeel, "Single Point of Entry and the Bankruptcy Alternative," in *Across the Great Divide: New Perspectives on the Financial Crisis*, ed. Martin Neil Baily and John B. Taylor (Stanford, CA: Hoover Institution Press, 2014), 315–16.

37. Ibid., 313.

38. See Thomas M. Hoenig and Charles S. Morris, "Restructuring the Banking System to Improve Safety and Soundness," white paper, November 2013.

39. For example, see Simon Johnson and James Kwak, *13 Bankers: The Wall Street Takeover and the Next Financial Meltdown* (New York: Vintage Books, 2011); Jonathan R. Macey and James P. Holdcroft Jr., "Failure Is an Option: An Ersatz-Antitrust Approach to Financial Regulation," *Yale Law Journal* 120, no. 6 (2011): 1368–418.

40. Hyman P. Minsky, *Stabilizing an Unstable Economy*, rev. ed. (New York: McGraw-Hill, 2008), 364. Recall that in Minsky's typology "speculative finance" and "Ponzi finance" refer to particular debt funding structures.

41. John Geanakoplos, "Solving the Present Crisis and Managing the Leverage Cycle," *FRBNY Economic Policy Review* 16, no. 1 (2010): 128.

42. Carmen M. Reinhart and Kenneth S. Rogoff, *This Time Is Different: Eight Centuries of Financial Folly* (Princeton, NJ: Princeton University Press, 2009), 278, 281.

43. See Atif Mian and Amir Sufi, *House of Debt: How They (and You) Caused the Great Recession, and How We Can Prevent It from Happening Again* (Chicago: University of Chicago Press, 2014), chap. 12.

44. Paul Krugman, "Bubbles, Regulation, and Secular Stagnation," *The Conscience of a Liberal* (blog), *New York Times*, September 25, 2013.

45. Paul H. Douglas et al., "A Program for Monetary Reform," memorandum, July 1939, 2, 19, 37.

46. Joseph E. Stiglitz, "Reconstructing Macroeconomic Theory to Manage Economic Policy," NBER Working Paper 20517, September 2014, 9.

47. Simon Wren-Lewis, "Will the Financial Crisis Lead to Another Revolution in Macroeconomics?" *Mainly Macro* (blog), January 19, 2014.

48. Charles I. Plosser, "Macro Models and Monetary Policy Analysis," remarks at the Bundesbank–Federal Reserve Bank of Philadelphia Spring 2012 Research Conference, Eltville, Germany, May 25, 2012.

49. Olivier Blanchard, "Where Danger Lurks," *Finance and Development* 51, no. 3 (2014), 31.

50. Tobias Adrian and Hyun Song Shin, "Financial Intermediaries and Monetary Economics," in *Handbook of Monetary Economics*, vol. 3A, ed. Benjamin Friedman and Michael Woodford (San Diego, CA: North-Holland, 2011), 602.

51. Adam Smith, *An Inquiry into the Nature and Causes of the Wealth of Nations* (1776), ed. R. H. Campbell and A. S. Skinner (Oxford: Clarendon Press, 1976), 1:321.

References

Acharya, Viral V., and Bruce Tuckman. "Unintended Consequences of LOLR Facilities: The Case of Illiquid Leverage." *IMF Economic Review* 62, no. 4 (2014): 607–55.

Ackerman, Andrew. "Some Asset Managers Avoid Brunt of New Money-Fund Rules." *Wall Street Journal*, July 23, 2014.

Admati, Anat R., Peter M. DeMarzo, Martin F. Hellwig, and Paul Pfleiderer. "Fallacies, Irrelevant Facts, and Myths in the Discussion of Capital Regulation: Why Bank Equity Is Not Socially Expensive." Rock Center for Corporate Governance at Stanford University Working Paper 161, October 22, 2013.

Admati, Anat R., and Martin F. Hellwig. *The Bankers' New Clothes: What's Wrong with Banking and What to Do about It*. Princeton, NJ: Princeton University Press, 2013.

———. "Does Debt Discipline Bankers? An Academic Myth about Bank Indebtedness." Rock Center for Corporate Governance at Stanford University Working Paper 132, February 18, 2013.

———. "The Parade of Bankers' New Clothes Continues: 23 Flawed Claims Debunked." Rock Center for Corporate Governance at Stanford University Working Paper 143, June 23, 2013.

Adrian, Tobias, and Adam B. Ashcraft. "Shadow Banking: A Review of the Literature." Federal Reserve Bank of New York Staff Report 580, October 2012.

Adrian, Tobias, and Hyun Song Shin. "Financial Intermediaries and Monetary Economics." In *Handbook of Monetary Economics*, vol. 3A, edited by Benjamin Friedman and Michael Woodford, 601–50. San Diego, CA: North-Holland, 2011.

———. "Liquidity and Financial Contagion." *Banque de France Financial Stability Review*, no. 11 (February 2008): 1–7.

Akerlof, George A., and Paul M. Romer. "Looting: The Economic Underworld of Bankruptcy for Profit." *Brookings Papers on Economic Activity*, no. 2 (1993): 1–73.

Allen, Franklin, and Douglas Gale. "Financial Contagion." *Journal of Political Economy* 108, no. 1 (2000): 1–33.

Allen, William R. "Irving Fisher and the 100 Percent Reserve Proposal." *Journal of Law and Economics* 36, no. 2 (1993): 703–17.

Appelbaum, Binyamin, and Neil Irwin. "Congress's Afterthought, Wall Street's Trillion Dollars." *Washington Post*, May 30, 2009.

Associated Press. "Sweden Moving towards Cashless Economy." CBSNews.com, March 18, 2012.

Bagehot, Walter. *Lombard Street: A Description of the Money Market*. 1873. Reprint, New York: John Wiley, 1999.

Baily, Martin Neil, and John B. Taylor, eds. *Across the Great Divide: New Perspective on the Financial Crisis*. Stanford, CA: Hoover Institution Press, 2014.

Bair, Sheila. Letter to Senators Christopher Dodd and Blanche Lincoln, April 30, 2010. *Congressional Record* 156, May 4, 2010 (daily ed.): S3069–70.

Baker, Dean. "Blame It on the Bubble." *Guardian*, March 8, 2010.

———. "What Krugman Said, with a Not So Small Addendum." *Beat the Press* (blog), Center for Economic and Policy Research, October 20, 2012.

Ball, Laurence, J. Bradford DeLong, and Larry Summers. "Fiscal Policy and Full Employment." Center on Budget and Policy Priorities, Full Employment Project, April 2, 2014.

Barnett, George E. "State Banks and Trust Companies since the Passage of the National-Bank Act." In *Publications of the National Monetary Commission*, 7:1–366. Washington, DC: Government Printing Office, 1911.

Basel Committee on Banking Supervision. "Amendment to the Capital Accord to Incorporate Market Risks." January 1996.

———. "Basel III: A Global Regulatory Framework for More Resilient Banks and Banking Systems." December 2010 (revised June 2011).

———. "Basel III Leverage Ratio Framework and Disclosure Requirements." January 2014.

———. "Basel III: The Liquidity Coverage Ratio and Liquidity Risk Monitoring Tools." January 2013.

———. "Basel III: The Net Stable Funding Ratio." October 2014.

———. "International Convergence of Capital Measurement and Capital Standards." July 1988.

———. "International Convergence of Capital Measurement and Capital Standards: A Revised Framework." June 2004.

Baumol, William J. "The Transactions Demand for Cash: An Inventory Theoretic Approach." *Quarterly Journal of Economics* 66, no. 4 (1952): 545–56.

Bayoumi, Tamim. "The Morning After: Explaining the Slowdown in Japanese Growth in the 1990s." *Journal of International Economics* 53, no. 2 (2001): 241–59.

Bernanke, Ben S. "Central Bank Independence, Transparency, and Accountability." Remarks at the Institute for Monetary and Economic Studies International Conference, Bank of Japan, Tokyo, May 26, 2010.

———. "Current Economic and Financial Conditions." Remarks at the National Association for Business Economics 50th Annual Meeting, Washington, DC, October 7, 2008.

———. *Essays on the Great Depression*. Princeton, NJ: Princeton University Press, 2000.

———. *The Federal Reserve and the Financial Crisis*. Princeton, NJ: Princeton University Press, 2013.

———. "The Financial Accelerator and the Credit Channel." Remarks at the Conference on the Credit Channel of Monetary Policy in the Twenty-First Century, Federal Reserve Bank of Atlanta, June 15, 2007.

———. Letter to Senator Christopher Dodd, May 12, 2010. *Congressional Record* 159, October 30, 2013 (daily ed.): H6922.

———. "Nonmonetary Effects of the Financial Crisis in the Propagation of the Great Depression." *American Economic Review* 73, no. 3 (1983): 257–76.

———. "On Milton Friedman's Ninetieth Birthday." Address at the Conference to Honor Milton Friedman, University of Chicago, November 8, 2002.

———. "Reflections on a Year of Crisis." Remarks at the Federal Reserve Bank of Kansas City's Annual Economic Symposium, Jackson Hole, WY, August 21, 2009.

———. "Some Reflections on the Crisis and the Policy Response." Remarks at the Russell Sage Foundation and the Century Foundation Conference on Rethinking Finance, New York, April 13, 2012.

Bhidé, Amar. *A Call for Judgment: Sensible Finance for a Dynamic Economy*. Oxford: Oxford University Press, 2010.

Binmore, Ken. *Natural Justice*. Oxford: Oxford University Press, 2005.

———. *Playing for Real: A Text on Game Theory*. Oxford: Oxford University Press, 2007.

Black, Fischer, Merton H. Miller, and Richard A. Posner. "An Approach to the Regulation of Bank Holding Companies." *Journal of Business* 51, no. 3 (1978): 379–412.

Blanchard, Olivier. "Where Danger Lurks." *Finance and Development* 51, no. 3 (2014): 28–31.

Blinder, Alan S. "Monetary Policy Today: Sixteen Questions and About Twelve Answers." In *Central Banks in the 21st Century*, edited by Santiago Fernández de Lis and Fernando Restoy, 31–72. Madrid: Banco de España, 2006.

Blinder, Alan S., and Robert F. Wescott. "Reform of Deposit Insurance: A Report to the FDIC." 2001.

Bordo, Michael D. "Comment on 'The Great Depression and the Friedman-Schwartz Hypothesis' by Lawrence Christiano, Roberto Motto, and Massimo Rostagno." *Journal of Money, Credit and Banking* 35, no. 6 (2003): 1199–203.

————. "The Lender of Last Resort: Alternative Views and Historical Experience." *Federal Reserve Bank of Richmond Economic Review* 76, no. 1 (1990):
18–29.

Bordo, Michael D., Angela Redish, and Hugh Rockoff. "Why Didn't Canada Have
a Banking Crisis in 2008 (or in 1930, or 1907, or . . .)?" *Economic History Review* 68, no. 1 (2015): 218–43.

Breckenridge, Roeliff Morton. *The Canadian Banking System, 1817–1890.* Toronto,
1894.

Briones, Ignacio, and Hugh Rockoff. "Do Economists Reach a Conclusion on
Free-Banking Episodes?" *Econ Journal Watch* 2, no. 2 (2005): 279–324.

Brunnermeier, Markus K. "Deciphering the Liquidity and Credit Crunch 2007–
2008." *Journal of Economic Perspectives* 23, no. 1 (2009): 77–100.

Bryan, Lowell L. "A Blueprint for Financial Reconstruction." *Harvard Business
Review*, May/June 1991, 73–86.

Buchanan, James M. "The Constitutionalization of Money." *Cato Journal* 30, no. 2
(2010): 251–58.

Caballero, Ricardo J. "The 'Other' Imbalance and the Financial Crisis." NBER
Working Paper 15636, January 2010.

Calomiris, Charles W. "Bank Failures, the Great Depression, and Other 'Con-
tagious' Events." In *The Oxford Handbook of Banking*, 2nd ed., edited by
Allen N. Berger, Philip Molyneux, and John O. S. Wilson, 721–36. New York:
Oxford University Press, 2015.

Calomiris, Charles W., and Gary B. Gorton. "The Origins of Banking Panics: Models,
Facts, and Bank Regulation." In *Financial Markets and Financial Crises*, edited
by R. Glenn Hubbard, 109–73. Chicago: University of Chicago Press, 1991.

Calomiris, Charles W., and Stephen H. Haber. *Fragile by Design: The Political Origins of Banking Crises and Scarce Credit*. Princeton, NJ: Princeton University
Press, 2014.

Calomiris, Charles W., and Charles M. Kahn. "The Role of Demandable Debt in
Structuring Optimal Banking Arrangements." *American Economic Review* 81,
no. 3 (1991): 497–513.

Calomiris, Charles W., and Joseph R. Mason. "Consequences of Bank Distress during the Great Depression." *American Economic Review* 93, no. 3 (2003): 937–47.

————. "Fundamentals, Panics, and Bank Distress during the Depression."
American Economic Review 93, no. 5 (2003): 1615–47.

Calvo, Guillermo. "Puzzling Over the Anatomy of Crises: Liquidity and the Veil of
Finance." Background paper for the Mayekawa Lecture at the Bank of Japan,
Tokyo, June 2013.

Carbaugh, Robert J. *International Economics*. 15th ed. Boston: Cengage Learning, 2013.

Carnell, Richard S., Jonathan R. Macey, and Geoffrey P. Miller. *The Law of Financial Institutions*. 5th ed. New York: Wolters Kluwer, 2013.

Carney, Mark. "The U.K. at the Heart of a Renewed Globalisation." Remarks at the 125th Anniversary of the *Financial Times*, London, October 24, 2013.

Chari, V. V., Lawrence Christiano, and Patrick J. Kehoe. "Facts and Myths about the Financial Crisis of 2008." Federal Reserve Bank of Minneapolis Working Paper 666, October 2008.

Checkland, Sydney G. *Scottish Banking: A History, 1695–1973*. Glasgow: Collins, 1975.

Chernenko, Sergey, and Adi Sunderam. "Frictions in Shadow Banking: Evidence from the Lending Behavior of Money Market Mutual Funds." *Review of Financial Studies* 27, no. 6 (2014): 1717–50.

Chodorow-Reich, Gabriel. "The Employment Effects of Credit Market Disruptions: Firm-Level Evidence from the 2008–09 Financial Crisis." *Quarterly Journal of Economics* 129, no. 1 (2014): 1–59.

Clark, Robert C. "The Soundness of Financial Intermediaries." *Yale Law Journal* 86, no. 1 (1976): 1–102.

Coase, Ronald H. "The Problem of Social Cost." *Journal of Law and Economics* 3 (October 1960): 1–44.

Coates, John C., IV. "Cost-Benefit Analysis of Financial Regulation: Case Studies and Implications." *Yale Law Journal* 124, no. 4 (2015): 882–1011.

Cochrane, John H. "Toward a Run-Free Financial System." In Baily and Taylor, *Across the Great Divide*, 197–249.

Cohen, Felix. "Transcendental Nonsense and the Functional Approach." *Columbia Law Review* 35, no. 6 (1935): 809–49.

Committee on Banking, Housing, and Urban Affairs, US Senate. "Comprehensive Deposit Insurance Reform and Taxpayer Protection Act of 1991," S. Rep. No. 102-67 (1991).

Conard, Edward. *Unintended Consequences: Why Everything You've Been Told about the Economy Is Wrong*. New York: Portfolio/Penguin, 2012.

Conti-Brown, Peter. "The Institutions of Federal Reserve Independence." *Yale Journal on Regulation* 32, no. 2 (2015).

Cook, Timothy Q., and Robert K. Laroche, eds. *Instruments of the Money Market*. 7th ed. Richmond, VA: Federal Reserve Bank of Richmond, 1998.

Cooper, Russell, and Andrew John. "Coordinating Coordination Failures in Keynesian Models." *Quarterly Journal of Economics* 103, no. 3 (1988): 441–63.

Cornett, Marcia M., Jamie J. McNutt, Philip E. Strahan, and Hassan Tehranian. "Liquidity Risk Management and Credit Supply in the Financial Crisis." *Journal of Financial Economics* 101, no. 2 (2011): 297–312.

Cornett, Marcia M., Hamid Mehran, and Hassan Tehranian. "The Impact of Risk-Based Premiums on FDIC-Insured Institutions." *Journal of Financial Services Research* 13, no. 2 (1998): 153–69.

Covitz, Daniel, Nellie Liang, and Gustavo A. Suarez. "The Evolution of a Financial

Crisis: Collapse of the Asset-Backed Commercial Paper Market." *Journal of Finance* 68, no. 3 (2013): 815–48.

Cowen, Tyler. "The Inequality That Matters." *American Interest* 6, no. 3 (January/February 2011).

Cowen, Tyler, and Randall Kroszner. "Mutual Fund Banking: A Market Approach." *Cato Journal* 10, no. 1 (1990): 223–37.

———. "Scottish Banking before 1845: A Model for Laissez-Faire?" *Journal of Money, Credit and Banking* 21, no. 2 (1989): 221–31.

Cox, Christopher. Hearing: "Turmoil in U.S. Credit Markets: Examining the Recent Actions of Federal Financial Regulators." Testimony before the Committee on Banking, Housing, and Urban Affairs, US Senate, April 3, 2008.

Currie, Lauchlin. "A Proposed Revision of the Monetary System of the United States: Submitted to Secretary of the Treasury Henry Morgenthau." 1934. In *The Supply and Control of Money in the United States* (1935), 195–226. Reprint, New York: Russell and Russell, 1968.

Curry, Timothy, and Lynn Shibut. "The Cost of the Savings and Loan Crisis: Truth and Consequences." *FDIC Banking Review* 13, no. 2 (2000): 26–35.

Datla, Kirti, and Richard L. Revesz. "Deconstructing Independent Agencies (and Executive Agencies)." *Cornell Law Review* 98, no. 4 (2013): 769–843.

Davis Polk & Wardwell LLP. "Dodd-Frank Progress Report: Five Year Anniversary Report." July 16, 2015.

DeLong, J. Bradford. "'Liquidation' Cycles: Old-Fashioned Real Business Cycle Theory and the Great Depression." NBER Working Paper 3546, December 1990.

Demirgüç-Kunt, Asli, and Edward J. Kane. "Deposit Insurance around the Globe: Where Does It Work?" *Journal of Economic Perspectives* 16, no. 2 (2002): 175–95.

Desan, Christine. "From Blood to Profit: Making Money in the Practice and Imagery of Early America." *Journal of Policy History* 20, no. 1 (2008): 23–46.

———. *Making Money: Coin, Currency, and the Coming of Capitalism.* New York: Oxford University Press, 2014.

D. E. Shaw Group. "The Basis Monster That Ate Wall Street." *D. E. Shaw Group Market Insights*, March 2009.

Diamond, Douglas W. Remarks at the Panel Discussion on Financial Regulation, Becker Friedman Institute, University of Chicago, November 6, 2010.

Diamond, Douglas W., and Philip H. Dybvig. "Bank Runs, Deposit Insurance, and Liquidity." *Journal of Political Economy* 91, no. 3 (1983): 401–19.

Diamond, Douglas W., and Raghuram G. Rajan. "Liquidity Risk, Liquidity Creation, and Financial Fragility: A Theory of Banking." *Journal of Political Economy* 109, no. 2 (2001): 287–327.

Diamond, Peter A. "Aggregate Demand Management in Search Equilibrium." *Journal of Political Economy* 90, no. 5 (1982): 881–94.

Dodd, Christopher. Statement on Comprehensive Deposit Insurance Reform and Taxpayer Protection Act of 1991. US Senate Floor. *Congressional Record* 137, pt. 24, November 27, 1991, 36131–32.

Douglas, Paul H., Irving Fisher, Frank D. Graham, Earl J. Hamilton, Willford I. King, and Charles R. Whittlesey. "A Program for Monetary Reform." Memorandum, July 1939.

Dudley, William C. "Fixing Wholesale Funding to Build a More Stable Financial System." Remarks at the New York Bankers Association's Annual Meeting and Economic Forum, New York, February 1, 2013.

Duffie, Darrell. "The Failure Mechanics of Dealer Banks." *Journal of Economic Perspectives* 24, no. 1 (2010): 51–72.

———. "Presidential Address: Asset Price Dynamics with Slow-Moving Capital." *Journal of Finance* 65, no. 4 (2010): 1237–67.

Dunbar, Charles F. "Deposits as Currency." *Quarterly Journal of Economics* 1, no. 4 (1887): 401–19.

———. *The Theory and History of Banking.* 3rd ed. New York: G. P. Putnam's Sons, 1917.

Eichengreen, Barry. *Golden Fetters: The Gold Standard and the Great Depression, 1919–1939.* New York: Oxford University Press, 1992.

Eichengreen, Barry, and Kris J. Mitchener. "The Great Depression as a Credit Boom Gone Wrong." In *Research in Economic History*, vol. 22, edited by Alexander J. Field, 183–237. Oxford: Elsevier, 2004.

Ellis, Diane. Memorandum to the FDIC Board of Directors from the Director of the Division of Insurance and Research: "Update of Projected Deposit Insurance Fund Losses, Income, and Reserve Ratios for the Restoration Plan," October 2, 2014. Available on the FDIC website.

Farmer, Roger E. A. *How the Economy Works: Confidence, Crashes and Self-Fulfilling Prophecies.* New York: Oxford University Press, 2010.

Federal Deposit Insurance Corporation. Final Rule. "Final Statement of Policy on Risk-Based Capital." *Federal Register* 54, no. 53 (March 21, 1989): 11500–18.

———. Interim Final Rule. "Orderly Liquidation Authority Provisions of the Dodd-Frank Wall Street Reform and Consumer Protection Act." *Federal Register* 76, no. 16 (January 25, 2011): 4207–16.

———. Notice; request for comments. "Resolution of Systemically Important Financial Institutions: The Single Point of Entry Strategy." *Federal Register* 78, no. 243 (December 18, 2013): 76614–24.

———. "Quarterly Banking Profile: Fourth Quarter 2014." *FDIC Quarterly* 9, no. 1 (2015): 1–35.

———. "Resolutions Handbook." 2003.

Federal Deposit Insurance Corporation and Bank of England. "Resolving Globally Active, Systemically Important, Financial Institutions." Joint paper, December 10, 2012.

Federal Reserve Bank of New York. Statement. "Update on Tri-party Repo Infrastructure Reform." February 13, 2014.

Federal Reserve Board. Final Rule. "Reserve Requirements of Depository Institutions Policy on Payment System Risk." *Federal Register* 75, no. 86 (May 5, 2010): 24384–89.

———. "Monetary Policy Report to the Congress." February 24, 2010.

Federal Reserve System. Final Rule. "Regulatory Capital Rules: Implementation of Risk-Based Capital Surcharges for Global Systemically Important Bank Holding Companies." *Federal Register* 80, no. 157 (August 14, 2015): 49082–116.

———. Final Rule. "Risk-Based Capital Guidelines." *Federal Register* 54, no. 17 (January 27, 1989): 4186–221.

———. "Guide to the Federal Reserve's Payment System Risk Policy on Intraday Credit." July 2012.

Financial Accounting Standards Board. "Statement of Cash Flows." Statement of Financial Accounting Standards 95, November 1987.

Financial Crisis Inquiry Commission. *The Financial Crisis Inquiry Report: Final Report of the National Commission on the Causes of the Financial and Economic Crisis in the United States.* Washington, DC: Government Printing Office, 2011.

Financial Stability Board. "Strengthening Oversight and Regulation of Shadow Banking." Consultative Document, November 18, 2012.

Financial Stability Oversight Council. *2014 Annual Report.*

Fischel, Daniel R., Andrew M. Rosenfield, and Robert S. Stillman. "The Regulation of Banks and Bank Holding Companies." *Virginia Law Review* 73, no. 2 (1987): 301–38.

Fischer, Stanley. "On the Need for an International Lender of Last Resort." Princeton University, Essays in International Economics, 220 (November 2000).

Fisher, Irving. "The Debt-Deflation Theory of Great Depressions." *Econometrica* 1, no. 4 (1933): 337–57.

———. *100% Money.* 3rd ed. New Haven, CT: City Printing, 1945.

———. *The Purchasing Power of Money.* Rev. ed. New York: Macmillan, 1913.

Flannery, Mark J. "Debt Maturity and the Deadweight Cost of Leverage: Optimally Financing Banking Firms." *American Economic Review* 84, no. 1 (1994): 320–31.

French, Kenneth R., Martin N. Baily, John Y. Campbell, John H. Cochrane, Douglas W. Diamond, Darrell Duffie, Anil K. Kashyap, Frederic S. Mishkin, Raghuram G. Rajan, David S. Scharfstein, Robert J. Shiller, Hyun Song Shin, Matthew J. Slaughter, Jeremy C. Stein, and René M. Stulz. *The Squam Lake Report: Fixing the Financial System.* Princeton, NJ: Princeton University Press, 2010.

Friedman, Milton. "The Euro-Dollar Market: Some First Principles." *Federal Reserve Bank of St. Louis Review*, July 1971, 16–24.

————. "Monetary Policy for the 1980s." In *To Promote Prosperity: U.S. Domestic Policy in the Mid-1980s*, edited by John H. Moore, 23–60. Stanford, CA: Hoover Institution Press, 1984.

————. *The Optimum Quantity of Money*. 1969. Reprint, New Brunswick, NJ: Transaction, 2006.

————. *A Program for Monetary Stability*. New York: Fordham University Press, 1960.

————. "Should There Be an Independent Monetary Authority?" In *In Search of a Monetary Constitution*, edited by Leland B. Yeager, 219–43. Cambridge, MA: Harvard University Press, 1962.

Friedman, Milton, and Anna J. Schwartz. "Has Government Any Role in Money?" In *Money in Historical Perspective*, edited by Anna J. Schwartz, 289–314. Chicago: University of Chicago Press, 1987.

————. *A Monetary History of the United States, 1867–1960*. Princeton, NJ: Princeton University Press, 1963.

————. *Monetary Statistics of the United States: Estimates, Sources, Methods*. New York: National Bureau of Economic Research, 1970.

Fuchita, Yasuyuki, and Kei Kodachi. "Managing Systemwide Financial Crises: Some Lessons from Japan since 1990." In *Rocky Times: New Perspectives on Financial Stability*, edited by Yasuyuki Fuchita, Richard Herring, and Robert Litan, 11–58. Washington, DC: Brookings Institution Press, 2012.

Fudenberg, Drew, and Jean Tirole. *Game Theory*. Cambridge, MA: MIT Press, 1991.

Gallatin, Albert. "Considerations on the Currency and Banking System of the United States." 1831. In *The Writings of Albert Gallatin*, edited by Henry Adams, 3:231–364. Philadelphia: J. B. Lippincott, 1879.

Geanakoplos, John. "Solving the Present Crisis and Managing the Leverage Cycle." *FRBNY Economic Policy Review* 16, no. 1 (2010): 101–31.

Glasner, David. "Endogenous Money." *Uneasy Money* (blog), April 11, 2012.

Golembe, Carter H. "The Deposit Insurance Legislation of 1933: An Examination of Its Antecedents and Its Purposes." *Political Science Quarterly* 75, no. 2 (1960): 181–200.

Goodfriend, Marvin. "Money Markets." *Annual Review of Financial Economics*, no. 3 (2011): 119–37.

————. "Policy Debates at the Federal Open Market Committee: 1993–2002." In *The Origins, History, and Future of the Federal Reserve: A Return to Jekyll Island*, edited by Michael D. Bordo and William Roberds, 332–73. New York: Cambridge University Press, 2013.

Gordon, Jeffrey N., and Christopher M. Gandia. "Money Market Funds Run Risk: Will Floating Net Asset Value Fix the Problem?" *Columbia Business Law Review*, no. 2 (2014): 313–69.

Gorton, Gary B. "Banking Panics and Business Cycles." *Oxford Economic Papers* 40, no. 4 (1988): 751–81.

———. "Bank Regulation When 'Banks' and 'Banking' Are Not the Same." *Oxford Review of Economic Policy* 10, no. 4 (1994): 106–19.

———. *Misunderstanding Financial Crises: Why We Don't See Them Coming.* New York: Oxford University Press, 2012.

———. *Slapped by the Invisible Hand: The Panic of 2007.* New York: Oxford University Press, 2010.

———. "Some Reflections on the Recent Financial Crisis." NBER Working Paper 18397, September 2012.

Gorton, Gary B., Stefan Lewellen, and Andrew Metrick. "The Safe-Asset Share." *American Economic Review: Papers and Proceedings* 102, no. 3 (2012): 101–6.

Gorton, Gary B., and Andrew Metrick. "The Federal Reserve and Panic Prevention: The Roles of Financial Regulation and Lender of Last Resort." *Journal of Economic Perspectives* 27, no. 4 (2013): 45–64.

———. "Regulating the Shadow Banking System." *Brookings Papers on Economic Activity*, Fall 2010, 261–97.

———. "Securitized Banking and the Run on Repo." *Journal of Financial Economics* 104, no. 3 (2012): 425–51.

Gorton, Gary B., and Guillermo Ordoñez. "Collateral Crises." *American Economic Review* 104, no. 2 (2014): 343–78.

———. "The Supply and Demand for Safe Assets." Working paper, August 2013.

Gorton, Gary B., and George Pennacchi. "Financial Intermediaries and Liquidity Creation." *Journal of Finance* 45, no. 1 (1990): 49–61.

Gorton, Gary B., and Andrew Winton. "Financial Intermediation." In *Handbook of the Economics of Finance*, edited by George M. Constantinides, Milton Harris, and René M. Stulz, 1A:431–552. Amsterdam: Elsevier/North Holland, 2003.

Government Accountability Office. "Large Bank Holding Companies: Expectations of Government Support." Report to Congressional Requesters, July 2014.

Graham, Frank D. "Partial Reserve Money and the 100 Per Cent Proposal." *American Economic Review* 26, no. 3 (1936): 428–40.

Greenfield, Robert L., and Leland B. Yeager. "A Laissez-Faire Approach to Monetary Stability." *Journal of Money, Credit and Banking* 15, no. 3 (1983): 302–15.

Greenwood, Robin, Samuel G. Hanson, and Jeremy C. Stein. "A Comparative-Advantage Approach to Government Debt Maturity." *Journal of Finance* 70, no. 4 (2015): 1683–1722.

Greenwood, Robin, and David S. Scharfstein. "The Growth of Finance." *Journal of Economic Perspectives* 27, no. 2 (2013): 3–28.

Gruber, Jonathan. *Public Finance and Public Policy.* 2nd ed. New York: Worth, 2007.

Hall, Robert E. "Why Does the Economy Fall to Pieces after a Financial Crisis?" *Journal of Economic Perspectives* 24, no. 4 (2010): 3–20.

Hamilton, Alexander. *The Report of the Secretary of the Treasury on the Subject of a National Bank*. 1790. Reprint, New York: S. Whiting, 1811.

Hamilton, James. "M3 or Not M3?" *Econbrowser* (blog), May 30, 2006.

Hammond, Bray. *Banks and Politics in America from the Revolution to the Civil War*. Princeton, NJ: Princeton University Press, 1957.

Hanc, George. "The Banking Crises of the 1980s and Early 1990s: Summary and Implications." In *History of the Eighties: Lessons for the Future*, 1:3–86. Washington, DC: Federal Deposit Insurance Corporation, 1997.

Hanson, Samuel G., Anil K. Kashyap, and Jeremy C. Stein. "A Macroprudential Approach to Financial Regulation." *Journal of Economic Perspectives* 25, no. 1 (2011): 3–28.

Hanson, Samuel G., David S. Scharfstein, and Adi Sunderam. "An Evaluation of Money Market Fund Reform Proposals." Working paper, May 2014.

Hardin, Russell. *Liberalism, Constitutionalism, and Democracy*. New York: Oxford University Press, 1999.

Hattori, Masazumi, Koji Koyama, and Tatsuya Yonetani. "Analysis of Credit Spread in Japan's Corporate Bond Market." Bank for International Settlements Papers 5, October 2001.

Hayakawa, Hideo, and Eiji Maeda. "Understanding Japan's Financial and Economic Developments since Autumn 1997." Bank of Japan Working Paper 00-1, January 2000.

Hayek, Friedrich A. *Denationalisation of Money*. 3rd ed. London: Institute of Economic Affairs, 1990.

———. *Prices and Production*. 2nd ed. London: Routledge and Kegan Paul, 1935.

He, Dong, and Robert N. McCauley. "Offshore Markets for the Domestic Currency: Monetary and Financial Stability Issues." Hong Kong Monetary Authority Working Paper 02/2010.

Herszenhorn, David M., Carl Huse, and Sheryl Gay Stolberg. "Talks Implode during a Day of Chaos." *New York Times*, September 25, 2008.

Hicks, John. *Value and Capital*. 2nd ed. 1946. Reprint, Oxford: Clarendon Press, 2001.

Hoenig, Thomas M. "Basel III Capital: A Well-Intended Illusion." Remarks to the International Association of Deposit Insurers 2013 Research Conference, Basel, April 9, 2013.

Hoenig, Thomas M., and Charles S. Morris. "Restructuring the Banking System to Improve Safety and Soundness." White paper, November 2013.

Hohfeld, Wesley Newcomb. *Fundamental Legal Conceptions as Applied in Judicial Reasoning*. New Haven, CT: Yale University Press, 1919.

Holmes, Oliver Wendell, Jr. Letter to Georgina Harriet Pollock, October 24, 1902. In *Holmes-Pollock Letters: The Correspondence of Mr. Justice Holmes and Sir Frederick Pollock, 1874–1932*, edited by Mark DeWolfe Howe, 1:108–9. Cambridge, MA: Harvard University Press, 1941.

———. "The Path of the Law." *Harvard Law Review* 10, no. 8 (1897): 457–78.

Holmstrom, Bengt. "Understanding the Role of Debt in the Financial System." Bank for International Settlements Working Paper 479, January 2015.

Hoover, Herbert. *The Memoirs of Herbert Hoover*. Vol. 3, *The Great Depression, 1929–1941*. New York: Macmillan, 1952.

Humphrey, Thomas M. "Lender of Last Resort: What It Is, Whence It Came, and Why the Fed Isn't It." *Cato Journal* 30, no. 2 (2010): 333–64.

International Accounting Standards Board. "Statement of Cash Flows." International Accounting Standard 7, December 1992.

International Monetary Fund. "How Big Is the Implicit Subsidy for Banks Considered Too Important to Fail?" In *Global Financial Stability Report: Moving from Liquidity- to Growth-Driven Markets*, 102–32. Washington, DC: International Monetary Fund, 2014.

———. "Safe Assets: Financial System Cornerstone?" In *Global Financial Stability Report: The Quest for Lasting Stability*, 81–121. Washington, DC: International Monetary Fund, 2012.

International Swaps and Derivatives Association. "Netting and Offsetting: Reporting Derivatives under U.S. GAAP and under IFRS." May 2012.

Isaacson, Walter. "How Steve Jobs' Love of Simplicity Fueled a Design Revolution." *Smithsonian Magazine*, September 2012.

Ivashina, Victoria, and David S. Scharfstein. "Bank Lending during the Financial Crisis of 2008." *Journal of Financial Economics* 97, no. 3 (2010): 319–38.

Ivashina, Victoria, David S. Scharfstein, and Jeremy C. Stein. "Dollar Funding and the Lending Behavior of Global Banks." *Quarterly Journal of Economics* 130, no. 3 (2015): 1241–81.

Jackson, Thomas H. *The Logic and Limits of Bankruptcy Law*. Cambridge, MA: Harvard University Press, 1986.

Jalil, Andrew J. "A New History of Banking Panics in the United States, 1825–1929: Construction and Implications." *American Economic Journal: Macroeconomics* 7, no. 3 (2015): 295–330.

James, William. *Pragmatism*. 1907. In *Pragmatism* and *The Meaning of Truth*. Cambridge, MA: Harvard University Press, 1978.

Jervis, Robert. "Cooperation under the Security Dilemma." *World Politics* 30, no. 2 (1978): 167–214.

Johnson, Simon. "Bank Leverage Is the Defining Debate of Our Time." *Bloomberg View*, September 3, 2013.

Johnson, Simon, and James Kwak. *13 Bankers: The Wall Street Takeover and the Next Financial Meltdown*. New York: Vintage Books, 2011.

Jones, David. "Emerging Problems with the Basel Capital Accord: Regulatory Capital Arbitrage and Related Issues." *Journal of Banking and Finance* 24 (January 2000): 35–58.

J. P. Morgan Securities Inc. "Short-Term Fixed Income Research Note." *U.S. Fixed Income Markets Weekly*, June 6, 2008.

Kahle, Kathleen M., and René M. Stulz. "Access to Capital, Investment, and the Financial Crisis." *Journal of Financial Economics* 110, no. 2 (2013): 280–99.

Kashyap, Anil K., Raghuram Rajan, and Jeremy C. Stein. "Banks as Liquidity Providers: An Explanation for the Coexistence of Lending and Deposit-Taking." *Journal of Finance* 57, no. 1 (2002): 33–73.

Kerr, Edmund H. "The Inadvertent Investment Company: Section 3(a)(3) of the Investment Company Act." *Stanford Law Review* 12, no. 1 (1959): 29–70.

Keynes, John Maynard. "An Economic Analysis of Unemployment." 1931. In *The Collected Writings of John Maynard Keynes*, edited by Donald Moggridge, 13:343–67. London: Macmillan, 1973.

———. *The General Theory of Employment, Interest, and Money.* 1936. Reprint, San Diego, CA: First Harvest/Harcourt, 1964.

———. "The Great Slump of 1930." 1930. In *Essays in Persuasion* (1931), 126–34. Reprint, New York: Palgrave Macmillan, 2010.

———. "A Self-Adjusting Economic System?" *New Republic*, February 20, 1935, 35–37.

———. *A Treatise on Money.* 2 vols. New York: Harcourt, Brace, 1930.

Kim, E. Han, Adair Morse, and Luigi Zingales. "What Has Mattered to Economics since 1970." *Journal of Economic Perspectives* 20, no. 4 (2006): 189–202.

Kindleberger, Charles P., and Robert Aliber. *Manias, Panics, and Crashes: A History of Financial Crises.* 6th ed. New York: Palgrave Macmillan, 2011.

Klomp, Jeroen, and Jakob de Haan. "Inflation and Central Bank Independence: A Meta-regression Analysis." *Journal of Economic Surveys* 24, no. 4 (2010): 593–621.

Kohn, Meir. *Financial Institutions and Markets.* 2nd ed. New York: Oxford University Press, 2004.

Konczal, Mike. "Sheila Bair: Dodd-Frank Really Did End Taxpayer Bailouts." *Wonkblog, Washington Post*, May 18, 2013.

———. "Why Keynes Wouldn't Have Too Rosy a View of Our Economic Future." *Wonkblog, Washington Post*, September 7, 2013.

Koo, Richard C. *Balance Sheet Recession: Japan's Struggle with Uncharted Economics and Its Global Implications.* Singapore: John Wiley, 2003.

———. *The Holy Grail of Macroeconomics: Lessons from Japan's Great Recession.* Rev. ed. Singapore: John Wiley, 2009.

Kotlikoff, Laurence J. *Jimmy Stewart Is Dead: Ending the World's Ongoing Financial Plague with Limited Purpose Banking.* Hoboken, NJ: John Wiley, 2010.

Krugman, Paul. "The Amnesiac Economy." *The Conscience of a Liberal* (blog), *New York Times*, October 26, 2011.

———. "Banking Mysticism, Continued." *The Conscience of a Liberal* (blog), *New York Times*, March 30, 2012.

———. "Bubbles, Regulation, and Secular Stagnation." *The Conscience of a Liberal* (blog), *New York Times*, September 25, 2013.

———. "End This Depression Now! A Politics and Prose Event." Remarks at Politics and Prose, Washington, DC, May 1, 2012. Available on YouTube.com.

———. "The Gold Bug Variations." *Slate*, November 22, 1996.

———. "If Banks Are Outlawed, Only Outlaws Will Have Banks." *The Conscience of a Liberal* (blog), *New York Times*, October 10, 2011.

———. "It's Baaack: Japan's Slump and the Return of the Liquidity Trap." *Brookings Papers on Economic Activity*, no. 2 (1998): 137–205.

———. "Letting Lehman Fail." *The Conscience of a Liberal* (blog), *New York Times*, February 19, 2014.

———. "More on Japan (Wonkish)." *The Conscience of a Liberal* (blog), *New York Times*, January 10, 2012.

———. *The Return of Depression Economics and the Crisis of 2008*. New York: W. W. Norton, 2009.

———. "Six Doctrines in Search of a Policy Regime." *The Conscience of a Liberal* (blog), *New York Times*, April 18, 2010.

———. "What Happened to Asia?" Unpublished manuscript, January 1998.

———. "What Janet Yellen—and Everyone Else—Got Wrong." *The Conscience of a Liberal* (blog), *New York Times*, August 8, 2013.

———. "Worthwhile Canadian Comparison." *The Conscience of a Liberal* (blog), *New York Times*, June 15, 2013.

Kryzanowski, Lawrence, and Gordon S. Roberts. "Canadian Banking Solvency, 1922–1940." *Journal of Money, Credit and Banking* 25, no. 3 (1993): 361–76.

LaCapra, Lauren T. "Goldman Names Schwartz CFO as Viniar Retires." *Reuters*, September 18, 2012.

Laidler, David. "The Price Level, Relative Prices and Economic Stability: Aspects of the Interwar Debate." BIS Working Paper 136, September 2003.

———. *Taking Money Seriously and Other Essays*. Cambridge, MA: MIT Press, 1990.

Lastra, Rosa M. *International Financial and Monetary Law*. 2nd ed. New York: Oxford University Press, 2015.

Laughlin, J. Laurence. *The Principles of Money*. New York: Charles Scribner's Sons, 1903.

Leijonhufvud, Axel. *On Keynesian Economics and the Economics of Keynes: A Study in Monetary Theory*. New York: Oxford University Press, 1968.

Lerner, Abba P. "Money as a Creature of the State." *American Economic Review* 37, no. 2 (1947): 312–17.

Levine, Matt. "Basel Makes Its Simple Leverage Rules … Simpler?" *Bloomberg View* (blog), January 13, 2014.

———. "Bill to Make Banking Boring Actually Might Be Kind of Fun." *Dealbreaker* (blog), May 1, 2013.

———. "Relatively Simple Basel Leverage Rules Still Pretty Complicated." *Dealbreaker* (blog), June 26, 2013.

Litan, Robert E. *What Should Banks Do?* Washington, DC: Brookings Institution Press, 1987.

Lucas, Robert E., Jr. "Monetary Neutrality." Nobel Lecture, December 7, 1995.

Lucas, Robert E., Jr., and Nancy L. Stokey. "Liquidity Crises: Understanding Sources and Limiting Consequences; A Theoretical Framework." *Region*, June 2011: 6–15.

Macey, Jonathan R., and James P. Holdcroft Jr. "Failure Is an Option: An Ersatz-Antitrust Approach to Financial Regulation." *Yale Law Journal* 120, no. 6 (2011): 1368–418.

Macey, Jonathan R., and Geoffrey P. Miller. "Nondeposit Deposits and the Future of Bank Regulation." *Michigan Law Review* 91, no. 2 (1992): 237–73.

MacLeod, Henry Dunning. *The Theory and Practice of Banking*. 4th ed. 2 vols. London: Longmans, Green, Reader and Dyer, 1883.

Madigan, Brian F. "Bagehot's Dictum in Practice: Formulating and Implementing Policies to Combat the Financial Crisis." Remarks at the Federal Reserve Bank of Kansas City's Annual Economic Symposium, Jackson Hole, WY, August 21, 2009.

Mankiw, N. Gregory. "Comments on Alan Greenspan's 'The Crisis,'" *Greg Mankiw's Blog*, March 19, 2010.

———. *Macroeconomics*. 8th ed. New York: Worth, 2013.

———. *Principles of Economics*. 7th ed. Stamford, CT: Cengage Learning, 2014.

Mankiw, N. Gregory, and Laurence M. Ball. *Macroeconomics and the Financial System*. New York: Worth, 2011.

Mann, Francis A. *The Legal Aspect of Money*. 5th ed. Oxford: Clarendon Press, 1992.

Martin, Robert F., Teyanna Munyan, and Beth Anne Wilson. "Potential Output and Recessions: Are We Fooling Ourselves?" *IFDP Notes*, November 12, 2014.

McAdams, Richard H. "Beyond the Prisoners' Dilemma: Coordination, Game Theory, and Law." *Southern California Law Review* 82, no. 2 (2009): 209–58.

McCulley, Paul. "Teton Reflections." *PIMCO Global Central Bank Focus*, August/September 2007.

McLeay, Michael, Amar Radia, and Ryland Thomas. "Money Creation in the Modern Economy." *Bank of England Quarterly Bulletin*, no. 1 (2014): 1–14.

Mehrling, Perry. *The New Lombard Street: How the Fed Became the Dealer of Last Resort*. Princeton, NJ: Princeton University Press, 2011.

Merton, Robert C. "An Analytic Derivation of the Cost of Deposit Insurance and Loan Guarantees: An Application of Modern Option Pricing Theory." *Journal of Banking and Finance* 1 (June 1977): 3–11.

———. "Financial Innovation and the Management and Regulation of Financial Institutions." *Journal of Banking and Finance* 19 (June 1995): 461–81.

Merton, Robert C., and Zvi Bodie. "Deposit Insurance Reform: A Functional Approach." *Carnegie-Rochester Conference Series on Public Policy* 38 (June 1993): 1–34.

Merton, Robert K. "The Self-Fulfilling Prophecy." *Antioch Review* 8, no. 2 (1948): 193–210.

Mian, Atif, and Amir Sufi. "Household Debt and the Great Depression." *House of Debt* (blog), March 15, 2014.

———. *House of Debt: How They (and You) Caused the Great Recession, and How We Can Prevent It from Happening Again.* Chicago: University of Chicago Press, 2014.

———. "What Explains the 2007–2009 Drop in Employment?" *Econometrica* 82, no. 6 (2014): 2197–223.

Miller, Marcus, Paul Weller, and Lei Zhang. "Moral Hazard and the US Stock Market: Analysing the 'Greenspan Put.'" *Economic Journal* 112 (March 2002): C171–86.

Miller, Merton H. "Do the M&M Propositions Apply to Banks?" *Journal of Banking and Finance* 19 (June 1995): 483–89.

Minsky, Hyman P. "The Financial Instability Hypothesis." Jerome Levy Economics Institute of Bard College Working Paper 74, May 1992.

———. "The Financial-Instability Hypothesis: Capitalist Processes and the Behavior of the Economy." In *Financial Crises: Theory, History, and Policy*, edited by Charles P. Kindleberger and Jean-Pierre Laffargue, 13–39. London: Cambridge University Press, 1982.

———. Foreword to *The Chicago Plan and New Deal Banking Reform*, by Ronnie J. Phillips. New York: M. E. Sharpe, 1995.

———. *Stabilizing an Unstable Economy.* Rev. ed. New York: McGraw-Hill, 2008.

Mises, Ludwig von. *The Theory of Money and Credit.* 1912. Translated by H. E. Batson, 1934. Reprint, New Haven, CT: Yale University Press, 1953.

Mishkin, Frederic S. *The Economics of Money, Banking, and Financial Markets.* 10th ed. Boston: Pearson, 2012.

Mitchell, Mark, and Todd Pulvino. "Arbitrage Crashes and the Speed of Capital." *Journal of Financial Economics* 104, no. 3 (2012): 469–90.

Modigliani, Franco, and Merton H. Miller. "The Cost of Capital, Corporation Finance and the Theory of Investment." *American Economic Review* 48, no. 3 (1958): 261–97.

Mulligan, Casey B. "Questions and Answers about the Book," n.d.

———. *The Redistribution Recession: How Labor Market Distortions Contracted the Economy.* New York: Oxford University Press, 2012.

Mundell, Robert A. "Monetary Unions and the Problem of Sovereignty." *Annals of the American Academy of Political and Social Science* 579 (January 2002): 123–52.

Nakaso, Hiroshi. "The Financial Crisis in Japan during the 1990s: How the Bank of Japan Responded and the Lessons Learnt." Bank for International Settlements Papers 6, October 2001.

Norris, Floyd. "Financial Perversions Sold during Credit Boom." *New York Times*, February 12, 2010.

Office of the Comptroller of the Currency. "Activities Permissible for a National
    Bank, Cumulative." 2011 annual edition.
———. Banking Circular 79, November 2, 1976.
———. Final Rule. "Risk-Based Capital Guidelines." *Federal Register* 54, no. 17
    (January 27, 1989): 4168–84.
———. Interpretive Letter re: Chase Market Index Investment Deposit Account,
    August 8, 1988.
———. Interpretive Letter 632, June 30, 1993.
———. Interpretive Letter 684, August 4, 1995.
———. Interpretive Letter 806, October 17, 1997.
———. Interpretive Letter 892, September 13, 2000.
———. Interpretive Letter to First National Bank of Chicago, March 2, 1992.
———. No Objection Letter 87-5, July 20, 1987.
———. No Objection Letter 90-1, February 16, 1990.
Office of the Comptroller of the Currency, Federal Reserve Board, and Federal
    Deposit Insurance Corporation. Final Rule. "Liquidity Coverage Ratio: Li-
    quidity Risk Measurement Standards." *Federal Register* 79, no. 197 (October 10,
    2014): 61440–541.
Ohanian, Lee E. "The Economic Crisis from a Neoclassical Perspective." *Journal
    of Economic Perspectives* 24, no. 4 (2010): 45–66.
Omarova, Saule T. "The Quiet Metamorphosis: How Derivatives Changed the
    'Business of Banking.'" *University of Miami Law Review* 63, no. 4 (2009):
    1041–110.
Philippon, Thomas, and Ariell Reshef. "Wages and Human Capital in the U.S. Fi-
    nance Industry: 1909–2006." *Quarterly Journal of Economics* 127, no. 4 (2012):
    1551–609.
Phillips, Ronnie J. *The Chicago Plan and New Deal Banking Reform*. New York:
    M. E. Sharpe, 1995.
Pitt, Harvey L., and Julie L. Williams. "The Convergence of Commercial and In-
    vestment Banking: New Directions in the Financial Services Industry." *Journal
    of Comparative Business and Capital Market Law* 5, no. 2 (1983): 137–93.
Plosser, Charles I. "Macro Models and Monetary Policy Analysis." Remarks at
    the Bundesbank–Federal Reserve Bank of Philadelphia Spring 2012 Research
    Conference, Eltville, Germany, May 25, 2012.
Posen, Adam. "It Takes More Than a Bubble to Become Japan." In *Asset Prices
    and Monetary Policy*, edited by Anthony Richards and Tim Robinson. Can-
    berra: J. S. McMillan, 2003.
Posner, Richard A. *A Failure of Capitalism: The Crisis of '08 and the Descent into
    Depression*. Cambridge, MA: Harvard University Press, 2009.
Pozsar, Zoltan. "Institutional Cash Pools and the Triffin Dilemma of the U.S. Bank-
    ing System." IMF Working Paper 11/190, August 2011.
Pozsar, Zoltan, Tobias Adrian, Adam Ashcraft, and Hayley Boesky. "Shadow
    Banking." *FRBNY Economic Policy Review*, December 2013, 1–16.

Pozsar, Zoltan, and Manmohan Singh. "The Nonbank-Bank Nexus and the Shadow Banking System." IMF Working Paper 11/289, December 2011.

Prescott, Edward C. Interview: "On the Economy with Tom Keene." *Bloomberg*, March 30, 2009.

Quiggin, John. "New Old Keynesianism." *Crooked Timber* (blog), January 22, 2014.

Rajan, Raghuram G. *Fault Lines: How Hidden Fractures Still Threaten the World Economy*. Princeton, NJ: Princeton University Press, 2010.

———. "Love the Bank, Hate the Banker." *Project Syndicate*, March 27, 2013.

Rehm, Barbara A. "FDIC's Own Experts Skeptical of Resolution Plan." *American Banker*, December 12, 2013.

Reinhart, Carmen M., and Kenneth S. Rogoff. "Recovery from Financial Crises: Evidence from 100 Episodes." *American Economic Review: Papers and Proceedings*, May 2014, 50–55.

———. *This Time Is Different: Eight Centuries of Financial Folly*. Princeton, NJ: Princeton University Press, 2009.

Reinhart, Vincent. "Secretary Paulson Makes the Right Call." *Wall Street Journal*, September 16, 2008.

Reis, Ricardo. "Central Bank Design." *Journal of Economic Perspectives* 27, no. 4 (2013): 17–44.

Richardson, Gary, and William Troost. "Monetary Intervention Mitigated Banking Panics during the Great Depression: Quasi-Experimental Evidence from a Federal Reserve District Border, 1929–1933." *Journal of Political Economy* 117, no. 6 (2009): 1031–73.

Ricks, Morgan. "Money and (Shadow) Banking: A Thought Experiment." *Review of Banking and Financial Law* 31, no. 2 (2012): 731–48.

———. "Reforming the Short-Term Funding Markets." Harvard John M. Olin Discussion Paper 713, May 2012.

———. "Regulating Money Creation after the Crisis." *Harvard Business Law Review* 1, no. 1 (2011): 75–143.

———. "A Regulatory Design for Monetary Stability." *Vanderbilt Law Review* 65, no. 5 (2012): 1289–360.

———. "A Simpler Approach to Financial Reform." *Regulation*, Winter 2013–14, 36–41.

Robbins, Lionel. *Autobiography of an Economist*. London: Macmillan, 1971.

———. *The Great Depression*. New York: Macmillan, 1935.

Rockoff, Hugh. "The Meaning of Money in the Great Depression." NBER Working Paper Series on Historical Factors in Long Run Growth, Historical Paper 52, December 1993.

———. "Parallel Journeys: Adam Smith and Milton Friedman on the Regulation of Banking." *Journal of Cultural Economy* 4, no. 3 (2011): 255–83.

Roe, Mark J. "The Derivatives Market's Payment Priorities as Financial Crisis Accelerator." *Stanford Law Review* 63, no. 3 (2011): 539–90.

Rogers, James Steven. *The End of Negotiable Instruments: Bringing Payment Systems Law Out of the Past.* New York: Oxford University Press, 2012.

Rogoff, Kenneth S. "Costs and Benefits to Phasing Out Paper Currency." *NBER Macroeconomics Annual* 29, no. 1 (2014).

———. "No More Creampuffs." *Washington Post*, September 16, 2008.

———. Panel Discussion: "Economic Forum: Policy Responses to Crises." Remarks at the 14th Jacques Polak Annual Research Conference, International Monetary Fund, Washington, DC, November 8, 2013.

Romer, Christina D., and David H. Romer. "Institutions for Monetary Stability." In *Reducing Inflation: Motivation and Strategy*, edited by Christina D. Romer and David H. Romer, 307–34. Chicago: University of Chicago Press, 1997.

Ross, Stephen A., Randolph W. Westerfield, and Jeffrey Jaffe. *Corporate Finance.* 8th ed. Boston: McGraw-Hill/Irwin, 2008.

Rothbard, Murray N. *America's Great Depression.* 5th ed. Auburn, AL: Mises Institute, 2000.

Rousseau, Jean-Jacques. *Discourse on the Origin of Inequality.* 1754. Translated by Donald A. Cress. Indianapolis: Hackett, 1992.

Rowe, Nick. "Banking 'Mysticism' and the Hot Potato." *Worthwhile Canadian Initiative* (blog), March 31, 2012.

———. "Medium of Account vs. Medium of Exchange." *Worthwhile Canadian Initiative* (blog), October 30, 2012.

———. "Money, Barter, and Recalculation." *Worthwhile Canadian Initiative* (blog), December 13, 2010.

———. "The Return of Monetarism." *Worthwhile Canadian Initiative* (blog), March 3, 2009.

———. "What Makes a Bank a Central Bank?" *Worthwhile Canadian Initiative* (blog), October 29, 2009.

Scharfstein, David S. "Perspectives on Money Market Mutual Fund Reforms." Testimony before the Committee on Banking, Housing, and Urban Affairs, US Senate, June 21, 2012.

Schelling, Thomas C. *The Strategy of Conflict.* 1960. Reprint, Cambridge, MA: Harvard University Press, 1980.

Schularick, Moritz, and Alan M. Taylor. "Credit Booms Gone Bust: Monetary Policy, Leverage Cycles, and Financial Crises, 1870–2008." *American Economic Review* 102, no. 2 (2012): 1029–61.

Schumpeter, Joseph A. *Essays: On Entrepreneurs, Innovations, Business Cycles, and the Evolution of Capitalism*, edited by Richard V. Clemence. 1951. Reprint, New Brunswick, NJ: Transaction, 1989.

Schwartz, Alan. Hearing: "Turmoil in U.S. Credit Markets: Examining the Recent Actions of Federal Financial Regulators." Testimony before the Committee on Banking, Housing, and Urban Affairs, US Senate, April 3, 2008.

Schwartz, Anna J. "The Misuse of the Fed's Discount Window." Homer Jones Memorial Lecture, St. Louis University, April 9, 1992.

————. "Real and Pseudo-Financial Crises." In *Money in Historical Perspective*, edited by Anna J. Schwartz, 271–88. Chicago: University of Chicago Press, 1987.

Scott, Hal S. "Interconnectedness and Contagion." Committee on Capital Markets Regulation, November 20, 2012.

Scott, Hal S., and Anna Gelpern. *International Finance: Transactions, Policy, and Regulation*. 19th ed. New York: Foundation Press, 2012.

Securities and Exchange Commission. Final Rule. "Money Market Fund Reform." *Federal Register* 75, no. 42 (March 4, 2010): 10060–120.

————. Final Rule. "Money Market Fund Reform; Amendments to Form PF." *Federal Register* 79, no. 157 (August 14, 2014): 47736–983.

————. Final Rule. "Valuation of Debt Instruments and Computation of Current Price per Share by Certain Open-End Investment Companies (Money Market Funds)." *Federal Register* 48, no. 138 (July 18, 1983): 32555–67.

————. No-Action Letter, Willkie Farr & Gallagher, October 23, 2000.

Selgin, George A. "Legal Restrictions, Financial Weakening, and the Lender of Last Resort." *Cato Journal* 9, no. 2 (1989): 429–69.

————. *The Theory of Free Banking: Money Supply under Competitive Note Issue.* Lanham, MD: Rowman and Littlefield, 1988.

Shleifer, Andrei, and Robert Vishny. "Fire Sales in Finance and Macroeconomics." *Journal of Economic Perspectives* 25, no. 1 (2011): 29–48.

Simons, Henry C. *Economic Policy for a Free Society*. Chicago: University of Chicago Press, 1948.

Singh, Manmohan, and James Aitken. "The (Sizable) Role of Rehypothecation in the Shadow Banking System." IMF Working Paper 10/172, July 2010.

Skeel, David A. "Single Point of Entry and the Bankruptcy Alternative." In Baily and Taylor, *Across the Great Divide*, 311–33.

Smallman, Joseph D., and Michael J. P. Selby. "Non-traditional Asset Securitization for European Markets." In *Issuer Perspectives on Securitization*, edited by Frank J. Fabozzi, 45–51. New Hope, PA: Frank J. Fabozzi Associates, 1998.

Smith, Adam. *An Inquiry into the Nature and Causes of the Wealth of Nations.* 1776. Edited by R. H. Campbell and A. S. Skinner. 2 vols. Oxford: Clarendon Press, 1976.

Solow, Robert M. "On the Lender of Last Resort." In *Financial Crises: Theory, History, and Policy*, edited by Charles P. Kindleberger and Jean-Pierre Laffargue, 237–55. Cambridge: Cambridge University Press, 1982.

Sommer, Joseph H. "Why Bail-In? And How!" *FRBNY Economic Policy Review* 20, no. 2 (2014): 207–28.

Stein, Jeremy C. "Evaluating Large-Scale Asset Purchases." Remarks at the Brookings Institution, Washington, DC, October 11, 2012.

————. "The Fire-Sales Problem and Securities Financing Transactions." Remarks at the Federal Reserve Bank of New York Workshop on Fire Sales as a Driver of Systemic Risk in Triparty Repo and Other Secured Funding Markets, New York, October 4, 2013.

———. "Monetary Policy as Financial Stability Regulation." *Quarterly Journal of Economics* 127, no. 1 (2012): 57–95.

———. "Overheating in Credit Markets: Origins, Measurement, and Policy Responses." Remarks at the Federal Reserve Bank of St. Louis, February 7, 2013.

Stewart, James B. "Eight Days: The Battle to Save the American Financial System." *New Yorker*, September 21, 2009.

Stiglitz, Joseph E. "Reconstructing Macroeconomic Theory to Manage Economic Policy." NBER Working Paper 20517, September 2014.

Stigum, Marcia, and Anthony Crescenzi. *Stigum's Money Market*. 4th ed. New York: McGraw-Hill, 2007.

Summers, Larry. "Fiscal Policy and Full Employment." Remarks at the Center on Budget and Policy Priorities, Washington, DC, April 2, 2014. Available on YouTube.com.

Sumner, Scott. "The Case for Nominal GDP Targeting." Mercatus Research, Mercatus Center at George Mason University, October 23, 2012.

———. "Eugene Fama Makes Me Look Like an MMTer." *TheMoneyIllusion* (blog), March 9, 2012.

———. "FAQs." *TheMoneyIllusion* (blog), n.d.

———. "An Idealistic Defense of Pragmatism." *TheMoneyIllusion* (blog), August 16, 2011.

———. "Keep Banks Out of Macro." *TheMoneyIllusion* (blog), January 22, 2013.

———. "Miron and Rigol on Bank Failures and Output." *TheMoneyIllusion* (blog), September 17, 2013.

———. "Misdiagnosing the Crisis: The Real Problem Was Not Real, It Was Nominal." *Vox*, September 10, 2009.

———. "The Real Problem Was Nominal." *Cato Unbound*, September 14, 2009.

———. "Where I've Failed (So Far)." *TheMoneyIllusion* (blog), December 6, 2012.

Sunderam, Adi. "Money Creation and the Shadow Banking System." *Review of Financial Studies* 28, no. 4 (2015): 939–77.

Sykes, Ernest. *Banking and Currency*. London: Butterworth, 1905.

Tarullo, Daniel K. "Evaluating Progress in Regulatory Reforms to Promote Financial Stability." Remarks at the Peterson Institute for International Economics, Washington, DC, May 3, 2013.

———. "Toward Building a More Effective Resolution Regime: Progress and Challenges." Remarks at the Federal Reserve Board and Federal Reserve Bank of Richmond Conference on Planning for the Orderly Resolution of a Global Systemically Important Bank, Washington, DC, October 18, 2013.

Task Force on Tri-party Repo Infrastructure, Payments Risk Committee. "Task Force Report." May 17, 2010.

Temin, Peter. *Did Monetary Forces Cause the Great Depression?* New York: W. W. Norton, 1976.

———. *Lessons from the Great Depression*. Cambridge, MA: MIT Press, 1989.

Tippetts, Charles S. "State Bank Withdrawals from the Federal Reserve System." *American Economic Review* 13, no. 3 (1923): 401–10.

Tobin, James. "The Case for Preserving Regulatory Distinctions." In *Restructuring the Financial System*, 167–83. Kansas City: Federal Reserve Bank of Kansas City, 1987.

———. "Commercial Banks as Creators of 'Money.'" In *Banking and Monetary Studies*, edited by Deane Carson, 167–83. Homewood, IL: Richard D. Irwin, 1963.

———. "Financial Innovation and Deregulation in Perspective." *Bank of Japan Monetary and Economic Studies* 3, no. 2 (1985): 19–29.

———. "The Interest-Elasticity of Transactions Demand for Cash." *Review of Economics and Statistics* 38, no. 3 (1956): 241–47.

———. "Money and Finance in the Macro-economic Process." Nobel Lecture, December 8, 1981.

———. "Price Flexibility and Output Stability: An Old Keynesian View." *Journal of Economic Perspectives* 7, no. 1 (1993): 45–65.

Tocqueville, Alexis de. "Paris on the Morrow of the 24th of February and the Next Days." 1850. In *The Recollections of Alexis de Tocqueville* (1893), translated by Alexander Teixeira de Mattos, 90–101. New York: Macmillan, 1896.

Todd, Walker F. "FDICIA's Emergency Liquidity Provisions." *Federal Reserve Bank of Cleveland Economic Review* 29, no. 3 (1993): 16–23.

US Treasury Department. "The Use and Counterfeiting of United States Currency Abroad." Report to the US Congress, Part 3, 2006.

Vanderlip, Frank A. "The Modern Bank." In *The Currency Problem and the Present Financial Situation: A Series of Addresses Delivered at Columbia University, 1907–1908*, 3–18. New York: Columbia University Press, 1908.

Volcker, Paul. Letter to Senator Christopher Dodd, May 6, 2010. *Congressional Record* 159, October 30, 2013 (daily ed.): H6922.

Wessel, David. *In Fed We Trust: Ben Bernanke's War on the Great Panic*. New York: Three Rivers Press, 2009.

White, Lawrence H. "Did Hayek and Robbins Deepen the Great Depression?" *Journal of Money, Credit and Banking* 40, no. 4 (2008): 751–68.

———. *Free Banking in Britain: Theory, Experience and Debate, 1800–1845*. 2nd ed., revised and extended. London: Institute for Economic Affairs, 1995.

———. *The Theory of Monetary Institutions*. Malden, MA: Blackwell, 1999.

Whitehead, Charles K. "Destructive Coordination." *Cornell Law Review* 96, no. 2 (2013): 323–64.

Williamson, Stephen. "Money Creation: Propagating Confusion." *New Monetarist Economics* (blog), March 27, 2014.

Wittgenstein, Ludwig. *Philosophical Investigations*. 1953. Translated by G. E. M. Anscombe. Oxford: Basil Blackwell, 1958.

Woodford, Michael. "Financial Intermediation and Macroeconomic Analysis." *Journal of Economic Perspectives* 24, no. 4 (2010): 21–44.

Wray, L. Randall. "Krugman versus Minsky." *EconoMonitor* (blog), April 2, 2012.
————. *Modern Money Theory: A Primer on Macroeconomics for Sovereign Monetary Systems.* London: Palgrave Macmillan, 2012.
————. *Money and Credit in Capitalist Economies: The Endogenous Money Approach.* Aldershot, UK: Edward Elgar, 1990.
Wren-Lewis, Simon. "Will the Financial Crisis Lead to Another Revolution in Macroeconomics?" *Mainly Macro* (blog), January 19, 2014.

Index